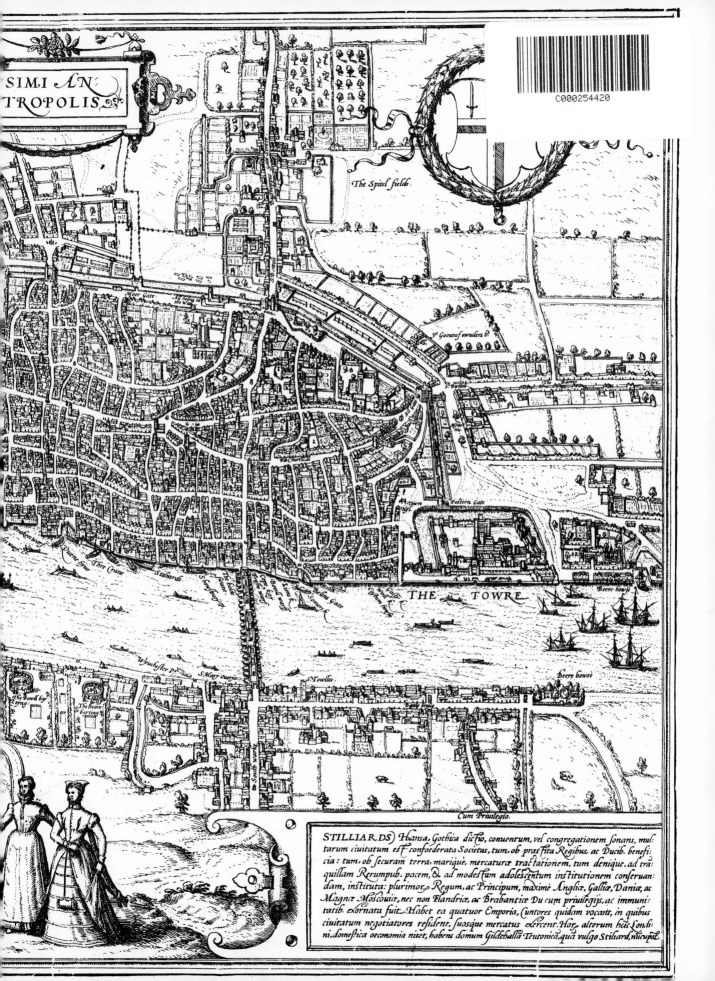

THE FREEDOM

FRONT COVER: The Arms of the City of London.

VERA EFFIGIES PRECLAR˜ DOMINI RICHARDI WHITTINGTON EQUI͗ AURAT͘

Huius sparsa viri totu benefacta per orbem   Potensa monstrant indice qualis era.

The true portraicture of RICHARD WHITTINGTON thrise Lord Maior
of London a vertuous and godly man full of good Works (and those famous) he builded
the Gate of London called Newegate which before was a miserable doungeon. He builded
Whitington Colledge & made it an Almose house for poore people Also he builded a
greate parte of y͞e hospitall of S. Bartholomewes in westsmithfield in London. He also
builded the beautifull Library at y͞e Gray Friers in London, called Christes Hospitall;
Also he builded the Guilde Halle Chappell and increased a greate parte of the East
ende of the saied halle, beside many other good workes.

Richard Whittington. (GL)

THE FREEDOM

THE PAST AND PRESENT OF THE LIVERY, GUILDS AND CITY OF LONDON

Valerie Hope BA

Clive Birch FSA FRSA

Gilbert Torry

assisted by

CAROLYN BIRCH

Foreword by

The Rt Hon the Lord Mayor
SIR CHRISTOPHER LEAVER GBE DMus

BARRACUDA BOOKS LIMITED
BUCKINGHAM, ENGLAND
MCMLXXXII

PUBLISHED BY
BARRACUDA BOOKS LIMITED
BUCKINGHAM, ENGLAND
AND PRINTED AND BOUND BY
NENE LITHO LIMITED AND
WOOLNOUGH BOOKBINDING
WELLINGBOROUGH, ENGLAND

LITHOGRAPHY BY
BICESTER PHOTOLITHO LIMITED
BICESTER, ENGLAND

JACKET PRINTED BY
CHENEY & SONS LIMITED
BANBURY, OXON

DISPLAY TYPE SET AND
TEXT SET IN BASKERVILLE 10½/12pt BY
BEDFORDSHIRE GRAPHICS LIMITED
BEDFORD, ENGLAND

ISBN 0 86023 136 4

Contents

Acknowledgements

This book owes its existence to the help, encouragement and public support of the Rt Hon the Lord Mayor, Sir Christopher Leaver, GBE DMus, without whom it would have been an impossible task, and to whom we are all deeply indebted. He will understand when we add to that our tribute to the officers and staffs at Guildhall and Mansion House, who have held our collective hand throughout.

In particular, we are grateful to the Corporation of the City of London for permission to reproduce the City's arms, and to the Town Clerk, S.J. Clayton, for his guidance; Godfrey Thompson, Guildhall Librarian, for his advice; Mr E.W. Padwick, Deputy Librarian and Messrs M.V. Roberts, Ralph Hyde, John Fisher and Jeremy Smith, all of Guildhall Library, for their patience, help and courtesy in tracing references and prints, and for their expert advice.

At Mansion House, we have had much support from the Lord Mayor's Assistant Private Secretary, Lt Cdr Brian Wright, City Marshall, Col John Howard, and outstanding help in research and information from Sophie Walpole.

We acknowledge also our considerable debt to all those who have chronicled the City and its Guilds and Livery Companies in so many different ways, by book, pamphlet and article. They are listed in the Bibliography.

Particular thanks go to Mrs Irene Shaw, Photographic Records Officer at the Museum of London for her help with their pictures, and to those who kindly read the typescript and offered constructive comment: Dr Hugh Chapman, Head of the Roman Department at the Museum of London, and Mr John Clark of the Medieval Department (Chapter 1); Miss Betty Masters, Deputy Keeper of Records, Guildhall (Chapters 2, 3 and 5) Dr Valerie Pearl, President of New Hall, Cambridge (Chapter 4); S.J. Clayton, Town Clerk (Chapters 7 and 8) and the Clerks, Archivists and other officers of the Guilds and Livery Companies (Chapter 6).

Our appreciation is also due to Mr R.G. Nation of the Port of London Authority; Mr C.A. Lodemore, Superintendent of Spitalfields Market; Miss Christine Button, Marketing Officer of Midland Bank Ltd; Mrs C.Y. Marshall, Information Division, Bank of England; and staff at Barbican Centre of Arts and Conferences, for their courtesy and for information.

The *City Recorder* has supported the project throughout in many ways, and we offer our thanks, especially to Editor John Naunton.

We owe a major debt of gratitude to the Masters, Wardens and Courts of the majority of Guilds and Livery Companies, for their positive support in informing their Freemen and Liverymen of this project, and we also thank them and their Clerks, Archivists and Librarians for making available their records. In this connection, we received particularly helpful responses from Janet Taylor, W.T.F. Rossiter, R.M. Simmonds, Reg Adams, Fredk. L. Rowe, B.W. Vigrass, J.R. Craig, W.E. Kingsland, Amanda Relph, Oliver Sunderland, Gavin Benbow, I.J. Kimmins, Derek Field, Roger Southcombe, David Reid, J.A. Nicholson, Andrew Hill, H.C. Weale, W.R. Spencer, Colin J. Eldridge, C.H. Baylis, F.E. Birch, Peter Oldak, Bernard Stroulger, Cdr P. Brook Cowan, A.K. Tudor, Maj Charles O'Leary, R.R.F. Cowe, A.G.P. Lincoln, Robert B. Hodgetts, John Green, H.J.

Lavington, D.E. Wickham, Air Commodore B.G. Frow, Richard Thompson, Capt K.G. Hamon, Lt Col Geoffrey Pearce, Robert C.G. Strick, Anthony Boyall, H. Wilson Wiley, C.P. de B. Jenkins, Miss Hare, Paul Harford-White, E.S. Earl, C.P.G. Chavasse, D.A.J. Taylor, John Edwardes Jones, R.B. Brayne, A.T. Langdon-Down, Anne F. Sutton, Brian P. Smith, Ray Tarrant, H.J. Maddocks, W.R. Crewdson, M.E.C. Lewis, J.M. Halford, H. Mott, Group Capt K.M. Oliver, E.C. Robbins, N.M.A. Evelegh, Col M. Woodhead, J.C. Peck, R.D. Ross, Raymond Cousins, Freda Sparke, J.W. Cross and R.S. Gothard.

In addition, Peter Herbage and Kenneth Mostyn went out of their way to provide text and illustrations of an extensive nature, for which we are particularly grateful.

John Armistead, our publisher's photographer, has helped the authors with illustrations, particularly in Guildhall Library Print Room.

The authors make formal acknowledgement, with their thanks, for provision of and permission to reproduce photographs and prints which are the copyright of the following: Guildhall Library, City of London; Corporation of London Records Office; Museum of London; British Museum; Mansell Collection; Handford Photography; the *City Recorder;* Bank of England, Barclays Bank Ltd, Lloyds Bank Ltd, Midland Bank Ltd, Peter Bloomfield, City of London Public Relations Department, Christ's Hospital, Anthony Coombs, Rev Geoffrey Harding (Rector of St Mary Woolnoth), Rev F.P. Coleman (Rector of St Andrew-by-the-Wardrobe), Rev Basil Watson OBE, MA, RN (Vicar of St Lawrence Jewry-next-Guildhall), Peter A. Sanderson ARIBA, National Westminster Bank Ltd, Martins Bank Ltd, David Liney (Hudson's Bay Company), Lloyds of London, Peter Marshall (Commissioner of Police of the City of London), S.A. Miller (Archivist, Port of London Authority), D.J. Noakes MBE (Superintendent, London Central Markets), Brien Reidy & Associates Ltd (London Metal Exchange), Paul Ridgway (Trinity House Service), Colonel W.W. Etches OBE, MC, and the Royal Regiment of Fusiliers Museum (Tower of London), London Stock Exchange, Rev Alan J. Tanner MA (Rector of St Botolph Without Bishopsgate), Universal Pictorial Press and Agency Ltd, D.R. Webb (Librarian, Bishopsgate Reference Library), Dep Bernard L. Morgan CBE, JP, Winckelmann Publications Ltd, British Insurance Association, Commercial Union Assurance, and all those Guilds and Livery Companies whose illustrations are reproduced.

In this last connection, formal acknowledgement is also made of the original sources of those photographs, in particular to *Country Life*; the Bodleian Library; Harry Margery; Gerald Sharpe; Bishop Marshall & Son; Woodyer Photography, and the School of Photography, Regent Street Polytechnic.

In addition, we are all deeply appreciative of the help we have received from our families and friends. Valerie Hope's husband, Michael, gave constructive criticism throughout and took modern City photographs; her son, Mark, drew the sketchmaps. Also, Clive Birch's thanks go to the Master, Wardens and Court of his own Company, the Carmen, for their fraternal support and encouragement throughout the project.

Finally, if any acknowledgement has been unwittingly omitted, the authors apologise and thank all those concerned for helping to make this book.

The Rt Hon the Lord Mayor, Sir Christopher Leaver GBE, DMus (1981-2). (UPPA)

10

Foreword

by The Rt Hon the Lord Mayor, Sir Christopher Leaver, GBE DMUS

During a conversation last year with my fellow Carman, Clive Birch, he mentioned his ideas for a modern record of our Companies, old and new. This had been in his mind for seven years — to produce a book which would contribute to a better understanding of the Companies' past and their modern role. This appealed to me. I believe they are not as widely known or understood as they deserve. I also felt such a book would be welcomed and it offered an exciting prospect for my year of office. I encouraged the project and offered the support of my Mayoralty.

The original intention was to find a single author but time was short, so I was delighted to recommend Valerie Hope, who was joined by Gilbert Torry, and Clive Birch himself, to enable the book to be published in 1982.

Between them they have produced a masterly summary, concise, informative and entertaining, with a wealth of fascinating illustration, in a handsomely presented volume. They have enjoyed help and co-operation throughout the City.

I am especially pleased that this book demonstrates so clearly the City's progressive attitude in welcoming new Companies — no less than nine since 1977 — as well as the continuing contribution of the older Companies.

Christopher Leaver

Court of Common Council in session, c1885. (GL)

Introduction

by Clive Birch, FSA FRSA

In 1974, I first conceived the need for a concise, illustrated book recording the past and present of the City and its ancient guilds and livery companies. In 1981 my fellow Carman and friend, then Mr Alderman Christoper Leaver, expressed our shared conviction that such a book could be an essential element in improving understanding by Citizens and outsiders of the multiple roles of the City and its freemen and liverymen. Both of us recognised the urgent need to provide clear information in an entertaining and attractive form, as a counter to the confrontation tactics of those antipathetic to the City corporate and otherwise, and as an encouragement to all those who believe in the manifold achievements, ever changing traditions and proven worth of this most marvellous of cities.

It is unfashionable in today's sometimes superficial society to embark on major projects for altruistic motives, yet such an approach is absolutely in line with much of the activity of the City of London. Nonetheless, we recognised that for such a project to be effective, it must be seen to have the support of the Citizens of London. To that end, with the full public support of Sir Christopher as Lord Mayor, I approached every Company and Guild for their cooperation, both with the information they alone could best provide about their past and present, and with the task of bringing the project to the attention of their freemen and liverymen.

The support has been substantial. The majority of the City's Companies and Guilds provided information, illustrations and active support, and many have been the expressions of goodwill while, in some cases, Masters, Clerks, Beadles and Archivists have considerably extended themselves.

It was our original intention to create an edition of 1,000 copies, but such has been the response, that we have separated the original arrangements, to present 100 copies to individuals and the guilds themselves in a special presentation edition, and we have extended the now separately numbered edition to avoid disappointing the subscribers to some 1,700 copies. We are privileged to present the first numbered copy of the presentation edition to Her Majesty the Queen, the second to the Rt Hon the Lord Mayor, the third to the Corporation and the fourth to Guildhall Library. The balance are numbered in order of precedence and will be given to each Livery Company or Guild.

I have been joined in this monumental task by three people who share my regard for the City. Valerie Hope assisted Sir Peter Gadsden with research during his Mayoralty, and has researched and written the first five chapters outlining the history of the City and the development of the livery companies. Gilbert Torry, a past Chairman of the Queenhithe Ward Club, has prepared the final two, dealing with the City today. My wife Carolyn has assisted me in my researches regarding the Companies and Guilds themselves, the records of which have been my responsibility. She has also created the index as an indispensable tool for those who come to use the book as a work of reference.

In sum, our brief has been to furnish a concise record of the City's past, a comprehensive guide to its present, explanation of its elective and selective procedures and government, and a summary of the past and present activities of each Company and Guild. We hope thereby to have provided in one readable, logical and attractive package, information, entertainment and reference, and perhaps one thing more — a book to keep and treasure. If we have succeeded in our aim *The Freedom* will have served the City, and we can wish for nothing more.

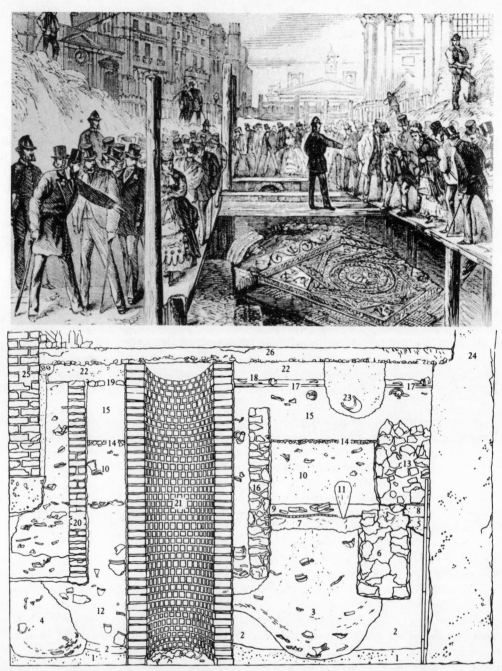

ABOVE: Drawing by Charles Roach Smith of the discovery in 1869 of the Bucklersbury mosaic pavement in Queen Victoria Street. (ML) BELOW: An imaginary section under a city cellar constructed as a wall in the Museum of London demonstrates 2,000 years of London's history.(ML) (1) Top of natural gravel; (2) Natural brick-earth; (3) and (4) First century pits; (5) Drainage gully, about AD 100; (6) Roman ragstone wall, about AD 100; (7) Roman floor of tile tesserae on concrete base, about AD 100; (8) Roman gravel surface, early 2nd century; (9) Burnt debris, 2nd century AD; (10) Roman and Medieval make-up; (11) Timber post-hole, probably Anglo-Saxon; (12) 13th century pit; (13) Chalk wall, 14th-15th century; (14) Chalk floor, 14th-15th century; (15) 16th and 17th century make-up; (16) Chalk-lined cess-pit, late 16th century; (17) 17th century tile floor; (18) Debris of Great Fire of 1666; (19) Cobble surface, 17th-18th century; (20) Brick-lined cess-pit, 18th century; (21) Brick-lined well, about 1800; (22) 18th-19th century make-up; (23) 19th century drain-pipe; (24) Concrete foundation, 19th century; (25) Brick party-wall, 19th century; (26) Concrete floor of cellar, 10 feet below modern street-level.

14

Genesis

Roman London lies beneath our feet as we walk the streets of the modern City. It is quite a long way down, around 20 feet below the present street level in some places. We can occasionally glimpse it on building sites, when yellow-helmeted archaeologists dig furiously to record the evidence of the past before the foundations of yet another office block are laid. In the Museum of London an imaginary section under a City cellar shows the deposits of 2,000 years of the City's history in a gigantic slice.

The Roman city is buried deep because of frequent destruction and reconstruction throughout that 2,000 years. London is now predominantly a place of stone and concrete, but since there were no natural stone deposits nearby, the majority of buildings up to the 17th century were of wood and so the City succumbed to several disastrous fires before the most famous of them all, in 1666. Prosperity and commercial activity have meant continual rebuilding since then, even without the German blitz of 1940-41, which destroyed a third of the City. New Londons have been piled upon the old with very little concern for the past, so that our knowledge is patchy and a map showing areas where archaeological evidence remains, or has been investigated, is like a jigsaw puzzle with most of the pieces missing.

Nevertheless, in the past Londoners were aware that theirs had been a Roman city. The Roman city wall was repaired and rebuilt several times, and in the 12th century William Fitzstephen described the landward defences, adding 'On the South, London was once walled and towered in like fashion, but the Thames . . . has in course of time washed away those bulwarks, undermined and cast them down'. He was referring to the Roman riverside defensive wall, the existence of which was doubted by experts right up to 1975, when excavations proved he was right. In 1595 John Stow described how 'a fair pavement like unto that above ground' had been uncovered about 15 feet deep on the corner of Bread Street and Cheapside. Sir Christopher Wren made several discoveries of Roman remains during the rebuilding of London after the Great Fire. However, it was not until the mid-19th century that a serious attempt was made to understand Roman London, in a period when major demolition for new buildings and roads began to uncover many Roman remains. The Corporation opened a public museum to house these in Basinghall Street (now part of the collection in the Museum of London). In 1869 the discovery of a magnificent Roman pavement in Queen Victoria Street aroused so much public interest that more than 50,000 people visited it in three days. Despite this interest, and the devoted efforts of several experts, it was not until the Department of Urban Archaeology was set up by the Court of Common Council over 100 years later, in 1973, that a systematic rescue of archaeological remains was begun. Knowledge of Roman London is constantly being extended today. In November 1981 a box-like structure, believed to be one of the piers of the Roman bridge, was found in Upper Thames Street — the earliest physical evidence of the bridge which was essential to the development of London.

There is no longer any doubt that it was the Romans who founded the first city. Fitzstephen followed an earlier 12th century chronicler, Geoffrey of Monmouth, in describing London as

'New Troy' founded by Brutus, a descendant of Aeneas, but this was pure fantasy. Although there were many Celtic settlements in the Thames valley they were further west, particularly near Heathrow, and there is no indication of any major habitation on the present City site. The southern British capital at the time of the Roman invasion was Colchester. It was there that the legions were heading when they reached the Thames on their way from Richborough in Kent, where they had landed in the spring of AD 43. On that occasion they may have crossed the river near Westminster, where it could be forded.

The site they chose for the city which they called Londinium had many advantages for the Romans, who did not regard the Thames as a boundary, since they controlled the areas to the north and south, and who had the engineering skill to bridge the river. Two thousand years ago, the Thames was wider and slower flowing than it is today, and the tide probably came no further upstream than around the present London Bridge. So it was a place which could easily be reached by ships from the continent, the lowest point unaffected by the ebb and flow of the tide, where a bridge could be built to serve as a focus for the Roman roads which radiated all over Britain. On the north, the gravel beds provided firm ground for a bridgehead; on the south, there was marshland with several sandbanks which the Roman engineers joined with piled logs, to form a causeway. The north bank was the obvious place for a city. It rose steeply 12 metres above the river to two flat-topped hills separated by the river Walbrook, which flowed into the Thames at that time, with the Fleet river beyond the western hill now crowned by St Paul's. On the eastern hill, known in the middle ages as Cornhill, the Roman city began.

Some historians believe that London was originally built purely as a military base; others think it more likely that from the beginning it was planned and developed as a commercial town. Certainly it grew swiftly as a trading centre. The first bridge must have been built by AD 50 and by the year 60 the Roman historian, Tacitus, was commenting that London was 'a place not indeed distinguished by the title of *colonia* (a town like Colchester or York for veteran soldiers with an administrative role), but was crowded with traders and a great centre of commerce.' Excavations have uncovered fine pottery and tableware from Italy and Gaul, and amphorae for oil and wine from Spain and Rhodes. Traces of what may be a market square have been found. Buildings and streets from the first London can be dated to this early period because, in AD 60, the town was burnt to the ground, leaving a 0.45m thick, red burnt layer.

This first destruction was the work of Boudica, Queen of the Iceni. She had good cause to turn on the Romans. On the death of her husband King Prasutagus, his estates and possessions were seized by the Romans. Boudica herself was flogged and her daughters raped. The infuriated Iceni, led by their Queen, looted and burnt Colchester and then marched towards Londinium. The Roman Governor Suetonius Paulinus was campaigning in Wales. He hurried back to arrive on the scene before the rebels, and well before the main body of his own troops. In the circumstances he had no alternative but to urge the inhabitants to abandon the town. Those who were either unable or unwilling to leave their homes were, in the words of Tacitus, 'massacred, hanged, burned and crucified with a headlong fury that was stimulated by the knowledge of forthcoming retribution.' Leaving Londinium in ruins, Boudica and the rebels turned North to Verulamium (St Albans) and sent that town up in flames. In a few weeks they had destroyed three major Roman towns and killed vast numbers of citizens, even if Tacitus' figure of 70,000 is a wild exaggeration, since the combined populations of all three cannot have been anywhere near that number at such an early date. Retribution soon followed. Paulinus had now gathered his forces, and they fell upon the Britons, slaughtering even their baggage animals. The Queen took poison to avoid the humiliation of capture.

The Romans might have followed this up by adopting a policy of severe repression but, in AD 61, the Emperor Nero sent a new Procurator (civil finance officer), Gaius Julius Alpinus Classicianus, who believed the Britons could be won over. He persuaded Nero to replace Paulinus with a less warlike and more statesmanlike Governor, Publius Petronius Turpilianus.

He and Turpilianus set about building a peaceful province. Classicianus made London his headquarters. His ashes were eventually buried in a cemetery near the present Tower of London, and today a copy of his massive tombstone, which had been set up 'by his sorrowing wife Julia', stands near the spot. The original was broken up in the 4th century and used in strengthening the city's defences against barbarian attacks. Fragments have, however, been recovered and the reconstructed tomb can be seen in the British Museum. (The Museum of London also has a copy).

It must have taken several years for London to recover from Boudica's devastation and the slaughter of its inhabitants. Nevertheless trade was booming in the Empire, and London had important advantages as a port and commercial centre. Agricola, who was Governor in AD 78-84, did much to foster the growth of towns in Britain, believing that the Britons would become enthusiastic Roman citizens when they could enjoy the comforts of Roman civilisation. He recognised they would be impressed by the dignified formality of Roman public buildings and, as well as temples, mansions and baths, London must have had its first Forum and Basilica by about AD 80. These were small compared with many Roman towns, but their presence does indicate some form of self-government at this early stage, as the Roman basilica was the administrative centre of a town.

London began to expand rapidly and, only forty years after the completion of the first Forum, this was replaced on the same site by a grand new Forum, with a Basilica over 150 metres long. The largest Basilica in the Empire north of the Alps, it would only just fit into St Paul's Cathedral today. Its massive walls were first discovered when Leadenhall Market was rebuilt in 1880. The possible justification for this handsome new civic centre was the visit of the Emperor Hadrian to Britain in AD 122. He may have ordered the building of the Forum and there was a fine, larger-than-life bronze statue of Hadrian which perhaps stood there. The head was fished out of the river at London Bridge in 1834 and can be seen in the British Museum (a copy is in the Museum of London). Other public buildings built or enlarged in the 2nd century indicate the importance of London in this period. Not only the Procurator but also the Governor was based in London. The Governor had a palace overlooking the river, where Cannon Street station now stands, with a fine garden and a huge ornamental pool. Very probably London Stone, which has been preserved as a piece of Roman London for centuries, and now reposes behind railings in a wall on the north side of Cannon Street, was part of the entrance to this palace. London had public baths at Cheapside and Huggin Hill, temples and fine houses with mosaic pavements. To the north-west of the city was the 12 acre Cripplegate fort, which could house 1,500 men, and may have been built as the headquarters of the guard, and perhaps used as a transit camp.

In AD 122 Roman Londinium was at the height of its prosperity and probably had a population of some 45,000. Of these, the wealthiest and most influential were Roman citizens: government officials, merchants and soldiers who had special legal rights and privileges.

Although some citizens were men of modest means, many Roman Londoners lived in spacious villas, with rooms overlooking a courtyard and sometimes a fountain playing in the garden. In such homes the walls were plastered and painted, and the floors, warmed by underfloor heating, were paved with tiles or mosaic. A high level of Romanisation is indicated by extensive finds of pottery, jewellery, hairpins and combs, bathing implements like the *strigils* used for scraping the skin after hot baths, and small bottles for cosmetics and perfume. These prosperous Roman households relied upon the labour of many slaves. On the whole, slaves were well treated, and some of them were educated people, who in time were able tō buy their freedom and set themselves up in business. As well as these, there were many native Britons who were free, although they lacked the status and privileges of citizenship. They were shopkeepers, labourers and craftsmen, many of whose tools have been found. Sets of carpenters', blacksmiths', cutlers' tools and even oculists' instruments were recovered from the river Walbrook, where they may have been thrown as votive offerings to propitiate the water gods. There were goldsmiths, metalworkers and leatherworkers. One tilemaker has been immortalised by a puzzled workmate, who scratched in Latin on a tile before it was fired, 'Austalis has been going off by himself every day these last thirteen days.'

London must have had the entertainments enjoyed by Roman citizens all over the Empire but, apart from some gaming counters and dice, little trace of these has been found. There is no sign of the amphitheatre which must have existed in London, as it did in every Roman town of any size. But in the Museum of London, there is a leather bikini which was probably worn by a young girl acrobat.

By the 2nd century London was already a cosmopolitan city, with the few ruling Romans greatly outnumbered by native Britons, soldiers from Gaul, Spain, North Africa and the Danube, merchants and financiers from all parts of the Empire. But it was a Roman city. Even labourers like Austalis were familiar with the Latin tongue and, as Tacitus tells us, the toga was everywhere to be seen. It was a busy and prosperous place, with traders coming in from all over Britain with pottery, lead, tin and building materials to sell, and eager to buy the luxury goods which London imported from Europe and the Eastern Mediterranean.

The city suffered its second great fire a few years after Hadrian's visit, in AD 122, when more than 100 acres were devastated. There is nothing to suggest that it was deliberately caused, but it must have spread easily among the huddled wooden buildings which housed the majority of Londoners. But, whereas after the Boudican destruction the city was soon rebuilt, it seems that a period of decline followed this second fire, and it is possible that although London continued to be the capital, the population of Roman London never again reached its earlier numbers. However, there was a positive effort to restore the city to its former size and importance about the year 200. It was about this time that London was for the first time protected by a wall, about six metres high and 2.4 metres thick, enclosing an area of 325 acres. On the outside was a ditch, and inside, a supporting clay bank. There were originally four gates, and bastions (projecting towers) were added later. Today the line of the wall can clearly be followed from the Tower, where part of it can be seen. There are several fragments at the eastern end, and then the curve formed by Dukes Place, Bevis Marks, Camomile Street, Wormwood Street and London Wall itself follows the wall exactly. At Cripplegate the Romans incorporated the NE and NW walls of the fort, part of which can be seen in a sunken garden in Noble Street. Then the wall swings west under the Post Office and down to the river past the Old Bailey. (In the Middle Ages it was extended to include Blackfriars).

There is no written record surviving of the building of the wall but the date has been pinpointed by coin finds to a period 190-225. The first date is marked by a coin dated 183-4 and sufficiently worn to suggest the year when it was dropped as about 190. But it was the hoard of a coin forger found on the site of the Old Bailey which gave archaeologists the clue to the second date. At the base of a small Roman tower on the city wall, excavators found two clay moulds for producing copies of coins issued between 210 and 215, as well as some new coins of about the same period. When the forger hid this incriminating material he can hardly have imagined how valuable it would be to 20th-century archaeological sleuths.

Although we can now say roughly when the wall was built, we cannot say under which of three Governors this was, or indeed why such a huge task was undertaken. No doubt it was necessary to provide some protection in a time of increasing unease and instability and, although the evidence is of a declining population in London, the building of the wall indicates the city's continuing importance. In the early 3rd century Septimus Severus, the Governor, divided Britain into two provinces, Britannia Superior and Britannia Inferior, and London was the capital of the former. Towards the end of that century, unrest in the Empire was echoed in Britain. In 287 Carausias, Admiral of the Channel Fleet, came to London, where he established himself and assumed the title of Emperor of Britain. He ruled for the next six years and set up a mint in London. In 293 he was murdered by his finance minister, Allectus, who was himself defeated two years later by the Emperor Constantius Chlorus. Allectus was killed in the battle and his Frankish mercenaries attacked and plundered London, which was saved by some ships from Constantius' invasion force. This episode was chronicled by a Roman writer, Eumenius, and commemorated by a gold medallion, struck in Trier and found in Arras. It is dated 296 and shows on one side the portrait of the Emperor Constantius Chlorus, and on the other, a picture of a woman personifying London kneeling at the city gate, with the Thames and a Roman warship in the background, welcoming Constantius. The inscription reads 'REDDITUR LUCIS AETERNAE' (Restorer of eternal light).

Although few remains have been found, it is clear that there was considerable building of villas and temples in 3rd century London. In the early period the official religion had been the Imperial cult, but now various Oriental mystery religions spread through the Empire. There was a temple to Isis and perhaps also to Cybele, but the most spectacular find was that of the temple of Mithras in 1954. It is of particular significance to the City, because the motto of the Stock Exchange 'My Word is My Bond' is a Mithraic concept.

It was only a small temple. Buried beneath the floors were its most precious treasures, marble sculptures and a silver canister now on view in the Museum of London. The temple itself could not be left on site as this would have interfered with building plans for Bucklersbury House, so it was reconstructed at street level just south of Queen Victoria Street, where it lies, as if stranded by the tide, far above the level of the Roman city. It is possible that the treasures were buried by the temple priests to protect them from destruction by Christians. There is little physical evidence of Christianity being practised in Roman London, though at this time it was overcoming Mithraism throughout the Empire, and a Bishop of London attended the Council of Arles in 314.

As the Roman Empire decayed from within and succumbed to barbarian attacks from without, so London declined. It was still sufficiently important to be renamed Augusta around the middle of the 4th century, and its defences were strengthened by the addition of bastions to the landward wall, and the building of a riverside defensive wall along the Thames. But the end seems to have come with a whimper rather than a bang. Once the Roman military protection was withdrawn at the beginning of the 5th century, the towns of Roman Britain were left to defend themselves. Roman civilization lingered on in London well into the 5th century, the city walls providing some sanctuary. According to the *Anglo-Saxon Chronicle,* written over 400 years later, the British fled into London after their defeat by mutinous German mercenaries at the battle of Crecganford in 457.

Even though the end of Roman London came slowly, there was a complete break in the city's development. The essential contribution of the Romans was the choice of site but, though they left much in stone, and the Anglo-Saxons little, it was the latter who gave the modern City of London its basic street plan and original structure of government. After the Roman era, a curtain of darkness descends on the history of Britain for nearly 200 years. People must have gone on living and farming, among the ruins of temples and villas, but they have left no trace.

London reappears on the pages of history at the beginning of the 7th century, with St Augustine's mission to convert the English. Sent by Pope Gregory the Great on this daunting task, he established his church at Canterbury, headquarters of the King of Kent, whose Christian wife persuaded him to meet the Papal emissary. The Pope had designated two archbishoprics based on the Roman provincial capitals of London and York. But owing to the influence of King Ethelbert in Kent and the later fame of St Augustine, it was at Canterbury that the Archbishopric was established and still remains. In 604 St Paul's Cathedral was founded as the Cathedral of the East Saxons, with Mellitus as Bishop. However, this first conversion of the heathen Londoners proved temporary, and Mellitus soon fled to Gaul, later returning to Kent where he became Archbishop of Canterbury. London was reconverted later in the 7th century and had its own bishop. The historian Bede, writing in the next century about this period, described London as an *emporium,* 'a mart for many peoples coming by land and sea'. Already there were probably several churches as well as St Paul's, and it is possible that the great Mercian King Offa had a palace on the site of the Cripplegate fort, and that he built St Alban's, Wood Street.

Lundenwic, as the Saxons called it, was now so prosperous that it attracted the next wave of invaders — the Vikings. They came in the 9th century and attacked London, sailing up the

Thames in their long ships. In 871-2 they spent the winter within the walls. During the next ten years they nearly overwhelmed the whole of England, until they were driven back by Alfred of Wessex. The *Anglo-Saxon Chronicle,* which Alfred began, records his occupation of London in AD 886: 'King Alfred occupied London: and all the English people that were not under subjection to the Danes submitted to him. And he then entrusted the borough to the control of Ealdorman Etheldred'. Perhaps to commemorate this event, Alfred issued a series of silver pennies bearing the monogram LONDONIA.

It would be difficult to exaggerate the achievements of Alfred the Great, not only as a military victor, but as an administrator, lawgiver, statesman, educator and town planner. Although his capital remained Winchester, he did much to establish a settled town life in London. The fortifications were strengthened and a new grid of streets laid. These took no account of the geometrical Roman street pattern, which must have disappeared, but they fixed the lines of many of the streets we know today. Two of the most important were West Cheap (Cheapside) and East Cheap, which followed an East/West line already established along the ridge above the Thames, and were developed as market streets.

The wharves along the Thames were busy with traders. There were merchants from Flanders, Normandy and Germany buying wool, fine embroidery and metalwork. Many luxuries were imported: gold, wine, olive oil, and silks, ivory, bronze and glass. Already in the 10th century London was the main English mint. The population grew and became more stable as grants of land were issued to bishops and noblemen. More churches were built.

During the late Saxon period the foundations of London government were laid. From a complex multitude of enclosed areas within the town — hagas, sokes and burgs as well as parishes — the wards began, although their boundaries were not fixed until the Norman period. Many of the central ward boundaries followed the tributaries of the river Walbrook, some stretching beyond the wall to take in a girdle of land all round the area of the Roman city.

The King's chief officer in London was the Portreeve. The office of Sheriff, also a Royal official, dates from about 1030 and at times the same person combined this with the office of Portreeve. Aldermen first appeared in Saxon times when the title could refer to any important Royal official and often described the headmen of the shires. In the towns there were aldermen of the guilds.

The citizens of London met at the Folkmoot in St Paul's churchyard three times a year, to transact general business and hear Royal decrees. Their tribunal was the Court of Husting (from the Viking 'House Meeting') which dealt with civil actions concerning the regulation of commercial practices and the supervision of property transactions. Guilds are also first to be found in Saxon London, with its *Frithgild* for mutual support and protection, and the *Cnihtengild* of the Portsoken. However, these were the forerunners, but not the direct ancestors of the medieval guilds.

By the mid-11th century, London was again an important city, although different from Roman London. It had spread beyond the Roman walls, but the population, around 12,000, was far smaller than that of Londinium at its peak. Despite having suffered several fires and Viking attacks since Alfred's time, it was thriving. One Norwegian prince, Olaf, is a hero to Londoners because he helped King Ethelred recapture the city from the more famous Dane, Canute. Six churches in London were dedicated to Olaf, of which only one, St Olave, Hart Street, remains. The nursery rhyme 'London Bridge is falling down' is an echo of the story told by the 12th century Icelandic historian Snorri Sturluson of how, finding the bridge was fortified against him, Olaf sailed under it, tied ropes round the supporting posts and hauled it down. The defenders fell into the river and the city was recaptured for Ethelred. However, on Ethelred's death Canute became King of England and the Londoners, who had originally supported his rival, Ethelred's son, Edmund Ironside, 'bought peace for themselves'. The monarchy was not necessarily hereditary yet and Londoners claimed a major part in electing a new king. On the death of Canute's son Harthacnut in 1042, 'all the people chose Edward as King in London'. Edward the Confessor, as he became known for his religious fervour, quit his palace in the City and concentrated on building a great abbey and a new palace at Westminster. This crucially important move established the duality of London, a capital with two great centres, Westminster the seat of the national government, and the City of London, a booming commercial centre in Saxon and Norman times and later the financial hub of the world.

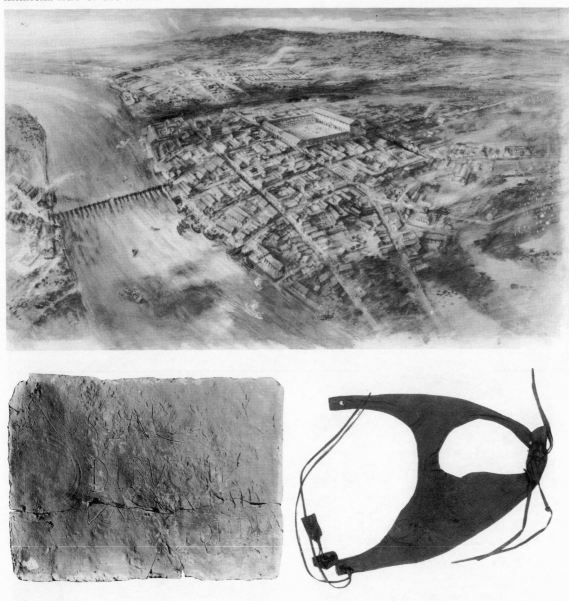

ABOVE: Imaginary reconstruction of Londinium in the time of the Emperor Hadrian, by Alan Sorrell (ML)
LEFT: Roman tile with Latin inscription about the workman Austalis. (ML) RIGHT: Roman leather bikini probably worn by an acrobat. (ML)

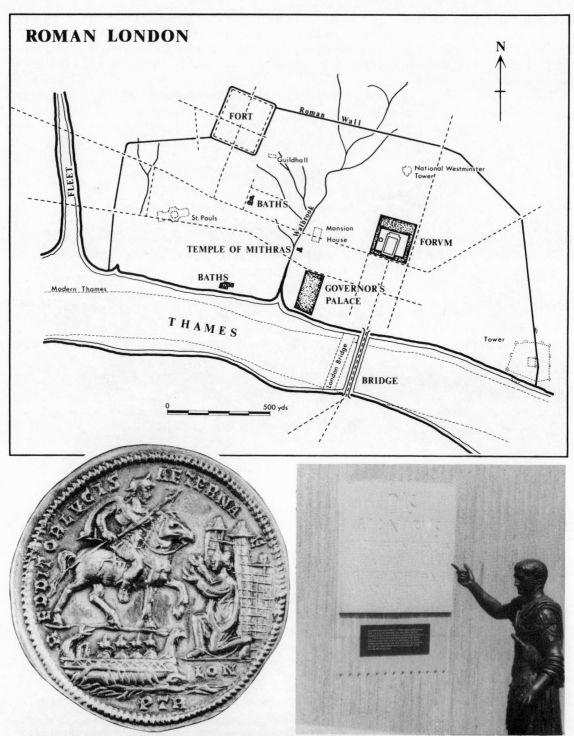

ABOVE: Sketch map of Roman London showing the lines of the roads and the walls and major buildings of which remains have been found. (MJH) LEFT: Replica of a gold medallion found in Arras commemorating Emperor Constantius Chlorus's relief of Londinium in 296. (ML) RIGHT: Copy of the reconstructed tomb of Procurator Classicianus behind Tower Hill Station with a statue of Emperor Trajan in the foreground. (JMH)

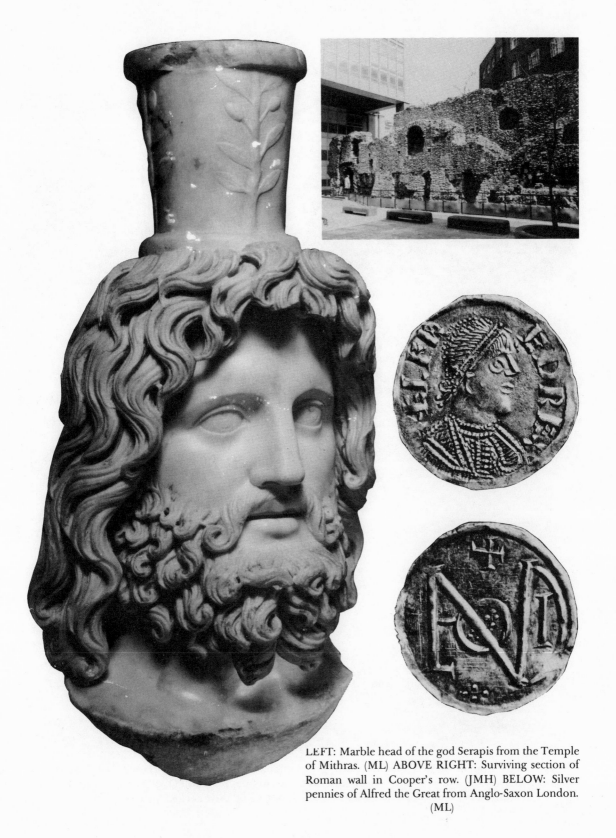

LEFT: Marble head of the god Serapis from the Temple of Mithras. (ML) ABOVE RIGHT: Surviving section of Roman wall in Cooper's row. (JMH) BELOW: Silver pennies of Alfred the Great from Anglo-Saxon London. (ML)

23

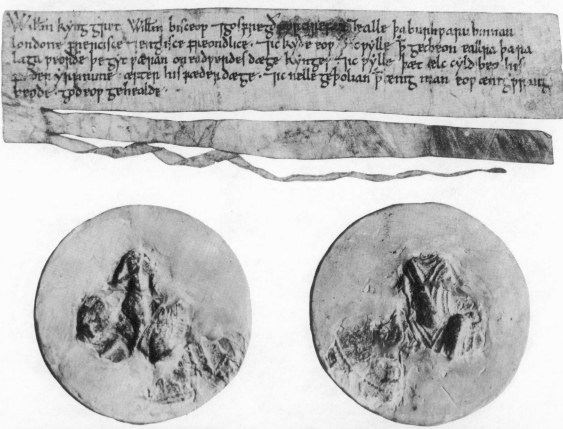

ABOVE: Scene from the Bayeux Tapestry showing the Londoners acclaiming King Harold at his coronation and then gazing at the comet, (since then identified as Halley's Comet). (MC) BELOW: The Charter given to the citizens of London by William I in 1067 acknowledging their ancient liberties. (GR)

The Custom of London

It is the City of London's proud claim that it is a Corporation by prescriptive right and that its constitution has been established 'from time immemorial' (ie before the year 1189). Already before 1066, the roots of government had taken such firm hold in London under the Anglo-Saxons, that the City was able to retain its individuality during the Norman conquest.

The catastrophic events of 1066 were the consequence of a dispute over the succession to the throne of England, in which the Londoners, not for the first or last time, backed a loser. Edward the Confessor died childless, and three ambitious and powerful men were determined to take his place — Harold Godwinson, Harald Hardrada of Norway, and William of Normandy. The citizens, together with the Witan (the Anglo-Saxon council of elders who traditionally chose the King) supported the English favourite, Harold, son of Earl Godwin. The Bayeux Tapestry shows him being acclaimed by the Londoners at his coronation in the brand-new Westminster Abbey. In the sky outside, a comet (Halley's) flares balefully, and the people regard it with dread as an evil omen, which indeed it proved to be. The first attack in the North by Harald Hardrada was swiftly and brilliantly quashed by King Harold at the battle of Stamford Bridge near York, where his army slaughtered the invaders. But there was no time to take breath after this victory, for news came of invasion from Normandy. Harold and his army, who had hastened over 200 miles south, met the Normans at Senlac near Hastings on 14 October. The fighting raged all day and, by evening, the King lay dead on the field. His army, among whom was a large contingent from London, was destroyed.

William had won the battle, but to control the kingdom he must first secure London. He moved round the coast and took Dover, where he improved the defences of the castle, then on to Canterbury which gave in without a murmur. Arriving at the south end of London Bridge he attacked, hoping the citizens would surrender. When they did not, he burnt Southwark and then swung west, crossing the Thames at Wallingford.

In London the Witan and other leading men anxiously watched his progress. Defiant at first, they proclaimed King the young Edgar Atheling, only survivor of the English Royal line: then, realising the cause was lost, they decided to make their peace with William. As the *Anglo-Saxon Chronicle* said 'all the best men from London' went out to meet William at Berkhamsted and accepted him as King. The terms they agreed are not recorded, but William entered London in peace and was crowned at Westminster Abbey on Christmas Day 1066. He ordered three castles to be built in the City 'against the restlessness of the vast and fierce populace'. These were the White Tower (in the East) and Baynard's Castle and Montfichet's Tower (in the West). The last two have disappeared though Baynard's Castle was rebuilt in the Middle Ages and the name survives today in a City Ward and on a pub. The White Tower remains, a symbol of the tense relationship which existed between the City and the Crown for hundreds of years. As a Royal palace, it soon ceased to be within the City limits. But London was far too rich and valuable for it to be worth William's while to damage it. Far better to conciliate the citizens. So within a year, the Londoners received from the King a charter which acknowledged and guaranteed their ancient rights and liberties. This small (6 ins by 1½ ins), ancient document is one of the City's greatest treasures. It is written in Anglo-Saxon and is addressed to the Bishop and Portreeve, as was the custom with English Royal decrees.

'William the king greets William the bishop and Geoffrey the portreeve and all the citizens in London, French and English, in friendly fashion; and I inform you that it is my will that your laws and customs be preserved as they were in King Edward's day, that every son be his father's heir after his father's death; and I will not allow any man to do you wrong. God keep you.' It is of interest that the two officials were French (the Bishop was a Norman appointed by Edward, the Portreeve was William's man) and it is assumed that the citizens were 'French and English'. Already there was considerable Norman influence in London, for Edward had lived in Normandy for nearly 30 years. Indeed it was a cosmopolitan city, with Norsemen, Flemings, Germans, Jews and French living within its walls. But the language of the document shows that the English predominated among the leading citizens and, although all over England in the shires the Normans replaced the Anglo-Saxon thegns, in the towns, especially in London, the English had to be taken into account. During the next 150 years London became the capital of a kingdom which included much of France, and whose rulers were constantly away in their efforts to control their domains. The Kings' necessity proved London's opportunity and the determined citizens won from the Crown a succession of charters which laid the foundations for the City government we know today.

In the early years of Norman England, identification of the people who ruled London is difficult, as the records are incomplete. It is known that Geoffrey the Portreeve was the same person as Geoffrey de Mandeville, the first Norman sheriff of London, but that does not mean that subsequent sheriffs, some of whose names are known, were also portreeves. There were aldermen, but again only some of their names are known. For a while there was an official called the Justiciar. During the 12th century the leading officials were the two Sheriffs, holding office jointly for London and Middlesex because of the City's close connection with that county. (The Local Government Act 1888 deprived Londoners of the right to elect a sheriff of Middlesex, so since then the two Sheriffs have been elected for London alone.)

They were Royal nominees responsible for the collection of Royal revenues. In other words they had the farm of the taxes, which they collected from the citizens, paying a fixed sum to the King every year. Obviously Londoners would have much more independence if they had a say in the choice of these officials. In Henry I's reign a charter of 1132 supposedly gave the citizens the right to choose their own sheriffs, but the surviving document is a later copy and its authenticity is in doubt, particularly since a strong king like Henry I would be unlikely to make such a concession. The right was not formally acknowledged until 1199.

After Henry's death the realm was torn apart by civil wars. His son and heir, William, had drowned tragically in the White Ship, which sank in the Channel when bringing him and his sister, Matilda, back from France. Matilda was saved, and in the next reign there was constant fighting between the supporters of a woman who was the King's daughter and those of his nephew, Stephen. It was a time, as one chronicler said, when 'God and his angels slept'. The Londoners supported Stephen, whom they claimed to have elected, and gave him considerable financial and military aid. They formed a commune, or sworn association of citizens, similar to those springing up on the continent at the time, but there was no official recognition of this yet. The accession in 1154 of Matilda's son Henry II ushered in a period of comparative stability, and the King granted London an important charter which upheld the City's judicial privileges and financial security. He made no concessions over its government, but the City prospered as trade flourished, while Henry's frequent absences on campaign meant that London became increasingly important as an administrative centre, based where the court and the Exchequer were, Westminster, and not in the City.

The relative peace of Henry's reign was shaken by his quarrel with the Archbishop of

Canterbury, Thomas Becket, which culminated in Becket's murder in his own cathedral on 29 December 1170 by a group of Henry's knights. Thomas Becket was canonised and an ever-increasing stream of pilgrims took the road to his shrine in Canterbury. He had been born in London, son of Gilbert Becket, a leading citizen who had been Sheriff, so London adopted him as patron saint along with St Paul, and his image appeared on the reverse of the City Seal. Another Londoner had been at Becket's side that fateful evening and had been wounded trying to defend him. This was William Fitzstephen who, when he wrote an account of the saint's life, prefaced it with a description of their native city. His pride in London is evident in the opening phrases: 'Among the noble cities of the world which Fame celebrates, the City of London, seat of the monarchy of England, is the one which spreads its fame more widely, distributes its goods and merchandise further and holds its head higher'. He wrote of London's encircling walls with the 'palatine fortress' of the Tower in the East; of its churches — over 100 — with fine schools attached to the greatest, and its 13 religious houses; its exotic trade with far-flung parts of the world; its many markets and fairs; its tradesmen and craftsmen. He described the City as a place for enjoyment, with football, jousting, bear and bull baiting, archery and wrestling. In winter the young men would tie bones to their feet and skate on the frozen marsh of Moorfields, while in the summer there were naval tourneys on the Thames, and when a contestant fell in, the spectators could 'laugh their fill'. He admitted there could be too much exuberance. 'The only plagues of London are the immoderate drinking of fools and the frequency of fires'. (Was one the consequence of the other?).

The description brings 12th century London vividly to life, and the only regret is that he was writing a few years too soon to include the great new stone bridge which was to be one of the wonders of Europe. It was started in 1176 by Peter of Colechurch, who himself did not live to see it completed, over 30 years later in the reign of King John. There were 20 piers supporting 19 arches of unequal width and the bridge itself was 20 feet wide. There was a chapel dedicated to St Thomas at the north end and a drawbridge and a stone gate at the south end. Soon it was crowded with houses and shops and, on several occasions in the middle ages, it was the scene of splendid pageants and processions.

It was in the reigns of Henry's sons, Richard and John, that the City's control over the choice of its rulers was established. Soon after his accession in 1189, Richard the Lionheart concentrated his energies on the Third Crusade, a costly failure, doubly so because the King was captured by the Austrians on his way home and only released on payment of a huge ransom by his loyal subjects. Richard's need for money was immense, and he is reputed to have said that he would sell London if a purchaser could be found. In his absence, William of Longchamp, Justiciar of England, was in control of Royal administration — a man with many powerful enemies, including the King's younger brother, Count John. Since Longchamp controlled the Tower, John decided to win over the City. On the night of 7 October 1191 a band of citizens welcomed John with lanterns and torches. The next night the bell of St Paul's summoned a great concourse of the citizens to meet Count John and the magnates of the realm. At this meeting Longchamp was deprived of his authority and the citizens offered John their support.

Then a Commune was granted to the City and all swore to maintain it so long as it pleased the absent King. Following the continental model, the leader of the Commune took the title 'Mayor' and the first person to fill this position was Henry FitzAilwyn, who held it until his death in 1212. His mayoralty is dated from 1192 and the following year he was busy helping to organise the collection of Richard's ransom. When the King returned to London in 1194, for a brief visit before going back to his French wars, he granted the citizens a charter repeating his father's grant. He said nothing specific about the Commune or the privilege of appointing their own sheriffs, but neither did he go back on John's concessions.

Richard was killed and buried in France in 1199 and his brother swiftly moved to take control. Shortly after his coronation, John granted the City three charters, the most important of which officially gave them the right to choose their own sheriffs. (In the 14th century it became customary for the Mayor to choose one of the sheriffs by toasting him at a banquet. The custom fell into disuse, was revived during the Quo Warranto dispute in the 1680s and finally stopped in 1694.) London paid heavily for this, but then even more onerous burdens were laid on the City in a period of increased taxation which, together with John's many other impositions, aroused resentment throughout the country. By 1215, with the majority of the barons in arms against him, John made an attempt to get the Londoners on his side, by granting them a charter giving them the right to elect their own Mayor every year. It stipulated that the Mayor, once chosen, should present himself to the King or, in his absence, the King's justices, and the annual journey to fulfil this duty became in time the Lord Mayor's Show. (The journey was originally to Westminster. In 1422 Mayor William Walderne made part of the journey by river and from the mid-fifteenth century until the mid-nineteenth century the custom persisted. It ceased in 1857, when the Thames Conservancy was set up. Since the Law Courts were built in the Strand in 1882, the procession now goes there.) The citizens had won the right to choose a ruler who was not a Royal official and, from this time on, the Mayor took over from the Sheriffs as the chief citizen and leader of the City. But all this availed John nothing. Perhaps it was too late, perhaps the Londoners themselves were too divided. Certainly, while John was still negotiating with the citizens, the rebel barons entered the City and fortified it against him. When, a few weeks later, John was forced to append his seal to Magna Carta, that document included confirmation of the City's liberties, and the Mayor was appointed one of 25 barons who were charged with seeing that the charter was implemented.

Londoners had thus played a major part in national affairs and had established their right to choose their own rulers. The struggle to retain these privileges continued for hundreds of years, and there were times when they were abrogated, but the citizens of London still choose their Mayor and Sheriffs to this day, and are unique in so doing. London's government was a model for other towns all over Britain, and now it is the only local government in the country which has not undergone substantial change over the centuries.

But who were these 'citizens'? William Fitzstephen was impressed by their visible importance. 'The citizens of London are universally held up for admiration and renown for the elegance of their manners and dress, and the delights of their tables. Other cities have citizens, London's are called Barons.' It is clear that he was describing an elite, and probably the actual citizens did not number more than five percent of London's population at that time. (Liverymen make up a similar proportion of the City's working population today.) The Common Seal of London which dates from the early 13th century has 'sigillum baronum Londoniarum' inscribed on it, but in 1321 the title 'Baron' was reserved for the aldermanic class.

By the end of the 12th century London was a hive of activity, with a growing and fluctuating population, which included many 'foreigners' (this indicated they were from the English countryside) and 'aliens' (from abroad). The whole municipal structure of the City was based on the status of freemen, who were the citizens. At first the limits of citizenship were vague, but as the privileges became more closely defined, and commercial groupings more permanent, the numbers were restricted. Some time after 1300 the freedom came to be a privilege of the members of the guilds (forerunners of the City livery companies) and while it could be inherited, 'patrimony', it was also open to newcomers through 'servitude' (ie apprenticeship to a craft or trade), or 'redemption' through which outsiders could buy their way in, usually in the early days to the wealthier merchant guilds. The earliest documentary mentions of freemen are references to an order for the enrolment of apprentices c1230, and to a register of freemen and apprentices of 1275.

The early medieval guilds were a development from the religious fraternities which grew up round the City's many churches. These associations provided townsmen with the security of a small, close-knit community. The Anglo-Saxon word 'gild' means 'payment' and from their members' subscription the guilds raised funds which could be used for support in time of trouble, to pay for funerals, and for other social and charitable purposes. Since men of the same trade or craft tended to live near each other, many of these developed into trade or craft guilds — the earliest known being that of the Weavers in 1130. During the middle ages there was constant change and fluctuation. Some guilds grew larger and more powerful, others disappeared altogether. Some amalgamated to former larger groupings, others split into fragments. The variety of type and size was great, their prestige considerable. Chaucer described a group of guildsmen in the Prologue to the *Canterbury Tales*. A Londoner himself, he knew the City and its people well.

> 'A Haberdasher, a Dyer, a Carpenter,
> A Weaver and a Carpet-maker were
> Among our ranks, all in the livery
> Of one impressive guild fraternity.
> They were so trim and fresh their gear would pass
> For new. Their knives were not tricked out with brass
> But wrought with purest silver, which avouches
> A like display on girdles and on pouches.
> Each seemed a worthy burgess, fit to grace
> A guild-hall with a seat upon the dais.
> Their wisdom would have justified a plan
> To make each one of them an alderman.'

As always Chaucer had his tongue in his cheek. These were worthy citizens, but they had social aspirations which they were not likely to realise, and the aldermanic rank to which they looked with envy was only open to a few.

In the 12th and early 13th centuries the wards were known by the names of their aldermen, and the consequent changing of names makes the early history of the City particularly confusing. However, it emphasises the importance of the aldermen in their wards, which were originally areas under their personal control. They were the lawgivers and administrators, concerned with the maintenance of order in time of peace and with defence in time of war. They were great lords, Royal officials and landowners referred to as 'worshipful', 'gracious' and 'wise', or by one anxious petitioner as 'your high wisdoms'. Men could be put in the stocks for insulting them. Their dignity was emphasised by the scarlet furred robes, to which their rank entitled them. Sumptuary laws passed in 1402 and 1406 classed Mayors and former Mayors and their wives with knights for wearing of gold and fine fur, and it is not surprising to learn that, when men hesitated to become aldermen because of the expense, their wives urged them on. As Chaucer commented

> 'They had the capital and revenue
> Besides their wives declared it was their due.
> And if they did not think so, then they ought;
> To be called 'madam' is a glorious thought,
> And so is going to church and being seen
> Having your mantle carried, like a queen.'

At first, entry to the aldermanic ranks was in the hands of a few powerful merchant families, but by 1249 (the date of the earliest known aldermanic election) the principle of election by the freemen of the wards was established. (Towards the end of the 14th century an attempt was made to enforce a system of annual elections on the aldermen, but in 1393 their right to hold office for life was established; now as magistrates they retire at 70.) Even so, the aldermen were still a restricted oligarchy, with the great merchant guilds firmly entrenched; in the 12th and 13th centuries all the aldermen came from the purveyors of luxuries, 'the few who catered for the few': mercers, drapers, goldsmiths, pepperers and vintners. The first outsider to break into the charmed circle was a fishmonger, in 1291. Skinners and corders followed, and as time went on, other craft and trade guilds also had their aldermen although, of 260 aldermen elected in the 14th century, only nine were citizens from lesser companies. Even in the 16th century most of the aldermen came from the great companies, and Stow said the Lord Mayor must be chosen from them 'because those of inferior rank are not capable of such dignitie'. It was not until the 18th century that an alderman no longer had to translate to a great company in order to become Lord Mayor. (In 1742 Robert Willimot, Cooper, refused to so change). They were predominantly English, but London was a magnet for talent and enterprise, and 'foreign' and 'alien' merchants soon found their way into the craft and trading companies, some of them becoming members of the City's ruling class.

The first Mayor, Henry FitzAilwyn, was an alderman and, apart from one or two among his immediate successors about whom there is some uncertainty, all London's Mayors have been aldermen, though it was not specifically stated they must be until 1435. An ordinance of the Court of Common Council of 1385 stipulated that every future Mayor should 'have previously been Sheriff so that he may be tried as to his governance and bounty before he attains to the Estate of Mayor'. (A wise provision but not always adhered to at first). The title 'Lord Mayor' was never officially granted but gradually came into use during the 15th century.

Powerful as they were in their wards, it was when the aldermen emerged as a collective body towards the end of the 12th century that they became the central authority in the City. Their earliest meetings were at the Court of Husting and, at some stage in the 12th century, they must have begun to use a hall near the present Guildhall, where they met daily to deal with the ever-increasing complexity and volume of City business. In the late 13th century they began occasionally to summon 'wise and discrete' men from the wards for advice and consultation. This was the beginning of the Court of Common Council. At first they were only summoned when the aldermen thought fit and were elected in the wards under their presidency. They gradually developed into a regular assembly and, from 1376, the Common Council was part of the constitution of the City. For some years the commoners were elected by the guilds, then partly by the guilds and partly by the wards. In 1384 'an immense commonalty' approved election by the freemen of the wards, and common councilmen have been elected annually by Wardmote ever since then (although the aldermen still had considerable influence over the elections until the mid-17th century). The first recorded numbers were 96. Membership grew until it reached a peak of 240 in 1826, then gradually reduced. In January 1982 there were 136.

Before the end of the 14th century the Court of Common Council secured jurisdiction in financial matters and obtained the City Seal. The Court assumed legislative functions and, under a charter granted in 1341, has the right to reform the civic constitution and customs. Participation of the commons in the City government was paralleled by the introduction of the commons into Parliament. As in that body the senior partners (Lords/Aldermen) were dominant until the seventeenth century. But, unlike Parliament where Sovereign, Lords and Commons only meet at the formal opening, the Mayor, Aldermen and Commons have always met together in the Court of Common Council.

At first, distinction in the City between assemblies for legislative and for elective purposes was blurred, though assemblies for elections were always larger. The ancient folkmoot had disappeared, but the citizens still met in a 'great concourse'. As the population grew, this became unwieldy, and from the 13th century only the 'more sufficient men' were summoned by the Mayor and aldermen to attend meetings known as 'the Congregation'. Then in 1467, following an act of the Court of Common Council, the Masters and Wardens of the Misteries (guilds and livery companies) and others of the 'wealthier and wiser' citizens were added. In 1475 only liverymen from the Misteries and the Court of Common Council were summoned to the Congregation. In time it became customary for liverymen alone to be summoned, and this was finally settled by Statute in 1725. Although this seems like chopping and changing, most of the Common Councilmen were also liverymen, and many of them are today.

For some time the Congregation had been called Common Hall and the title first appeared in the records in 1738. The assembly no longer had legislative powers, but the citizens could use Common Hall to exercise influence in national affairs, through petitions to the Throne and Parliament, as they did in the 18th and 19th centuries. From the 16th century until the Reform Act of 1832 they also elected the City's Members of Parliament there. In 1406, the custom whereby the Commonalty chose two aldermen for the Court of Aldermen to elect the Mayor was established. This was the year when Richard Whittington was elected for the second time, and the first occasion when a religious service was held beforehand — it is said this was to put the electors in a peaceable frame of mind.

During the 13th and 14th centuries the City had been far from peaceable. There were violent feuds between rival guilds, outbreaks of xenophobia, struggles of the commoners against their oligarchical rulers and conflict between those rulers and the Crown. There were times of hardship — wars and rebellions, famine and plague. In the thick of it all were London's Mayors. They had considerable authority and many outward signs of dignity. Wearing his distinctive robes, surrounded by his guard of honour, preceded (from the late 14th century on) by his Swordbearer and his Serjeant-at-Arms bearing the mace, the Mayor stood out as the chosen leader of his colleagues and the City's representative in the Kingdom.

The right to elect their own Mayor granted to the citizens by John in 1215 did not mean any immediate democratic advance, and for many years the office remained in the hands of a few families. The craft guilds struggled to gain a foothold and they found a champion in Thomas FitzThomas, who was Mayor from 1261-5. He took the step of submitting important questions to a general assembly of the citizens for their approval, thus making the Commune a reality. During his term of office, relations with Henry III were fraught with difficulty because of the King's exorbitant demands for money. When in 1263 the City refused the King a loan, his son Prince Edward seized money and jewels held in the Temple. The Londoners were furious and vented their rage on the Queen, threatening her from London Bridge when she attempted to sail from the Tower to Westminster. 'Greatly moved to anger against the city', the King instructed his justices not to receive the re-elected Mayor when he presented himself at Westminster that autumn. Meanwhile Henry, like his father, John, had been having trouble with the barons, now led by Simon de Montfort. Once again the citizens joined with the barons and a contingent of Londoners fought at the battle of Lewes in 1264, where de Montfort was victorious. In the period of reconciliation which followed, FitzThomas did fealty to Henry in St Paul's, but he made it clear that loyalty could not be one-sided, saying 'My Lord so long as you are willing to be to us a good king we will be to you faithful subjects.'

De Montfort's triumph was shortlived, and the following year he was defeated and killed at the battle of Evesham. FitzThomas went with other citizens to confer with the King at Windsor and was never seen again. The King appointed a Warden to govern the City and the Mayoralty was suspended for five years until 1270 when John Adrien was elected. The next Mayor, Walter Hervey, was popular with the citizens, who re-elected him the following year in the teeth of aldermanic opposition. When the aldermen attempted to put in their nominee, Philip le Taylour, the citizens shouted 'We are the Commune. We ought to elect the mayor. Hervey is our man'. The aldermen wanted to appeal to the King for support but he was on his deathbed, so they gave way, although later in the year they degraded Hervey from his aldermanry.

Two notable Mayors ruled the city alternately for the next 12 years, Henry le Walleis and Gregory de Rokesley, but in 1285 Edward I deposed the Mayor and appointed a Warden. Edward took this action because of the violence of factions in the City and only restored its liberties on condition that the foreigners who supplied him with loans and the City with capital should enjoy security and freedom of trade. The citizens' rights were restored in 1298, when Henry le Walleis was again elected and the City paid a large sum into the Royal coffers, sadly depleted by Edward's campaigns in Wales and Scotland.

Edward I expelled the Jews from England in 1290, thus depriving himself of a valuable source of finance, though the Italian bankers after whom Lombard Street is named soon filled the gap. Resentment of foreigners (aliens) built up during Edward II's reign and the disturbances which resulted, combined with insistent demands by the City that the King repay his loans, led to suspension of the Mayoralty again in 1321. The King's unpopularity increased throughout the country, and Londoners supported his estranged Queen Isabel and the disaffected barons in the final crisis of the reign, which led to Edward's deposition in favour of his son in 1327. There were riots in the City for a month and the Mayor, Hamo de Chigwell, an experienced and popular man, was unable to control them. Things were so bad that, when his term of office expired that autumn, there was no election for some weeks, until the Queen authorised a free election and Richard de Betoyne was chosen.

The reign of Edward III was dominated by the war with France which began in 1337 and was to drag on for 100 years. The City was in sympathy with the King's commercial aims and provided massive support — money, ships, provisions and fighting men. In 1348 the Black Death reached England and in a few months killed about one third of the population. The death rate in London's crowded, insanitary circumstances must have been at least as high. It was believed that 50,000 bodies had been cast into vast burial pits on the site where the new Charterhouse monastery was built in 1371, but that is impossible, since estimates of the entire population of the City at that time suggest this was about 40,000. Whatever the extent of the disaster — there are no records for London — the City's vitality enabled it to recover quickly, though plague was to come again many times until the last outbreak of 1665.

It was in the reign of Richard II that London suffered the greatest dissension, which reflected the tensions in the realm. People were in a turmoil over the teachings of Wycliffe and oppressed by heavy and unjust taxes. In the City there was violent rivalry between the victualling and the manufacturing guilds. The King was a boy — only 14 years old — when the Peasants' Revolt broke out in 1381 over the hated poll tax. The Mayor, William Walworth, found himself in charge of a city with two rebel armies at its gates, and many of the people in sympathy with the rebels. Some of these supporters let the men of Kent onto London Bridge; others opened Aldgate to the men of Essex. The rebel leader Wat Tyler had ordered that there should be no looting, but the destruction and bloodshed were terrible. Mayor Walworth mustered two mass meetings of the citizens with the rebels, at the King's command, one at Mile End, which proved inconclusive, and the second fateful one at Smithfield, where, infuriated by Tyler's insolence to the King, the Mayor struck him down with his dagger (now in the Fishmongers' Hall). The King showed his gratitude by knighting Walworth and two other leading citizens: John Philipot, Mayor in 1378, who had fitted out ships at his own expense to clear the sea of pirates, and Nicholas Brembre, Mayor in the first year of Richard's reign, 1377. He was Mayor again from 1383-5 but got too involved with Royal politics, was tried for treason by Parliament in 1388 and executed at Tyburn — the only Mayor of London to meet this fate.

As Richard's reign drew towards its sombre close, he quarrelled with the City over a loan, and in 1392 deposed the Mayor and sheriffs (the last time the City was 'taken into the King's hands' in the Middle Ages). Although this estrangement lasted only a year, the City's relations with the King never recovered, and Londoners supported Henry Bolingbroke, son of John of Gaunt, when he ousted Richard in 1399.

OPPOSITE ABOVE: The White Tower. (ML) LEFT: The Norman Choir of St Bartholomew-the-Great. (JMH) RIGHT: 13th century stone entrance arch to the nave of St Bartholomew-the-Great with Tudor half-timber superstructure. (JMH)

33

ABOVE LEFT: First page of William Fitzstephen's Description of London reproduced in the *Liber Custumarum*. (GR) RIGHT: King John's Charter of 1215 granting the citizens of London the right to elect their own Mayor. (GR) BELOW: The 13th century City Seal with St Thomas Becket and the inscription 'Sigillum Baronum Londonarium'. (GR)

LEFT: A drawing of Old St Paul's from a 14th century Lambeth manuscript. (MC) RIGHT: View of 15th century London showing the White Tower, shipping and the Bridge. (BM) BELOW: Whittington Stone, Highgate, marks the spot where 'Dick' Whittington heard Bow Bells calling him back to the City of London. (JMH)

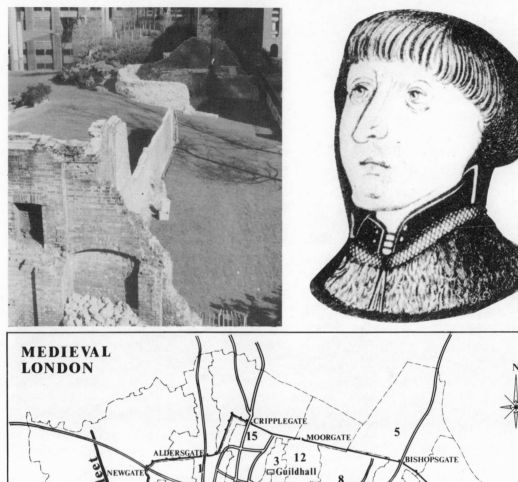

MEDIEVAL LONDON

LEFT: Surviving section of medieval city wall seen from the high walkway, Barbican. (JMH) RIGHT: Sir Ralph Jocelyn, Lord Mayor in 1464 and 1476, who repaired the city walls. (ML) BELOW: Sketch map of medieval London showing the ward boundaries. (MJH) (1) Aldersgate; (2) Aldgate; (3) Bassishaw; (4) Billingsgate, (5) Bishopsgate; (6) Bread Street; (7) Bridge; (8) Broad Street; (9) Candlewick; (10) Castle Baynard; (11) Cheap; (12) Coleman Street; (13) Cordwainer; (14) Cornhill; (15) Cripplegate; (16) Dowgate; (17) Farringdon Within; (18) Farringdon Without; (19) Langbourn; (20) Lime Street; (21) Portsoken; (22) Queenhithe; (23) Tower; (24) Vintry; (25) Walbrook.

36

The Rise of Capitalism

In 1319 Edward II granted London a charter, which finally established the guilds as the exclusive avenue to the freedom of the City, with the privileges and responsibilities which that entailed. In effect, only the citizens could trade or practise a craft in the City and only the citizens could have a share in its government. 'At this time', commented the *French Chronicle of London,* 'many of the people of the trades of London were arrayed in livery and a good time was about to begin.'

Considering the problems of 14th century London, that seems an over-optimistic prediction. But it was during the 14th century that the guilds strengthened their position and, from the 1390s, the great companies began to acquire their Royal charters of incorporation, and in time were known as Livery Companies. The term 'livery' originally described an allowance of food and clothing (granted to his household by a nobleman or bishop) but it had come to mean simply distinctive clothing. In the Middle Ages, livery was frequently worn by members of the guilds and fraternities. On special occasions everyone would wear the same livery, or uniform clothing, with badges to distinguish the separate groups. For example, 600 citizens rode out to meet Queen Margaret, second wife of Edward I, 'in one livery of red and white, with the cognizances of their misteries embroidered on their sleeves'. At times the use of a uniform was regarded by the Crown as a possible rallying point for political agitation, but the guilds were exempted from statutes of Edward III and Richard II against liveries. Nevertheless, they took care to have their right to a livery stated in their charters of incorporation.

Later, the right to wear a livery became the perquisite of the senior members of the companies, who bore the greater part of the expense and difficulty of achieving incorporation, and were responsible for the finances and administration of the company. So they were the liverymen and below them were the main body of freemen with, in some of the older companies, an intermediate rank of yeomanry who were not yet fully privileged. Inevitably these class distinctions within the companies hardened, and in some cases the yeomanry formed their own associations. The governing body of a company was chosen from the liverymen, and by the mid-16th century, each of the larger companies was administered by a Court of Assistants, which included the Master, Wardens and ex-Masters. They co-opted new members of the Court from the ranks of the liverymen and chose new liverymen from the yeomanry or freemen.

The medieval guilds already controlled their trade through powers of search, which enabled them to maintain standards and keep out interlopers. Their new charters confirmed and strengthened these powers, and this was their paramount concern in seeking incorporation. But they were at the same time religious and social organisations, and in the Middle Ages, the only reputable motive for association was religious or benevolent. It was that aspect therefore which featured predominantly in the guilds' petitions for charters of incorporation. So the Mercers urged the need to provide for the dependants of those who suffered shipwreck, while the Goldsmiths pleaded to be better able to help 'those who by fire and the smoke of quicksilver have lost their eyesight'. As the historian of the guilds, George Unwin explained, the declaration of a religious motive was 'a more or less conscious device for securing liberty of action'. However, it is interesting that today many of those great companies are primarily benevolent institutions, having lost their connection with a trade, and that even those which maintain a trade interest give considerable weight to their charitable responsibilities.

They are in a position to maintain their charitable work because of the wealth which has accumulated over the centuries. As corporate bodies, the livery companies could hold lands and property in mortmain — in other words the members of the company had the right to perpetual succession. Thus the companies' wealth and consequent prestige and influence were assured. They began to acquire halls, at first buying a nobleman's mansion or the buildings of a religious community, later purpose-building their own, with perhaps a chapel, reception rooms, buttery, pantry and stables as well as the main hall. In Richard II's reign two or three companies had halls; when Richard III began his brief reign a century later, there were 28 livery halls and others were being built.

Incorporation was a lengthy and expensive business, only possible for the wealthy trading companies in the early days. Many of the smaller craft guilds disappeared completely. Others were absorbed by stronger companies with related trades, or two or three guilds in the same field of activity amalgamated to form a company. As guilds fought for their position, or for their very existence, violent quarrels frequently broke out and there were pitched battles in the streets of London. The great companies armed their retainers like feudal magnates and much blood was shed as goldsmiths fought tailors, tailors fought drapers, pepperers fought goldsmiths — and so on. Many of these struggles were over the vital question of precedence and often the Mayor had to settle the dispute. By the time Mayor Robert Billesdon delivered his famous judgement of 1484 over whether the Skinners or the Merchant Taylors should take sixth or seventh place, the worst of the fighting was over. The order of precedence was settled in 1516, when the Court of Aldermen issued a list of companies and guilds in order of importance. At the head were the great twelve: Mercers, Grocers, Drapers, Goldsmiths, Fishmongers, Skinners/Merchant Taylors, Haberdashers, Salters, Ironmongers, Vintners, Clothworkers, (in 1516 these were still the Shearmen, whose amalgamation with the Fullers in 1528 formed the Clothworkers' Company.)

Although incorporation was always granted by Royal charter, the civic authorities were careful to maintain control over the livery companies. From 1437, charters had to be presented to the Mayor and Aldermen for approval, and from 1560, when the Stationers prayed to have a livery 'like other companies', application for the grant of a livery had to be made to the Court of Aldermen. From the beginning of the 17th century, guilds were expected to obtain a licence to sue for incorporation, and the Court of Aldermen has limited the number of every company granted a livery since 1712. So the Mayor and aldermen kept their influence over the companies who were, as A.L. Rowse put it, 'bone of their bone'.

In the 15th and 16th centuries the livery companies grew in numbers, in importance and in usefulness. They were an essential part of the close-woven fabric of London society which made provision for so much as yet neglected by the state: welfare, internal security, defence in time of war, supply in times of emergency. These matters were dealt with by the citizens themselves acting through the wardmote, the parish vestry and the guilds and livery companies. Obeying mayoral precepts, the companies mustered troops against Jack Cade in 1450, the Pilgrimage of Grace in 1536 and Wyatt's rebellion in 1554. They fitted out ships against the Spanish Armada in 1588. They raised endless loans for the Crown. Through their control of their trade they enforced government economic regulations. In times of shortage, the people were supplied with grain and fuel which had been bought in and stored by the companies. They dealt with everything from the maintenance of buildings to the settlement of disputes.

Then as now, they played a vital part in pageantry, particularly when Royalty was welcomed to the City. In 1486, when Henry VII's queen, Elizabeth of York entered the City, 'all the streets through which she should pass by were cleanly dressed and beseen with cloths of tapestry and arras and some streets such as Cheap, hung with rich cloth of gold, velvet and silk. Along the streets from the Tower to St Paul's stood in order all the crafts of London in their liveries'. When she sailed up the river, she was accompanied 'by the mayor, sheriffs and aldermen of the city and many worshipful commoners chosen out of every craft in their liveries in barges freshly furnished with banners and streamers of silk richly beseen with the arms and badges of their crafts'. Archbishop Thomas Cranmer, in a letter to the English Ambassador at the Imperial court, described the overture to Anne Boleyn's coronation, when 'the King and Queen being at Greenwich, all the Crafts of London thereunto well appointed, in several barges decked after the most gorgeous and sumptuous manner, with divers pageants thereunto belonging, repaired and waited all together upon the Mayor of London; and so, well furnished, came all unto Greenwich, where they tarried and waited for the Queen's coming to her barge; which so done they brought her unto the Tower, trumpets, shawms, and other divers instruments playing and making great melody, which as is reported was as comely done as never was like in any time nigh to our remembrance'.

The river was part of the setting for the Lord Mayor's Procession from the mid-15th century, but this did not become the major civic occasion until the late 16th century, reaching a peak of splendour in the early 17th century. Before then, the outstanding procession in London was the Midsummer Marching Watch, which Stow remembered from his childhood, when 'every man's door being shadowed with greene Birch, long Fennel, Saint Johns wort, Orpin, white Lillies, and such like, garnished upon with Garlands of beautiful flowers, had also Lampes of glasse, with oyle burning in them all the night, some hung out braunches of yron curiously wrought, contayning hundreds of Lampes light at once, which made a goodly shew . . .'. The march was lit with 700 cressets, 500 being found by the companies, the other 200 by the Chamber of London. 'Besides the which lights every Constable in London, in number more then 240 had his cresset.' More than 2,000 men took part in the watch: old soldiers, gunners, archers, pikemen, whifflers, drummers and fifes, standard and ensign bearers, sword players, trumpeters, morris dancers — and many more, and finally the Mayor and the Sheriffs with their entourages. In 1539, Henry VIII forbade the Midsummer Watch, because of the expense and, though it was revived occasionally, it died out, and by the end of the 16th century the Lord Mayor's Procession had taken its place, with the livery companies providing marvellous and elaborate pageants.

The pageantry was an outward and visible sign of London's prosperity and importance. On civic occasions the companies vied with each other to do honour to the Mayor with lavish and ingenious displays. On Royal occasions the display was a demonstration of loyalty and an acknowledgement of the interdependence of the City and the Crown. For, despite the turbulence of the Wars of the Roses in the 15th century, and the disruption of religious changes in the 16th century, the old struggles between the Kings and the City government were played out, and the troubles of the 17th century were yet to come. The civic government had become part of the nation's establishment. The City's position was assured, its privileges protected by Royal charters. The weak government of Henry VI offered no threat. The strong government of Edward IV and the Tudors provided conditions for flourishing trade and, from the wealth generated by that trade, the City was able to provide the finance needed by the Crown.

One of the favourite legends about Richard Whittington is how, when he gave a banquet for Henry V and his French bride Catherine, he not only cast costly spices on the fire to perfume the air, but also £60,000's worth of Royal debts. If not to be taken too literally, the story does symbolise the beginning of the happier relationship between the Crown and the City. However, such a grand gesture would be a rare public relations exercise. The whole question of lending and borrowing was complicated in the Middle Ages by the attitude of the Church to what was then called usury. In religious terms, lending money for interest was a sin. In commercial terms, it was a necessity, and was practised despite the Church's condemnation. The moral dilemma was less when moneylending was in the hands of the Jews but, after their expulsion from England, Italian and then English capitalists took over. The great City merchants controlled wide financial empires and were adept in the techniques of speculating in futures and buying on credit. The face of capitalism might be unacceptable, the whole idea of 'unearned' profit at odds with the ethics of the time, but it was a fact of life. The medieval attitude to capitalist finance was ambivalent for, while an individual who charged interest on a loan might be accused of usury, the international money market continued its activities unhindered, and kings, feudal magnates, bishops, abbots and even Popes regularly used the great banking houses.

With the industrial and commercial progress of the 16th century, the official attitude to the taking of interest had to change, and gradually the argument moved from whether charging any interest was a sin to what was a fair rate. In England a statute of 1545, while condemning usury, allowed that a limited interest might be allowed in certain circumstances, for example when repayment was delayed. In 1552 an act prohibited all taking of interest as 'a vice most odious and detestable', but the statute of 1571 allowed the taking of moderate interest (up to 10%). However, it was many years before the idea was generally accepted. Shakespeare's audiences sympathised with 'the noble Antonio' who took no interest while Shylock demanded his pound of flesh, if he was to forgo interest on his loan to Bassanio.

In that same year (1571) Queen Elizabeth rode into the City in state to inspect a great new commercial venture. Sir Thomas Gresham had built in London an exchange for merchants, to rival the Antwerp Bourse, and now that usury was no longer a crime, he was able to transfer the business of the Royal loan from Antwerp to London. The idea of a London exchange had been mooted by Gresham's father in Henry VIII's reign and such a building was long overdue. Richard Clough, writing from Antwerp in 1561, exclaimed, 'Considering what a city London is and that in so many years they have not found the means to make a bourse! but must walk in the rain when it raineth more like pedlars than merchants!'. Indeed, unless merchants met in St Paul's, they had to discuss business walking up and down Lombard Street.

Gresham's Exchange was a fine Renaissance building with columned arcades round a spacious paved quadrangle. The ground floor was given over to wholesalers and there were retail shops in the upper galleries. Traders were hesitant about this new departure and many shops were still empty the day before the Queen was expected. So Gresham offered the unlet premises rent-free for a year to the existing tenants, if they would stock and light them in time. It worked. The Royal visit was a great success, and the delighted Elizabeth ordered the herald to proclaim that it would henceforth be known as the Royal Exchange.

It was high time a more realistic attitude to capitalism was adopted, for Europe was undergoing the birthpangs of the modern world. Technological advance had promoted remarkable developments. Designs for ocean-going ships, navigational aids like the compass and the astrolabe, and the adventurous spirit of men like Columbus and Da Gama had opened up new worlds to European traders. The printing press had enabled the ideas of the Renaissance and Reformation to spread far beyond the narrow circles of those who could afford manuscript books. Gunpowder and firearms were revolutionising warfare. The unity of the medieval world was giving way to the emergence of nation states with powerful and ambitious rulers. Countries on the Atlantic seaboard like Spain, Portugal, France, the Netherlands and England were poised to compete for the riches of the Americas and the East.

England's foremost trading company until the mid-16th century was the Merchant Adventurers. The members were merchants concerned with the export of cloth, many of them from the greater livery companies, and their headquarters was the Mercers' Hall. Although they had a monopoly of the English cloth trade, they faced fierce competition from the Germans of the Hanse, who were established at the Steelyard in Dowgate. These merchants, who had won their privileges from the Kings of England since Henry III's time, in return for financial assistance, were greatly resented by the English, but they were useful for the economy while English merchant shipping was inadequate. By the late 16th century this was no longer the case, and they were finally driven out in 1598. Henry VII and Henry VIII had encouraged shipbuilding and, by Elizabeth's reign, England was well on the way to becoming a maritime nation. New companies were formed to open up routes to the wealth of the East but, since Spain and Portugal still controlled the southern sea lanes, English explorers attempted to find a way round the north. Voyages seeking a NE passage to Cathay led to the founding of the Muscovy Company in 1555, which opened up trade with Russia and Persia. Attempts to find a NW passage were not immediately fruitful, but ultimately led to the formation of the Hudson's Bay Company a century later. Meanwhile the Guinea Company traded in Africa and in 1578 two London merchants, Edward Osborne (Lord Mayor in 1583) and Richard Staper 'seriously considering what benefit might grow to the commonwealth' formed the Levant Company to trade with Turkey. Five years later they helped to finance an epic land journey to the East, led by John Newbery and Ralph Fitch, which opened up communications with India. In 1589 a group of London merchants applied to the Privy Council for permission to send a trading expedition to the Indies, and this led to the formation of the East India Company, which was granted its charter of incorporation in 1599. As far as America was concerned, the only way for the English to get at the gold and silver which flowed into Spain was through privateering which, since it was directed against the national enemy, was winked at by the Queen. Drake's great voyage round the world from 1577-80 received Royal as well as City finance, and proved a splendid investment, bringing an alleged 300% profit. Drake received a knighthood from Elizabeth in 1581 and was made an honorary member of the Drapers' Company in October 1588, after the defeat of the Spanish Armada.

Spain had been England's ally at the beginning of the 16th century, when Catherine of Aragon came to marry Henry VII's son. But soon after that, Europe was torn by the religious controversy of the Reformation, and Catholic Spain became Protestant England's mortal enemy. Protestant ideas had survived in England, particularly in London, since Wycliffe's time, but it was Henry VIII's desire for a divorce from Catherine of Aragon which made the government break with Rome. The trial of the case against the King's marriage was opened by Cardinal Wolsey and the papal legate, Campeggio, in the palace of Bridewell, but was unable to reach a conclusion. The King's Great Matter dragged on while Parliament, led by Thomas Cromwell, passed a succession of statutes which severed the Church of England from Papal control. When Anne Boleyn was already expecting her first child, the newly consecrated Archbishop of Canterbury, Thomas Cranmer pronounced the King's first marriage null and void. All men of importance in the Kingdom, including the citizens of London, had to take the Oaths of Succession and Supremacy, acknowledging the King as head of the Church and Anne Boleyn's heirs as his rightful successors. Then Henry and Cromwell turned on monasteries, nunneries and friaries all over the kingdom, confiscated their property and sent the monks, nuns and friars packing. There were a great many of these religious houses in the City of London: the Greyfriars of Newgate, the Dominicans or Blackfriars, the Whitefriars, Austin Friars, Crutched Friars. There were the great priories of St Bartholomew and St Mary Overy, Southwark, the monastery of the Charterhouse, the nunneries of St Helen's in Bishopsgate and of the Poor Clares in Minories. One of the first to be founded and the first to go was the priory of the Holy Trinity just within Aldgate. By 1540 all the religious houses in the country had been dissolved and their property disposed of. In London, areas which had been outside the City's jurisdiction as liberties of the Church, were sold off or granted to Royal favourites. Some became great men's houses; others, like St Helen's, whose hall was bought by the Leathersellers', became livery halls. Warehouses, glass manufactories and arms stores took over. The Blackfriars' church became a storehouse for the properties of pageants.

Although he despoiled the Church, Henry VIII was not a Protestant, but his son Edward VI was, and so were the influential members of his council, notably the Duke of Somerset and later the Duke of Northumberland. New laws introduced English church services throughout the land. As they were religious foundations, the livery companies and guilds were affected by legislation which abolished chantries for saying masses for the souls of the dead, since they had many trust funds for this purpose. They had to pay a rent charge to the Crown covering those revenues which were intended for the chantries, but later they were compelled to buy up the rent charges, and so acquired the property free from the obligation of religious duties. For many companies it must have been a great relief not to have to attend so many anniversary services. They still maintained a strong religious association, held their own guild services and of course provided for the funerals of their members, with the coffin covered by a treasured company pall. Liverymen attended these services in their gowns and hoods and the yeomanry 'in cleanly apparel and without their aprons', as a record of the Pewterers states.

The City was closely involved with the troubles which followed the death of Edward VI at the age of 16. By his father's will, he should have been succeeded by his sister, Princess Mary, daughter of Catherine of Aragon and a fervent Catholic. Fearing a reversal of his policies, the Duke of Northumberland persuaded the dying Edward to alter his will in favour of Lady Jane Grey, a Protestant and newly wed at the age of 15 to Northumberland's son. Among the signatories were the Lord Mayor and Aldermen, but they had no part in the proclamation of Queen Jane, which was received without enthusiasm in the City. When Northumberland set off to confront Mary, who had retreated to Norfolk, the Lord Mayor and Aldermen met with the Lords of the Council at Castle Baynard and agreed to support the rightful Queen. The citizens were jubilant when Mary was proclaimed at Cheapside, and a few days later she entered the City in triumph. But they had not anticipated the religious excesses which followed. At a stroke, England became Catholic again, and those who professed the Protestant faith were persecuted. The civic authorities conformed, and remained loyal to Queen Mary who, at the height of her unpopularity, made a courageous defence of her marriage to King Philip of Spain and her treatment of heretics, before the citizens in Guildhall. But the fires of Smithfield, in which so many Protestant martyrs perished, strengthened Protestant feeling, and must have contributed to the extraordinary enthusiasm of the City's welcome to Elizabeth when she became Queen on Mary's death in 1558.

Elizabeth rode through London on her way to her coronation in January 1559, and the chronicler Holinshed compared the City to 'a stage wherein was showed the wonderful spectacle of a noble hearted princess towards her most loving people'. Everywhere she was greeted by carefully staged pageants glorifying her accession. Children declaimed verses lengthily and sometimes inaudibly above the excited throng, but Elizabeth strained to listen . . . 'for so much as the noise was great by reason of the presse of people so that she could scarse hear the child which did interpret the said pageant' (in Gracechurch Street). All along the streets from Fenchurch Street to 'the high end of Cheap' stood the companies of the City 'enclosed with rails hanged with cloths and themselves well apparalled with many rich furs and their livery hoods upon their shoulders in comelie and seemly manner'. When the Recorder presented her with a crimson satin purse, richly wrought with gold and containing 1,000 marks in gold the Queen replied 'I thank my lord mayor, his brethren and you all. And whereas your request is that I should continue your good lady and queen, be ye assured that I will be as good to you as ever queen was to her people'.

The reign of Elizabeth was a time of great opportunity, growth and expansion. The possibilities seemed boundless; the achievements were remarkable. It was also a time of great danger and hardship. Elizabeth's skilful diplomacy averted war for 25 years, but the threat was always present and the Queen's life often in danger from would-be assassins. From 1585 until Elizabeth's death in 1603, England was at war with Spain and faced a series of rebellions in Ireland. The City's resources were called on as never before to meet the demands for ships, troops, provisions and money. The citizens responded magnificently, though it was hard to keep it up. In the late 1590s they tried to resist a Royal request for a loan, pleading scarcity. Elizabeth sharply suggested the livery should do less feasting — and an order of the Court of Aldermen went forth accordingly.

The economic problems of the time were severe and in some ways remarkably similar to our own. The Elizabethans also suffered from accelerating inflation and widespread unemployment. The causes of inflation in the 16th century were little understood at the time and are disputed by historians today. The gold and silver flooding in from the New World were partly to blame; so were earlier attempts to mint more money by Wolsey and Henry VIII, which only debased the currency. Probably, the swift rise in population was the most influential factor. But whatever the causes, it was distressing and bewildering to people who still believed that everything should have a just price. The increase was uneven, reaching a peak in mid-century, but over the whole of the Tudor period, prices went up about 500%. Stow commented wrily on inflation when describing the cost of the repairs to London Bridge a century before his time '. . . by which accompt then made may be partly gessed the great charges and discharges of that Bridge at this day when things be stretched to so great a price'.

Wages lagged behind prices in an age when there were no unions to protect the interests of the workers. The livery companies, which have sometimes been described as early trade unions, did care for their members' interests in many ways, but they were run by master craftsmen and employers, who benefited from the higher prices they received for their products. The government intervened with the Statute of Apprentices in 1563 which recognised that 'wages are in divers places too small and not answerable to this time' and gave the JPs the authority to regulate wages according to the conditions in their area. It also regulated terms of apprenticeship, but it was more concerned to make sure that everyone did the work that was available to them, than with tackling unemployment. Those who were fit to work and yet had no employment were regarded as 'sturdy beggars' and a danger to public order. Legislation for relief of the poor ordered 'sturdy beggars' to be punished by 'whipping until their body be bloody', boring through the ear, the stocks and in persistent cases, death.

The population increase was seen most dramatically in London. In 1509 the inhabitants of the City and its immediate surroundings numbered about 50,000. By 1558 there were nearly 90,000 and by the end of Elizabeth's reign the population of the metropolitan area was about 250,000. People poured into London from the countryside. Some of them had been dispossessed of their livelihood by enclosures for sheep farming or the dissolution of the local monastery. Others simply came to seek their fortunes in the capital City, which had far outstripped all other towns in England. Refugees from religious persecution in the Netherlands and France came in huge numbers, bringing with them valuable skills in textiles and glassmaking. Soon the open spaces left after the closure of the religious houses were filled up, gardens and fields were built over and great houses let off into small tenements. Stow's description of the suburbs is punctuated by regret for the open fields which he remembered from his childhood now 'encroached upon by building of filthy cottages'. In 1580 a Royal proclamation charged the Lord Mayor to see that no new houses should be built within three miles of the gates of the City 'where no former house hath been known to have been in the memory of such as are now living'. It also forbade crowding more families into existing houses, and hopefully suggested that people should go and live in 'other places abroad in the realm where many houses rest uninhabited to the decay of divers ancient boroughs and towns'.

The attempt to limit the growth of London was doomed to failure, but the City of London remained within its ancient boundaries, for its rulers were not interested in attempting to govern areas where they could not exercise control through the livery companies and the wards. By the 14th century, the boundaries of the wards were fixed, and bars across the main roads beyond the walls marked the outer limits of the City, as at Temple Bar and Holborn Bars. The huge ward of Farringdon in the west was divided into Farringdon Without and Farringdon Within in 1393/4 because 'the governance thereof is too laborious and grievous for one person to occupy and duly govern the same'. The City authorities had long been concerned with the borough of Southwark, for all too often it harboured refugees from City justice who fled across the bridge. In 1550 Edward VI sold the borough to the City and it became the ward of Bridge Without, but the inhabitants were not citizens of London. Their alderman was appointed by the Court of Aldermen and they sent no representatives to the Court of Common Council. The wards were the most important of the self-governing communities in the City, which also included parishes and

43

precincts. Their affairs were managed by the Wardmotes, whose meetings were recorded in Wardmote Inquests. In the Wardmote the heads of households met to run the affairs of the ward, settle disputes, watch over the conduct of the inhabitants and see to the lighting of the streets by individual householders. From among themselves they appointed beadles, scavengers to remove the rubbish, watchmen, and constables to keep the peace. (Southwark was separated from the City of London by the London Government Act 1899. The Aldermanry of Bridge Without was reserved for the Senior Alderman, until it was abolished in 1978. The City still retains a traditional link with Southwark through the ancient courts of its three manors. The Recorder of London, as High Steward, and the Secondary and Undersheriff, as High Bailiff of Southwark, attend these courts once a year.)

Within its boundaries, the City of London was ahead of all other towns in making some provision for the poor and for education. In the Middle Ages much of this had been left in the hands of religious organisations like the guilds or the monasteries. When the latter were dissolved, the Royal intent was to found new schools and hospitals in their place, and in London the City authorities took the lead, providing endowment for five hospitals: St Bartholomew's for the sick, St Thomas's for the infirm, Christ's Hospital for the education of orphans, St Mary Bethelem (later known as Bedlam) for the insane. The palace of Bridewell, which Edward VI had sold to the City, was set up as a house of correction for vagabonds or 'sturdy beggars'. City merchants endowed schools all over the country as well as in London, and several of these were direct foundations by the livery companies and are still associated with them today. Between 1541 and 1600 London citizens also built 37 almshouses, and some of them are still providing for old people. In Elizabeth's reign, government legislation began to recognise that provision for the poor was not only a social necessity but a public responsibility. The Elizabethan Poor Law established the principle of corporate provision for relieving poverty, and ordered the parishes to levy a compulsory poor rate, and to use it to provide for the needy and set the fit to work.

'London thou art the flower of cities all' wrote William Dunbar in 1501. By the end of the century Stow was regretting the changes he had seen in his lifetime. But Elizabethan London, though much more crowded than in Dunbar's day, was still a beautiful city. Dominating the whole was St Paul's, minus, alas, its great steeple (at 490 feet the highest in Europe) which was struck by lightning in 1561 and never replaced. But London's skyline was still indented with the towers and spires of nearly 100 churches. In the heart of the City towered the great roof of the Guildhall, which the citizens built in the early 15th century with its own chapel and library. The spaces left by the religious houses were taken up with great houses and the halls of livery companies. The walls, which had been repaired throughout the Middle Ages, still circled the City from the Tower in the East to the extension of the Roman wall, which took in Blackfriars, bringing them down beside the mouth of the Fleet river. West of the Fleet were the Inns of Court, straddling the boundary between the City of London and Westminster. They were now full of gentlemen's sons completing their education, by getting a smattering of the law and incidentally taking part in some of the earliest secular dramatic productions. The drama flourished in Elizabethan London in a miraculous way, despite the disapproval of the authorities, whose outlook tended to be Puritan. Licensed companies of players performed in inn yards in the City, but the theatres were built outside, at Shoreditch and on the south bank, where they competed with the Bear Garden and the Bull Ring. (There was also a theatre at Blackfriars, but that was still a 'liberty' outside the City's jurisdiction). The theatres provided wonderful business for the London watermen, who would row patrons across when the flag went up and the trumpeter heralded the performance of another of William Shakespeare's plays at the Globe. The river was always thronged with shipping of all sorts: sometimes great processions of barges as on Lord Mayor's Day, or when the Queen sailed down to her favourite palace at Greenwich. There were barges and lighters unloading at the wharves at Queenhithe, Dowgate and Billingsgate; fishing smacks, eel ships, coal boats from Newcastle, pleasure boats. The historian Camden wrote that the Thames was 'like a wooded grove'. On the north, the City was still surrounded by fields, providing opportunities for sports, archery practice — and a place to dry the laundry. To the west beyond Temple Bar great men's houses stretched along the Strand, linking the City with the centre of Government: the Royal Palace of Whitehall and the Palace of Westminster where Parliament sat, with an increasingly active and articulate House of Commons. In the next century the conflict between Crown and Parliament was to split the nation in a struggle which closely involved the City of London.

Woodcut of London from the *Chronycle of Inglande* printed by Wynkyn de Worde 1497. (ML)

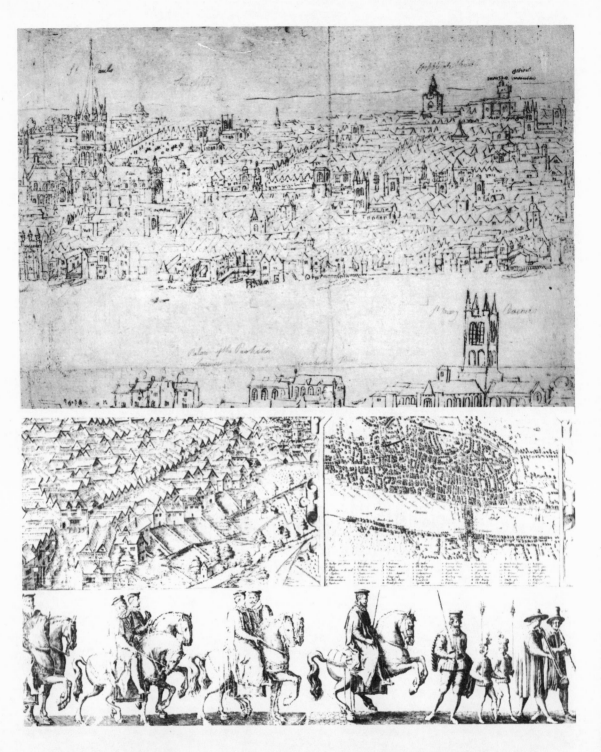

ABOVE: Detail from drawing of London by Wyngaerde 1543-44 showing Old St Paul's before the spire was destroyed. (GL) BELOW: Aldermen in procession from John Norden's map of London. (GL/JA)

ABOVE: Edward VI riding in procession through the City to his coronation. (ML) BELOW: Sir Thomas Gresham's Royal Exchange. Engraving by Hollar. (ML)

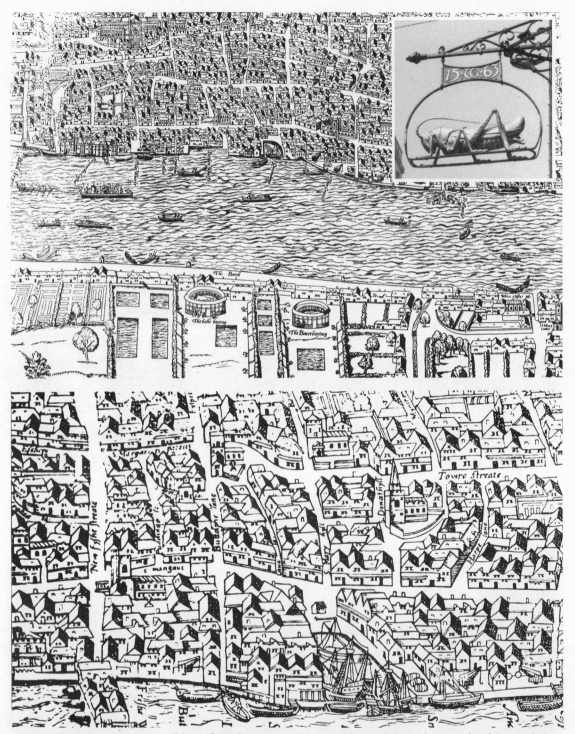

INSET: Gilded grasshopper, emblem of Sir Thomas Gresham outside Martin's Bank in Lombard Street where Gresham's house used to be. (JMH) ABOVE: Detail from Ralph Agas's map of London c1561. (GL) BELOW and OPPOSITE ABOVE: Enlarged detail from Agas. (GL) BELOW: The NE section of the City showing archery practice and laundry on Moor Field. Detail from an anonymous copperplate map of 1558. (GL/JA)

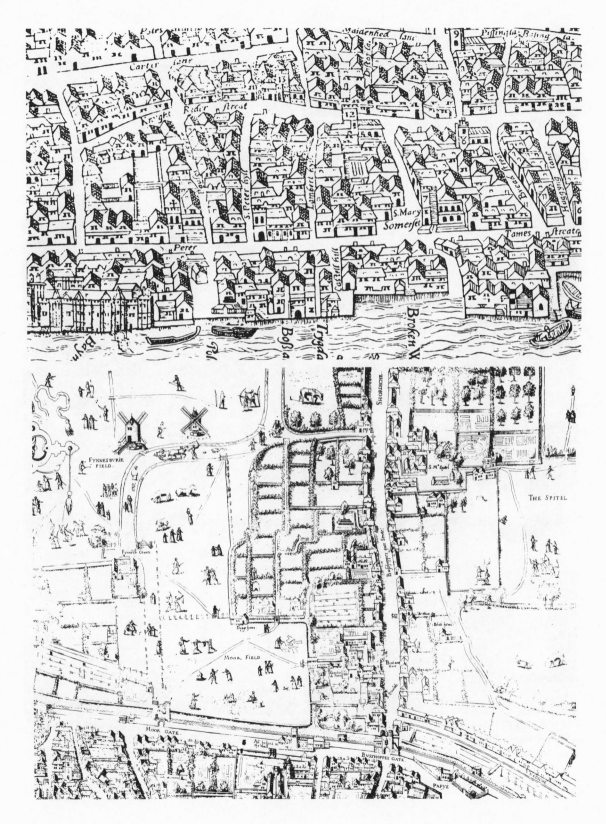

ABOVE LEFT: Memorial in St Andrew Undershaft to John Stow, author of the *Survey of London,* (d1605). At an annual service the Lord Mayor replaces the quill in his hand. (JMH) RIGHT: Bust of William Shakespeare in the garden of St Mary Aldermanbury; (monument to John Heminge and Henry Condell of the parish, to whom we owe the first Folio of 1623). (JMH) BELOW LEFT: Carefully preserved 16th century buildings at Staple Inn, High Holborn. (JMH) RIGHT: Statue (1586) of Queen Elizabeth I in a niche on St Dunstan-in-the-West, originally over Ludgate. (JMH)

The Melting Pot

In April 1603 King James VI of Scotland left Edinburgh and took the road south. As he rode through his new Kingdom, the City of London prepared a lavish welcome, but an outbreak of the plague prevented their demonstration of loyalty. The splendid pageants which Ben Jonson had arranged for the usual procession through the City streets had to be postponed. However, Lord Mayor Robert Lee was knighted at Greenwich and the aldermen at Whitehall — a new departure, for Elizabeth was as sparing of honours as she was of money. There was a grand reception in the City the following year and the Londoners soon had another opportunity to express their enthusiasm for the King after the Gunpowder Plot, in November 1605. Bonfires were lit in the streets for deliverance from 'this most horrible treason' and the heads of the plotters were displayed in customary fashion on the spikes at the Southwark end of London Bridge.

Pageantry was dear to the heart of James, who believed in the divinity of kings, 'For kings are not only God's lieutenants on earth and sit upon God's throne, but even by God himself they are called Gods', as he informed Parliament in 1610. This view of the monarchy was reflected in the masques, which were characteristic of Stuart court entertainment. They were a medley of poetry, music and dance set against a background of brilliantly ingenious scenery, all combining to glorify the Crown.

Emulating the court, the livery companies' displays for the Lord Mayor's Show reached a peak of elaboration. In 1613 the Grocer, Sir Thomas Middleton, was elected on the day that his brother, Sir Hugh Middleton, celebrated the opening of his New River scheme to bring fresh water to the City, in which the King had half shares. Sir Thomas's pageant for Lord Mayor's day was designed and written by his namesake, the dramatist Thomas Middleton. In Soper Lane the Lord Mayor was greeted in blank verse by 'a Grave Feminine Shape' with long white hair and a model of steeples and turrets on her head representing London. On the river floated five islands 'artfully garnished with all manner of Indian fruits, trees, drugs and spiceries' and, when he arrived at the Great Conduit on his return, there was a mountain wreathed in clouds which were dispersed by Truth's Angels clad in white. In 1616 Anthony Munday's pageant for the Fishmonger, John Leman, had the King of the Moors on a golden leopard (a sign of the Fishmongers' friendship with the Goldsmiths) hurling gold and silver among the crowd on one float, while on another a pelican stood under a lemon tree feeding her young with her blood, thus symbolising 'the cherishing love borne by the mayor to the citizens' and yet another showed Sir William Walworth in his bower. John Webster's pageant for the Merchant Taylors in 1624 had 'a fair terrestrial globe circled about in convenient seats with seven of our most famous navigators'.

The explorations of men like Frobisher, Drake, Hawkins and Gilbert in the sixteenth century led to the beginnings of colonisation in James I's reign, and the livery companies were involved in the first settlement in Virginia. Raleigh's earlier attempts to establish a colony there had ended in failure but, in 1606, the Virginia Companies of Plymouth and London were chartered with the intention of 'propagating all Christian religion to such people as yet live in Darkness'. It was also recognised that this was a practical way of disposing of surplus population, and the livery companies were urged by mayoral precept and example to contribute. Fifty six of the companies responded, and seven ships sailed across the Atlantic in 1609 with the first 'Virginians'. More money for the project was raised by public lottery in 1612 and the companies invested again, though they were now involved in a colonising venture in Ireland.

The rebellion in Ulster, which had troubled the last years of Elizabeth's reign, had finally been quelled, and the government was desirous of maintaining the peace by introducing settlers from the mainland. But where was the money to come from? James turned to the City of London and at first met with little enthusiasm. However, they agreed to send an inspection party of 'grave, wise and discreet citizens' who were royally entertained. No effort was spared to convince them of the advantages of the good agricultural land on which they could settle poor people from London's superfluous population. They were persuaded — some said hoodwinked — and in 1610 the Irish Society was formed. The twelve great companies were all induced to participate, and each of them brought minor companies into the venture. The town of Derry was built up, fortified and renamed Londonderry, and the companies began to develop those lands which had been allotted to them. The Irish Society was granted a Royal charter in 1615 but the companies made a loss for many years and the work of settlement proceeded slowly — too slowly for the King's liking.

The seventeenth century was fraught with difficulties for the livery companies, particularly because of the ever-increasing financial demands of the Crown, but it was also a time of great expansion. Many new companies were incorporated by James I and Charles I, who found this a convenient way of supplementing their income, since the companies paid handsomely for their charters. Some of these incorporations were of old companies like the Butchers, Horners, Plumbers and others; some were breakaway groups from established companies like the Feltmakers who separated from the Haberdashers, the Glovers from the Leathersellers and the Apothecaries from the Grocers. As well as these, there were many companies representing new trades, like the Coachmakers, Gunmakers, Glass Sellers and Spectacle Makers. The imports from Virginia led to the founding of the Tobacco Pipe Makers Company, granted a charter by James I, who conveniently ignored his own 'Counterblast against Tobacco' in which he had utterly condemned the habit of smoking. More new companies were incorporated during the reigns of the first two Stuarts than in any comparable period, many of them before receiving the permission of the Court of Aldermen, to the latter's great annoyance.

With the expansion of London, the companies were in danger of losing their influence as workers moved out into the suburbs, but several of them sought and acquired powers of search over wider areas. There was an attempt in Charles I's reign to incorporate the new suburbs, but it was unpopular in the City and the plan was dropped. Thus a growing area of London was left without any satisfactory government. Within the City limits the proportion of freemen was higher than ever before. This was owing to the growth in the numbers of companies and the expansion within them. In the early 16th century the cost of 'redemption' into the companies had been greatly reduced. It has been estimated that about three-quarters of the adult male population in mid-century were citizens. The companies were also concerned to regain control over workers in their craft since, under the 'custom of London', freemen of a buying and selling guild were free of any other, though the manual trades were more strictly regulated. Also because of patrimony, many freemen had no link with their trade. Throughout the seventeenth century the City government supported the movement to gather the citizens into their proper trades and many acts of Common Council were passed to this end. But already several of the greater companies were more concerned with social organisation and City government than with trade.

Charles I succeeded his father in 1625 and again the City was afflicted with a severe outbreak of plague. When he brought his French bride Henrietta Maria to London for the coronation, the citizens dutifully lined the banks to cheer the Royal pair as they sailed up the Thames in an open barge, and all were soaked by a violent hailstorm although it was June. A graver indication of the climate of the times was the attitude of Parliament to the new King. Instead of making the customary grant of tonnage and poundage for life, they voted it for one year only. Charles was already involved in war with Spain and he turned to the City of London for a loan but, although the City merchants had as yet no quarrel with the King, their willingness to lend was tempered by their concern for securities until his revenue from Parliament was assured. A grant of Crown lands solved that problem, but Charles was driven to a series of financial expedients, including forced loans and unparliamentary taxation which, together with his religious policy, brought his relations with Parliament to the breaking point. In 1629 he dissolved his third parliament and hoped he would not have to call another.

During the next eleven years the King extracted money from his subjects in devious ways. The most unpopular was Ship Money, originally levied on seaports for defence, but now demanded all over the country. John Hampden became a national hero because of his refusal to pay, famous trial and consequent imprisonment. Calling titles, privileges and charters into question was another way for the Crown to raise money. Both James and Charles had expressed impatience with the progress of the Ulster plantation, and in 1630 the Irish Society and the livery companies were attacked in Star Chamber, for failure to build houses and send out settlers and Protestant clergy. The charges were unjustified, but judgement was given against the Society in 1635, on the grounds that it had broken its charter. The Irish estates were seized by the Crown and a fine of £12,000 was imposed on the companies. (The Society was reinstated by Oliver Cromwell in 1656 and reincorporated by Charles II in 1662.)

Despite the exactions and injustices of these years the City magnates remained loyal to the King. Most of the aldermen were closely linked with the court as office holders, farmers of customs, and holders of monopoly patents. Many of them were connected with the landed gentry and had the patronage of lucrative City offices. They were the counterpart in the City to the King and court. But among the mass of the citizens, anti-Royal feeling was growing, and many of the smaller City merchants, whose business had been affected by Royal depredations, were turning against the King. There was also resentment of the religious policy pursued with fervour by Charles and William Laud, Archbishop of Canterbury. The Anglican church services which they promoted seemed to City Puritans dangerously Roman Catholic in tone. Aldermen might contribute to Laud's restoration of Old St Paul's, even though their sympathies had been Puritan — so did most of the great livery companies — but the citizens would rather listen to the Puritan lectures which Laud suppressed.

It was this policy which led to the King's downfall, for Charles and Laud's determination to force the English church service on the Presbyterian Scots led to the outbreak of war in 1639, nicknamed the 'Bishops War'. Now really large sums of money were needed and the King was forced to summon Parliament in April 1640. His minister, the Earl of Strafford, was confident of his ability to manage the Commons, but soon found he was mistaken. Led by John Pym, they demanded redress of grievances before they would vote for any subsidies, and in less than three weeks the 'Short Parliament' was dissolved.

The King now tried to force a loan out of the City of London. The Mayor and aldermen were ordered to produce lists of the richest men in London from whom the money could be raised. Seven of the aldermen refused to cooperate, their attitude expressed by Alderman Soames, who told the King's Bench that 'he was an honest man before he was an alderman and desired to be an honest man still'. An exasperated Strafford told the King that he would have to make examples of some of the aldermen and four were imprisoned. By now the City was in a ferment. Another demand for Ship Money came in and the Mayor and aldermen went from house to house trying to collect it, but only got one man to pay. When Charles appealed to the livery companies for a contribution, they declared that the Londonderry plantations 'had consumed all their stocks'. With the Scots army encamped in the north of England there was nothing for the King but to call Parliament again and on that surety a loan was raised in the City, since they could expect taxation would provide for repayments.

So in November 1640 the Long Parliament met — so named because an act was passed which ensured it could only be dissolved with its own consent. In the event it went on for twelve years. The City's four MPs, elected by the livery in Common Hall, had suggested it was necessary to give Parliament some form of permanence, if loans were to be raised in the City to pay off the Scots. The members of the Long Parliament were in a black and determined mood and they set about dismantling the authoritarian powers the King had assumed during the 'eleven years tyranny'. In the attack upon the King's policies and ministers, the Puritan opposition in the City was crucial. The citizens put forward unofficial petitions for church reform 'root and branch'. They demanded the exclusion of the bishops from the House of Lords. With cries of 'prentices, clubs' the mobs of London apprentices gathered and descended on Westminster. Londoners were in a frenzy over the detested Strafford, whose 'evil counsels' they blamed, rather than the King. They were determined to have him executed, and 5,000 demonstrators, merchants and tradesmen as well as apprentices, surrounded Westminster Hall, where the terrified House of Lords passed an Act of Attainder condemning him. After the King had signed his loyal servant's death warrant, many thousands of Londoners cheered his execution on Tower Hill and then rushed through the streets shouting 'His head is off, his head is off'.

There was a swing of sympathy towards the King in the summer of 1641 when Charles visited Scotland to win back the allegiance of his northern kingdom. On his return in November, the City organised a splendid welcome, with wine running from the conduits. The liverymen lined up in their gowns and there was a loyal address from the Recorder. Charles was delighted. 'I see' he said, 'that all those former tumults and disorders have only risen from the meaner sort of people, and that the affections of the better and main part of the City have ever been loyal to my person and government' and he knighted the Lord Mayor Richard Gurney, the Recorder, five aldermen and the Sheriffs. He also promised to restore trade, uphold the City's liberties, maintain the true Protestant religion and restore the Irish estates to the City.

Charles could not have kept the last promise even with the best of intentions, because a serious rebellion had broken out in Ireland, and the struggle over whether the King or Parliament should control the army which was needed to deal with it was to lead to the outbreak of civil war.

The King was deceived in thinking he had the support of the City, or at any rate in discounting 'the meaner sort of people'. For it was they who won control at the Common Council elections in December 1641 when, as the Royalist historian Clarendon wrote, 'All the grave and substantial citizens were left out and such chosen as were most eminent for opposing the government and most disaffected to the church, though of never so mean estates'. The new Puritan councilmen were so keen to participate that they took up their seats before the traditional Plow Monday and so were in Guildhall on 5 January, when Charles came to demand the return of the five members of the House of Commons, who had escaped to the City when he had attempted to arrest them at Westminster the day before. The few loyal cries of 'God save your Majesty' were drowned by angry shouts of 'Privileges of Parliament'. Charles retired to dine with the Lord Mayor and sheriffs, but he had lost the City and so had they. On 10 January the King left London, and the five members returned in triumph to Westminster.

In the City a Committee of Safety elected by Common Council took control. Parliament and the King both endeavoured to summon the militia, Parliament by issuing a Militia Ordinance, the King by Commissions of Array. The Lord Mayor, Sir Richard Gurney, was dismissed for attempting to comply with the Royal demands. At first he refused to surrender the mayoral insignia, saying they were locked in his house and he 'could not come at them', but they were seized and he was sent to the Tower where he died in 1647. One of the City MPs, Alderman Isaac Pennington was elected Mayor in August. The Royalists called him 'the pretended Lord Mayor' but, with his election, the Parliamentarians had captured the City government. During the period 1640-42, Puritan sympathisers replaced several of the Royalists on the Court of Aldermen.

Charles never re-entered the City. After the battle of Edgehill, the Royalist army advanced towards London and took Brentford but, confronted by the City trained bands at Turnham Green, it turned away. There was no further serious attempt to take London, although in January 1643 Charles ordered a blockade of the City. There were shortages of food and fuel, but morale was high and the citizens worked enthusiastically to build 18 miles of fortifications round London and the suburbs. Their ardour was more to preserve their City than for the parliamentary cause, for feeling was divided there as elsewhere in the country. The trained bands distinguished themselves in the relief of Gloucester, but they were a citizen army and soon tired of fighting away from home. (They had been started as a home defence force by Elizabeth. Until the civil war they were often a butt for jokes. The London Trained Bands were led and trained by the Honourable Artillery Company, which perhaps explains their notable performance in the civil war, when they numbered over 16,000 men.)

With Oliver Cromwell reorganising and inspiring the Parliamentary armies, the tide of war turned against the King and, after his defeat at Naseby in 1645, his cause was lost. Over three years later, after endless negotiations, proposals for alternative government, quarrels between Parliament and the army, and invasion by the Scots, the King was brought back to London. He was tried in Westminster Hall by a commission on which several aldermen sat, (notably Isaac Pennington and Thomas Andrewes), and declared 'a public enemy to the Commonwealth of England'. On 30 January 1649 he was executed on a platform specially constructed outside the splendid new Banqueting House in Whitehall built for him by Inigo Jones.

Now Oliver Cromwell was in charge, and for the rest of his life he tried to set up a workable government. The House of Lords and the monarchy were abolished and England became a Commonwealth ruled by a Council of State. The City retained its civic government, but the powers of the Lord Mayor were curtailed and the aldermen were deprived of their veto in the Common Council. The Lord Mayor was obliged to summon Common Council if ten members requested it, and they could only be dissolved or adjourned by their own consent. In June 1649 they entertained the members of Parliament and the Council of State in the Grocers' Hall. The civic sword was surrendered to the Speaker by Lord Mayor Thomas Andrewes, and golden gifts were presented to Cromwell and Fairfax. Parliament gave Richmond Park to the City. (They returned it to Charles II in 1660).

Life was austere, for parliamentary taxation was even heavier than the King's had been and the City was suffering from its losses during the war. Some of the livery companies had lost forever huge sums loaned to the government. Of course, life went on and two new companies were incorporated — the Framework Knitters and the Needlemakers. Less money was spent on lavish entertaining but the expenses provided for the Lord Mayor and sheriffs were so severely cut back that it was difficult to find men willing to take on the job. Trade had suffered badly during the wars, but recovered in the 1650s, thanks to Cromwell's vigorous foreign policy against Britain's trade rivals, the Dutch.

The Long Parliament had been so heavily purged by the Army that it was nicknamed the Rump and in 1653 Cromwell, the defender of Parliament, was driven to expel the members with armed force. (Cromwell did call other parliaments, but found them very troublesome.) He was made Lord Protector, and was royally entertained in the City, where he knighted the Lord Mayor. He was criticised for acting like a king but, when City MP Sir Christopher Pack (Lord Mayor in 1654) presented him with a paper inviting him to assume 'the name, style, title and dignity of King' he refused, knowing that if he accepted he would lose the support of the Army. When he died in 1658, the same allowance for mourning cloth was made to the Lord Mayor and City officers as for a sovereign, and the heralds proclaimed his son Richard his successor as Lord Protector.

Once Oliver Cromwell had gone, the desire for a restoration of the monarchy grew. A period of confusion ended when General Monck marched down from Scotland and occupied London with the approval of the reinstated Rump. Its members at last dissolved themselves and a new Parliament was called, which invited Charles II to return to his Kingdom.

In the Declaration which Charles II sent to Parliament from the Dutch town of Breda, he promised to allow freedom of worship and to let Parliament settle the country's finances and decide who should be punished for their part in the rebellion. He wrote to the City of London, saying he counted on its assistance in re-establishing the fundamental laws of the Kingdom. Samuel Pepys, who had recently been made Clerk of the Acts in the Navy Office, recorded in the diary which he began on 1 January 1660, 'the City of London have put out a declaration wherein they do disclaim their owning any other government but that of King, Lords and Commons'. Some people had cause to be apprehensive, but the predominant mood was joyful. 'More bonfires than ever' wrote Pepys, 'and ringing of bells and drinking of the King's health upon their knees which methinks is a little too much.' Common Council voted the King a gift of £10,000 and on 8 May in the City, the Lord Mayor proclaimed Charles II King.

Pepys was with the fleet which brought the King to Dover and so did not see his rapturous reception in London. John Evelyn described the scene in the city on 29 May, the King's thirtieth birthday . . . 'the ways strewed with flowers, the bells ringing, the streets hung with tapestry, fountains running with wine; the Mayor, Aldermen and all the Companies in their liveries, chains of gold and banners; Lords and Nobles clad in cloth of silver, gold and velvet; the windows and balconies all set with ladies; trumpets, music and myriads of people flocking'. There were 20,000 people in the procession, which crossed London Bridge and wound through the City past Temple Bar to Whitehall.

Charles II was a different person from his high-minded, unbending father. Pleasure-loving and witty, he was amused that he met no-one 'who did not protest that he had ever wished for his return' and said it must be his own fault he had stayed away for so long. The greyness which had descended on London during the Interregnum lifted. The theatres reopened, and for the first time actresses took the women's parts, much to Pepys' approval. Goldsmith Sir Robert Vyner was commissioned to provide new regalia for the coronation (as the old crowns and sceptres had been destroyed in 1649) and they have been used ever since. The Lord Mayor held his banquet again in Guildhall and the King watched the procession from Cheapside.

The surviving regicides were tried and executed. Pepys, who as a boy at St Paul's school had seen the execution of Charles I, went to watch Major General Harrison being hanged, drawn and quartered at Charing Cross, 'he looking as cheerful as any man could do in that condition'. An even more gruesome spectacle could be seen at Tyburn, where the exhumed corpses of Cromwell, Ireton and Pride were hung up. In January 1661 the City was disturbed by an uprising of one of the strange sects left over from Cromwell's time, the Fifth Monarchy Saints, who ran amok shouting 'King Jesus and their heads upon the gates' and killing all who got in their way, until order was restored. When the Common Council elections came round that December, Charles wrote to the Court of Aldermen requesting a peaceable election and 'a choice of such persons as are every way well affected to the Established Government both in church and state'. It was twenty years since the fateful election which had turned the City away from his father.

Despite its happy opening, Charles II's reign was not an easy one, even without the two huge natural disasters for which it is famous. In the blazing hot summer of 1665 the third and most terrible outbreak of plague in the 17th century began. It took its worst toll from June to September, and the City became a ghost town, with half its population fled, and others shut up in their houses, with red crosses on the doors to show the plague was there. The Lord Mayor, Sir John Lawrence stayed and ordered the aldermen to do the same. Everyone anxiously watched the weekly Bills of Mortality for a sign that the epidemic was abating but, although the worst was over by December (on the 19th the total within the walls was 9,887) deaths were still being reported in the summer of 1666. Then, in the early morning of 2 September, a fire started in a baker's in Pudding Lane, which did not immediately attract great attention. Fires were common enough in London. So perhaps it is unfair to record the first reaction of Lord Mayor Sir Thomas Bludworth who dismissed it with 'Pish, a woman might piss it out'. However, a particularly dry summer and a strong east wind meant the fire spread fast and was soon out of control. People fled from their houses, taking what valuables they could carry. The King and the Duke of York took charge of the fire-fighting and worked furiously among the Londoners, but the 'horrid, malicious, bloody flame' consumed all in its path. The Lord Mayor had hesitated to create a gap by blowing up houses but eventually this was done and at last the wind dropped. The fire had raged for three days and destroyed four fifths of the City within the walls. St Paul's, the Guildhall, the Royal Exchange and the Customs House were burnt; so were 44 livery halls. Over 200,000 people were homeless; many of them camped out in the fields to the north. 'London was and is no more,' wrote John Evelyn, but he was one of the first to produce a plan for rebuilding, though he was beaten by Christopher Wren, whose plan was ready on 10 September.

The City authorities feared a permanent loss of population and were anxious to rebuild and get business moving again as soon as possible. The would-be planners saw a marvellous opportunity to create a spacious new city. The King wanted the City rebuilt 'with more decency and conveniency than formerly,' and in the event that was achieved. The competing claims of individual owners made it impossible to redraw the lines of the City, and it arose on the old street plan. But streets were widened, King Street and Queen Street opened a new highway between Guildhall and the river, and proper spaces were made for the markets. Regulations governed the building of the new houses, which were of brick and stone, and conformed to a regular pattern, with flat facades free of the medieval protrusions which had cluttered the old streets. Wren's St Paul's Cathedral and the steeples of his new churches rose beautifully above the skyline.

A coal tax paid for some of the rebuilding, but a heavy burden fell on the livery companies, who contributed generously to the rebuilding of the Royal Exchange, as well as finding the money to replace their own halls. Craftsmen with building skills were so much in demand that guild restrictions were lifted and they were allowed to work in the City for seven years without becoming freemen.

There were fewer houses in the more spacious City but years later many of them were still unlet for, as the authorities had feared, some of the City's population had gone for good. Merchants moved away, some to other towns like Bristol, others to the growing suburbs in the west, which were developing round the fashionable squares in Covent Garden, Leicester Square and Bloomsbury. The aldermen were ordered to return to the City but no pressure could be put on private individuals. Craftsmen and workers found life less expensive in the suburbs to the east and south, and the immigrants who fled from Louis XIV's persecution of the Huguenots settled in Spitalfields. Before the Fire, the majority of Londoners had lived in the City. By 1700, its population was about 200,000 and that of London as a whole over 600,000. The tendency of the City to become a business centre rather than a place of residence had begun.

The favourite gathering places of businessmen in London were the coffee houses. The first houses were opened in the City in the 1650s and the taste for the new drink soon caught on. By the end of the century there were nearly 150 coffee houses within the walls, where merchants, lawyers, writers, stockjobbers, shippers and politicians could meet and read the papers, get news of shipping and keep up with world events. From these gatherings several of the City's most famous institutions evolved: Lloyds, the Stock Exchange, the Baltic Exchange, even the earliest postal services. In 1675 a Royal proclamation attempted to suppress the coffee houses, for they were also the resort of the political opposition.

Like his predecessors, Charles II was always in financial straits, and in 1672 he ordered the suspension of all payments from the Exchequer, where the goldsmiths who were the bankers deposited their reserves. The stoppage was only for a year but many wealthy merchants were bankrupted. Charles was at odds with his parliament over the succession to the throne, for he and his Queen, Catherine of Braganza, had no children and the King would not countenance any suggestion that his illegitimate son, the Duke of Monmouth, should succeed him. The rightful heir was his brother James, Duke of York, an ardent Catholic. Feeling against Catholics was strong, as could be seen when the Monument to the Fire was erected, with an inscription laying the blame on them. (It was removed in 1831). A party built up in Parliament which was determined to prevent James from succeeding to the throne. They were led by the Earl of Shaftesbury, and known as the Country Party, until they acquired the epithet 'Whigs', after a group of Scottish republicans. Their Green Ribbon Club had its headquarters in the King's Head Tavern at Temple Bar and they met there and at coffee houses all over the City. The Court Party were known as 'Tories', after a gang of Irish rebels.

Charles stood firm over the succession, even when the storm of the Popish Plot broke over his head. It raged from the summer of 1678, when one Titus Oates began to spread the story of a Catholic plot to kill Charles and make his brother King. Although Charles never believed it, thousands did, and there was panic in the country and turmoil in Parliament. In the City, two thousand men were kept at arms day and night. It looked as if the nation was on the verge of a revolution, but gradually the excitement died down during the next two years, while Shaftesbury strove to use the crisis to force an Exclusion Bill through Parliament. Charles would not budge, though he was driven to summoning Parliament to Oxford in 1681 to escape the influence of London.

In all this the City had been with the opposition, and Charles now turned on them. When he brought Shaftesbury to trial, a Whig jury picked by the City Sheriffs acquitted him. So in 1682 Lord Mayor Sir John Moore, a Tory, was encouraged to revive the old mayoral privilege of choosing one of the new Sheriffs by toasting him at a banquet. Then in Common Hall at Midsummer, the Common Cryer called upon the livery to confirm the Lord Mayor's choice and elect the other Sheriff, but the gathering roared their disapproval and elected two Sheriffs of their own. There followed a series of adjournments until at last the Royal nominees were declared elected, but Guildhall had to be guarded by a detachment of the trained bands when they were sworn in.

The King wanted to govern the corporations of London and of other towns because they controlled the election of the majority of members of Parliament. Earlier in 1682 he had issued a writ of Quo Warranto questioning the City's rights, on the grounds that they had infringed their charters. After a year in which the City's lawyers attempted to prepare a defence, the case opened in 1683 and judgement was given against them. They had to surrender their charters and for the next five years the Lord Mayor, Sheriffs and other officers were chosen by a Royal commission. The livery companies were treated in the same way, for they elected the City's members of Parliament.

The City's liberties were at their lowest ebb. When James II became King in 1685 the worst fears of the Protestant opposition were soon realised. In three short years James managed to range most of the nation against him, until even the Church of England found itself opposed to the monarch, when he brought the Archbishop of Canterbury and six bishops to trial for refusing to read his Declaration of Indulgence in the churches, on the grounds that it was an illegal document. In spite of Royal influence in the courts they were acquitted amid scenes of public rejoicing. The birth of a son to James's Catholic second wife was the final straw. In a last bid to recover the loyalty of the City of London, James hastily restored their charters, but it was too late. William of Orange and his wife Mary, James' Protestant daughter, were invited to rule England. James fled, throwing the Great Seal of England into the Thames as he went, but it made no difference. The Glorious Revolution had taken place with no blood shed.

The City's liberties and franchises and the charters of the livery companies were finally restored by Act of Parliament in 1690. The country was at war with Louis XIV and financial demands were greater than ever. Then in 1694, the Bank of England was founded. Merchants and bankers were invited to subscribe to a loan of £1,200,000 at 8 per cent. Lists were opened at the Mercers' Hall and the demand was brisk; the money was raised in twelve days. The subscribers were incorporated as the Governor and Company of the Bank of England and Sir John Houblon, Lord Mayor in 1695, was the first Governor. They met in the Grocers' Hall until the Bank was built in

1734. It was the first English joint-stock bank and could issue notes and discount bills. The loan did not have to be repaid so long as the interest came in regularly, and so the national debt was founded. It ensured the permanence of the Glorious Revolution, for those whose money was vested in the government had no interest in trying to overturn it. The influence of Parliament was safeguarded by a clause in the act of foundation, making it illegal for the Bank to lend to the Crown without its consent. The Bank helped England to win the war against France and laid the foundations for the City's future as the financial centre of the world. London, now the second largest city in Europe after Paris, was at the beginning of a period of great expansion and prosperity.

Detail from Wenceslas Hollar's panorama of London (1647) showing Old St Paul's without its spire. (GL/JA)

ABOVE: Sir William Walworth's Bower, and BELOW: the Golden Leopard, both from the Fishmongers' Pageant of 1616 by Anthony Munday. (GL/JA)

LEFT: Early 17th century tomb statue of an alderman in St Olave, Hart Street. (JMH) RIGHT: Statue of Captain John Smith, Citizen and Cordwainer, in Bow Churchyard. 'First among the leaders of the settlement at Jamestown, Virginia, from which began the overseas expansion of the English speaking people.' (JMH) BELOW: Marie de Medici's procession in Cheapside in 1638. (ML)

61

Woodcuts of Charles I's reception in the City from John Taylor's *England's comfort and London's Joy,* 1641. (GL/JA)

ABOVE: A painting by Dirk Stoop of Charles II's triumphal procession through the City in 1660. (ML)
BELOW: A print by Schut and Visscher of the Fire of London 1666. (ML)

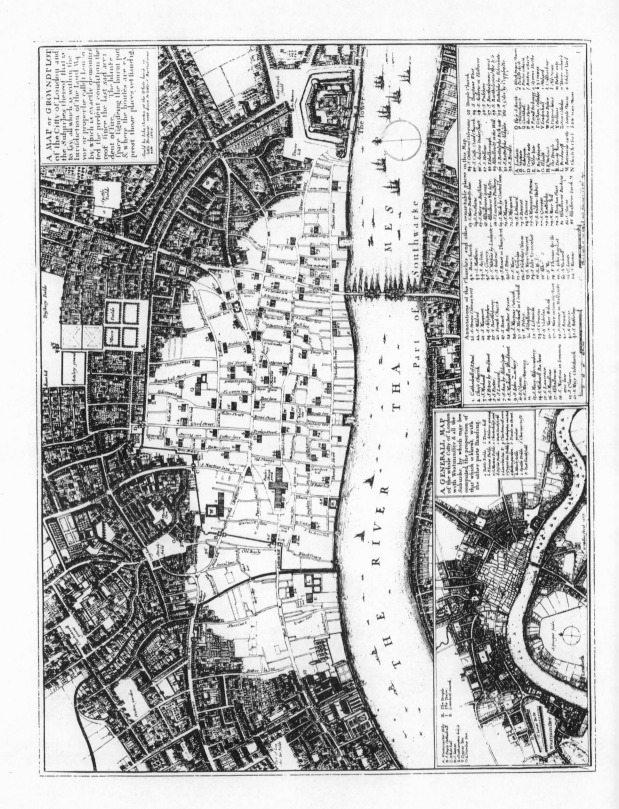

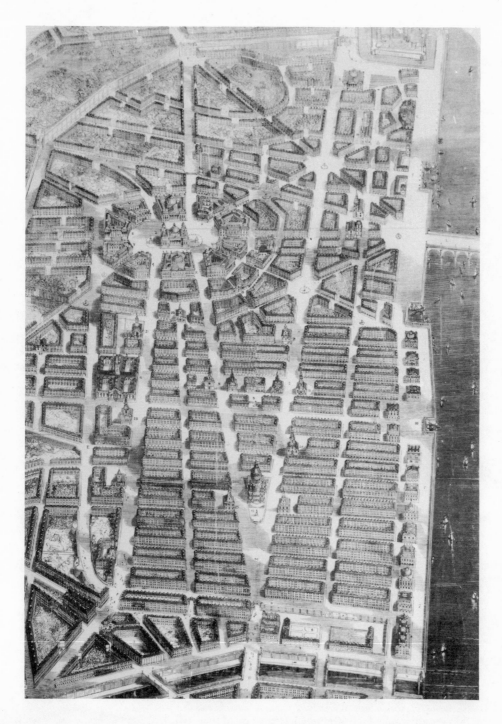

OPPOSITE: London after the Fire, by Wenceslas Hollar 1666. (GL) ABOVE: A 19th century engraving of the City of London as it would have looked if reconstructed according to Christopher Wren's plan. (GL)

ABOVE: An 18th century print of the Monument to the Fire of 1666. (GL/JA)
LEFT: The Golden Boy of Cock Lane, Smithfield, where the Fire stopped. He is
supposed to show that the Fire was caused by gluttony as it started in a baker's in
Pudding Lane, and stopped here at Pie Corner. (JMH) CENTRE: Late 17th
century house in Cloth Fair, St Bartholomew-the-Great. (JMH) RIGHT: A
Wren steeple: Christchurch, Newgate Street. (JMH)

66

Sir John Houblon, Lord Mayor 1695 and first Governor of the Bank of England. (GL/JA)

Wren steeples: LEFT: St Bride's, Fleet Street; RIGHT: St Stephen Walbrook. (JMH) BELOW: London Bridge, from Southwark.

Lord Mayor and Aldermen. Frontispiece to De Laune 'Present State of London' 1681. (MC)

City Corporate

By the middle of the 18th century London had outstripped Paris as the largest city in Europe. Early in the 19th century the population passed the million mark and, by the beginning of the 20th century, it had reached 4½ millions. During the same period, the population of the City dropped from an estimated 200,000 at the beginning of the 18th century to 26,897 in the census of 1901. This decline in residents did not indicate any lessening of the City's importance. The exodus was part of the metamorphosis by which the City, begun as a market town in a far-flung province of the Roman empire, became the financial and commercial centre of the world. Wealthy merchants and bankers moved west to live in more spacious and fashionable suburbs, workers moved east, south and north where the rents were lower and they could escape the restrictions of the City guilds. But the banks, insurance companies, trading companies and exchanges became concentrated in the City.

From this time on the story of London's development is concerned less with the ancient City and more with the suburbs, where the majority of Londoners found their homes and where London's new industries were based. As a commercial centre, the City grew in wealth and influence but that influence was vested in corporations like the Bank of England, and the great trading companies — the East India Company, the Russia and the Levant Companies, the Hudson's Bay Company. The livery companies no longer commanded London's commercial activity. Although freemen alone could practice handicrafts or pursue a retail trade within the City boundaries, there was no such restriction on wholesale trade and finance. Many of the new City men chose neither to live in the City nor to take up the freedom and become involved in municipal government. Of course, some of them were liverymen, and there was no shortage of people to carry on the City's civic life and traditions. The livery companies which had survived the trials and financial strains of the 17th century were still active. But their role was diminishing.

As London grew, it became more and more a place of extreme contrasts. The beauty and elegance of the squares and terraces at 'the polite end of town', west of the City, seemed to belong to a different world from the seething rookeries of Holborn and St Giles, hardly a stone's throw away from their handsome Georgian facades. The grand offices of banks, exchanges and insurance firms in the 19th century City were one aspect of eastern London. The other was the hovels of the silk weavers in Spitalfields, the watchmakers in Clerkenwell and the dockers in Bermondsey and Wapping. The depopulated commercial City became a buffer zone between London's west end and the east end.

Daniel Defoe divided the nation into seven major groups from 'the great who live profusely' to 'the poor that fare hard' and 'the miserable, that really pinch and suffer want'. Although for the rich, London was an immensely civilised place, violence, squalor and degradation were never far from the surface. Crime was widespread and punishments were brutal. There were frequent floggings in the streets and public hangings at Tyburn were a popular attraction. In 1746 the heads of the leaders of the '45 Jacobite rebellion were displayed on Temple Bar, and some were still there 25 years later.

The most common form of social protest in the 18th century was the riot. For the mass of the people who had no vote, no trade unions, no organisation to represent them, the riot was the only way to make their views heard. In London the mob was often out on the streets for a variety of causes. There were riots of those whose livelihood was threatened — sailors and watermen, coalheavers and silk weavers, hatters and tailors. There were many disturbances over political issues — against Dissenters, Catholics and the Irish; against the Gin and Excise Acts; over the Wilkes affair. There were even theatre riots in protest against the price of seats or the presence of French actors. At Drury Lane and Covent Garden the actors had to be protected by a row of iron spikes along the front of the stage. Although the mobs might issue bloodcurdling threats, saying they would 'blow your brains out' and 'pull your house down' they rarely killed anyone, but they did a great deal of damage. They suffered more casualties themselves, since riots were put down by the militia using muskets. Also there were many executions.

However, conditions did improve during the 18th century, and London became cleaner, healthier and more orderly. The worst overcrowding had been experienced during the 17th century, when most people tried to crowd into the City and its immediate surroundings. Now the population continued to grow but London expanded to accommodate them. From 1750 the death rate began to fall and this trend accelerated towards the end of the century when, for the first time, the number of baptisms exceeded burials. A crucial factor in this improvement was the final passing of the Gin Act after years of resistance by vested interests and the poor themselves, who did not know or care what was bad for them. The land-owning Whigs in Parliament used their surplus corn for distilling. The charter of the Distillers' Company was overridden by Act of Parliament so there was no control over distilling or retailing of spirits in London. The scenes of appalling drunkenness so vividly depicted by Hogarth became memories of the past, once cheap gin was no longer available.

The streets of London became safer and cleaner in the 1760s when the authorities began to pave them and to remove picturesque but hazardous shop signs. The Fleet ditch, which had become a stinking abomination, was filled in, and sewers and drains were improved. In the City the wardmotes had been concerned with policing, lighting the streets and clearing rubbish, but gradually their responsibilities were taken over by the Corporation. In Westminster and the metropolitan parishes outside the City boundaries there was no overriding authority, and the vestries obtained local Acts of Parliament, giving them powers to administer their areas. It was a haphazard system, but administration did improve and policing gained tremendously from the work of the Fielding brothers at Bow Street, and from the Thames Police Office set up by Patrick Colquhoun in 1798. By the end of the 18th century, London's orderliness as well as its size and splendour were the admiration of foreign visitors.

Another reason for improvements in conditions and behaviour was the awakening of a social conscience and the growth of a more humanitarian spirit. There was a greater awareness of the condition of the poor and realisation of the need to ameliorate their state. In his 'Proposal for making an effectual provision for the poor' Henry Fielding pointed out that 'the sufferings of the poor are indeed less observed than their misdeeds . . . They starve and freeze and rot among themselves, but they beg, steal and rob among their betters'. Charitable associations of various kinds were formed to give help. The main London hospitals were built in the first half of the century, including Guy's Hospital, founded by a Lombard Street bookseller. St Thomas's was rebuilt as a hospital in the early 1700s and St Bartholomew's was extended and improved in the 1790s. Captain Coram set up the Foundling Hospital in Bloomsbury in 1739. After 1769 dispensary doctors visited patients in their homes and so gathered much useful information about the conditions of the poor, when giving more effective treatment.

The Methodists did much to awaken the public conscience to the needs of the poor. John Wesley was first converted in a house in Aldersgate Street in 1738 where, as a plaque recalls, 'he felt his heart strangely moved'. His earliest sermons were given in City churches and, when he took to preaching in the open, his headquarters for many years was a disused foundry in Moorfields. Wesleyan ministers did much to bring religion to the poor, visiting them in their garrets, comforting prisoners in Newgate and riding with the condemned to Tyburn.

One of the most serious problems facing the London parishes was the number of deserted children — foundlings, illegitimate children and those abandoned by their parents. Provision for them by the workhouse or the parish nurses was so terrible that a death rate of 50 percent in mid-century, after the work of the Foundling Hospital and others had made considerable improvements, was considered by the reformer Jonas Hanway quite an achievement. He obtained an act of Parliament in 1762 which obliged parishes to submit an annual register of infants to the Company of Parish Clerks, who made an abstract. On the basis of the information thus obtained, an act of 1767 enforced more enlightened care of pauper children and there was an immediate reduction in deaths.

For those children whose parents were too poor to provide an education, the charity schools, set up by the Society for Promotion of Christian Knowledge gave some training, though their aims were limited to teaching the children to be good citizens and know their place in society. By 1800 there were 32 of these schools in the City for boys, and 24 for girls. A few of their delightful statues can still be seen, for example outside the Fanmakers' Hall.

Already by the late 17th century London had become a centre of conspicuous consumption. As it grew, the demands of its vast population provided employment all over the country. In 1724 Defoe wrote of 'the general dependence of the whole country on London for the consumption of its produce'. Although there was much poverty, Londoners on the whole earned relatively high wages and had more to spend, while the wealthy lived in great luxury. Quantities of provisions came into London every day — fish and coal to Billingsgate, fruit and vegetables to Covent Garden, the Borough Market and Spitalfields. Corn came up the river to Bear Quay and Queenhithe, while most of London's meat was driven in great herds along the dusty roads to Smithfield. London's own industries grew up in the suburbs: silk weaving, brewing, clock-cabinet- and brick-making, glass manufacture. The constant demand for new buildings was enough by itself to keep thousands in work.

In the City few houses were built, but a home for the Lord Mayor was long overdue. Suggestions for a Mansion House had been included in the plans for rebuilding after the Great Fire of 1666, but there were years of delay before a site was at last agreed at the Stocks Market, opposite the Bank of England and the Royal Exchange. The foundation stone was laid by Lord Mayor Micajah Perry in 1739, but building operations dragged on, and it was finally ready in time for the inauguration of Crisp Gascoygne in 1752. The architect was George Dance, the City's Clerk of Works. One of his sons, George Dance the Younger, followed in his father's footsteps, rebuilt Newgate prison and remodelled the porch of Guildhall. The first Bank of England was completed before the Mansion House, but a splendid new Bank was built by Sir John Soane at the end of the 18th century. Since then the Bank was been rebuilt within its outer walls.

New bridges were built. In 1750 the City lost its monopoly of Thames crossings when Westminster Bridge was opened. Jealous of the fine new bridge, the Corporation improved London Bridge, by widening the roadway and taking down the remaining houses. Congestion on the bridge had been so bad that, in 1722, the Lord Mayor ordered that all carts, coaches and other carriages from Southwark to the City should keep to the west, and those going the other way to the east. It is said that this was the beginning of driving on the left in Britain. Blackfriars Bridge was opened to wheeled traffic in 1769.

The demands of a large and prosperous population stimulated developments in the arts, and London dominated the cultural scene with its theatres and concerts, its pleasure gardens, its artists and writers. 'He that is tired of London is tired of life' said Dr Johnson, 'for there is in London all that life can afford.' Johnson was a City man and it is appropriate that his statue should stand gazing down Fleet Street. It was in the City that the Press developed. In the 17th century the printing press had been active, particularly during the Commonwealth period, with broadsheets and pamphlets. It was strictly controlled by government licensing Acts, which entrusted control of the presses to the Stationers' Company. But when the last licensing Act lapsed at the end of the century, the Commons refused to renew it. There were already 25 journals and periodicals in London when the first newspaper, the *Daily Courant* came out in 1702, followed by the *Evening Post* in 1706. Steele and Addison's weekly journals the *Tatler* and the *Spectator* were founded in 1709 and 1711. By 1800 there were 278 newspapers, journals and periodicals being published, including the *Times,* founded in 1785, and the Sunday *Observer,* founded in 1791. In this period too, the political cartoon came into its own, employing talents of a high order — Hogarth, Rowlandson and Gillray.

During the 18th century politics were complicated, but in general it is true to say that until 1760 the ruling party were the Whigs, but after the accession of George III, the 'King's friends' were various shades of Tory. For most of the time the City was aligned with the opposition to the Court. The river race started by the actor Thomas Doggett to celebrate the accession of George I was rowed on the Thames every year, but relations between the City and the Hanoverian monarchs were not cordial. Naturally there were divisions of opinion. The usual tendency of the moneyed interest was to side with the government, which meant that many of the aldermen were Whigs in the first half of the century. The Common Council, composed mostly of ordinary tradesmen and craftsmen, formed the Tory opposition.

There was considerable strife between the two parts of the City government in the early years of the 18th century. The Court of Aldermen succeeded in enforcing a veto on Common Council legislation and there was a period of over a year in the 1720s when the latter did not meet at all. However, they joined forces in opposition to Walpole, of whom the Whig Lord Mayor, Sir John Fryer wrote 'he is detested in the City of London for he never did anything for the trading part of it'. The power of Common Council steadily increased as it took on responsibility for the day-to-day administration of the City as well as its legislation. The volume of work increased with the City's growing commerce, its new markets and prisons, the paving and cleansing of the streets, the building and maintenance of the Mansion House. Committees were set up and salaried staff taken on. It was on the way to developing, in the words of the Webbs 'from a sort of consultative legislature dependent for its executive upon the Lord Mayor and Aldermen into a supreme organ of administration, itself wielding the whole power of government and reducing the Lord Mayor and Aldermen to a mere magistracy'.

The City's most radical assembly was Common Hall. The exclusive right of liverymen to attend was confirmed by Act of Parliament in 1725. It is particularly interesting that the livery should be so influential politically at a time when in other ways they were at a standstill. After the formation of the Fanmakers' and the Loriners' companies in the early 1700s there were no new grants of livery until the 20th century. The fortunes of the great companies revived as their property increased in value, but many of the smaller companies had a struggle to survive, though they made a vigorous effort to keep control over their trade by forcing traders and craftsmen to take up the freedom. From 1835 it was no longer necessary to belong to a company to be a freeman. An act of Common Council in 1856 ended the freemen's monopoly of the crafts.

The influence of liverymen in Common Hall was exerted in two ways, as an elective body and as the mouthpiece of the City. They played the same part in the election of the Lord Mayor and the sheriffs as they do today, though the choice of Lord Mayor was sometimes a more tumultuous business than would be acceptable now. More important, they not only elected the City's four Members of Parliament, but frequently instructed them on the policy they should pursue. The weight of City opinion was also brought to bear on the government through Common Hall's right to present addresses to the throne. In the 18th century these often expressed strong disapproval of government policy, though the customary loyal and congratulatory addresses (ie on the birth of

Royal princes and princesses) were sent too. The City's support of William Pitt the Elder, was an important factor in his return to power in 1757.

The first twenty years of the reign of George III, who succeeded in 1760, saw the strongest expression of City radicalism in Common Hall, in Common Council and even among some of the aldermen. Three names stand out: John Wilkes, William Beckford and Brass Crosby. Each of them became Lord Mayor, Beckford twice (then a rare honour), and each made a stand against the government on matters of principle. John Wilkes achieved national fame (or notoriety) when he criticised the government in No 45 of the *North Briton*. His subsequent imprisonment, duel, exile, re-incarceration and release fired the popular imagination. Through his persistence and that of the Middlesex electors, who re-elected him three times in defiance of the House of Commons before he finally took his seat in 1774, he established the principle that Parliament had no right to reject an elected MP. When he won the election in 1768 which was annulled by the Commons, the London mob roared through the streets shouting 'Wilkes and Liberty' and smashing the windows of any house not lit up in his honour, including those of the Mansion House. When he was finally elected Lord Mayor in 1774 they gave him their favourite accolade by unharnessing the horses from the mayoral coach and drawing him back to the Mansion House in triumph.

William Beckford was a friend of William Pitt, and a popular Lord Mayor in 1763 who was pressed to serve for a second time in 1769. In 1770 he presented a remonstrance from the City to the King about the government's attitude over the Wilkes election, to which the King made an ungracious reply.

The normal procedure after delivering the address was for the Lord Mayor to kiss the Royal hand and bow his way out, but Beckford stood his ground and delivered the short homily which is inscribed on his statue in Guildhall. 'Permit me, Sir, to observe that whoever has already dared, or shall hereafter endeavour, to alienate your Majesty's affection from your loyal subjects in general, and from the City of London in particular, is an enemy of the public peace, and a betrayer of our happy Constitution, as it was established at the Glorious Revolution'. It may not seem very daring today, but that it was said at all astounded everyone present. Pitt said Beckford had expressed 'the spirit of old England'. George III afterwards testily described the livery as 'those fellows in fur'.

Later that year, when Brass Crosby was Lord Mayor, the City clashed with the Commons over the printing of Parliamentary debates. The Commons summoned the printers of several newspapers to the bar of the House. Two failed to appear, and the messenger sent to seize one of them in the City was himself arrested and brought before the magistrates at Mansion House. They happened to be Lord Mayor Crosby, Alderman Oliver and Alderman Wilkes. Deciding to leave Wilkes, who was not yet an MP, the Commons summoned Crosby and Oliver (both MPs) to the House and then sent them to the Tower. They were released a few weeks later and escorted to Guildhall by a triumphal procession of 53 carriages, carrying most of the Common Council, and greeted by a salute from the Honourable Artillery Company. There was no further attempt to stifle the printing of Parliamentary debates.

Over these issues the London mob had appeared as an ally of the reformers, but the situation got out of hand in the Gordon Riots of 1780, which were a violent expression of anti-Catholic feeling. Mobs rampaged through London for a week, terrorising the inhabitants and causing great damage. In the City the authorities were slow to organise resistance, but the wards were ready with the London Military Association by the time an attack was made on the Bank of England. (After this the nightly Bank Picquet by the Guards was introduced until it was stopped in 1973.) Wilkes was prominent in leading the defence. When it was all over, 450 prisoners had been taken, of whom 25 were hanged. The military had killed about 200 rioters and nearly as many were wounded. (These were official figures; probably over 800 died). About 50 buildings had been seriously damaged or destroyed. It was a traumatic experience for London and, because of its undertones of class hostility, it broke the link between the reformers at Guildhall and popular feeling expressed by the mob.

During the period of the French wars the City supported William Pitt (the younger) and it was not until after his death that it became radical again, by which time the reforming movement was growing more strongly in Westminster and Middlesex. Common Hall and the Common Council opposed governmental restrictive measures — the Corn Laws, the suspension of Habeas Corpus (after the Spa Fields meetings) and the repressive Six Acts (after Peterloo). They were in the van in the campaign for Parliamentary reform. This reached a head when William IV succeeded George IV in 1830. The Duke of Wellington, who was then Prime Minister, was so unpopular in the City because of his opposition to reform, that he was advised not to accompany the King to the annual Guildhall banquet. In the event, neither he nor the King attended, and this tension contributed to the fall of Wellington's government. Lord Grey then took over the knotty problem of a Reform Bill, which could not pass the House of Lords unless the King was prepared to create enough Whig peers to outvote the Tories. The King refused, so Grey resigned and Wellington came back with a watered-down bill which the public would not accept. There were nationwide protests, and Common Hall sent the King an address expressing dismay at Grey's resignation. Common Council instructed the City MPs to refuse to vote supplies. Finally a concerted run on the banks with the slogan 'to stop the Duke go for gold' forced the King to give way and the Reform Act was at last passed in 1832.

In the City, the Parliamentary franchise was extended to householders and occupiers of the annual value of £10. The rights of liverymen were preserved, providing they lived within seven miles of the City (extended to 25 miles under the 1867 Act). The 1918 Act abolished the right of liverymen as such to the Parliamentary franchise but allowed those with business premises in the City to be entered on a separate register. The 1948 Act abolished this last qualification and united the constituencies of the City and Westminster.

After the Reform Act the City ceased to be a radical force in politics, although both the Chartist movement and the trade union movement began in London, and the City did support the second Reform Act in 1867.

There was especial pressure for Parliamentary reform because the industrial revolution had led to the growth of towns in the North and the Midlands, whose citizens had no Parliamentary representation, and where there was considerable urban misery. London played an important part in the country's industrial growth, both as a consumer and as a provider of capital. But having no coal mines, steel foundries, cotton mills or potteries it did not suffer the worst conditions which industrialism brought. Nevertheless building continued to spread further and further into the countryside, swallowing up villages as it went. In 1801 the young Wordsworth wrote of the view of London from Westminster Bridge:

'Earth has not anything to show more fair
Dull would he be of soul who could pass by
A sight so touching in its majesty:
This City now doth, like a garment, wear
The beauty of the morning; silent, bare,
Ships, towers, domes, theatres and temples lie
Open unto the fields, and to the sky,
All bright and glittering in the smokeless air.'

Sixty years later the scene was different. Henry Mayhew went up in a balloon and saw 'the Leviathan with a dense canopy of smoke hanging over it . . . it was impossible to tell where the monster city began or ended'.

Improved communications made this spread of London possible. New bridges — Vauxhall, Waterloo and Southwark, opened up south London. In 1831 the historic London Bridge was finally replaced. People travelled to work in horse 'buses, private carriages, hackney coaches or by steam boat. The coach builder Shillibeer began to run a horse omnibus from Paddington Green to the Bank in 1829 and by 1856, when the London General Omnibus Company was formed, over

1,300 omnibuses were running in London, organised into Associations, or cartels to control stages, fares and frequency of service. By then railway mania was well under way. The first line from London to Greenwich was opened in 1836 and carried half a million passengers in the first year. By 1842 the London and Croydon, London and Brighton and South Eastern were all running into London Bridge station. During the 1850s London was connected by rail with the Midlands, the North, the East and the principal South Coast towns. In the 1860s the development of the underground railway system began. In 1862 the Metropolitan Railway Company ran the first underground train in the world from Paddington to Farringdon Street. By 1866 four railway bridges crossed the Thames into Victoria, Charing Cross, Farringdon Street and Cannon Street.

For the City the most remarkable expansion was that of the London docks. At the beginning of the 18th century, London was already the largest centre of shipping and international trade in Europe, and it soon became the greatest ship-building centre in the world (and remained so until the mid-19th century). By the end of the 18th century the trade of the Port of London had trebled in value and in the number and tonnage of ships. The river downstream from the bridge was literally a forest of masts. The congestion had become totally unacceptable. The Corporation was reluctant to countenance extending the Port further downstream, but the war with France forced its hand. It co-operated in planning new docks and within five years the West India, the London, the Surrey and the East India Docks were built. This was the beginning of the development of dockland which led to the setting up of the Port of London Authority in 1909.

All these developments contributed to the astounding growth of the new trades of London — banking, insurance and the exchanges. 1844 was a particularly significant year, when Queen Victoria opened the new Royal Exchange and the Bank Charter Act was passed, which led to the development of central banking principles by the Bank of England. By 1858 it was said that 'the trade of the world could hardly be carried on without the intervention of English credit' and that of course meant the City of London. The mid-19th century saw a tremendous growth in the activities of the Stock Exchange and the beginning of many new insurance companies — marine, fire, accident and life. All these companies built themselves palatial offices. It has been estimated that four fifths of the City's buildings were replaced in the second half of the 19th century.

In the 19th century City government became the object of a swelling tide of criticism. Its powers extended beyond the City boundaries into Middlesex and Southwark; it had a monopoly of markets within a radius of seven miles; it collected coal duties over a wide area, and it governed the Thames for 80 miles, including the Port of London. But already, by the 1811 census, nine tenths of London's population lived outside the City's boundaries. The City Corporation refused to concern itself with the administration or welfare of the suburbs, and had quashed the 17th century attempt to give them a corporation of their own. Whereas it was possible to regard the City as a proudly independent authority in the 17th and even the 18th centuries, by Victoria's reign the epithets 'antiquated', 'complacent' and 'replete with privilege' were being bandied about.

The need to give the suburbs a proper local government was urgent because the huge population had inadequate housing, burial grounds and sewerage. Nor was there any proper police system. The City was organised, but in the suburbs the parish vestries coped as best they might with their increasing problems. The City resisted any suggestion that it should be included in the 19th century reforms and reorganisation. The Metropolitan Police set up by Peel in 1829 left alone the City, with which Peel said he was 'afraid to meddle', and the City Corporation formed their own police force on the model of the Metropolitan Police ten years later. The Municipal Corporation Reform Act of 1835 left the Corporation of London unreformed and it was exempted too from the Public Health Act of 1848. But, threatened by cholera, the City did decide to follow Liverpool's example and appoint a Medical Officer of Health. They chose well in Dr John Simon, whose first annual report was a devastating document ruthlessly analysing the Corporation's shortcomings.

The improvements he made during the next five years meant that the City had far fewer deaths per head than the rest of London when the cholera struck again in 1854. Meanwhile nothing had been done for the majority of London's people, whose appalling living conditions were so vividly described by Charles Dickens and Henry Mayhew.

A Royal Commission was set up to enquire into the Corporation in 1852. Its report, produced in 1854, recommended abolition of the Court of Aldermen and Common Hall and the amalgamation of the City and the Metropolitan Police. But it stopped short of extending the City boundaries, fearing that 'a municipal administration of excessive magnitude would be created'. The idea of a 'Corporation of Greater London' had its supporters right into the 20th century, but was resisted not only by the City but also by the government, which hesitated to create such a powerful body. Instead, the 1854 scheme envisaged the separate incorporation of the suburbs, but failed to come up with a workable arrangement, so no act reached the statute book.

Instead of a reorganisation of local government, the Metropolitan Board of Works was set up in 1855, with the prime aim of giving London a proper system of sewerage. Its powers were inadequate, and no positive action was taken until June 1858, when the stench from the Thames was so bad that the windows of the handsome new Houses of Parliament had to be covered with curtains soaked in chloride of lime. Then at last a main sewer was constructed to carry all the sewage generated in London away downstream. The other main achievement of the Board was the construction of the Thames Embankments. In 1857 the City's responsibility for the Thames ended, when the Thames Conservancy was set up (and the Lord Mayor's Show stopped using the river). In 1867 the franchise in the wards, previously limited to freemen, was extended to £10 householders and occupiers. Otherwise the Corporation remained untouched by change.

The livery companies too were criticised, for their wealth and secrecy. They were suspected of using their magnificent entertainments as social bribes to cover their misuse of their trusts. They were regarded as an anachronism. In 1872 Froude wrote of 'certain ancient societies, the members of which may occasionally still be seen in quaint gilt barges pursuing their own difficult way among the swarming steamers; when on certain days, the traditions concerning which are fast dying out of memory, the Fishmongers' Company, the Goldsmiths' Company and the Mercers' Company make procession down the river for civic feastings at Greenwich or Blackwall. The stately tokens of ancient honour still belong to them and the remnants of ancient wealth and power — But for what purpose they were called into being . . . few people now care to think or enquire'.

In fact the livery companies were administering their charities faithfully and responsibly as they had always done. But they probably were too comfortable and, from 1870 onwards, the City began to awaken to the need to make a more positive contribution beyond its own immediate concerns. Already in 1871, Common Council had approached the government over the possibility of the Corporation buying unenclosed parts of Epping Forest, as a recreation ground for the people. In 1872 a meeting was held at the Mansion House to consider how the City Guilds could revert to their old function of directing the arts and manufactures of the country.

Their traditional involvement with education took on a new lease of life with the expansion of higher education at this time. Some companies founded their own colleges, others fostered new departments at the universities and, in 1878, a group of 16 companies, together with the Corporation, subscribed to the formation of the City and Guilds of London Institute for Technical Education. Their membership began to pick up too, because some Tory politicians, fearing the tide of liberalism, began to buy their way into the livery companies and the Liberals accused them of trying to resuscitate their guilds on political lines. However, the 1884 Royal Commission of enquiry vindicated the livery companies and found they were administering their funds properly.

In 1884 Sir William Harcourt tried to bring in a Bill for unifying London but he failed, and in 1889 the Local Government Act set up the London County Council, leaving the City untouched. Another Royal Commission in 1895 argued for a central council for London, but again without success. The 1899 London Government Act swept away the vestries and set up 28 metropolitan boroughs under the LCC but left the City alone. Since then there have been many critics of the City's government but the last Royal Commission in 1960 decided it should stay. 'If we were to be strictly logical' it stated 'we should recommend the amalgamation of the City and Westminster. But logic has its limits and the City lies outside them'. They decided that the City was an 'institution of national importance' and that even though it was an anomaly 'this anomaly should continue'. In 1965 London government was reorganised under the Greater London Council with 32 Metropolitan Boroughs. The Corporation makes the 33rd, retaining its ancient Corporation and traditions, and from its wealth making a major contribution to the revenues of the rest.

The livery companies are alive and well too. Numbers of liverymen rose from about 8½ thousand in 1900 to double that number in 1968 and today there are about 20,000. In 1929 the Master Mariners were the first new company to be granted the livery since the beginning of the 18th century, and their example was followed by the Solicitors in 1944. Since then 14 new companies have been granted the livery and the momentum has increased in recent years.

In one way these new companies are more traditional than those which originated in the Middle Ages, because all their liverymen must be practising members of their trade. However, many of the older companies have sought and found ways of becoming re-involved with their trade, if only through a modern development, like the Horners with plastics and the Carmen with modern transport.

Several members of the Royal family are liverymen and take a keen interest in the activities of the companies. Since the accession of Queen Victoria, relations between the City and Crown have been singularly happy and the City can recall many splendid occasions, from Queen Victoria's first attendance at the Lord Mayor's Banquet in 1837 to her Jubilees in 1887 and 1897. In recent years there have been the luncheon given to the Queen and Prince Philip in Guildhall to celebrate the Silver Jubilee, the special thanksgiving service in St Paul's for the 80th birthday of Queen Elizabeth the Queen Mother and, of course, the wonderful Royal Wedding of 1981. On all these occasions and countless others the City has demonstrated its genius for pageantry. Just as the pageantry of state arises from traditions of Royal and Parliamentary government, so that of the City stems from the history of its ancient Corporation. We should all be the poorer without them.

However it cannot be said of the Corporation of London that it looks only to the past. The task that confronted it after the devastation of the war was immense. About a third of the City had been destroyed. Guildhall stood roofless but with its walls and crypt intact, and has since been completely restored, thus preserving the City's heritage. Many of the livery companies rebuilt their halls; many of Wren's churches were restored. But the Corporation felt it was important to bring the City alive with its own resident population. The result was the Barbican, which has been described as 'a unique achievement' by William Robson, whose book *The Government and Misgovernment of London* published just before the war, severely criticised the City government and recommended the abolition of the Corporation. But in an article on central London planning in 1977 he wrote: 'All in all some of the best planning for the future and the most welcome revival of civic design is now to be found within the square mile of the ancient city'. This year that achievement has been crowned by the opening of the Barbican Centre by Her Majesty the Queen. It will be a focus for the lives of the City's residents and a splendid Arts and Conference Centre for London, Britain and the world.

Doggett's Coat and Badge Men (accompanying Sir Christopher Leaver on Lord Mayor's Day 1981). (VFH)

LEFT: Statue of a charity boy in a niche on St Botolph's Aldgate Church Hall, now the Fanmakers' Hall. (JMH)
CENTRE: Hogarth's caricature of John Wilkes. (MC) RIGHT: Statue in Guildhall to William Beckford. (JMH)
BELOW: Print of Mansion House in the 18th century. (GL/JA)

ABOVE: The Gordon Rioters attacking Newgate Gaol. (MC) BELOW: 18th century caricature of the City Trained Bands. (GL)

79

ABOVE: 18th century caricature of Lloyd's Coffee House 1798. LEFT: Statue of Sir John Soane in the wall at the back of the Bank of England facing St Margaret's Lothbury. (JMH) RIGHT: Panorama of London 1749; S. & N. Buck. (V&A)

ABOVE: View of the City from Somerset Gardens. 18th century print. (GL) LEFT: The Lord
Mayor's Dinner at Guildhall, 9 November 1829 by G. Scharf. (GL/JA) RIGHT: The Arms of the City of London,
(on Tower Bridge). (JMH)

ABOVE: Old and New London Bridges; drawing by E. & W. Cooke. (MC) BELOW: Relief on the monument at Temple Bar showing the surrender of the Pearl Sword to Queen Victoria, as she entered the City to attend the Lord Mayor's Banquet in 1837, the year of her accession.

ABOVE: The Silent Ceremony in 1856 when Thomas Q. Finnis was sworn in as Lord Mayor. (MC) BELOW: Engraving by T.H. Shepherd 1855 of Guildhall Porch from *Mighty London Illustrated.* (GL/JA)

ABOVE: The Presentation of the Freedom in Guildhall to Lord Beaconsfield and Lord Salisbury, 1878. (GL/JA)
BELOW: The Barbican Centre Lakeside Terrace. (JMH)

84

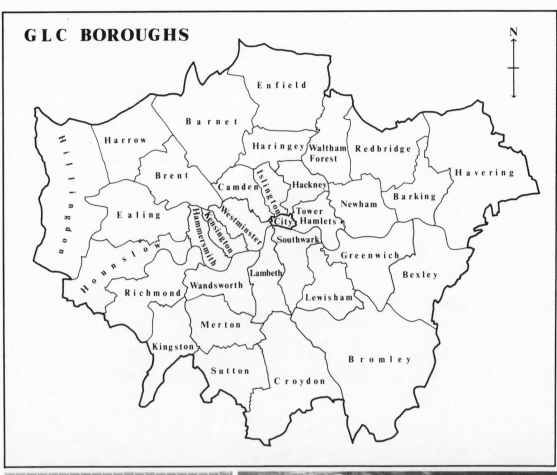

GLC BOROUGHS

N

Hillingdon

Harrow

Enfield

Barnet

Brent

Haringey

Waltham Forest

Redbridge

Havering

Camden

Islington

Hackney

Ealing

Westminster

Newham

Barking

Hammersmith

Kensington

City

Tower Hamlets

Southwark

Greenwich

Bexley

Hounslow

Lambeth

Richmond

Wandsworth

Lewisham

Merton

Kingston

Sutton

Croydon

Bromley

ABOVE: The City and the Greater London Boroughs. Boundaries drawn 1965. (MJH) LEFT: Contrast in the modern City. Reconstructed Girdlers' Hall backed by the IBM tower. (JMH) RIGHT: The Barbican Centre Lakeside Terrace (close-up). (JMH)

85

St Paul's Cathedral, in the days of horse traffic. (GL)

The Freedom
The Livery and Guilds

The preceding five chapters have unfolded the story of the City's past and the development of the Guilds, Companies and Livery. In turning now to the past and present of each of these, except in particularly significant instances, recurrent facets such as the depredations of Tudor monarchs, interference of the Stuarts, restrictions of the Protectorate and successive charters, have been largely omitted, in the interests of brevity, clarity and avoidance of repetition. Where extensive records have been available, relevant detail has been included to lend force to the otherwise largely chronological parade of significant milestones. In general, the inevitably more comprehensive records of recent times have been summarised. In every possible case, details have been included of current activities. By definition, some Companies have a simpler tale to tell, and some, whose available records are relatively sparse, have been represented briefly.

Each Company or Guild has been recorded in order of precedence, and is separately listed, with the number of that precedence, at the back of the book. For ease of reference, each is entered in the index alphabetically. Thus the story of each organisation may be read consecutively in the following narrative, or individually consulted.

What emerges with the greatest possible force is the great diversity of origin, development and activity of the City's ancient Guilds, and the impressive scope of their modern endeavours. More than that, there emerges also the unique contribution that the City's Freemen have made to society — in local government, fellowship, education, charitable work, trade and industrial practice, professional qualification and standards, and in cultural and technological innovation. Here is the foundation and continuity of an astonishing complexity of contemporary institutions and practices, a contribution to modern life the like of which cannot be attributed to any other collective institution. The debt that the nation and indeed the world owes to London's ancient Guilds would be beyond belief, were it not recorded here for all to read. This is the story of the Freemen and Liverymen of the City of London, and in so many ways, of that other freedom of choice we all take so much for granted in our contemporary society. Root and Branch, may both Freedom and freedom continue and flourish for ever.

The Mercers. In 1347 new ordinances were drawn up for the conduct of the already existing Company — these represent the oldest surviving records. A Mercer was a merchant, trading in small wares, rather than a specific craftsman with a later emphasis on wool and cloth, later luxury fabrics, though when Elizabeth I asked the Company why silk was so dear, they could not help, since no Mercer then traded in that commodity.

The Mercers were early concerned with charity and from the 16th century the Company's prime function was charitable. Thrice Master, Dick Whittington, Mayor of London for 3½ years, rebuilt the church of St Michael Paternoster Royal, and Newgate Prison, repaired the City conduits and helped rebuild St Bartholomew's Hospital. Under his will Whittington College, a college for priests, was founded in 1424, and an almshouse for thirteen poor citizens was also created. On his deathbed, he entrusted these to the Company and, on the Reformation, the college was dissolved and the name passed to the almshouse. This was destroyed in the fire of 1666 and rebuilt in 1670. In 1824 a new building was sited in Highgate. It was again resited at Felbridge outside East Grinstead in 1965, extended in 1978 and 1981, with an adjoining development. Forty five people, over 55, mostly women, live in flats or bungalows. The Whittington Charity also grants some 300 out-pensions. One other benefaction from Richard Whittington's estate was the establishment of a library at Guildhall.

Henry Howard, Earl of Northampton, in 1614 founded a hospital or almshouse at Greenwich and, though not a Mercer, he entrusted its management to the Mercers. This was Trinity Hospital. That same building now provides 21 modern flats for old men, and the trust provides almshouses at Shotesham, Norfolk, and various pensions and allowances.

Mercer John Colet, Dean of St Paul's, founded St Paul's School in 1509, which the Company subsequently administered. Originally in Old Change, it moved in 1884 to Hammersmith and in 1968 to Barnes. In 1904 St Paul's Girls' School was founded at Hammersmith. Mercers School, now closed, was founded in 1542. The Company is still concerned with Collyers Sixth Form College, Sussex and Dauntsey's School, Wilts — both founded by Mercers.

Mercer Sir Thomas Gresham founded the Royal Exchange in 1566 and by his will in 1575, Gresham College — both are managed by the Mercers and the Corporation who appoint the seven Gresham professors. The Company also makes grants for other charitable and educational purposes.

The Company is closely associated with HMS *London* and the Royal Regiment of Fusiliers and No 6 Squadron, Royal Air Force.

Originally the Mercers met in the Hospital of St Thomas a Becket, born nearby; the buildings became the Company's Hall in 1542 until their destruction in the 1666 fire. Rebuilt 1672-1682, the Hall was blitzed in May 1941, its modern successor opened in 1958. Among those who first met or were founded there were the Merchant Adventurers, the East India Company, the Bank of England, the Royal Exchange Assurance and the City and Guilds of London Institute. The Hall houses a private chapel — the only one possessed by a City Livery Company.

The Grocers. The Pepperers' Guild is first recorded in 1180, but it seems likely that the Pepperers had connections with important London moniers who built, c1100, what became the Guild church of St Antonin.

The dedication comes from Spain and may link them with imports of gold, as well as with other Mediterranean goods and spices, from which they took the name. A Pepperer Mayor, Andrew Aubrey, repressed a riot between the Skinners and Fishmongers, allegedly executing two of the latter. The Pepperers inhabited Soper's Lane (now Queen Street), and they bought and sold or 'engrossed' merchandise. They garbled and cleansed spices and drugs, and nominated the officer in charge of the King's Beam, which weighed heavy goods in the Port of London. They were the forerunners of the Grocers, first recorded in 1345.

At their first meeting, twenty dined at the house in St Mary Axe of the Abbot of Bury St Edmunds. They agreed to pay 1 d each to maintain a priest and drew up ordinances, to provide for an annual mass, dinner, election and crowning of wardens (which last still occurs every July), and to help one another. They regulated apprenticeships, and agreed 'that every member having a wife or companion should bring her to dinner or a lady in her place should she be ill . . .'. A beadle was to be appointed. In 1373, the Fraternity was first called the Company of 'Grossers' and in 1376, the Grocers of London.

Grocers John Philipot and Nicholas Brembre were knighted by King Richard for services during the Wat Tyler riot; both were Yorkists. Philipot was Mayor in 1378 and his fleet swept the pirates from Channel and North Sea. Brembre was Mayor in 1377 and 1383, but was executed in 1388 for treason.

In 1426 the Grocers bought a property in Old Jewry, completing their Hall in 1431, with extensive gardens including a bowling green, lost when Princes Street was built some three centuries later. In 1428 Henry VI granted their first Charter, referred to in the Company's 'Blake Boke' as their Patent of Capacity. In 1376 came the first mention for any Company of a governing Court of Assistants. A Clerk was first recorded in 1450. During the 15th century the Company furnished twenty Lord Mayors.

In 1609 the Grocers paid £5,000 for lands in Ulster under pressure from James I, selling out in 1872. Mounting Crown pressure for 'loans' culminated in an impost in 1642 of £9,000, to meet which the Company had to sell its plate. The Company supported Parliament in the Civil War and subsequently Monck's Restoration of the monarchy.

A 1607 bequest led to the purchase of four church benefices in 1620, 1663, 1762 and 1786, followed by others, so that today the Company is Patron of several benefices, including the shared patronage of St Stephen Walbrook and St Mary-le-Bow.

The 1666 Great Fire brought the Company's worst calamity — the destruction of their Hall, though a turret in the garden survived and with it the Company's archives. This, coupled with the Company's debts and the loss of rentals from other properties destroyed, brought a century of struggle. With Sir John Cutler's help, the Hall was partly rebuilt but, in 1673, Christ's Hospital took possession as creditors. In 1682, with Sir John Moore's help, the Hall was completed, but let out to provide income.

In 1689 King William III accepted the office of Sovereign Master, the Company prospered and in 1694 the Bank of England was founded, shortly afterwards occupying the Hall until 1734. Past Master Sir John Houblon was the first Governor.

In 1800 the Hall was again rebuilt — badly. In 1888 it was replaced.

By his will of 1556 Sir William Laxton, Lord Mayor in 1544 and eight times Master, had endowed and thereby revived a grammar school and almshouse in Oundle. In 1573 the Wardens took formal possession; in 1876 the school was divided into two and later extended to three.

Today there are three schools — Oundle Public School, Laxton (which derives from the original Grammar School) and Laxton Junior School. In addition, Witney Grammar School was founded by Grocer Henry Box in 1660 and the Company was appointed Governors. In 1901 the Oxfordshire County Council took over. In 1876 the Company established a school at Hackney Downs, merged into the London County Council system in 1902.

In 1940 the Hall was damaged, though the records survived again. They escaped the final disaster of the fire of September 1965, which destroyed the Hall. The fifth and present Hall was opened in 1970.

The Drapers. In 1364 Edward III granted Letters Patent to the Mistery of Drapers, an already existing gild, giving rise to unrest and opposition in the City, principally from the Tailors. The Drapers were the principal dealers in cloth and also caused materials to be made up into drapery. In 1385 the Company purchased property in St Swithin's Lane, and in 1405 it gained control of the Blackwell Hall cloth market. That year the Company drew up ordinances for its government and that of the market. By this time it had provided more than one Mayor. In the year of Agincourt, the Drapers, with an incoming and outgoing Mayor, presented the victorious King with gifts worth £1,500. In 1425 they built their first Hall in St Swithin's Lane, finished in 1430. Eight years later the Company was incorporated by Royal charter. In 1439 they received one of the earliest Grant of Arms. Its three crowns represented a heraldic tripling of the imperial crown of Our Lady. The Tailors reacted to the Drapers' new powers and again in 1447. In the 1470s the two misteries joined forces to control the quality of English cloth wares, thus ensuring their supreme reputation throughout Europe.

The troubles between the two misteries erupted again in 1502, the Merchant Taylors gaining incorporation the next year, and to these were added the rival claims of the Haberdashers. In the 16th century the Company's charitable activities included the building, by four times Master Sir John Milborn, of almshouses near the Crutched Friars, and the foundation, by six times Master George Monoux, of Walthamstow Free Grammar School. In 1543 the Company bought Thomas Cromwell's great house in Throgmorton Street — to become their new Hall. But taxes, the Reformation and Chantry Acts were to ensure the Company's financial embarrassment and the 16th century brought 'sore decay'. In mid-century the export trade in cloth reached saturation, and slump followed. To add to their troubles, the Crown requisitioned their Hall. The Elizabethan era brought further financial imposts and repeated calls for military service, but some stability followed and, after the Spanish Armada was vanquished, the Company elected Sir Francis Drake a member. In 1574 William Lambard founded Queen Elizabeth's College at Greenwich, built in 1576 and entrusted to the Drapers as Governors. The almshouses were rebuilt in 1817-18 and subsequently modernised. The Lambard Cup, presented by William Lambard in 1578, stands before the Master at all functions. In 1607 a new charter was obtained, which operated for over three centuries. The Company was by then more concerned with administration than its original trading purpose.

With the colonisation of Virginia and Ulster the Drapers made substantial contributions — in the latter, laying the ground for Drapers' Town and Moneymore. In 1640 they challenged the King — refusing his request for money. Royalist Masters gave way to Parliamentarians. However, during the Commonwealth, the Drapers were mortgaged to the hilt and lacked enthusiasm for the Lord Protector. By the Restoration, their affairs were more prosperous and the Company had emerged from a purely trade guild to a self-perpetuating oligarchy of magnates.

The Great Fire destroyed the Company's Hall and much of its property. Its replacement on the same site was occupied in 1671. The Drapers had founded the Lucas Hospital at Wokingham in 1663; their other charitable interests included Walter's Almshouses at St George's and Stoke Newington, Kirkham School near Preston, Lancs, and Barton School. In 1772 fire again all but destroyed the Hall, which was shortly thereafter rebuilt. As the century drew to a close the Company conferred the freedom on Nelson, Duncan and St Vincent.

By 1817 the Drapers' Irish rent roll was worth over £10,000 pa.   Leases were falling in and decisions were imperative. It was decided to enlarge holdings, fund better clothing and apprenticeships, build an inn and market house, provide a doctor and surgery, and to support all churches, of whatever religion, improving Catholic chapels and rebuilding the Presbyterian meeting house. The Drapers' disinterested liberalism would be considered enlightened even today.

By 1837 the Charity Commissioners' report recorded forty eight charitable Drapers' trusts. One effect of the reform of charities at that time was an action brought against the Drapers over Howell's Trust for orphans, founded c1537. The Drapers were held to have misapplied the trust incomes, and that their Hall was therefore the property of the trust. In 1846 they repurchased it. In 1860 the Company opened Howell's Schools at Llandaff and Denbigh. By 1866, after spending £25,000 on the Drapers' School at Tottenham, they had accumulated a surplus of £99,000, with funded property worth £97,000. They decided to refurbish their Hall, spending nearly £113,000 by 1871. Too great a realisation of capital drastically reduced incomes.

In 1877, after approaches by other Companies, the Drapers joined in a concerted effort to create the City and Guilds of London Institute. They also gave money for technical education in other ways. By 1880 the Institute was under way. In 1884, £50,000 was voted for Bancroft School's removal from Mile End to Woodford. In 1888 the Company withdrew its support from the Institute as a result of disaffection with that body's growing departure from its original policies. By the end of the 19th century, the Drapers disposed of most of their Irish interests, following a serious deterioration in landlord-tenant relationships.

In 1890 they amalgamated the Tottenham school with their small school nearby at Elmslea. The People's Palace — a day boy institution on the old Bancroft School site, run by the Beaumont Trust — was in debt, so the Company in 1890 voted £6,000 a year for ten years for what was to be known as the Drapers' Company's Institute. As the century turned, they donated 20,000 gns to the rebuilding of Radcliffe Library, Oxford, and they contributed to the reorganising of London University.

In 1908 Middlesex County Council took over the Tottenham schools, and in 1913 the Drapers modified their connection with the People's Palace, from which sprang the East London College, to which they gave conditional support. By 1922 they were contributing some 10,000 gns a year. The school at Llandaff having been taken over by the local authority in 1894, the Drapers made substantial grants and loans in 1925, and transferred Elmslea pupils to Denbigh. In the early 1930s fire destroyed the People's Palace and the Company concentrated its support on East London College. In 1934 it became Queen Mary College.

In the blitz of 1940/41 many of the Company's properties were destroyed and their Hall damaged. In 1947 Princess Elizabeth took up her freedom of the Company by patrimony. By 1951 the connection with Kirkham's School was ended. Ten years later, the Drapers pioneered nine Commonwealth scholarships, and reinforced their links with Oxford, Cambridge, Howell's and Bancroft's Schools, contributing to the new Portland Place HQ of the City and Guilds of London Institute.

Today the Company acts as trustee of two schools, four almshouses, a block of flats for the elderly, pension charities and educational grants, but its main function lies in its support of many objects, chiefly educational, medicinal and artistic, through its Drapers' Charitable Fund, here and abroad.

The Fishmongers. An organised community before their first charter of 1272, the Fishmongers were, by this and two subsequent charters, empowered to control the sale of fish, limit fish markets and ensure the quality of fish sold in the City. Successive charters in nine reigns incorporated the Company and provided its ordinances. By the 14th century the Fishmongers held a monopoly for what was one of the staples of medieval diet. They had furnished three ships for Edward I's navy and mounted impressive pageants for the monarch.

During the 14th century the Company headed the Victualling Guilds, in the conflict with the Craft Guilds to protect monopolies in foodstuffs, where the latter sought free trade, but protection for their trade in manufactured goods. In 1381 Sir William Walworth was a Prime Warden and Mayor of London. Walworth stabbed Wat Tyler to death in the historic confrontation with the young Richard II — the dagger he used is preserved in the Company's Hall and features in the present coat of arms of the City.

In 1383 Common Council withdrew the Fishmongers' jealously guarded monopolies, and this was confirmed by Parliament, but Richard II's 1399 charter restored their privileges. Until the end of the century the Fishmongers held their own *Leyhalmode* (court) to settle all disputes in their trade, but in the following century their monopoly disappeared.

By the late 14th century the shoreline by today's Fishmongers' Hall had been gradually extended by Roman, Saxon and medieval merchants, to become the marine traders' wharf and warehouse area. Here the Fishmongers plied their trade. One piece of land became home and business premises of fish merchants and Mayors John Lovekyn, Sir William Walworth and William Askham — between Thames Street and the river. Each enlarged the premises, which included a great hall. During 1433-44 the property was acquired for the Company, with the help of John Cornwall, Lord Fanhope, Henry IV's brother-in-law.

When the saltfishmongers and stockfishmongers sank their differences in 1536, the premises were partially rebuilt, alongside the wharf. A dining hall was added in Elizabeth I's reign.

In 1555 Sir John Gresham founded a school at Holt in Norfolk. He left funds for its administration to the Company. Gresham's School is still largely supported by the Company, who predominate on its governing body.

In 1666 the Hall was destroyed by fire. In 1668 rebuilding started, on an enlarged site and the following year, the foundations were begun for a new dining hall. In 1788-90 the interior was renewed and in 1827 the siting of the new London Bridge meant the loss of twenty feet of the then Hall. That part of the building was demolished and rebuilt between 1827 and 1831.

In 1831 Henry Roberts designed a new Hall, with Gilbert Scott's help. A concrete raft was laid to stabilise the riverbank, and the shell erected by William and Lewis Cubitt in 1833, who completed the interior in 1835. In 1940 the Hall suffered grievously from bomb damage, and restoration was completed in 1951.

HRH The Prince Philip is a Member of the Court and a past Prime Warden; in 1971 HRH The Prince of Wales became a freeman by patrimony and was elected to the Livery and in 1972, HRH The Princess Anne followed suit.

Today the Company is still actively involved in fisheries and fishing. Fishmeters (chartered by James I) still examine all fish coming into London and, where necessary, implement the Food and Drugs Act of 1955. The Company has statutory powers under other Acts. It maintains a rigorous watch over salmon fisheries and imports, helped to set up the Atlantic Salmon Research Trust and supports the Anglers' Cooperative Association; it is also a founder member of the National Anglers' Council. It formed the Shellfish Association of Great Britain in 1907 and its bacteriologist regularly examines shellfish samples. The Company set up the Central Council for Rivers Protection to end river pollution and represent water supply, amenity and fishery interests. The Fishmongers help fund the Marine Biological Association of the UK and its Scottish equivalent.

The Company maintains almshouses and pensions, provides exhibitions and scholarships, and administers various charitable and other trusts. It was instrumental in starting the City and Guilds of London Art School Limited. The Company awards an annual trophy for outstanding achievement to a member of the Parachute Regiment, with which, and the RNR, it maintains close links.

The Goldsmiths. A fraternity of Goldsmiths existed by the 12th century. In 1327 the Company received its first charter and in 1462 was incorporated as 'The Wardens and Commonalty of the Mystery of Goldsmiths of the City of London'. Long before that, the ancient examination of the coinage was formalised in the Trial of the Pyx (mint box), first recorded in 1282. The Company's records of this surviving activity date from 1604. Under the Coinage Acts, the Mint provides samples, which are judged by a jury of goldsmiths sworn in by the Queen's Remembrancer annually, at Goldsmiths' Hall.

From their beginnings, the Goldsmiths have exercised statutory powers to search workshops and prosecute workers in low standard metal, and makers of below quality goods, as well as binding apprentices — to this day.

The Goldsmiths are the oldest hallmarking authority in the country. The word hallmark derives from a mark applied at Goldsmiths' Hall to denote the quality of gold and silver and platinum since 1975. All British-made articles successfully tested in the Assay Office at the Hall are marked with the oldest of marks — the leopard's head.

Goldsmiths' Hall has stood on the same site since Edward III's time. The original, possibly altered Hall was rebuilt between 1634 and 1636 and damaged in the Great Fire thirty years later. It was demolished in the 1830s and rebuilt by 1835 to Philip Hardwick's design. Damaged again in 1941, it was repaired by 1951, and further improved since.

In 1564 the Company funded its first University scholarship. Benefactions include grants to libraries, museums and art collections. It contributes to hospitals, convalescent homes and to the training of the disabled; provides recreation grounds and supports youth clubs. The almshouses erected in the 19th century at Acton have been modernised as Goldsmiths' Buildings, and the Company has built flats for the elderly.

A leading contributor to the foundation of the City and Guilds of London Institute in 1878, the Company has ever since lent its support. It founded Goldsmiths' College at New Cross, now part of London University, and endowed the Goldsmiths' Chair of English at Oxford, of Metallurgy at Cambridge and of Medical Microbiology at The London Hospital. It offers open awards to school teachers and scholarships in medicine, nursing and the arts.

The Company still keeps a strong connection with its craft. The Company's Antique Plate Committee examines antiques, and the Company maintains and lends part of one of the most comprehensive collections of antique and modern plate for exhibitions. It sponsors design competitions, makes grants to metalwork departments of colleges of art, grants travelling awards and, under a Director of Research, runs a technical advisory service for industry.

The Merchant Taylors. John Stow recorded 'the Guild and Fraternity of St John the Baptist, time out of mind called tailors and linen armourers of London'; in 1327 the Guild received Letters Patent from Edward III. Four years later John de Yakeslee, the King's pavilion maker, acquired a mansion, (sited between today's Threadneedle Street and Cornhill) which in 1347 was transferred to Trustees for the Guild. By the end of that century the Guild had regulated its affairs by ordinance and acquired a livery garment; in 1400 the Common Hall was in use on the site of today's Livery Hall, known five years later as 'Taillourshalle' with the enlargement of the site. One year later a chapel and crypt existed, and within twenty years the Great Kitchen, in continuous use ever since.

In 1481 Clarenceux King of Arms made the first Grant of Arms to the Fraternity and four years later the quarrel for precedence with the Skinners was settled by Mayor Billesden, with priority granted in alternate years. During that century, almshouses were erected to the east of the Hall and in later years, an embroidered hearse cloth or pall, made for the Guild, was first recorded; with another of 16th century Italian origin. It survives.

The Guild was first recognised as the Merchant Taylors by charter of Henry VII in 1503 and, in 1586, the second Grant of Arms was made to the 'Art or Mystery of Merchant Taylors of the Fraternity of St John the Baptist'. In 1547 the Act of Suppression of Chantries spelt the end of the Chapel which, by 1555, was replaced by the Bachelors' Chamber used by the Yeomen Taylors.

At the end of the 15th century the Guild still controlled its area of trade but by the 17th its connection with tailoring had virtually ceased, its nature essentially philanthropic and social. In 1512 Sir Stephen Jenyns founded Wolverhampton Grammar School, making the Company Trustees — the beginnings of this great Company's centuries of contribution to English education. In 1555 Sir Thomas White founded St John Baptist College, Oxford, and in 1561 Merchant Taylors' School was founded in Suffolk Lane. In 1592 the Guild's almshouses were transferred to Tower Hill.

When James I dined at the Hall in 1607 Dr John Bull played, 'God Save the King' — perhaps its first public performance. The Hall itself was gutted in the 1666 Great Fire and subsequently rebuilt. Meanwhile, in 1617 Matthias Springham founded a free school in Londonderry (now Foyle and Londonderry College), and John Harrison founded Merchant Taylors' School, Crosby in 1620. Merchant Taylors' School was itself destroyed in the Great Fire and rebuilt in 1674, while Henry Colborn founded Merchant Taylors' School, Ashwell, Herts in 1681 (the Further Education Centre from 1947).

Earlier in the 17th century the Irish Society granted the Company an estate in Ulster (sold in

1727). In 1676 the Festival of the Corporation of the Sons of the Clergy was first held at the Hall — an annual event maintained there to the present day. Much of the Company's plate not destroyed in the 1666 fire was sold to finance the King's Civil War demands, but there survive the Corporate Seal of c1502, the early 16th century Cloth-yard, the mace and two late 16th century rose-water dishes. The Company's records go back to the 14th century, including the Books of Account, starting in 1397.

In 1683 Christopher Boone endowed almshouses at Lee, Lewisham — four houses and a chapel, still standing. In the early years of the 18th century the Hall was let to the East India Company and later the ill-fated South Sea Company; it was repanelled in 1729 and much restored in 1793. In 1964, 28 modern almshouses, with a matron's house and gardener's lodge, were completed on a new site. During the 18th century a number of scholarships at Oxford and Cambridge were endowed for boys from the Company's School, which was moved in 1874 to Charterhouse Square and in 1933 to Moor Park, near Rickmansworth in Herts. In 1767 the Company's Tower Hill almshouses were rebuilt, and in 1825 moved to Lee, in south east London, while in 1870 a convalescent home was opened in Bognor, which closed in 1953.

In the 19th century the Hall was altered, the Court Room and Library rebuilt in 1879. Enemy action destroyed much of the complex in 1940, and rebuilding and restoration were completed by 1959. Boone's almshouses now comprise 39 self-contained flats. Dowe House in Blackheath was opened in 1968, to provide 37 wardened flats for elderly and infirm people.

Today the Master, Wardens and Court are still the Governing Body of their School at Rickmansworth, and the Company continues its association with two schools at Crosby and one at Wolverhampton. The Company are patrons of the churches of St Helen's, Bishopsgate and St Paul's, Swanley, and provide pensions, grants, scholarship and prizes among their many acts of benevolence.

The Skinners. Trade in furs goes back to Celtic times. A skinner, or *pelliparius,* was a trader in peltry, the use of fur in the manufacture or trimming of clothing for those privileged to wear such a mark of distinction. An association of skinners was chartered by Edward III in 1327 and reconstituted a Livery Company by Richard II's 1392 charter. By 1380 a Skinners' Hall stood in Dowgate Hill, where the trade became concentrated by the 15th century. In 1484 the dispute over precedence with the Merchant Taylors on great civic occasions, settled by Mayor Billesden, possibly gave rise to the phrase 'to be at sixes and sevens'. One of the Mayor's provisions is still observed — that the two Companies entertain each other on their alternate years of priority.

In the 15th century and until the Reformation the Guild was associated with two religious fraternities — those of the Body of Christ and of Our Lady's Assumption. In the following century the Company controlled the London fur trade, for example admonishing one for 'the foulness of his fats' and in 1594 searching Bristol Fair. A Coat of Arms was granted in 1550 but in 1562 one of three ducal coronets replaced the chalice and host — a reflection perhaps of the more secular usages of the period. In 1560 a 'worshipful dinner' included 'spice-bread, cherries, strawberries, pippins, and marmalade and suckets, comforts and portingalles and divers other dishes, Hippocres rhenish wine, claret wine and beer and ale great plenty and all was welcome' though by 1580 the election dinner was 'laid by' and in 1587 there was only 'a cup of ale or beer and a sermon'.

In 1588 a Skinner, Sir James Lancaster, commanded the *Edward Bonaventure* against the Armada under Drake and Sir Andrew Judd, Lord Mayor in 1550, a Muscovy Merchant born in Tonbridge and apprenticed a Skinner, founded in 1553 'the stately free school' in the town of his birth. He died in 1558, when the Company became the school's governors. During that same century the Skinners tried to protect their rights against the Tawyers and the Artezan Skinners without success. By then fur was less a mark of distinction and the Company was evolving towards its present role. True to their concern to 'advertise' through civic pageantry, the Skinners in 1535 hired from the Wardens of St Sepulchre's Brotherhood 'their giant and puppets and angels' wings and albes'.

Following the Elizabethen incursion into Ireland and James I's plea to the City to invest there, the Company contributed to the Irish Society and, with the Stationers, Girdlers and Bakers acquired what has been described as the twelfth 'and worst lot' of five separate portions totalling 44,000 acres, 24,000 of which were moor and bog. The main settlement was Dungiven, by coincidence 'the stronghold of the skin'. This became the Pelllipar Estate. By 1872 a Company deputation found the town 'susceptible of considerable improvement. . . The interiors of most of the houses combine every element of discomfort . . .'. A light railway was constructed, but gradually the estate was sold piecemeal. Even the Skinners Arms changed its name. In 1933 old contacts were renewed, but the old order had passed.

By the early 17th century the Company had acquired its two major charities for 'setting young men on work' and for poor relief through almshouses and pensions, including subsequently a major charity covering much of Kent, from a Haberdasher, Sir Thomas Smythe, first Treasurer of the Virginia Company, who was the grandson of Judd.

In 1666 the Hall was destroyed by the Great Fire and rebuilt. The present facade was erected in 1778 to Jupp's design. The Hall was let to the East India Company, and the Company met, as Macaulay states 'in a parlour renowned for the fragrance which exhaled from a magnificent wainscot of cedar'.

In 1727 the Company opted out of yet another conflict with the Artezan Skinners. In the 19th century it helped to found the City and Guilds of London Institute and also helped establish the Northampton Institute in Clerkenwell, now the City University. It took an interest in the Yorkshire College at Leeds, since Leeds University, and removed its two almshouses to Palmers Green, founding Judd School at Tonbridge and the Skinners' School at Tunbridge Wells, together with the Skinners' Company School for Girls at Stamford Hill. In 1806 Tonbridge School was rebuilt — today a major public school and the Company's principal interest.

These associations continue, together with the presentation of two scholars to Christ's Hospital and divers other educational activities. In 1954 the Company adopted what is now the 39th (City of London) Signal Regt (Volunteers), which bears the Company's lynx crest as its emblem and has in turn adopted a lynx at London Zoo. Sixteen charities, rationalised in 1890, form the basis for other aspects of the Company's benefactions.

The Haberdashers. During the reign of Edward I, customs dues refer to *hapertas* and *haberdassherie,* probably related terms. *Hapertas* was a coarse cloth worn under armour and haberdashers were dealers in such cloth and later in underwear and other clothing. In 1378 a haberdasher's inventory included leather laces, caps, hats, purses, spurs, beads, daggers, pincases, children's woollen boots and linen thread. The Haberdashers were originally part of the Mercers' Guild and they operated in Cheapside, under two heads — as *hurrers* or *haberdashers* of hats and *cappers* or haberdashers of small wares, otherwise *millianers* (milliners) from their importation of goods from Milan. In 1371 the Haberdashers issued their first ordinances.

Henry VI chartered 'his well beloved liegemen of the Mystery of Haberdashers as 'The Fraternity of Saint Katherine the Virgin' in 1448, and in 1502 the Hatters, Cappers and Hurrers were united with the Haberdashers as 'Merchant Haberdashers'. Agreements with two carpenters, Walter Tylney and Robert Wheatley for the building of a hall were recorded in 1597. The present site of the Hall was left to the Company by William Baker in 1478. The Grant of Arms issued in 1446 was the second to a City Company, and this was replaced by that of 1498, extended in 1570. The Company's earliest charity is that of Henry Somer in the early 16th century.

The Company's new 'merchant' status was withdrawn by Henry VIII's 1510 charter, but its powers and privileges were extended. Cheapside saw Haberdashers' shops blossom with foreign wares, and in the Elizabethen era their trade in pins accounted for some £50,000 in imports. Essential to the well dressed woman, whose husband made her suitable allowance, the trade gave rise to the expression 'pin money'. The Company's charitable activities increased with Roger Jeston's 1575 bequest of properties (sold in 1890 to Whitbread's), and in 1594 they founded the Free Grammar School of Bunbury, Cheshire which became a Primary School in 1958 and is today partly managed by Company appointees. Some 41 past Lord Mayors of the Company included Sir George Bond (1587) whose nephew, Capt Martin Bond commanded the Trained Bands at the time of the Armada threat, and Billesden.

The Haberdashers were involved in James I's Irish adventure to the tune of £4,724 but theirs was the first City Company to extricate itself from this reluctant commitment. They also invested unsuccessfully in Virginia and by 1673 were owed £60,000 by Parliament. The Hall was totally destroyed by the Great Fire, and Sir Christopher Wren was commissioned to design its replacement, completed by 1668.

Haberdashers Sir John Lawrence and Henry Cornish led the non-conformist and Whig movement against Charles II and his Court. Lawrence was Lord Mayor in 1664. Cornish was elected Sheriff in 1680 despite Court opposition, but failed to secure the Mayoralty in 1682. When James II annulled City charters in 1685, Cornish spoke out against the King and he was arrested, tried and executed in Cheapside for high treason, and accused of a drunken speech on the scaffold. William Penn witnessed this and declared it the honest resentment of an outraged man. The Company staged nine pageants in that century, furnishing for one of these 'a faire Pageant Chariot and a Lion, two gallies, fireworks, streamers and all other things . . .'.

In 1613 William Jones, a Liveryman and a Merchant Adventurer of Hamburg, gave the Company £6,000 for almshouses and a preacher at Monmouth, leaving a further £3,000 by his will for a 'free school' and £5,000 for the poor of Newland (Glos) and a preacher there. With many changes over the centuries, these bequests resulted in three schools at Monmouth and Pontypool, the latter transferred to the County Council and the former now among the best of their kind, as Independent Schools on which over £2 million has been spent since 1956.   The Jones bequest also supports almshouses in Monmouth and Newland, and lectureships.

Other 17th century charities include that of William Adams, now reflected in a Grammar School at Newport (Salop), to which the Company appoints Governors, and of Robert Aske, who gave £20,000 for almshouses and a school, which became four schools by the late 19th century. These are now Haberdashers' Aske's School and Haberdashers Aske's School for Girls, both at Elstree; Haberdashers' Aske's Hatcham Boys' School, and Haberdashers' Aske's Hatcham Girls' School, to which the Company appoints Governors while also remaining Governors of the Haberdashers' Aske's Charity. Throckmorton Trotman, not a Haberdasher, nonetheless by his will of 1663 left £4,000 to the Company 'whereof I should have been free had I taken up my freedom', now reflected in exhibitions for Greater London secondary students and under-graduates. Both Thomas Aldersey and Edmond Hammond left money for the patronage of churches at Bunbury and Awre and Blakeney .

During the Commonwealth, soldiers were quartered at the Hall, but attempts by Lord Fairfax to seize the Company's funds, and threats to their plate were thwarted by a blank refusal on the one hand and the quiet removal of the latter on the other.

Other grants and scholarships include the Arno Bequest of £300,000 by Thomas Arno in 1937.

In 1840 the Hall was seriously damaged by fire, rebuilt and again burnt in 1864. In 1940 it was demolished by enemy action. Plate, records and wine survived, but much else was lost. In 1956 the Hall was rebuilt.

LEFT: The Mercers' Arms. (M) CENTRE: Bargemaster's Badge, Grocers' Company. RIGHT: The Lynde Cup of the Grocers' Company (1607). BELOW: The Grocers' Second Hall. (G)

LEFT: The Old School House, Oundle, 1798. (G) RIGHT: William Lambard, founder, Queen Elizabeth's College. (D) BELOW: Fishmongers' Hall. (F)

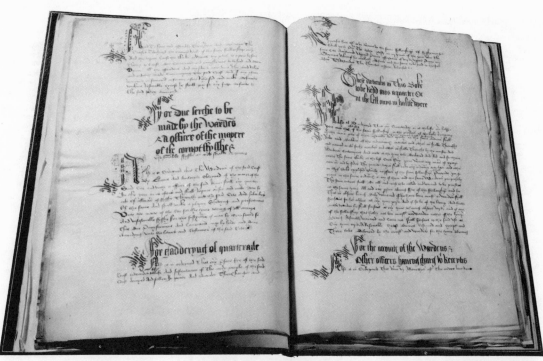

AL' WORSHIP BE TO GOD ONLY

PARVÆ · RES

CONCORDIA · · CRESCUNT

IN CHRISTO FRATRES

ABOVE: The Fishmongers' Book of Ordinances, 1509, and LEFT: their Arms. (F) CENTRE and RIGHT: the Merchant Taylors' Arms 1481 and 1586. (MT) BELOW: the Skinners' Arms. (S)

LEFT: St Katherine of Alexandria, Patron Saint of the Haberdashers, from a 1509 book of bye laws. (H) RIGHT (top to bottom): the Arms of the Salters, (ST) Ironmongers, Vintners, (V) and Dyers. (DY)

100

The Salters. The existing guild was founded by a licence granted by Richard II in 1394 to the Fraternity and Guild of Corpus Christi in the Church of All Hallows, Bread Street, composed of all those who followed the trade of salter, whether or not they lived in the parish. Further licences followed in 1467 and 1510, and in 1559 Elizabeth granted the Company's Charter of Incorporation, while in 1607 the Charter of James I reincorporated the 'art or Mystery of the Salters of London'. Salters dealt not only in salt but as drysalters, in flax, hemp, logwood, cochineal, potashes and chemical preparations.

In 1454 the first Hall was rebuilt. This was destroyed by fire in 1539, and rebuilt. The third Hall, at London Stone in the Parish of St Swithin, was bought in 1641, burnt down in 1666 and rebuilt two years later. It was demolished in 1824 and the fifth Hall completed in 1827. This was also destroyed by fire — in May 1941. It was not until 1976 that the Company finally 'came home' again, to its sixth and present Hall in Fore Street, designed by Sir Basil Spence, and comprising a banqueting hall, committee and court rooms, and offices.

The Salters administer several charities; among these are the almshouses at both Maidenhead and Watford. In 1918 the Company founded the Salters' Institute of Industrial Chemistry, as a link with its former trade. Initially the Institute helped young chemists complete their training after serving in the Great War; then it fostered and funded Salters' Fellowships and Scholarships to young chemists and chemical engineers of high academic and personal standards.

The Salters also assist research projects relevant to industrial chemistry at universities and technical colleges, and help to fund training programmes. More recently they have given grants towards Salters' Exhibitions from specific public schools and book grants, and have organised conferences for science teachers, aimed at updating their knowledge of the most modern teaching methods and latest research findings.

The Ironmongers. Well established as a craft and fellowship in the 13th century, the Ironmongers were granted armorial bearings in 1455 as 'The Honurable Crafte and felasship of the ffraunchised men of the Iremongers of the Citie of London'. Two years later the Guild, as it still was, purchased buildings in Fenchurch Street and converted them into its first Hall. In 1463 the Company was incorporated. The Hall was rebuilt in 1587, and escaped the Great Fire of 1666, but was once more rebuilt in 1745.

In 1606 Nicholas Leat, three times Master of the Company, was appointed engineer to a major project to the north of the original 13th century boundary of the City. Here, outside Aldersgate, lay the great marsh which was first drained in 1211-13, and caused continual problems throughout the next three centuries. Leat's job was to fill the marsh and raise the ground level. His task was done by 1616.

After a bomb had damaged the Company's Hall in 1917, the site was sold and the building pulled down. Land was bought in Shaftesbury Place, Aldersgate Street in 1922 and, during excavations, Nicholas Leat's work was rediscovered and the fringe of the marsh exposed. Thus a former Master literally prepared the ground on which his Company's Hall stands over three centuries later. The new and present Hall was completed in 1925.

In 1703 Master Sir Robert Geffery founded almshouses in Kingsland Road, now the Geffrye Museum; in 1912 the almshouses moved to Mottingham, Kent and were damaged during an air raid in the last war. Under this same trust, a school is maintained at Sir Robert's birthplace at Landrake in Cornwall. The Mottingham almshouses were relocated in 1976 as flats for 38 elderly people at Hook in Hampshire. In 1723 Thomas Betton, once a victim of the slave trade, left half his estate 'for the redemption of British slaves in Turkey and Barbary'. The Company administered the trust until the abolition of slavery, and now Betton's bequest funds annual grants to Church of England Aided schools and independent schools, as well as the relief of poverty.

In 1940 the Hall narrowly escaped destruction when the heat from surrounding buildings, all of which were destroyed, melted its windows. In 1963 the Company set up a new charitable fund, one of the effects of which has been an annual award for distinction in the iron and steel foundry industries, and another the award of grants to the National Trust for the restoration or preservation of examples of craftsmanship in iron in the Trust's properties.

The Company nominates pupils to Christ's Hospitals and Haberdashers' Aske's Schools, grants Exhibitions to both Oxford and Cambridge, and makes annual grants for research at Sheffield University.

The Vintners. The toast of the Company is traditionally 'The Vintners' Company may it flourish, root and branch for ever with Five and the Master' — the *Liber Niger* of Westminster Abbey of 1485 recorded the feasting of 'Five Kings' by Henry Picard, citizen and vintner which, tradition has it, took place in 1363. The guild was first chartered in 1364 and granted a monopoly of trade with Gascony, with duties of search throughout England, which find an echo in the new charter of 1973 authorising the Company to set up The Wine Standards Board, to which the Government delegates responsibilities for enforcing certain EEC wine laws.

Among the Company's archives are deeds dating from 1288. The first deed relating to a Hall was witnessed by Geoffrey Chaucer's father, John.

The 1364 charter gave the Company the right to buy herrings and cloths for sale to the Gascons. By 1437, estates by the gifts of benefactors facilitated incorporation and, throughout the Middle Ages, the Company controlled the London wine trade and dominated that of the rest of the country. That year the Company appointed a 'Bedel'. In 1446 Guy Shuldham bequeathed the site of the Hall. A year later the Company was granted a coat of arms.

King Edward VI's Act of 1553 severely curtailed the right to sell wine, and this and the suppression of the chantries reduced its activities and prosperity. Yet, in 1537 a Clerk was appointed, and in 1539 the Company acquired a hearse cloth by gift of John Hussey; a tapestry showing St Martin and the Beggar dates to 1466 — both are still in the Company's possession, together with a stoneware jug of 1563 and a coconut cup of 1518.

The byelaws of 1594 include the oldest surviving example of the Company's seal, the matrix of which is still in the Company's possession, with St Martin and the Beggar on the obverse and a wine tun on the reverse, resembling Wykeham's 1386 seal for New College.

The Company's right to own swans on the river Thames is by prescription and the account book of 1507-22 mentions a payment in 1509 for looking after them in the frost of that year.

With the depredations of the Stuarts and Parliament and the fire of 1666 the Company suffered financially and lost its Hall. The new Hall was first used in 1671. The staircase was carved by a Mr Woodroffe in 1673. The cost was largely met by selling off the Company's plate, but thereafter it was gradually replaced, such as by a silver gilt salt and cover of 1569 given by John Powel, Master in 1702, and two silver gilt cups and covers given in 1682-3 by another Master, Sir Thomas Bloodworth. Sir Thomas was Master in 1659 and Lord Mayor during the year of the Great Fire.

The Vintners' Song was written for a pageant given by Sir Samuel Dashwood in 1702 to entertain Queen Anne, and it now precedes the toast of the Company, and is followed by five cheers in memory of the Feast of the Five Kings.

In 1725 the duty of search was abandoned, and the Company became less involved with the wine trade, while increasing its charitable activities. By 1799 the exclusive right of the Wine Porters to lower and set up all wines imported into the City had been largely superseded by the West India and London Dock Companies, though it was not until 1963 that the porters ceased practising their ancient craft. During the 18th century the Company acquired the Master's Chair. The Vintners were involved in James I's Ulster colonisation schemes and owned estates there known as Vintners' Manor or Bellaghy until 1737.

Guy Shuldham's 15th century bequest of the Hall site included 'thirteen little mansions' burnt down in the Great Fire, rebuilt at Mile End, and again, through the generosity of Benjamin Kenton and his heir David Pike Watts, in the 18th and 19th centuries. During the last war they were again burnt down and rebuilt at Nutley in Sussex, and these and other Vintners' charities are amalgamated in a scheme known as Vintners's Gifts. Every five years the Company recalls Kenton with a special church service.

In 1822 the widening of Upper Thames Street involved demolition of part of the Hall; the present facade dates to 1910. The banqueting hall ceiling was renewed in 1932. The Hall escaped significant damage in the last war but was refurbished shortly afterwards. The Vintry Ward Schoolboy statue was put on the west wall in 1949 — it originally stood outside the Vintry Ward Charity School of 1840.

The Vintners' swans are marked by two nicks in the beak, and are counted annually on the July Swan Upping voyage. A Swan Feast is held each November. Today the Company retains another ancient right — the privilege of selling wine without licence in London, within three miles of its walls, and in specified ports and towns between London and Berwick and London and Dover. Only freemen by patrimony or apprenticeship may exercise this right.

In 1926 the Company created a yearly scholarship in the wine trade; a bursary was added in 1958 and in 1953 the Company founded the Master of Wine examination with the Wine and Spirit Association. It has made a substantial annual grant to the Wine and Spirit Education Trust for training purposes. Five Kings House in Kennet Wharf Lane was specially built for the use of the Wine and Spirit Association, the Wine and Spirit Education Trust, the Wine and Spirit Benevolent Trades' Society, the Guild of Sommeliers and the Wine Development Board.

The Clothworkers. The Shearmen ranked twelfth among the 'great twelve' Livery Companies. Incorporated in 1508, together with the Fullers, who were incorporated in 1480, they were branches of the Weavers and merged to combat their rivals, and as Clothworkers, took over Shearmen's Hall in Mincing Lane. Chartered in 1528, their first ordinances were signed in 1531 by, among others, Sir Thomas More. Their craft was the finishing of woven cloth; the practice of stretching cloth over a hooked frame or 'tenter' gave rise to the phrase 'being on tenterhooks'.

The site of the original Hall was conveyed in 1456 to individual shearmen, and it was built about 1472, rebuilt in 1548/9 and enlarged in 1608. Early clothworkers included Adam Winthrop, Master in 1551, ancestor to the Puritan Winthrop governors of Massachusetts and Connecticut. William Lambe, Master 1569, founded Sutton Valence School in Kent and brought water to that part of London later crossed by Lamb's Conduit Street. Samuel Pepys was Master in 1677 and presented three of the Company's greatest treasures — a silver-gilt ewer, rosewater dish and a loving cup.

In the early 17th century the Company was forced to make loans towards the resettlement of Ulster. The Hall was rebuilt in 1633 and destroyed in the Great Fire of 1666. Pepys wrote: 'But strange it was to see Cloathworkers-hall on fire these three days and nights in one body of Flame — it being the cellar, full of Oyle'. Two years later a new Hall had risen from the ashes of the old, but it was based on the previous foundations, which in 1855 had 'mouldered and trembled', and it was pulled down.

Meanwhile the Company administered charitable trusts such as that of James Finch of 1508, and contributed a £5 scholarship to Christ Church, Oxford as early as 1551. In 1577 Richard Hakluyt, the historian, received a grant from the Clothworkers, as did Thomas 'Little Tommy' Tucker in 1607. Between 1718 and 1724 John West, Master in 1707 and his wife Frances endowed several trusts to help the blind.

During the Industrial Revolution the clothmaking trade moved to Yorkshire and the Company gradually lost its trade associations but, with the Mastership of Thomas Massa Alsager, a manager of *The Times* and founder of its City page, the Company's fortunes improved. The fifth Hall was opened by the Prince Consort, an Honorary Liveryman of the Company, in 1860. In 1874 the Company built the Department of Textile Industries, later the University of Leeds, and helped to set up the City and Guilds of London Institute. In 1883 it grant-aided the establishment of a Department of Dyeing and Tinctorial Chemistry, later the Department of Colour Chemistry and Dyeing, at Leeds. Other educational benefactions included those to the North London Collegiate School, Camden School for Girls, and women's colleges at Oxford and Cambridge.

In 1941 the Hall was destroyed by fire as a result of a May air raid. The present Hall was opened in 1958. Today the Company continues charitable and educational work, with particular emphasis on help for the blind, the University of Leeds and many other established charities.

The Dyers. First mentioned as a Guild in 1188, the Dyers acquired powers of self-regulation from Mayor Richer de Reffham in 1310-1311 and were incorporated in 1471. In 1390 Chaucer, (who was a Vintner) wrote: 'An Haberdasher and a Carpenter,

> A Webbe, a Dyer and a Tapiser
> Clothed in oo liveree
> Of a solemne and great fraternitee.'

In common with the Vintners, the Dyers have 'a Royalty of a game of Swans of the Thames'. This custom is said to go back to the 1480s; each July the cygnets are marked once on the beak in the annual Swan Upping voyage.

In 1422 and 1423 the Company hired the Brewers' Hall for 1s 6d or 2s on four occasions. By 1482 they had their own Hall in Anchor Lane, St Martins Vintry. A century earlier John of Northampton, a follower of Wycliffe and also Mayor, who had a dyehouse in All Hallows, although he was in fact a draper, was supported in military matters by men of the 'Misterie of Dyers'.

Sir Robert Tyrwhitt gave The Three Stars in Upper Thames Street to the Company in 1545 and Dyers' Hall stood there until it was burnt down in 1666. Its replacement also burnt down in 1681. It was Tyrwhitt who founded the Company's first London almshouses.

Originally twelfth in precedence, the Dyers followed the Vintners, and this was confirmed in 1515 only to be changed a year later, when it was adjudicated that 'the Wardens and Fellowship of the Dyers shall charitably and lovingly follow next the Wardens and Fellowship of Shearmen in all processions, goings, standings and ridings, without any further strife or debate'.

In 1518 the Dyers had to find four bowmen 'to awayt the Mayore in the Watch every of the said nights' on the Vigils of St John and St Peter. In 1585 they furnished forty men for the City Militia in anticipation of a Spanish invasion. In 1577 the Company was awarded a Grant of Arms with the motto 'Da Gloriam Deo'.

The Company's Dowgate Hill estate included two houses which were adapted in 1731 for use as a Hall, but they fell down thirty-seven years later and a new Hall was built on the same site by 1770. That too was destroyed in 1838 when it was found to be structurally unsound, and the present Hall was in use by 1842. Damaged in the last war, it was renovated in 1948 and restored during the period 1955-1965.

Prime Warden Dr Gerald Tattersall Moody left the Company sufficient funds in 1936 to substantially increase its charitable activities. Tyrwhitt's original almshouses had been gradually augmented until there were 26 by 1739, on different sites in London. In 1840 these were brought together with 26 new houses at Balls Pond, Islington, and in 1939 these in turn were sold, and 10 new homes built at Crawley, Sussex. The Moody bequest made possible another 16 in 1952, to which were added four more in 1971.

Since 1948 the Company has been closely associated with King Edward VI Grammar School, Norwich, in particular making good war damage and helping low-income parents, through the Dyers' Scholarship Fund. In 1957 the Company adopted the 10th (V) Battalion The Parachute Regiment and in 1960, the 30th Signal Regiment.

The Dyers have long been involved with the Department of Colour Chemistry and Dyeing at the University of Leeds and, in 1966, founded a housing association for short-term staff and retired people there. It has also helped re-equip the Dyehouse and awards an annual prize to the most meritorious student. In 1973 the Company established a Scholarship at the City of London School. Five years ago the Dyers provided a Music Room at the King Edward VI School, opened by Lady Barbirolli and called the Barbirolli Room after their Honorary Liveryman, Sir John Barbirolli.

A founder member of the City and Guilds of London Institute, the Company awards prizes in dyeing, and an annual gold medal for papers of merit published in the *Journal* of the Society of Dyers and Colourists. A Trust Fund publishes text books and helps students attend courses. Grants are made to the Wool Industry Research Association.

The Brewers. In the City Letter Book for 1292 it is recorded that the Brewers lodged a complaint against the Sheriffs; they were recorded as infringing the prices and measures laid down for the sale of ale. In 1406 they won the right to control their own trade and in 1437 they were incorporated, receiving their first Grant of Arms in 1468 — impaled in turn with the coat of arms of their patron saint St Thomas a Becket. William Porland was Clerk to the Company 1418-1441 and he kept a minute book which survives as the oldest of its kind in the City.

In 1420 Mayor Richard Whytington took umbrage when he learned that the Brewers 'had fat swans at their feast . . . when he had none at his' and he made them sell ale at the ridiculously low price of 1 d a gallon for a day. Then he fined them £20 in 1421 with a caveat that it would be £100 if they failed to pay in time. Fortunately they managed to delay until a new Mayor accepted £10. In conflict again with Whytington, they collected 'voluntary taxation' to petition Common Council against his ordinances. It was spent thus: '£20 to Robert Whetynham, Sheriff; £7 3s 4d for 2 pipes of Red Wine To Richard Whytington's butler; 20s to John Carpenter the Mayor's Clerk; 32s for 2 butts of Malmsey wine to Tho. Fakonere, Alderman and Recorder; Porterage 6s 8d; Writing of the Petition 6d; Spent in collecting the money 6d; Left for Common use 40s 4d.'

Though the Company has deeds to land in Addle Street leased from the Dean and Chapter of St Paul's in 1291, the first mention of a 'Brewers halle' occurs in 1403. Porland was given a 'free and quiet dwelling' there and recorded hirings to, among others, the Footballplayers — who paid less than everyone else. This is one of the earliest references to the game.

After the Reformation, due to the inadvisability of association with so prominent a member of the old Church as Becket, the Company omitted his Arms when they obtained a new Grant of Arms in 1544.

Like so many other companies, the Brewers lost their Hall in the Great Fire of 1666 and spent £5,827 16s 8d on its replacement in 1673, making a levy of £5 a member, payable in four instalments, and pawning their plate and pictures, which were never redeemed. Its builder, Captain Caine, was admitted to the Livery for 'his care and diligence in building the Hall.'

In 1599 Alderman and Brewer Richard Platt of the Old Swann Brewery, Garlickhythe appointed the Brewers as trustees and governors of the grammar school and almshouses he had founded at Aldenham in Hertfordshire, with Letters Patent obtained four years before. He ordered that 'neyther the Maister nor Ussher shall gyve themselves to games nor haunting of Alehowses and Taverns unbeseeminge places such Persons as governe others leaste theire evill examples breede nott onlye discredit to the Schoole but infection also to the Schollers to whome I woulde have them patternes of vertue honestie and pyetie.'

Dame Alice Owen founded the Company's other school in 1613. Out one day in the Islington fields, she narrowly escaped death from an arrow, which pierced her hat as she rose from milking a cow. She vowed to one day commemorate this 'astonishing deliverance', and after outliving three husbands, two of them brewers, she bought Ermitage Fields in Islington, and established a school for 30 boys and almshouses, entrusting their government to the Company. In 1886 a girls' school was added.

In 1940 the Company's Hall was demolished in the blitz, only some leaded window panes surviving. A new Hall was completed in 1960 for a cost of £133,000 — the panes are displayed there. In 1970, the 800th anniversary of Becket's death, the Company commissioned a piece of music for performance in Canterbury Cathedral and in 1973 a new secondary school, The Dame Alice Owen's School was opened in Potters Bar. It was completed in 1976 and formally opened by HRH Princess Anne. The two Islington schools had meanwhile amalgamated and finally closed in 1976. The Aldenham almshouses are now housed in new buildings, and the public school continues to enjoy the Company's support.

Today the Brewers are unusual in continuing to restrict membership to those practising their trade, membership being normally confined to directors of brewery companies which brew in the City or within eight miles thereof, or which own at least 100 licences within the area. Until recently the Company has not had an active Livery membership for many years — members took up their Freedom and were elected to the Livery and the Court at one and the same time, with the result that the Livery comprised, almost without exception, retired Court members. Some years ago, Member companies were invited to nominate candidates for the Livery who would serve on the various committees. These are eligible for nomination to the Court when vacancies occur. The Livery is also open to a certain number of directors from brewery companies outside London, but they do not normally participate in the Company's working activities.

Mainly through the Trade Committee established in 1972, the Company is as active in its trade today as it was eight centuries ago.

The Leathersellers. Tanners and producers of leather were established in the 12th century near Moorgate. Originally two earlier fraternities, of Grey Tawyers and Whittawyers, were associated with, but junior to the Pelterers or Skinners, but in 1275 two Whittawyers were sworn in before the Mayor as Correctors or Licensed Brokers of Leather — Girard de Brie and John de Lincoln. In 1372 'men of the Mistery of Lethersellers', together with the Craft of Pursers, asked the Court of Aldermen to regulate against fraudulent practices in dyeing and staining of inferior leather. Four Supervisors were appointed. In 1398 the Guild obtained articles for the regulation of their craft, which stipulated a fine of 40s 'if any one be found a defaulter' in 'that no manner of Shepeslether nor Calveslether be tinged in the manner of Rolether'.

The Guild's powers increased, and in 1440 its authority was extended: 'alle manner rough felles and tawed, that commyth to this Cite to be solde, from this day forward be brought plenerly to the Selde whiche is ordeyned therfor, on the Northside of the Yeldhalle, there to be discharged, serched, assaid, and solde, and nowher elles'. Four years later the Company was incorporated and its powers of search extended throughout England. In 1445 the Company acquired premises adjoining the City Wall, further extending its estate by 1477. One of the larger buildings became the first Hall. The first Grant of Arms was made in 1479.

By then, the Leathersellers were experiencing problems with the Glovers and the Pursers. In 1498 these two guilds merged as the Glovers-Pursers and in 1502 they in turn merged with the Leathersellers. In 1540 the Company outgrew its original Hall, and three years later concluded the purchase of the Priory of the Black Nuns of St Helen in Bishopsgate — a victim of Henry VIII's dissolution of the monasteries.

The Company grew in power and influence, with an extended 1559 charter and another in

1604, the year in which Parliament defined leather: 'the hides and skins of Ox, Steer, Bull, Cow, Calf, Deer, red and fallow, Goats and Sheep, being tanned or tawed, and every salt hide is, shall be and ever hath been, reputed and taken for Leather'. In 1634 the Company's motto was confirmed: 'Soli Deo Honor et Gloria'. In 1638 the Glovers seceded from their union with the Company and reformed as a separate Guild, and later the Pursers followed suit.

In 1652 the Vicar of Lewisham, Rev Abraham Colfe founded Colfe's School in Horn Lane, south east London and in 1659 the Company were appointed Foundation Trustees. In common with other Companies, the Leathersellers suffered from the financial depredations of Tudor and Stuart monarchs, and in 1685 paid dearly for a new charter. When William III came to the throne, the Company formally repudiated the charter of Charles II, tearing the Great Seal from its foot and breaking it into small fragments.

In the last year of the 18th century, the old Hall at Little St Helen's, as the Company's estate was known, was suffering from structural decay, so the buildings were demolished and a nearby old house temporarily used as a Hall. This was burnt down in 1819 and a new Hall built on the original site by 1822. In 1878 a fifth Hall was erected.

In 1909 the Company established Leathersellers' Technical College in Tower Bridge Road, Bermondsey. In 1926 its Hall was extended, but in 1941 those premises were severely damaged and their contents virtually destroyed by enemy action. In 1944 the same fate befell Colfe's School. Temporary school accommodation was provided from 1949 to 1964. The Company's present Hall was completed in 1959 off St Helen's Place.

In 1951 the college in Tower Bridge Road was re-established as the National Leathersellers College. In 1962 the Company established two scholarships at St Catherine's College, Oxford, and in 1966 two more at Fitzwilliam College, Cambridge. In 1964 a new building was completed for Colfe's School, and in 1977 the school moved from voluntary aided status to full independence. A preparatory school was opened in 1978 and the Company awards five annual £100 Leaving Exhibitions.

In 1978, by means of a half million pound grant by the Leathersellers, a new building known as the National Leathersellers Centre was completed — two years before this, the old technical institution had been transferred to within Nene College, Northampton as the National Centre for Leather Education. This is the only institution of its kind in the English-speaking world. In 1979 a Research Fellowship in Industrial Engineering was established at Jesus College, Oxford. Leathersellers act as Governors of the Prendergast Grammar School for Girls at Catford and the Company has helped to fund new buildings there. It has also endowed flats for elderly people associated with the Company, at Barnet.

The Pewterers. Pewterware was first introduced into Britain by the Romans. In the 11th century it grew in popularity and use. Pewterers were already organised into a Guild by 1348 when the 'goodfolk, makers of vessels of pewter' were formally recognised. They attended every year at the Austin Friars, and held a feast in the hall of the monastery. The Company's records date back to 1451, and in that year it achieved its first Grant of Arms. In 1474 the Company was incorporated, and granted wide powers of search, inspection and the right to impose penalties or forfeit against badly wrought ware or ill-mixed metal. The 'mix' was scrupulously controlled and defined in three grades: 'fine metal' for flatware was made of tin with 'so much copper as it would absorb', probably 2%; 'lay metal' for hollow-ware could include an additional 10% lead, and 'trifle' for stills, candle moulds, buttons and toys contained up to 25% lead. Bad wares were marked with a broad arrowhead.

Pewter had little competition as table ware for two centuries. Goods were sold 'by the garnish', comprising effectively twelve place settings of platters, dishes and saucers. Less elegant items were sold by the pound, then valued as 'six or seven pence, or peradventure eight pence'. From the granting of the first charter, before a pewterer could set up shop he had to record his 'touch', or trade mark on large pewter sheets retained at the Company's Hall. In 1484 the Pewterers acquired a site in Lime Street and completed its first Hall in 1496.

The trade reached its zenith in the 17th century. Then changing fashion, new techniques and the introduction of tea drinking brought decline. 1666 saw the destruction of the Hall and all the early 'touch' plates in the Great Fire. A new Hall rose on the same site in 1670, and was often let out to dissenters as well as for dancing, fencing, funerals and meetings.

In 1801 the Company could no longer justify the cost of the Hall, and it was let on a permanent basis, the Company meeting and dining instead in one of its houses facing Lime Street. Fire damaged that building in 1840, but it survived until its demolition in 1932.

Since 1879 the Pewterers have supported the City and Guilds of London Institute among many charitable and educational activities. In 1940 the Company planned to build a new Hall in Queen Victoria Street, but the Corporation acquired the property and a site in Oat Lane was sold to the Company. In 1960 the foundation stone of the present Hall in Oat Lane was laid and the building opened a year later. It contains a fine collection of antique British pewter, and records of over 1,000 'touch' marks.

In 1970 the Pewterers sponsored manufacturers to set up the Association of British Pewter Craftsmen, thus forging new links with its old trade. The Association echoes the original Guild's principles, with its own ABPC mark, and in 1979 the Company encouraged the Association to join with European pewterers in forming the European Pewter Union. Today, the Company's other activities include housing for the elderly, support for neurological research, scholarships for pupils at City schools and Dulwich College, and support for research into metals at the City University.

The Barbers. The Barbers existed as an unincorporated guild in the 13th century. In 1308 the Master was Richard le Barber. Barbers also practised as surgeons and the first recorded admission of one to the guild was in 1312. At the same time a Surgeons' Gild existed, and furnished Master Surgeons to examine the work of those in practice and to report defaults. The Barbers' Guild also successfully applied to the Mayor and Aldermen for the right to control surgical practice. In 1376 Lawrence de Weston and John de Grantone were appointed Masters for that purpose.

In 1462 the Barbers' Company was incorporated — it was by far the more powerful and prosperous of the two apparently competing guilds. Edward IV's charter granted a significant exemption: 'that neither the said Master or Governors and Community of the said Mystery of Barbers, nor their successors, nor any of them shall hereafter in any wise be summoned or appointed in any assizes, juries, inquests, inquisitions, attainders or other recognizances within the said City . . .'.

The Company's first Hall was built in the 15th century in Monkwell Street, near the hermitage of St James-in-the-Wall. In 1493 the Company and the Surgeons' Guild agreed to commonise surgical practice within the City. Each would select two Masters, the four to act as directors of surgical matters. A system of 10s and 20s fines and referral to the Mayor and Aldermen was established. In 1497 the first known diploma in surgery was granted to Robert Anson, bearing the seal of both organisations. The 1499 charter referred to the 'Mystery of Barbers and Surgeons'.

In 1511 an Act of Parliament placed the approbation and licensing of surgeons in the hands of the Bishop of London and the Dean of St Paul's and in 1512 the Company's charter was confirmed. The Gild of Surgeons and the Company of Barbers were formally joined by Act of Parliament on 24 July 1540, which also required that the bodies of four criminals should be made available for dissection at the Hall. At the time of the Union, the Barbers had more freemen than any other Company.

In 1605 the hall was extended, and in 1635 it was decided to build an anatomical theatre. This was designed by Inigo Jones. All except the theatre was destroyed in the 1666 fire and a new parlour and Court room were built at a cost of £4,292. The theatre was demolished in 1784. In 1745 an Act of Parliament separated the Barbers and Surgeons once again. In 1869 only the Court Room was retained. In 1940 the Hall was razed by enemy action, and the present Hall was opened in 1969 by HM Queen Elizabeth the Queen Mother, now an Honorary Freeman.

The Cutlers. The word 'cutler' comes from the Latin *cultellarius* and old French *coutelier* and signifies a maker or seller of knives or other cutting instruments. The trade or art is lost in antiquity, but cutlers are recorded as far back as the 12th century and early in the 13th century the Cutlers regulated their own affairs under articles approved by the Mayor and Aldermen. The first recorded cutler was appropriately called Adam. In 1416 'the poor people of the craft of Cutlers within the City of London' achieved incorporation. There were then distinct branches of the art or mystery — bladers, bladesmiths or knifesmiths made the blades; hiltsters the hilt; sheathers the sheath; the cutler completed the weapon or instrument. The grinders and furbishers were also involved.

Until 1441 the Sheathers existed as a separate craft but shortly after they united with the Cutlers; until then the Cutlers had occasion to complain about their bad workmanship more than once.

Although the original Guild met regularly to transact business at 'a house of the Cutlers' opposite the Conduit in West Cheap as long ago as 1285-6, and the colony of craftsmen in the neighbourhood was known as the 'Cutlery', the Fraternity probably met at a monastic lodge or a tavern. They paid Roger de Northwode £12 a year for the building's use. By the early 15th century the Company met at a Hall in Horseshoe Bridge Street (later Cloak Lane), and owned the site by 1451 — they may well have owned it earlier than 1416. Close to the Walbrook, the building suffered from damp and needed frequent repair. The property included almshouses and other tenements. In 1548 the cost of paving the road frontage of some 130 feet was 13s.

In 1462-3 the Cutlers were 17th in order of precedence; in 1483, 15th, but in 1515 they were placed 18th. In 1476 the Company obtained a Grant of Arms, which included as its crest, an elephant — a possible heraldic reference to the use of ivory in hafting weapons. Earlier, in 1470, the accounts record 'Paid for the amendyng of the bassell of the Master with the Olivaunt in the prynte'. The elephant and castle were granted as the Company's crest in 1622. The Company's motto was originally 'Pervenir a bonne foy' which later became 'Pour parvenir a bonne foy' — 'To succeed through good faith' — one of only two Company mottoes in French.

In 1660 the Company decided its Hall was inconvenient and in bad condition. A loan of £400 was raised for a new building, which in the event cost £2,733 2s 7d, took four years to build and was just paid for when it was totally destroyed in the Great Fire. Fifteen days later the Company met in the Bear Tavern 'att the Bridge ffoote' and ordered a chest to contain its records and treasures. The plate was sold towards a new Hall and meanwhile Loriners' Hall was hired. The numbers of the Livery were increased, fines raised and a committee of nine formed to organise rebuilding. In 1670 the new Hall was in use. A year later there were £475 of workmen's bills outstanding and a £500 mortgage was raised. Eventually an enforced contribution from members and a loan by the Master resolved the problem. It was then let for weddings, funerals and to other Companies.

By the mid-18th century the Company had ceased to have any real control over its original trade, much of which had moved to Sheffield, though it continued to control aspects of manufacture and import of swords, and granted marks to swordmakers. In 1882 the District Railway Company acquired its site in connection with the building of Cannon Street Station, and for six years the Cutlers met at Salters' Hall.

In 1886 the Company bought what was from 1674 to 1825 the site in Eldenslane or Old Dean's Lane, now Warwick Lane of the Royal College of Physicians from Charles Tylor and others for

£14,000. Over £20,000 was spent on the new Hall, which was opened in 1887. The facade included a terra cotta frieze illustrating the processes of the cutlers' art — the only known example of its period. It was executed by Creswick, a young Sheffield craftsman 'discovered' and helped by Ruskin.

In 1940 the Hall miraculously escaped destruction during a major air raid. Beadle and Hallkeeper Fred Hall watched as two fires raced towards the Hall, and firemen stood by powerless, because the water pressure had failed. Hall watched to see what would happen and 'to keep a eye on the wine cellar'. Warwick Lane was ablaze and the next and opposite buildings were a wall of flame, when suddenly the water came on and the firemen doused the Hall from the roof, saving it from all but minor damage. Said Fred Hall afterwards: 'I looked down the Lane at the old Jumbo (the metal sign of the elephant hanging over the door) to see whether he'd stand up to it — and, Master, he did'. But the Hall's escape was short-lived for, six months later, an HE bomb took away the north wall, destroyed the dining room and damaged the main hall. Within months the north wall was restored and in 1949 more repairs were made; in 1954 the building was finally and fully restored.

Today the Company fosters apprenticeships in the surgical instrument-making industry, awards annual prizes to apprentices, gives annual scholarships at Keble and St Peter's Colleges, Oxford and St John's, Corpus Christi and Queens' Colleges, Cambridge, under the wills of John Craythorne and Nathaniel Bucke, and by way of a trust established by Macdonald Beaumont. It grants musical scholarships and a City of London School scholarship. The Company also awards travelling scholarships for the study of modern languages in the name of Captain Francis George Boot, Master in 1894. Once a year, by his will and direction, a banquet is held as near as possible to his birthday, when the Company and its guests dine together and drink to his memory, hear an extract from his will and, as he instructed, 'the viands, wines and appointments shall be the best of their kind and . . . hospitality be dispensed with no niggard hand'. The Company also makes a £500 Surgical Award annually for advances in surgical technology, by recommendation of the Association of Surgeons of England.

The Bakers. As early as 168 BC, bakers were the only craftsmen in Rome who were freedmen of the City, all other trades being conducted by slaves. The whole craft was incorporated in a college of bakers — *collegium pistorum* — and was of such high repute in affairs of state as to be represented in the Senate. It is clear that a craft fraternity must have existed in London during the Roman occupation.

However, the first record of such an organisation in London is in the Pipe Rolls of Henry II, which listed the yearly 'farm' paid to the Crown and which show that the bakers of London *(bolengarii)* paid one mark of gold to the King's Exchequer from 1155. Since only the Weavers were recorded before that, the Bakers claim to be the second oldest Guild, as others which may have existed did not pay a tax and were not recognised, being classed as adulterine and fined accordingly.

Known originally as the 'Fraternity of the Guylde of Our Lady and St Clement', the Bakers' main function was to administer the Assize of Bread. Enacted in 1266, the Assize laws probably go back to Saxon times. Under the Bread Assize the price of a loaf remained constant but the weight might vary according to the market price of grain and other costs. The nineteen articles included such edicts as 'Every baker must imprint his mark upon his loaves' and 'no baker of brown may bake white, and vice versa'. The Assizes continued for nearly 600 years until eventually abandoned in 1815, when responsibility for regulating the sale of bread passed to the Government.

During those years there were many disputes between the White and Brown Bakers and in the early 14th century they split into separate Guilds. The White Bakers received their first proven charter in 1486 — though it has been claimed that this merely replaced an earlier one of 1307 — and were incorporated in 1509. They had hired a tenement in Dowgate in 1490 as their first Hall, until a large mansion was acquired in Sigrymes (now Harp) Lane in 1506. This was rebuilt after its destruction in the 1666 fire and burnt down again in 1715, to be built anew in 1722, and lost for a third time in the 1940 blitz.

Meanwhile the Brown Bakers had obtained a distinctive coat of arms in 1572, incorporation in 1621 and their own Hall in Aldersgate in 1635. They were reunited finally with the White Bakers in 1645. The shield of the White Bakers of 1461 formed the basis for their Grant of Arms of 1536.

Offenders against the Bread Assize laws were brought to the Hall to appear at the bar of the ancient 'Court of Halimote' to be tried by the Master and Wardens, with a jury composed of Assistants of the Court. Some of the offences and fines were, to say the least, extremely odd. 'Hitting the Clerk in the teeth' cost a penny; yet a shilling was imposed on Mr Dixon 'for saying of Steward Smith he snorted like a horse', with an extra twopence 'for saying he shall snort like an asse if he will the next time'. Others were fined 'for telling Richd. Thiknes he had a thicke skull', 'Mr Slye for sleeping in the roome and for brawling with the Butlers', 'Mr Dixon for leaning on his elbow and playing with his beard', and 'Mr Goodman for saying of another that though he came late he came not unprovided for he robbed his wife's purse of all the farthings', and again 'Mr Stubbes for calling Mr Miller the base string of a Welshe harpe'.

Records show that the diminishing 20th century practice of some Companies of excluding the ladies at functions was not tolerated by the Bakers in the 18th century. Once in 1710, when for some reason, the ladies were unwilling to attend, the dinner was cancelled since 'no dinner is to be provided for next Election Day if the wives of the Court do not come'.

The present Bakers' Hall was opened in 1963 and has two distinguishing features: in the Court Room a curious low balustrade has been retained, dividing the room in two. This echoes the old halimote. The other comprises three stained glass windows by John Piper in the Livery Hall, symbolising the three fires which destroyed previous Halls.

Today the Company maintains educational and charitable links with the industry it reflects which, together with allied traders, provides around a third of the membership. In 1977 The Bakers' Livery Society was formed to further the interest of its Liverymen in the history and traditions of their Company, the 'trade' and the City.

The Wax Chandlers. The business of The Wax Chandlers was the preparation and sale of beeswax and wax products — mainly candles, and also tapers, torches and images as well as seals for documents. Beeswax candles were used primarily by the Church, Court and nobility and were made by servants and by monks. The earliest reference to a commercial wax chandler is that to William le Sirger in 1298. By 1330 the craft was organised and in 1358 obtained its own ordinances, fifteen years after four members were appointed to investigate the mixing of wax. In 1371 rules were laid down for pricing and makers' marks. In 1422 the business of providing candles for funerals was highlighted by the provision of iron candlestands by Simon Prentot for Henry V's funeral procession, at a cost of £300 12s 6d. In 1470 the Guild was required to provide twenty-one men for the City watch. At the 1478 Wax Chandlers' feast on Lord Mayor's Day, the fare included a loin of beef, a leg of mutton, two loins of veal and of mutton, a goose, capon, pig and rabbit, a dozen pigeons, a hundred eggs, a gallon of wine and a kilderkin (16-18 gallons) of ale — total cost 7s. In 1484 the Company was incorporated and a year later received its first Grant of Arms.

At the turn of the century, the Company acquired a house in Aldersgate Street and in 1501 it obtained property in Maiden Lane, now Gresham Street, for £36. This consisted of a brewhouse, The Cock on the Hoop and other buildings, and 24 years later these had been converted into a Hall — the site dates back to Roman times and the present Hall stands on part of it. In 1508

Thomas Field started a wax bleaching business at Lambeth — his family like others with early freemen, retains links with the Company to this day. In 1514 new ordinances specified a two-year term for Master and Wardens — now almost unique among City companies — and in 1527 John Thompson bequeathed property at Queenhithe for poor relief. The 1530-2 accounts reflect the dinner fare for a dinner for forty — 'A Buck and Fetching of another', a rump of beef, half a lamb, six marrow bones, seven shoulders of mutton and suet, 18 pike, two fresh salmon and a salmon trout, a ling and a side of salt fish, three barrels of ale, a kilderkin of beer and 'wine at the Cardinal's Hat' — total cost £4 13s 8d.

The Company contributed two men to the City's force of 264 bowmen and billmen to subdue the Pilgrimage of Grace in the north in 1536 and that same year the plate was sold for £40 and bought in by a warden, William Baynard. In 1542 property in Coleman Street was left to the Company in trust, and in 1544 the Hall and buildings were conveyed to the Company. In 1547 the Reformation's prohibition of candles, tapers and images in church lost the Company its major customer, and the Fraternity of Jesus in St Paul's, with which the Company had been closely associated, was suppressed. In 1559 William Kendall, Past Master, bequeathed property in Old Change, the basis for the Company's most important charity. In 1581 Parliament brought the wax and honey trades under national regulation.

In 1606 the Company sold its mark and game of swans for '£14 of good money of England' thus relinquishing its swan marking rights and the custom of swan-upping. Three years later the Wax Chandlers contributed £80 to the Ulster resettlement programme. In 1622 William Parnell gave a house in Puddle Dock for poor relief. In 1634, when the Grant of Arms was confirmed, the motto 'Truth is the Light' appeared for the first time.

In 1657 the Company extended and partly rebuilt its Hall, and the Vicar of Bexley, Nicholas Frankwell, entrusted the Company with a charity for the poor of that village. The 1663 charter and 1664 ordinances extended the trade monopoly to a ten mile radius and laid down procedures reflected in today's Company, but thenceforth it gradually lost control of a declining trade. That year the plate was sold again and £25 borrowed to lend to the King for the war with Holland. In 1665 the plague made Assistants hard to come by and in 1666 the Great Fire destroyed the Hall, and the reduced Court met at 'the sign of Redd Cross in Little Britain'. By 1670 the Hall was rebuilt at a cost of over £500. Dinner by 1669 was more expensive and more lavish. £7 11s 3½d bought 'A Sr Loyne' and four ribs of beef, four legs of mutton, four shoulders of veal, 10lb of bacon, 9lb of butter, 'Carrets and Collyflowers', three gallons of beans, bread, wine, oranges and lemons, strawberries, sugar and tobacco, and paid for the cook and 'The House Bill'. In 1684 the charter was surrendered to the King, and a new and more restrictive one purchased for £161 16s 10d a year later, to be 'lost' in 1688 and anulled in 1689 when the previous one was reinstated. In 1686 the Company sold its Irish holdings, reserving the fishing, hunting and mining rights to the Irish Society.

In 1791 the Court decided to demolish and rebuild the Hall, said to be 'in ruinous condition'. This was completed in 1793 for £1,429 15s. In 1799 Elizabeth Applegarth was admitted to the freedom — until recently the last woman to be free of the Company. In 1837 Master John Cowan became Lord Mayor and received Queen Victoria on her first City visit. In 1852 the Hall was yet again rebuilt, this time at a cost of £4,417; of this £4,014 was received as compensation, due to the widening of Gresham Street. In 1884 the Company was a foundation donor of the City and Guilds of London Institute.

In 1906 the Master was elected President *ex officio* of the British Bee Keepers Association, Patron in 1922, and of the Central Association of Beekeepers in 1945. In 1940 the Hall was largely destroyed in the blitz. In 1958 a new Hall was completed — cost £57,900. That year the Company undertook to supply candles for the new high altar in St Paul's in perpetuity. In 1962 the Company presented a donor governor of Christ's Hospital and three years later instigated an annual award to successful candidates for the Central Association's exams. Today the Company maintains its charitable and educational activities, supplementing income from its ancient trusts with grants from corporate funds.

The Tallow Chandlers. The first reference to the craft occurred in the early 13th century: 'the house which Edward the oynter used and occupied'. An *oynter* (or *unctuarius*) was a tallow melter who rendered the rough fat supplied by the butchers; such men were also called *candelarii* or chandlers, the term also embracing the makers of candles. In 1283 oynters occupied shops and *seldae* (stalls) in the market place known as West Chepe (now Cheapside), among them Roger and Stephen le Chaundeler. Suppliers to the Royal Household of wax and tallow candles were called chandlers, and their department the Chandlery, but as beeswax came into commercial use, those concerned became *ciergers* and the tallow trade retained the term chandler, later tallow-chandler. The earliest reference to a Guild is in 1300. In 1362 and 1373 orders regulated the prices of tallow and candle, and the sale of tallow by butchers. The Guild originally derived from the Fraternity of Our Lady and St John in the Church of St Botolph; an early lease in Chaunderllers' Alley 'pertenynge to the crafte of Tallough Chaundellers' referred to the Fraternity of St John the Baptist of the craft of Tallow Chandlers of London.

Tallow chandlers also dealt in other commodities: vinegar and sauces, oil, soap, herring and cheese. In 1339 a number of Chandlers were sworn to prevent bad liquor in mustard, sauces and saxifrage, and although later that century the Vintners carried out duties of search, Chandlers are known to have accompanied them. In 1419 existing conflict with Salters, who also made tallow candles and dealt in sauces, came to a head. (Chandlers were traditionally associated with saucers (*salsarii*), and the two terms *sauser* and chandler were often interchangeable occupational surnames.) The Tallow Chandlers sought to 'assay weights and measures used by Salters'. The Mayor and Aldermen ruled in favour of the Salters. In 1404 City inhabitants were ordered to hang out 'lanthorns' with candles 'lit to burn as long as they will last'. Tallow was used for these, the City stipulating that it should not be used for soap, though there were soapmakers among the ranks of the Tallow Chandlers.

In 1456 the Tallow Chandlers obtained a Grant of Arms, and the fellowship was incorporated in 1462, with powers of search. By December 1464 the Company rented a Hall bearing its name near Austin Friars at the junction of Throgmorton Street and Old Broad Street. The site of the present Hall in Dowgate Hill was bought for £166 13s 4d in 1476, three years after the 'Wardeyns of the Craft of Taloughchaundlers' were ordered to seek out Tallow Chandlers and others using the craft whose candles were made 'disceyvably with flotice (surface scum in boiling) and grece'. The order stipulated that wicks should be made of clean cotton and not of 'threde and flox (coarse tufts of cotton and wool waste)'. Offenders went to prison. 'Others' using the craft included Barbers, Cutlers, Fishmongers, Leathersellers, Saddlers, Salters, Tailors, Vintners and Wax Chandlers. The Tallow Chandlers were the watchdogs, but the City encouraged adequate supplies by permitting these 'others' to practise the craft. In 1474 further regulations forbade the butchers to trade in or melt tallow or to make candles except for themselves. The 1473 regulations allowed search in mustard, vinegar and other sauces.

In 1512 a statute authorised the Tallow Chandlers to regulate the import of oils into the City, and six years later the Company sought to search Salters who made candles, and it was ordered that 'from henceforth two of the Wardeyns of the Salters and two of all the Wardeyns of the Taloughchaundlers' should 'lovingly and charitably at all times convenient together make search of all persons of both Fellowships as sell any tallow candle or sauce'. Six years later this was revoked and the right restricted to the Company. In 1538 the Tallow Chandlers attempted to claim quarterage from anyone 'occupying the craft' and the right to search for 'Oyles, sawse and Weyghates, Talough and Candyll' — this was opposed by the Salters and, after eleven years, the independent right of search was confirmed, but quarterage could only be collected from the fellowship and those 'content to pay'.

By the mid-16th century the Vintners had adopted the practice of 'presenting' wines unfit to drink to the Company to assess their suitability as vinegar for sauces. Herring was mentioned in early ordinances and in 1558 a Mayoral 'Proclamation for Vyctualles' sought 'reasonable rates and pryces' for tallow candles, cheese, butter and herring dealt in by tallow chandlers, and others using their 'art or occupacion'.

Successive charters and Letters Patent confirmed or changed the Company's powers, including the contentious 'Tyler's Patent' of 1577, which appointed the Company 'searchers, waighers, examyners, viewers and tryers of all sope, vyniger, barrelled butter, oile and hoppes', which was opposed by the Mayor and Aldermen and other Companies. In 1603 the Company obtained a Grant of Supporters to the Arms, and a second crest intended as a correction of the first, but the Company has ever since borne both. In the 17th century the Company was granted a succession of charters, culminating in that of William and Mary. In 1690 candles were superseded by oil for street lighting with the introduction of lamp lights, or *lucidiaries*.

The Tallow Chandlers lost their Hall in the Great Fire of 1666, but within ten years a new Hall and other buildings had been completed on the same site.

By 1709 the Company's grip on the trade had all but disappeared, though in 1693 and again in 1784 other companies attempted to regulate the Tallow Chandlers. In 1868 the Hall ceiling was replaced, and in 1883 the Company's four houses on Dowgate Hill were replaced by an office block. In the last half of the 19th century tallow was virtually replaced by paraffin wax in candle manufacture, though tallow found many other industrial applications. The Hall survived the blitz.

Now the Company maintains links with the changed trade and associates itself with the oil industry. It has admitted to its freedom members of the old London Oil and Tallow Trades Association, and those of the Federation of Oils, Seeds and Fats Association as well as establishing a special relationship with the National Edible Oil Distributors' Association.

The Company provides, among other charitable endeavours, pensions for poor people sponsored by the Oilseed, Oil and Feedingstuffs Benevolent Association, and awards annual grants to craft apprentices and students of BP Oil.

The Armourers and Brasiers. The Guild of St George of the Armourers was first formalised in 1322 and a lease acquired in 1346 of the 'Dragon and two Shoppes' in what is now Coleman Street. In 1428 the freehold was acquired, and this was conveyed to the Company on its incorporation in 1453 by charter of Henry VI, himself a Brother of the Fraternity.

The first Grant of Arms was made in 1556, with the motto 'Make All Sure'. In 1528, William Vyneard, Master in 1531, gave the Company a 'George of Complete Armor on horseback' which disappeared at the end of the 18th century. The Company in 1975 purchased a 30 inches high, 16th century mounted figure of St George in armour believed to be the selfsame article. Forced to sell much of its plate to finance Henry VIII's campaigns, the Company retained a stoneware pot known as the Owl Pot, given in 1537 by Vyneard's widow — it is the oldest example of Rhenish stoneware in the world. In 1557 the Company received its greatest treasure — the Richmond Cup presented by John Richmond, three times Master, and his wife, Esabell. Each year the Master drinks his successor's health at the election day banquet in this vessel.

Successive charters included that of 1619 which gave the Company control of all who made brass and copper articles, edged tools, and guns and armour.

In 1708 Queen Anne's charter incorporated the Brasiers with the Armourers, granting control of all brass and copper work made in the City and within a radius of five miles, whether by the Company's members or by others. The arms of both Companies were joined, and the motto 'We

Are One' added. The charter granted 'full power and authority to have, use and enjoy for ever a Common Seal for the affairs and business of the said Corporation', and that silver seal remains in use today.

Towards the end of the 18th century the Hall was sorely delapidated, and was virtually rebuilt; in 1840 it was demolished and the present Hall built. Both in 1666 and 1940 fire came within a few yards, but each time the building escaped destruction. The Hall contains a representative collection of English and foreign arms and armour, some of the former bearing the Company's hall mark.

Though the Company's trade no longer exists, it maintains its traditional association with metalworking through its charities and educational awards. Funds are provided for research fellowships in metallurgy, scholarships and exhibitions in metallurgy at Oxford, prizes and travel awards to Sheffield cutlery apprentices, and likewise for students of engineering and metallurgy at Sheffield College of Technology, together with a grant to the City and Guilds of London Institute and prize awards to students of engineering.

Not surprisingly, the Company has strong links with the forces. The City of London Yeomanry (Rough Riders) which was formed in 1900, was affiliated to the Company between 1938 and 1961 and, on amalgamation with the Inns of Court Regiment, the affiliation was maintained with the combined Inns of Court and City Yeomanry, now a Signal Squadron of the Territorial Army. The Company also gives prizes to the best officer or cadet from each term at Sandhurst joining the Royal Armoured Corps, with which it has been associated since 1955, and for marksmanship to Armourers serving in the Corps of Royal Electrical and Mechanical Engineers, as well as to the most promising officers on training courses of the Royal Armoured Corps. Since 1957 the Junior Leaders Regiment of the Royal Armoured Corps has been affiliated to the Company, which also awards prizes and medals to armourers qualifying at HMS *Excellent* and in the RAF.

The Girdlers. The craft consisted of making the girdle or belt which was worn outside gown or tunic to gather the garment or suspend the purse, wallet or side arms. The Girdlers are permitted to present the sword belt for the Sword of State at each sovereign's Coronation. The craft overlapped others and the Company has been associated with the Pinners, Cordwainers, and the Gold and Silver Wyre Drawers. In 1209 a licence was granted by King John to Gerard de Seinturer, in 1216 Benet le Seinturer was made Sheriff and in 1327 Letters Patent regulated the trade on the petition of 'the Girdlers of our City of London'. In 1431 the Guild acquired the site for a Hall from Andrew Hunt, Girdler, and in 1449 the Mystery of Girdlers was incorporated. Two years later the Lord Mayor recognised an association of Girdlers with the Pinners and Wireworkers, which was formalised by the charter of 1567.

In 1454 a Grant of Arms was achieved, with three gridirons or girdle-irons and a crest depicting the patron saint, St Lawrence, who was martyred by burning on a girdle-iron. The Company has long-standing connections with St Lawrence Jewry-next-Guildhall. In 1574 the Master, Cuthbert Beeston, presented a crown which is used on the election of the Master and eight years later he bequeathed land for an almshouse charity. The year following, Henry Flycke, who had been Master in 1551, gave the George Inn, Hammersmith and other land there to the Company and, in 1610, George Palyn, who was Master in 1595, left money for an almshouse charity. In 1634, twice-Master Robert Bell commissioned and presented to the Company the Lahore Carpet.

In the Great Fire the Hall was destroyed but the carpet was saved. It was rebuilt in 1681 at a cost of £1,428 2s 10d. Successive charters and ordinances culminated in that of 1682.

During the succeeding centuries the Company's trade disappeared, and its prosperity reduced until the 19th century brought better times; by 1860 both Beeston's and Palyn's almshouses had been rebuilt on their present sites. In 1878 the Hall was enlarged.

A Readership in Economics at Cambridge was instituted in 1911 — one of the early holders was

J.M. Keynes. In 1911 the Company presented the Girdle and Stole Royal for the Coronation of George V. On 6 February 1933, the anniversary of the signing of the Treaty of Waitangi, the Company began its long association with the New Zealand Society by entertaining the members to tea — now an annual event. In 1937 a new charter was obtained — three years later the Hall was blitzed into oblivion, but the famous carpet, the Company's silver and the 1462 charter were saved.

In 1954 the Company founded the New Zealand Scholarship to enable an undergraduate to go to either Oxford or Cambridge, and in 1961 the Hall was rebuilt, virtually on the original 1431 site. The Company has since extended the New Zealand Scholarship to fund three students at Corpus Christi College, Cambridge, new almshouses have been built at Peckham, and there are two distributions of money to charity each year.

The Butchers. With their basic trade recorded in 150 AD and Stow's record of a Hall outside the walls where butchers met in 975 AD (though there is no supporting evidence), the Butchers were first recorded as a Guild in 1179: 'Gilda bocheiorum unde Willelmus Lafeite est aldermannus debet 1 m'. They congregated in Eastcheap, the hub of the City, and gradually moved westwards, to form the shambles of St Nicholas (now Newgate Street), recorded in 1196. A third market house between the two locations was established in 1283, called 'les Stokkes'. In 1266 legislation prevented the sale of 'infectious' meat, and prevented 'forestalling' — the practice of selling meat before it reached the market stalls. Weights, measures and prices were specified.

In 1299 ordinances were enforced and, in 1319, surveyors of meat markets appointed. By 1300 the authorities had empowered seven freemen to control prices. In 1345 some butchers set up in Poultry, forcing the City to restrict the trade to its original marketplaces. Thirteenth and 14th century development of Common Council saw increasing representation by the Butchers, but their undoubtedly anti-social trade handicapped them compared to the other great companies. In 1361 a Parliamentary ordinance required slaughtering to be done outside the City limits, which the Butchers resisted. The Butchers were constantly subject to complaints. The Eastcheap tradesmen had slaughterhouses behind their shops but those in St Nicholas Shambles were less well placed. The Greyfriars took them to law for flushing offal and other refuse into the streets. In 1343 they had been moved to Seacoal Lane by the Fleet River. The Prior of the Hospital of St John of Jerusalem objected in 1354 to the stench, which he claimed was injurious to health, especially those in Ludgate prison. They were moved again near to Blackfriars. In succeeding years the problem constantly erupted, with ordinances, complaints to the Crown, action by the authorities, and they were moved to Butchers Bridge on the Thames, to Holborn, back to Queenhithe and then Pudding Lane. In 1371 an Act attempted to move slaughtering of animals outside the City — without much success — at Stratford and Knightsbridge. Offal was supplied to the dogs in the City's doghouse and for the King's bears at Bankside, Southwark. When the Butchers moved from Seacoal Lane the practice of giving a boar's head ceased, though it was revived in the 17th century as a presentation to the Lord Mayor, and in modern times. By 1423 the Butchers had hired their own Hall. By 1450 the Butchers leased the northern half of Stocks Market — '£40 received from the Wardens of the Butchers craft for rent of half the London Stocks on the north side...'. In 1507 the authorities committed 'Wardens of the bochery of Estchepe' to Newgate for disobedience and contempt. A year later, the 'Wardens and Felyasship of bochers of Eastcheap' found their control of particular markets terminated. By 1533 they were using Leadenhall Market. In 1541 they obtained a Grant of Arms and in 1544 they occupied St Giles Hall in Whitecross Street.

St Giles Hall went with the supression of chantries, and in 1547 they acquired the parsonage house of St Nicholas, by King Edward Street (formerly Butcher Hall Lane, Fowle Lane, Stinking Lane or St Nicholas Lane). The first charter of 'the ancient Society or Mistery of Butchers' conferred incorporation in 1605 and in 1607 the new Company was enrolled at Guildhall. Successive charters followed.

Daniel Defoe, son of a butcher, recorded the plague from first hand knowledge; the Fire of 1666 resolved some of these problems as well as the growing dissension between City and country butchers, competing for custom in the City's markets. The new markets were established at Newgate, Honey Lane and Woolchurch — an enlarged Stocks Market, but without provision for slaughterhouses. The original ordinance of 1361 forbidding slaughter in the City only eventually became operative in the 20th century.

In 1666 the second hall was destroyed by fire, and in 1668 replaced in Pudding Lane. In 1829 it was destroyed by fire. By the following September it had been rebuilt for £2,890 12s 4d, and in 1883 the Metropolitan Railway and District Railway acquired the premises for their Cannon Street-Aldgate extension. In 1885 a new Hall was opened on a new site — Bartholomew Close, close to Smithfield. It was enlarged in 1913 and bombed in 1944. The present day Hall was opened in 1960 on the same site.

The oldest charitable bequest goes back to 1357, the Poor Box increasing in use in the 18th century, and today the Company administers a wide range of benevolence, including the George Lonsdale Memorial Scholarships, endowed in 1969, which enable students to work abroad in the meat trade. A grant is made annually to the Institute of Meat and a medal presented to the highest marked Institute student. Three medals go each year to students of the Smithfield College which holds its annual prizegiving at Butchers' Hall. The Company supports the London Meats Trades Association, the Butchers' Charitable Institution, the Market Clerks Benevolent Society and other causes, trade and City.

Since the last war the Butchers have not only built their new Hall but also completed a unique undertaking — the Golden Book, a record of outstanding inscriptions and occasions with details of the Company's past Masters, Clerks, Honorary Freemen and distinguished visitors, and signatures of Royalty, including HM Queen Elizabeth the Queen Mother, an Honorary Freeman. The Golden Book was stolen when the Hall was burgled in 1981. A comparable volume was accepted by the Queen.

The Saddlers. The Company originated as an Anglo-Saxon Guild and may well therefore be the oldest of all City Companies. The evidence lies in an 1160 Convention between the Convent of the Church of St Martin-le-Grand and the Guild of Saddlers which refers to 'custom of old . . . when Sir Aernaldus was Alderman'. The name Aernaldus is Anglo-Saxon. The first charter, now lost, dates back to 1272, and the Company was incorporated in 1395, with confirmation or amendment by later charters up to the final effective one of 1607.

In 1383 William de Lincolne bequeathed 10 marks on condition that a Common Hall be built within three years, though the first reference to such a Hall did not emerge until 1479.

Early charters gave the Company rights of control over the trade, and of search throughout the country, though this was reduced in 1559 to within a two mile radius of the City. This right is still exercised quarterly. In the 14th and 15th centuries, the Saddlers were involved in sometimes bitter disputes with associated guilds such as those of the Joiners, Loriners, Painters and Girdlers, usually resolved by the Mayor and Alderman, but once by the monarch himself. At one time the Company ranked among the first twelve Companies.

Among the Company's treasures is a 1508 crimson brocade funeral pall and the ballot box of 1619 made for the East India Company, but used since 1676 to elect the Master and Wardens. The Company's Freedom Roll records all freemen since the 16th century.

The original Hall was burnt down in the 1666 Fire of London and replaced within four years, only to be damaged by fire in its turn in 1815 and burnt out in 1821. This Hall was destroyed in 1940 and the present Hall in Gutter Lane, Cheapside was erected in 1958, extended (upwards) in 1970 and modified in 1979. The Company lost its traditional Cheapside frontage by compulsory purchase for the sum of 10s.

The Company maintains its association with Saddlery, mainly through the Society of Master Saddlers, and supports saddlery training courses at Cordwainers Technical College and those sponsored by the City and Guilds of London Institute and Council for Small Industries in Rural Areas. It holds an annual Saddle, Bridle and Harness making competition and awards saddlery prizes at equestrian competitions recognised by the British Equestrian Federation; it also grants funds to the Federation to train young riders of promise. Saddles of Honour are presented to overall winners of major equestrian events — in 1971 HRH The Princess Anne won the Company's Saddle at Burghley. That year the Company installed Her Royal Highness as a Yeoman — an honour reserved for distinguished users of the saddle. Two years prior to that, the Company presented HM The Queen with a side saddle for ceremonial use.

The Company maintains close links with The City University, successor to the old Northampton Institute, of which the Saddlers and Skinners were foundation benefactors, and has provided a covered Sports Centre for the use of staff and students. It is also associated with Alleyns School at Dulwich, where Saddlers Scholarships are awarded annually. Charities funded by bequest help elderly and indigent saddlers or their widows. The Company keeps close links with the modern saddlery trade, centred on Walsall. The Saddlers help to fund projects of the Riding for the Disabled Association, and recently contributed to a stabling block and additional riding school at the National Equestrian Centre, Stoneleigh.

The Carpenters. A 1271 document gives the first reference to a Guild or Fraternity of Carpenters with its mention of 'The Master Carpenter'. The Fraternity met in the Church of St Thomas of Acon and that of St John the Baptist of Holywell beside London. In 1388 the King required Guilds to give an account of themselves and the Carpenters lodged at Guildhall their 'Boke of Ordinances' of 1333. Significantly one of its clauses reads 'Also it is ordained that if any brother go idle for default of work and another brother have work whereon he may work with his brother, and that work be such that his brother can work it, then shall he work his brother before any other thing and give him as another man would take of him for the same work'. The carpenter's wage was then 6d per day for the half year and 5d for the other half. The carpenters were then the builders of London's houses.

The Company built their Hall on a site adjoining the City wall, between Bishopsgate and Moorgate, and in 1477 they were incorporated. They virtually controlled the City's buildings and maintained proper standards of timber used. In 1666 their Hall escaped damage from the Great Fire, but the replacement of so much of London with brick heralded a serious decline in their fortunes. Their Hall was let to several Lord Mayors while their own mansions were rebuilt. As with so many Companies, the Carpenters fell out with other trades and crafts. They joined issue at different times with the Bricklayers, Woodmongers, Joiners and Sawyers. In 1672 they set down their view of the Joiners, asserting 'that it was our trade and customary work ffully to compleat and finish all that may be said to goe to the building, compleating and finishing of houses or other edifices, both as to strength and ornament'. They went on: 'there were found some ingenious men who, to secure their bodies from hard labour, took upon them to make moveable goods for furnishing of houses, and thereby considering that the name Carpenter was to gross a title for them whose employment was so weak that . . . they obtained a Patent to become a Guild and . . . gave themselves two names, viz: Joyners and Cielers — Joyners as they made boxes and casketts and Cielers (as they pretended) for nailing up boards under roofes of houses and under some ffloors, thereby to hinder the Plaisterers in their trade . . . And now thinking themselves famous by vertue of this their new names, they thought there was more work to be done and more names to be got they fall to the work and now call themselves Shop Joyners, House Joyners, Cabinett Makers, Frame Makers, Box Makers, Upholsterers etc., and now would faine be called Carpenters to boot, in prosecution of which they have and doe thrust themselves to doe much of the work belonging to the Carpenters' trade'.

In 1456 the Hall was settling and 10s was paid for 'underpinning the house and paving of the kitchen'. In 1619 Richard Wyatt left land and money for almshouses at Godalming, erected two years later. In 1769 the Company used 3,000 gns from bequests to buy 70 acres at Stratford-by-Bow. In 1841 more almshouses were built, this time at Twickenham. In 1876 the old Hall was pulled down and a new one built on part of the site by 1881.

Evening classes in handicrafts on the Stratford estate were augmented in 1891 by a day school, closed in 1905, then enabling the Company to develop the Trades Training School in Great Titchfield Street, started some years before. Scholarships were funded to Oxford and Cambridge and in 1897 Sir Henry Harben, a Past Master, built and partly endowed the Rustington Convalescent Home for 'persons of the working class and others'.

The Hall was gutted in 1941 and the Stratford estate was seriously damaged. Other Company properties escaped the bombs. The Trades Training School became The Building Crafts Training School. During the last war the Company helped to train many soldiers. The School reopened in 1947. The Rustington Convalescent Home was also closed for the duration but re-equipped and reopened in 1948. In 1974 the Twickenham almshouses were replaced by the Borough with flats and the occupants rehoused. The Company's new post-war Hall was opened in 1960. The Stratford estate was scheduled for redevelopment and acquired by the Borough, except for the factory.

Today the Company still vigorously supports its craft, principally through the Titchfield Street school, maintains its Godalming almshouses and Rustington Home (for men and women) and, in collaboration with its sister Company in the City and County of Philadelphia, USA, runs an exchange scholarship programme for architects and builders. The Company co-sponsors the Carpenters' Award, and helps other charitable and educational causes.

The Cordwainers. The Cordwainers (Shoemakers) take their name from *cordwan*, a goatskin leather from Cordova, Spain, famed from the 8th century for its fine skin and filigree work, brought back by Crusaders. Already organised as a Guild, the Cordwainers were first recognised by ordinance in 1272. They were centred on Cordwanestrate and were the first craftsmen after whom a ward was named. The craft was strictly regulated as to hours and areas of selling and the number of journeymen allowed to each Master Cordwainer. In 1303 the journeymen complained about their low wages. In 1387, such was their rebellious attitude that they were forbidden to conspire against their masters. Nonetheless they formed their own guild, though with no say in the affairs of the Mystery proper. Conflict was not confined within the craft: in 1267 the Cordwainers joined in the pitched battle between the Tailors and the Goldsmiths. They also quarrelled with other craftsmen, especially the Cobblers.

Cobblers repaired rather than made shoes, but there was a grey area between repair and renewal; in 1434 Ralph John, a cobbler, went to prison 'having for the maintenance of his family made certain pairs of shoes'. Earlier, the 14th century crisis caused by the Black Death and consequent inflation in food prices and scarcity of labour, led to civil disturbance, culminating in the Peasants' Revolt and its reforming aftermath. When some of the guilds high-handedly forced a conservative Mayor on the City, the Cordwainers, led by John Constantyn, rioted. Constantyn was siezed, tried on the spot and beheaded in the street. The Cordwainers then attempted to petition the King, without success.

In 1439 the Cordwainers were incorporated. They probably met before then in a 'tenement with cellars solars and outbuildings' granted to John Payn in 1364 by John de Trumpeton, Cordwainer, and a 1440 deed mentions 'Cordwayners Hall, adjoining a dwelling . . . belonging to William Payn'.

This formally became the Company's Hall that year. In 1445 the Cordwainers provided 24 men for the Watch. By 1528, when the Cordwainers petitioned against the number of master shoemakers in London, their numbers had dwindled from 140 to 20. In 1608 they insisted that all

Cordwainers free of the Curriers and Embroiders should make a 'proof piece' at their Hall — otherwise known as a 'master-piece' — to ensure the quality of apprentices' work and restrain wage earners from threatening to flood the craft elite.

Imported leather was insufficient for the needs of the trade by this time, so the Cordwainers allowed their employees to treat leather, thus creating conflict with Curriers. The Cobblers had now merged with the Cordwainers. Five Acts were passed between 1548 and 1558 to control the leather trade, and the Statute of Leather in James I's reign was precise — the right to search in the boot and shoe trade was vested in the Cordwainers' Company. In 1547 John Fisher, a clothworker, gave the Company his house, The Sign of the Falcon, for poor relief. Cordwainer Thomas Nicolson left funds for the poor and for a 'more apte and better common howse', and in 1577, the Cordwainers 'built a faire new Hall'.

In the 17th century the Cordwainers initially invested £250 in the Irish estates, and a further £1,200 by 1654 — their return was an annual rent of £7. They sold out to the Goldsmiths for £150 in 1679. In 1627 the poorer Cordwainers had once again petitioned the King's Council to examine the Company's controlling elite, and that of related Companies, to prevent the rich exploiting the poor. At that time Richard Minge, James Shawe and Richard Pendrey left or gave the Company property or funds. By contrast the Stuarts and Parliament cost the Cordwainers dear — they paid £800 towards Cromwell's Army alone. In 1666 the Great Fire took a heavy toll, destroying the Hall and other Company property. With debts of £1,338 18s 4d, the Company decided to sell the plate its Clerk had saved from the holocaust. In 1670 a new Hall was completed for £2,213 13s 5d. Ten years later that Hall was nearly sold to meet debts. In the 1730s the Cordwainers were again at loggerheads with the Curriers, desperately trying to save their monopoly at a time when the trade was moving out of their control. The Flaying Act of 1803 stemmed the tide for a while and brought the two crafts together in common cause. In 1815 together they petitioned unsuccessfully for the preservation of the old Statute of Leather.

Towards the end of the 18th century Past Master John Came sent anonymous sums of £100 and £200 to the Company for the relief of widows of clergymen. On his death in 1796 he left £37,300 for the same purpose and for the blind, deaf and dumb. In 1788 the Company built a new Hall in Distaff Lane.

In 1825 the Company was still active in its trade, but facing the age-old problems with its workforce, and Northampton was fast becoming the new and competitive centre for the trade. It resisted mechanisation as evidenced by Marc Isambard Brunel's Battersea Boot Factory and a Sussex shoemaker's invention to reduce the cost of threadwork. In the 19th century the accent was on entertainment, but the Company nonetheless faithfully administered its charities and made funds available for scholarships. In 1877 the Cordwainers provided £250 for the foundation of the City and Guilds of London Institute, which early on established the Leather Trades School with their support. In 1913, with help from the LCC, the Cordwainers took responsibility for what became the Cordwainers Technical College. In 1909 the foundation stone was laid for a new Hall — at a cost of £39,111 17s 4d. In 1941 it was burnt down by enemy action. In 1923 the Cordwainers College had moved to St John's Lane, Finsbury, but that, too, was bombed out in 1940. In 1946 it moved again to Mare Street, Hackney, and was rebuilt in 1957. In 1973 major redevelopment enabled the Company to sell Richard Minge's Southwark land profitably. Back in 1951 the old Hall site had been purchased by the Corporation. The Company now considered building a new Hall, but decided instead to move its offices to the Fleet Street property which was once The Sign of the Falcon.

Today the Company still helps the blind, deaf and dumb and clergymen's widows, the poor, and ex-servicemen. It administers almshouses in Shorne, Kent, and in 1976 acquired five almshouses at Chesham, Bucks, once the property of the Francis family, lawyers for three centuries in that town. It also supports the Church of the Holy Sepulchre. Grants are made annually to theological colleges, the Royal Free Hospital School of Medicine and the Institute of

Dental Surgery, as well as awards and medals to nurses. Over £41,000 has been contributed to the City and Guilds of London Institute over the years. The major Company interest remains the Cordwainers Technical College.

The Painters (otherwise Painter-Stainers). It is believed that the original art of the Stainer was that of painting on woven fabrics. Painted cloths imitated tapestry. Stainers painted flags, banners and streamers, and devised pageant and procession decorations. The already existing Fraternity of Stainers was first recorded when they rioted with other Companies in 1268. The Painters existed as a Guild by 1283.

In 1433 the Painters (Peyntours) and Stainers (Steynours) were first associated, when Richard Davy, a Painter of Gloucestershire, petitioned the Mayor. In 1434 two Masters of each craft were 'sworn for the mistery' of the other. In 1466 the Painters were granted ordinances and in 1469 they contributed twenty men to the Watch; the Stainers sent fourteen. In 1486 Arms were granted.

In 1502 the two crafts again petitioned the Mayor that whereas 'the said craftes beyng separate after divers and many assemblies and communications betwixt them hadde for reformacion and weall of the said craftes and for perpetuall amite, concorde and unite thereafter betwene them to be hadd and kept', and they were 'knyt joyned and uynd to giders'; in 1581 the united Guild was incorporated. Between 1588 and 1738 the Painter-Stainers and the College of Heralds were at issue over the right to paint arms. In 1530 the original Arms were illegally replaced. In 1532 Sir John Browne, sergeant-painter to Henry VIII, left his premises in Little Trinity Lane within Queenhithe Ward to his Guild, and these became Painters' Hall. In 1666 Charles II, Samuel Pepys and others are believed to have disembarked at Queenhithe Stairs during the Fire of London, to tour the City and to direct demolition of buildings and retrieval of property. They repaired to Painters' Hall to rest. The King sat down to a meal with an appetite 'such as the most magnificent banquet could not, under other circumstances have provoked'. He summoned the Lord Mayor, Sheriffs and Aldermen to discuss blowing up buildings to check the fire. They opposed this, and the King, unprepared to take sole responsibility, did not press the point. Thus Painters' Hall was doomed. The story is not substantiated but has, with due reservation, become part of the Company's lore.

The Hall was rebuilt in 1670 and repaired in 1776-7.

Arguments with the College of Heralds led to Painters being charged at the Court of Chivalry, and some went to Marshalsea Prison. After the confusion of the Civil War the College sought a Royal declaration in their favour and again in 1738, but the Attorney and Solicitor General 'found no good reason to recommend any alteration to the Charter granted to the Painter-Stainers' Company'.

In 1766 the Company obtained powers to control the trade of painting, and three years later established a labour exchange for house painters at 2 Ironmonger Lane. In 1775 action was taken to restrain the inroads of the Plaisterers, and journeymen's rates were revised in 1799, with further revisions in 1836 and 1851. From 1823, the Company took legal action against infringements of their rights but, in 1829, the courts ruled against the Painter-Stainers and their campaign gradually lost momentum. In 1880 a new wing was added to the Hall.

In 1781 John Stock, a benefactor to the Company, left £55,000 in trust for the blind and distressed and in the 1790s this was supplemented by bequests by Mrs Jane Shank, Mrs Dorothy Smith and Mrs Anne Yeates, as well as in 1806 by Mrs Mary Grainger. That year John Fairchild left £1,000 for the Company's poor. In 1877 the Company presented prizes and medals to the City of London School, Freemen's Orphans' School, Commercial Travellers' School and the City and Spitalfields School of Design. In 1893 a technical class was established in the Carpenters' Trades Training School and in 1899 the Incorporated Institute of British Decorators was formed in the Hall.

In 1914-16 the Hall front was reconstructed and new buildings erected on the adjoining site. In 1930 the south wall, a survivor from the Great Fire, was condemned and its replacement involved a major reconstruction. Eleven years later the Germans destroyed the building. Twenty years after that the present Hall was opened on an enlarged site. In 1972 the Company reverted to use of the 1486 Arms.

The company continues to administer its charitable bequests and awards prizes and medals to students through the City and Guilds of London Institute, and to winners in Advanced Crafts Examinations, through twelve London colleges. It also awards prizes in calligraphy, bursaries to art students at the Institute and the Royal Academy Schools of Painting, a plaque and prize to the best third year student at the Royal College of Art and grants to art departments of six City schools. In certain cases the winner is also admitted to the Honorary Freedom of the Company. The Company also jointly sponsored the Children's Royal Academy exhibition, now discontinued.

Prizes are awarded to Licentiates and Associates of the British Institute of Interior Design, travelling bursaries to students of dyeing and printing of textiles, and to the best final-year undergraduate textile print student at Leeds University.

The Company annually helps to fund a production of the Guildhall School of Music and Drama and, with the City Heritage Society, sponsors a conservation award in the City. The Painter-Stainers house a number of fine paintings in their Hall, and have in recent years commissioned others. The Company maintains a tradition of electing Presidents of the Royal Academy to the Court.

The Curriers. The Currier derived his name from the Latin *corium,* the middle layer of skin between flesh and epidermis. His craft comprised dressing and preparing the raw material for leather. Curriers were not as settled as other crafts, and moved about the city until the early 16th century — there was a Curriers Arms Inn Yard near Goswell Street, a Curriers Alley by Puddle Dock and another Curriers Alley in Shoe Lane. The earliest reference is in the 1270s — an inquest on a drunken currier's wife who fell, broke her leg and died. By 1299 curriers' prices were regulated.

In 1388 the Curriers responded to the King's order to Fraternities to define their activities, by pretending to be a good deal poorer than they must have been, by virtue of numerous charitable bequests by their members. They were by then associated with St Mary of the Carmelites in Fleet Street, probably since 1367. One of the first Lollards to be arrested was a Currier called John Cleydone, who had caused to be copied a book called the 'Lanterne of Light'. He could not read, but he was nonetheless tried, and burnt at Smithfield, in 1415. Three weeks later the 'good men of the Mistery of Curriers' came before the Mayor to seek recognition.

As the various subsidiary crafts in the leather trade were absorbed by the Leathersellers during the 15th century, the Curriers alone stood out as independent, due to the skills involved in their craft. By 1485 the Curriers had their own Hall built into London Wall, while in 1484 it was laid down by statute that tanners were not to be curriers and vice versa. In 1493 further ordinances were granted. In 1503 the craft gained the right of search. In 1516 Thomas Sterne gave the Guild a property called the Boar's Head in the parish of St Alphage Cripplegate.

After Henry VIII's death, various statutory attempts to tighten control of the leather trades threatened the Curriers' monopoly. The first Act 'for the true currienge of Leather' suggests that 'through the covertise of Tanners in overhastinge their works by divers subtill and craftie meanes, by neglicence of the serchers and collusion of the corryars . . . the Kinges subjects are not onely in their goods but also in the helthe of their bodyes much endomaged by occacion of yll Shoes and Bootes made of evell Lether . . .'. Following statutes further restricted the curriers' rights to 'make up' the price of tanned leather, but these endeavours failed, simply by strangling trade, creating unemployment and thereby short supply. The Curriers won back their right to wholesale their product, but not for long. Further legislation restricted them. Shoes shot up in cost, and finally, sixteen acts were repealed in 1559 and it was ordered that since 'Leather was never woorse taned curried or wrought than nowe a dayes' the Curriers alone should curry leather.

By 1587 the Curriers had occupied a Hall on the site of the Boar's Head. Fours years earlier the Company had obtained a Grant of Arms. The Curriers paid their share of Crown imposts — £4 towards the fleet that 'singed the King of Spain's beard' and doubtless something towards the staggering £4,000 that the Queen demanded, to call in a patent granted to Edward Darcie to search and seal leather throughout the realm. Soon afterwards the Curriers and Cordwainers concluded an agreement that the Curriers would 'have the dressing of all leather bought in Leadenhall and Southwark markets and three miles compass of London'. Eventually the statute of Leather of 1603 closely defined the Curriers' rights and obligations. In 1605 the Curriers were incorporated.

The Company contributed an initial £44 to the Irish estates, through the Vintners, and subsequent smaller payments, together with a further £150. They got back £172 15s, in 1737, over and above some earlier repayments. In 1666 the Curriers' Hall was destroyed, though the crypt of the Carmelite Priory where they first met survived, and exists today. The Curriers rebuilt in 1670. After the fire they sold much of their surviving plate, and turned to the Dissenters, who had used their Hall during the Commonwealth, for income. In 1672 Edmund Calamy rented the Hall to preach to his flock, followed by two other Anabaptists and Joseph Taylor, a Baptist.

Financial difficulties set in with the final years of the Stuarts, and members refused to pay their fines. William Cole 'swore Four Oathes and Cursed and refused to pay his quaretridge . . .'. The Company dined frugally and at a tavern, because their Hall was 'encumbered with formes and pewes and the Kitchen not in order'. Labour problems bedevilled them, and the Pattenmakers leased the Hall for seven years for £5 annual rent. By 1704 the Company was well in debt.

By the 18th century, the Currier was a skilled and highly paid craftsman, whose ability to drive tallow into hides gave rise to the term 'elbow grease'. He did not retail his products. He also lacked capital. The Cordwainers, on the other hand, were a wealthy merchant group, and their trade was expanding. They laid a complaint against a currier, Thomas Carpenter, and the Curriers decided to defend him. Armed with incomes from a fortuitous bequest, they were then faced with attempted legislation, but secured a truce. Finally, by raising loans, they secured a Bill before Parliament in their favour.

As the 18th century drew to a close, the Curriers faced open rebellion among their journeymen, culminating in their seeking the help of outside curriers. In 1792 the Company accumulated sufficient evidence to prosecute them for conspiracy, and the journeymen gave in. But in 1796 they distributed a pamphlet, 'Articles of the Curriers' Tramp Society'. The Company's response was the Flaying Acts which once again brought them together with the Cordwainers, and they opened the floodgates to apprentices.

They lost control of their craftsmen with the repeal of the Statute of Leather and the 19th century saw the workforce effectively move towards trade unionism. In 1819 the Company built a new and larger Hall for £1,000. By 1827 its chief asset was the Sun Tavern, which was let to Charles Calvert MP for £200 a year, with other buildings. Within 25 years of their dispute with the journeymen, the Company ceased to control their trade. The craftsmen themselves established a National Conference of Curriers. In 1872 the Company decided to build a new Hall but, no sooner was it finished, than they were offered a new Hall as part of a deal which would give the original Boar's Head site to an expanding commercial enterprise. They agreed. The new Hall was completed in 1876 and Messrs Rylands took up their lease. Within ten years their factory was destroyed by fire, but the Hall survived. By the end of the century the Curriers were in financial difficulties, mainly through the running costs of their Hall. Then an 1892 bequest saved them. In 1920 they sold the Hall, and agreed with the Cordwainers to have the use of theirs, for twenty years. When the Chartered Institute of Secretaries took over the old Hall, they offered the freehold to the Curriers, but this was declined. In 1940 it was destroyed by enemy action.

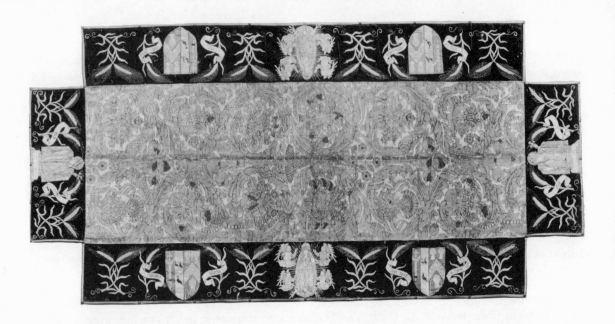

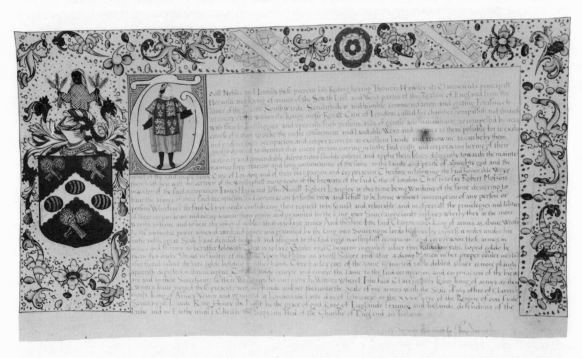

ABOVE: Brewers' Company pall at the Victoria and Albert Museum. BELOW: the Brewers' Grant of Arms of 1544, and OPPOSITE ABOVE LEFT: their second Coat of Arms, on the Bargemaster's Badge of 1727, now a snuffbox lid. RIGHT: Brewers' Beadle John Church petitioned for a rise in 1800, and BELOW: the Court Room at Brewers' Hall. (B) CENTRE LEFT: the Leathersellers' Arms, (L) and BELOW: those of the Pewterers. (P)

To the Master and Wardens and Court
of Assistants of the Worshipful Company
of Brewers

The Petition of John Crouch Beadle

Most humbly Showeth

That the Salary of Beadle of
this Worshipful Company near a Century
ago was £ 17..5..0. a Year

That in the Year 1752. it was raised
£ 3..10..0. more making it £ 20..15..0. at
which it still continues

That between the Years
great number of Annual Gifts and Gratuitys
were given by the Court not only to the
Clerk but to the Beadle

That your Petitioner presumes he
need not mention the Difference of living
between the Year 1752 and the present time
in every Article of Consumption

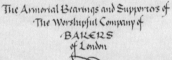

The Armorial Bearings and Supporters of The Worshipful Company of BAKERS of London

NEERE TO THIS PLACE LYETH BVRIED THE BODY OF SIMON BVRTON, CITIZEN AND WAXCHADLER OF LONDON, A GOOD BENIFACTOR TO Ỹ POORE OF THIS PARISHE; WHO WAS 3 TYMES MASTER OF HIS COMPANY; AND ONE OF THE GOVERNORS OF SͭThomᴬˢ HOSPITALL. AND OF THE COMON COVNSELL OF THIS WARD XXIX YERES, HE HAD 2 WYVES, ELIZABETH AND ANN, AND HAD ISSVE BY ELIZABETH, I SONN AND III DAVGHTERS; HE DECEASED Ỹ 23 OF MAY 1593. BEING OF Ỹ AGE OF 85 YERES. IN WHOSE REMEMBRANCE HIS LOVEING DAVGͭER ALYCE COLDOCK ERECᴾED THIS MONVMENT

ABOVE LEFT: The Barbers' Arms, (B) CENTRE: the Armourers' and Brasiers' Arms, (AB) and RIGHT: those of the Bakers. (BK) CENTRE: the Cutlers' Arms, (C) BELOW LEFT: Wax Chandler Simon Burton and his family (1593), (W) and RIGHT: the Courtyard at Tallow Chandlers' Hall. (TC)

126

ABOVE LEFT: Arms of the Tallow Chandlers, (TC) RIGHT: those of the Carpenters, (CP) CENTRE LEFT: Bas relief of a pork butcher's shop AD 150 and RIGHT: the Butchers' old Hall in Pudding Lane. (BR) BELOW: the Saddlers' Arms. (SD)

ABOVE LEFT: Saddlers' Hall. RIGHT: their ballot box. BELOW LEFT: the King's Champion Saddle and
CENTRE: another example of the saddler's craft. (SD) BELOW: Painter-Stainers' Arms. (PS)

ABOVE LEFT: the 19th century entrance to Painter-Stainers' Hall. (RJG) RIGHT: the sixth Hall of the Curriers. (CR) CENTRE: the Masons' Arms (MN) and BELOW: the Innholders' Arms. (IN) RIGHT: the Carpenters' Grant of Arms. (CP)

The Masons. The Masons' origins are among the most ancient; Roman remains in the City and elsewhere clearly reflect this. London's first stone bridge was started in 1176; in 1189 an assize of buildings determined the thickness of stone walls; in 1209 London Bridge was complete and 1220 is the supposed date of foundation of the original fellowship. London masons repaired and fortified the Tower in 1240 and in 1257 the City walls and gates were rebuilt by them. In 1272 two were chosen with two master carpenters to inspect the walls and gates but, although masons appear throughout contemporary records, it was stated in 1356 when mason hewers and mason setters were in dispute that they had not properly regulated their trade as others had done. Ordinances were drawn up to control apprenticeships and contractors and to protect the customer.

Although there are oblique references to a fraternity of St Thomas of Acon in 1389, and to a livery gown in 1418, the Masons appear relatively unorganised until 1463, when they acquired land for a Hall: the Prior and Convent of the Church of Holy Trinity, Aldgate, leased them ground in what is now Mason's Avenue, near Guildhall, for 99 years. In 1472 the Guild obtained a Grant of Arms: '. . . the Hole Crafte and felawship of masons corogeowsly meoved to exercise and use gentill and commendable guydyng in such laudable maner and fourme as may best sounde unto gentrice by the whiche they shal mowe with goddis grace to atteigne unto honoure and worship. . .' Three years before that they provided 28 men-at-arms for the Watch.

New ordinances were drawn up in 1481 and a livery granted, to the Fellowship of Free Masons in the City of London. In 1509-10 the 'hoole felliship of the craft mistere or science of Fremasons enfraunchesed within this Cittie' petitioned the Mayor and Aldermen for an assize of freestone, marblestone and hard stone of Kent. The term 'freemason' was in use as far back as 1376, but this is the first use of it collectively to describe the Guild. In 1501 the Masons had contributed Kentish ragstone to pave Guildhall's kitchen.

Masons in mediaeval times ranged from the great architects and master masons, through the skilled stone-worker, overseer, building contractor, and dealer to the rough mason. In the middle ages, over 7,000 major ecclesiastical buildings were constructed in stone, apart from churches, castles, town walls, bridges and public buildings. The freemason was a skilled worker in free stone, the rough mason a layer of stone or brick. It was the freemasons, for example, who carved and cut fan vaulting.

In 1521 further ordinances were agreed, and in 1580 a further Assize was successfully requested for 'a kynde of pavinge stone not before used in this cytie called Purbeck stone or Purbeck pavinge'. In 1563 the Masons bought their Hall and in 1585 they absorbed the Marblers or monumental masons.

In the first decade of the 17th century the Masons revised their ordinances, and admitted to the livery 'accepted masons' — the forerunners of the modern freemason. In 1618 they contributed to the Ulster resettlement programme under the auspices of the Mercers and, two years later, records refer to speculative masonry — mason shopkeepers who dealt in statuary and stonework. In 1655 the fellowship considered petitioning for incorporation but the 1666 fire of London put paid to that when their Hall was destroyed. For four years the Company laboured to replace it — at a cost of £400. The Fire posed other problems, principally the incursion of foreign or non-member masons, due to the massive rebuilding required. An Act of 1667 allowed other than freemen to work in the City mainly to rebuild its churches, and this weakened the fellowship's power. With related crafts, they unsuccessfully petitioned the authorities.

In 1626 Nicholas Stone became Master Mason to the King and in 1633 Master of the Company. He was both sculptor and mason-contractor. In 1670 Thomas Strong, mason-contractor at St Paul's under Christopher Wren, was admitted to the freedom of the Company. Seven years later he laid the first stone for the new Cathedral. That year the Company was incorporated.

In 1694 it was in parlous straits, the influx of outside masons and the abuses even of its own members reducing its fortunes and dissipating its powers. The Masons decided to act. They sought remedial legislation and obtained it, but the times were against them, and the Company's hold over its craft was virtually ended by the close of that century. (They tried twice more — in 1719 and in 1822 — to resurrect their powers, but to no avail.) In 1681 Thomas Strong had been succeeded by his son, also Thomas, as mason-contractor at St Paul's, and Edward, his brother, succeeded him, becoming Master in 1696 and laying the final stone, or so it is said, on the cathedral dome, in 1708.

In 1865 the Company's Hall was sold, though no one knows why. In 1909 the Irish estates were sold but in 1947 the Company once again joined with the Mercers, this time to invest in Rhodesia. In 1958, on the rebuilding of Mercers' Hall, the Company presented a Master's Chair made from old timbers from Guildhall, and the Baptismal Font in Mercers' Chapel. The Masons resumed meeting at Mercers' Hall that same year.

Today the Company makes a grant towards the cost of tools or books to every apprentice mason in London, Chichester and at Portland, actively supports the Building Crafts Training School, and encourages apprentices with prizes through The London Association of Master Stone Masons. For 241 years the Clerkship of the Company has stayed within the same solicitors' partnership.

The Plumbers. Craftsmen who dealt in lead articles must have existed in Norman times, but there is no evidence of the Guild of Plumbers until their first ordinances of 1365, which showed they worked in gutters, conduits, tap-troughs, furnaces, belfries, roofing and cisterns. These also required 'that no one of the said trade shall buy stripped lead of the assistants to tilers, laggers or masons, or of women who cannot find warrant for the same. And if any one shall do so, himself or by his servants, or if any one of them shall be found stealing lead, tin or nails, in the place where he works, he shall be ousted from the said trade for ever, at the will and ordinances of the good folks of such trade'. In 1371 they hired a plot in Eastcheap as a melting furnace. In 1488 further ordinances required every journeyman accompanying a plumber to bring his own tools. These were confirmed in 1520. In 1588 the Company obtained a Grant of Arms with the motto 'Justicia et Pax'. In 1611 the Company was incorporated with the usual successive charters culminating in that of William and Mary. The Company acquired the right of search.

From 1532 the Company rented the Vintners Hall in Palmers (Anchor) Lane, until 1639, when they held Court for the first time in their own Hall in Chequer Yard, Bush Lane. Unhappily, the Great Fire claimed the building in 1666, but it was rebuilt three years later.

In 1599 the privilege of stamping weights was taken over by Guildhall, but James I's charter restored it to the Company. Records of 1664 show that freemen paid 20s on admission in lieu of a silver spoon, but usually the fee was paid in addition to the spoon. Other accounts reflect the costs of paying for assay work: 6d for tin and lead 'to make an essay' in 1679 and 8 gns in 1694 'Paid allowed Mr Man for himselfe and servante for 2 years, and mending the beame scales and weights, with 10s expenses . . .'. Apprentices were ordered: 'According to your carriage expect your reward for good or ill from God and your friends'. No apprentice could be taken if he was 'greatly disfigured in any part of his body'.

The Charter required solder or lead in weights to be impressed with the image of St Michael the Archangel, the Plumbers' patron saint. In 1687 the Company was concerned that 'mill lead' used in shipbuilding was being applied to roofing, against the law; it was proposed that the Plumbers install their own 'Engine to Mill Lead', but the Court demurred.

In the 18th century the Company was still looked to in matters of its craft: Parliament directed the Master and Wardens to inspect the milled lead roof of Greenwich Palace when serious defects developed. In 1808 a new seal was made for sealing solder.

The Company's Hall was demolished in 1863 to facilitate the building of Cannon Street Station.

In 1875 the Company's attention was drawn to recurrent complaints in the press about bad plumbing in houses. At that time the apprentice system had fallen into disuse, and labourers learnt what they could from plumbers and then set up on their own. In 1879 the Company decided to offer the freedom to competent plumbers of 15 years' standing, and diplomas to those of 10 years' standing who could prove their ability. Shortly after, these principles were formalised through the City and Guilds of London Institute examinations. By 1886, after much discussion, public debate and various conference and other decisions, the Company formed a Register of Plumbers on a national basis. In 1893 arrangements were made with King's College for training, and a museum and workshop established. Appropriately, the site chosen was found to contain a veritable network of insanitary and ancient drains and these were replaced. In the next few years the Company attempted many times to push legislation through Parliament to give the force of law to their Register and training proposals. However, by 1909, the voluntary register contained 14,250 names, and the Company set up the General Council for the National Registration of Plumbers. During the first World War the need arose to rapidly expand munitions plant, for which one of the essential techniques was lead burning. Few were proficient in the skills required, and the Company offered its help to the Government. Initially, it was politely snubbed, but in 1915 Lloyd George urgently begged it to set up a training scheme. Special workshops were set up at King's College and so the Plumbers made a major contribution to the war effort. In 1921 the Company helped with the establishment of the Plumbing Trade National Apprenticeship Council. By 1950 there were 25,000 registered plumbers. Three years later the Council became the Registered Plumbers Association. The Register is now maintained by the Institute of Plumbing. Today the Company presents a gold medal annually to the student with most potential as a future spokesman for the industry and the St Michael medallion for outstanding contributions to the art and craft of plumbing. The Company is represented on Government and Trade Committees. A pleasant tradition has evolved, whereby a silver ladle is presented to the outgoing Master, which has become known as the Ladle Dinner.

The Innholders. The first inns were wayside alehouses. By the end of the 13th century the professional *herbegeour* appeared (after the King's harbinger), sometimes known as a haymonger or hosteller — providing bed and board for man and horse. By 1309 a Guild had been formed, for every hosteller took an oath to 'oversee alle maner marchandise that any alien merchant had under his said hostage'. This was to enforce the law that required foreign merchants to dispose of their goods within forty days. In 1371 charges were regulated — 2½d for feeding a horse for a day and a night; 2d for a gallon of best ale; 1d for a pot of three pints of best ale; 6d for a bushel of oats. Only ale brewed on the premises was to be sold retail and no bread sold, except that made and stamped by the City's bakers. In 1379 hay for a horse was pegged at 2d a day and night. In 1382 the hostellers were ordered to collect 'ferlings' (farthings) from Guildhall so that they had sufficient change. They were also required to ensure their guests laid aside their swords and introduced no strangers for whom they could not vouch.

In 1422 came the first mention of the 'Mistery of Hostillers', and in 1446 they were granted powers of search and obliged to have an open sign outside their premises. By 1473 the word 'hosteller' had been corrupted (ostler) to denote the servant of the innkeeper. The Guild petitioned successfully to be known as Innholders. In 1514 it was incorporated as 'the Art and Mistery of St Julian le Herberger of Innholders of the City of London'. St Julian was the patron saint, though not connected with any religious fraternity.

By 1522 the Innholders had their own Hall, assessed at £22. In 1598 it was recorded as standing in Elbow (Bow) Lane. A Grant of Arms was achieved in 1634. In 1663 their second charter extended the Innholders' powers to within three miles of the City. Three years later the Great Fire destroyed the Hall, the following year the site was cleared at a cost of £18 1s 0d and in 1671 a new Hall completed for £1,211 8s 10d. The bricklayer was paid £500, the carpenter £344 and 'ye workmen for extraordinary pains, 2s 6d' this clearly being a gratuity. Fortunately the Company's plate escaped the fire, for the year prior, the Master had been charged with looking after it, and Robert Bridges, who kept the Ram Inn at Smithfield, had it in his safekeeping. It was at his hostelry that the Company met while without its Hall. The Company suffered the usual successive charters of the Stuarts until the Act of 1683 restoring their 1664 third charter. In 1757 the Company ceased to exercise their 'three mile' jurisdiction.

In 1885-6 the Hall was partly rebuilt, suffered some damage in the first World War and was badly damaged in the second, to be restored in the early 1950s. In the late fifties it was extended.

In 1962 a home for the elderly was opened in Wimbledon, in 1978 a nursing home was opened at Tunbridge Wells, and a second one in the town in 1980, in conjunction with the Distressed Gentlefolks' Aid Association, who manage both. Funds for these were and are provided by past and present Liverymen, and the complex is known as John Bentley Park in memory of the Previous Clerk. In 1978 the Company revived its trade links by instituting the Master Innholders Award for certain carefully selected hoteliers. There are now twenty such Master Innholders.

The Founders. In 1365 the Guild of Founders successfully petitioned for their ordinances to be enrolled at Guildhall. They worked in brass, and brass or tin alloys, and made small cast items such as candlesticks, lavers (ewers), pots and pans. They congregated in or near Lothbury, using St Margaret's, Lothbury, as their Guild church. The original fraternity was possibly associated with St Lawrence Jewry, and known as the Brotherhood of St Clement. In the 16th century John Stow wrote: 'This street is possessed for the most part by Founders that cast candlesticks, chafing dishes, spice mortars, and such like copper or laton works, and do afterwards turn them with foot and not with the wheel, to make them smooth and bright with turning and scrating (as some do term it) making a loathsome noise to the by-passers that have not been used to the like, and therefore by them disdainfully called Lothberie'. A Saxon origin seems more likely.

The first ordinances granted powers of search. In 1587 all users of small brass weights were ordered to take them to Founders' Hall for approval, and stamping with the Company's mark. Defective weights were destroyed. The mark was the Laver-Pot which figures in the Company's arms, granted in 1590. The Hall itself was acquired in 1531 when 18 members of the Company joined together to buy two houses and some land in Lothbury, formerly the property of the Augustine Friars. The site is still Founders' Court. Conversion continued until 1549.

The Company held some 90 members between 1498 and 1568, in two classes — Masters and Yeomen, some of them women and a few French exiles from religious persecution. One of these, Peter Baude, developed a new process of iron-founding and produced the first iron cannon in this country. In 1614 the Company was incorporated by charter and suffered from both Stuarts and Cromwell, selling all its silver spoons, except one. Presented by Humphrey Bowen, it was inscribed 'If you Love Me, Keep me Ever. That's My Desire and Your Endeavour'.

Friction between Founders and their more numerous Yeomen flared in 1651, when sixteen petitioned the Cromwellian government, complaining that 'we have for many years been extremely trodden and kept under foot by the power and will of the Master, Wardens and Assistants' with other grievances. They also alleged 'The major part of them are notoriously disaffected to the present Government and upon all opportunities have manifested their malignity in words and deeds, particularly in choosing one Mr Pilchard, Upper Warden this present year, being a man twice sequestered for delinquency and served the late King at Oxford during the wars. Not much good to be expected from Men so qualified'. The Court riposted at 'perverse, proud, and peevish minds' and defended its record, adding for good measure that the rebels had not paid their contributions to poor relief, and that some had themselves received such help.

The Hall went up in flames in 1666 but was rebuilt and then let to Nonconformist preachers to recoup some of the heavy expense. In 1753 the Company tried to extend its jurisdiction but was successfully challenged in 1830. Its powers of search continued, until eventually local authorities and public inspectors took over, though the 'sizing' of weights continued at Founders' Hall until 1914. The Court still elects a 'Sizer' and 'Searcher', but these are nominal appointments.

The Hall in Founders' Court was rebuilt in 1845 and property was also bought in St Swithin's Lane. The Hall was leased to the Electric Telegraph Co in 1853 and a new one built on the new property in 1877. Twenty years later there was a curious echo of the old Grant of Arms, when the Court learnt that J.C. Chase, a Liveryman, as Civil Commissioner for the District of Aliwal North in Cape Colony had adopted the Arms for his colonial charge. The Court was delighted, and sent him a faithful copy of the original.

The Hall escaped the blitz, and for a while was partly let. Today it is entirely occupied by the Company, though the Founders Court premises were sold in 1964 to Brown, Shipley, who had leased them since 1921.

In 1929 Wilson Wiley was admitted to the Livery and has served as Clerk since 1936. Five years before that, Charles Fountain was appointed Beadle; his son John now occupies that position. Both were made Freemen of the Company.

Many new Liverymen are modern founders in the industrial sense, and the Company supports the industry through scholarships, fellowships, prizes for training and research, and in 1979 sponsored a seminar at Founders' Hall to discuss the financial implications of technological advance. There are also spring tours of foundry centres at home and abroad. Aid to industry has been largely financed through a trust fund bequeathed by a Past Master, Robert Warner, in 1933. His family's association dates to 1767, and ten of its members have served as Master.

Today the retiring Master of the Founders drinks to his successor in a painted Venetian glass goblet left by Richard Weoley, Master in 1631 and 1640, in the terms requested by him: 'And I do hereby wish that my means were agreeable to my will, then should they record me a better Benefactor; and I shall ever wish the whole Body may ever live in Unity, Concord, and Brotherly Love which is pleasing to God and Man. Even thus the God of Heaven Bless Them All. Amen.'

The Poulters. By the 13th century the sale of poultry was localised at the east end of Cheapside, in what came to be known as Poultry. Poulterers were subject to price control and other regulations from at least 1274; twenty two species were rated, and middlemen discouraged. It was an offence to forestall, that is, to purchase goods on their way to market and mark them up to enhance the ultimate price. By 1299 the Poulters supervised their own trade but, in 1321, faced with fixed rates imposed by the Itinerant Justices through an Assize of Poultry, they closed their shops and refused to sell at those laid-down rates. Some were imprisoned, the assize was amended and the King intervened in favour of sensible pricing — but the Poulters lost their right to control the trade for fifty years. They secured ordinances in the 1360s and by 1422 appear to have met in Brewers' Hall.

The Poulters over a period, with the Fishmongers and Butchers, spread along Cornhill, and began to display their live birds in stalls and pens outside their premises. In 1345 there were complaints of highway obstruction and they were confined to their shops. Ten years later they were allowed to rent land under the south wall of the church of St Nicholas, Shambles, at 4d a foot, with 13 plots totalling 74 feet. The average stall was 8 feet long and 34 inches in depth. 'Foreign' poulters, allowed by authority to ensure sufficient supplies, were to sell only through the market, initially Leadenhall.

Poulters were restricted to certain days and hours of sale and purchase, and in other ways. In 1444 Common Council was petitioned against 'the grete and noyous and grevous hurt which that long tyme come and allway cometh to the comon people of thys Citee and lordes and ladies of this reaume by the pultrie biside the stokkes and in the principal stretes and weyes . . . thrugh the evel rule and demenyng of the pulters kepyng wythin hem Swannes, gees, heronsewes and other pultrie wherof the ordure and standyng of hem is of grete stenche and so evel savour that it causeth grete and parlous infectyng of the people and long hath done'. The Poulters were moved to London Wall. Prison was the reward for Poulters who sold unfit stock. They were after all engaged in a luxury trade that only the wealthiest could afford, when one considers the price of a swan at 3s 6d or a pullet at 1d against a skilled worker's wage at 4d a day.

It has been assumed that the Company was incorporated by charter in 1504 but there is no direct evidence for this. Ordinances were approved in 1440, 1513, 1543 and 1550. By 1601 the Company enjoyed premises leased to Robert Warden in Blanchappleton, a tenement in Fenchurch Street. In 1616 the Guild obtained the lease, 'Provided that they substantially build the same for their Hall . . .', to which end they had been storing members' contributions in a chest. The meeting chamber was some 370 square feet, with an outside staircase, and upstairs kitchen, buttery, chamber, closet 'with a little room by it,' and a garret. There was a garden plot and a passageway. The members sat on fourteen stools with green cushions round a trestled table; the floor was carpeted with green cloth and strewn with rosemary and bays and the chest was triple-locked. The walls were decked with streamers bearing the Royal, City and Company arms. The Hall was not rebuilt. Between 1587 and 1591 the Company achieved its own coat of arms, and by 1501 the Poulters had achieved their own livery by prescription. Their Grant of Arms was made in 1634. Twenty years later they were given a silver seal by retiring Master George Robinson and in 1665 'meere poulters or selling pultry wares' within seven miles of the City were incorporated as Poulters London. The final charter was granted in 1692, requiring new ordinances which were never in fact presented. Thus the Poulters have for nearly three centuries been governed by strictly speaking, illegal bye laws.

The Company consistently failed to rebuild its tenement in Fenchurch Street, despite renewed leases and demands, and in 1630 they moved to a tenement in Butcher's Hall Lane (previously Chicken or Fowl Lane, and even earlier, Stinking Lane), leased from Christ's Hospital by Anthony Hawkes, Poulter. In 1636 Hawkes left the lease to the Company. In 1664 the Company started to negotiate better terms, having spent money on the building, but in 1666 it was destroyed by fire. Subsequently it variously used other Company Halls and taverns, or coffee houses. In 1767 it commenced using a room at Guildhall, and then in 1952 removed to the Hall of the Armourers and Brasiers.

By the mid-18th century the Company had effectively ceased to control its trade. Meanwhile the Poulters had been involved in most of the financial depredations of the monarchy and Parliament. Since the 15th century they had traditionally provided prizes for wrestling contests. In the 17th century it was recorded that '. . . he that gyveth a fall shall have a Cony and he that taketh a fall shall have a Cheken, and God Save the Kyng'. The Poulters were one of few Companies to actually make a profit on their investment in Ulster.

From time to time they intervened in public affairs, such as when they opposed the establishment of Covent Garden Market, the restrictions on export of cony wool and hair in the Hudson Bay Bill, and Acts for the preservation of game. The Company administers numerous bequests for the benefit of old or poor freemen or their widows and their major charity, Nepton's Trust, the product of property left in 1724 by Thomas Nepton, which has been largely devoted to educational purposes.

The Cooks. The cookshops of London were established by 1170, when Becket's Clerk, Fitz-Stephen referred to *publica coquina* on the north bank of the Thames, where 'at any hour of the day or night' victuals of all kinds might be found to take home or eat on the spot. 'It is a public eating house and is both highly convenient and useful to the City and is clear proof of its civilisation.' In 1212 King John ordered that cookshops be whitewashed and plastered and their partitions removed, following the great fire of that year. That first community of cooks was in Vintry, though they later spread elsewhere in the City.

In those days meat was chopped or ground and heavily spiced as most food was salted for the winter and cooks, as specialists, held to the secrets of their craft. The Cooks obtained ordinances in 1379 having probably organised themselves into two fraternities in Estchepe and Bredstret by 1311. The Cooks were first regulated in 1312. Chaucer referred to the offence of twice cooking the same meat or fish:

> 'For many a pastee hastow taken blood,
> And many a jakke of Dovere hastow sooled,
> That hath been twies hoot and twies coold.'

The Guild was incorporated in 1482 and, although it has been suggested that the cooks, pastilers and piebakers were merged by 1420 into one Guild, the Pastilers obtained separate ordinances in 1495. In 1421 Walter Maungeard was sworn as a Master of Pastelers yet his will refers to him as 'citesen and Koke of London'. In 1538, among listed Pastelers was John Armestronge who, by his will of 1554, left money to the Company of Cooks. It therefore appears that the cooks, pastelers and piebakers did merge into one Guild, but when is not clear. Perhaps the terms pasteler and cook became interchangeable by the time of the 1538 listing, which is taken to reflect the Company of Cooks. Certainly in 1378 and 1379, ordinances referred to Cooks preparing meats, cooks and piebakers, and pastelers or piebakers making pasties.

In 1461 the Cooks received their Grant of Arms. Altogether nine charters were granted, that of 1482 referring to the 'manifold pains and labour' they expended on the preparation of Royal and other feasts. It also laid down two Masters for the Company — the only City Company with this distinction. There are also two conflicting traditions to explain this: one, that the King required the Master to accompany him the same day he was due to attend on the Lord Mayor; the other, more likely explanation, that one Master was needed to attend the King in person while the second supervised the kitchen, since both needed to guarantee the Royal party's safety from poison. In 1530 Richard Roose, Cook to the Bishop of Rochester, was boiled to death for poisoning 16 people with broth intended for his master. The Company for centuries effectively provided the Royal, Corporation and other Company cooks.

Cook's Hall was built in 1500 in Aldersgate Street, and extended in 1674. It had been repaired in 1666 after slight damage by the Great Fire. The new Hall was consumed by fire in 1764, though the original building escaped. In 1771 the entire complex was destroyed by fire, and the ground let to this day. Thereafter the Company met at Guildhall or various taverns, and more recently at Innholders Hall.

By 1570 the Company's ancient crowning ceremony was first recorded, when 'Wm. Stokes, Coke, in the Cokes Hall, did verie cruelly and disrespectfully, to the evell example of evell doers, pull the garland from the head of one Robynsone, Coke, elected one of the Wardens . . .' The ceremony lapsed in the 19th century but has since been restored, and takes place at the annual Election Dinner.

Benefactions to the Company go back to that of Walter Maungeard of 1421, and include that of John Phillips of 1674 which allows the Company to present two children to Christ's Hospital, and of Samuel Birch, Cook, dramatist and Lord Mayor in 1815 (he was Master in 1799) whose business was acquired by Ring & Brymer in 1830. By then the Company had ceased to regulate its trade.

The Cooks contributed some £300 to the Irish estates under the aegis of the Mercers and the association was renewed in 1948 when they subscribed to Charter Estates Ltd, to develop Rhodesian property, again through the Mercers. The Company also retains links with the owners of two farms left in 1676 by Edward Corbett, and sold this century.

The Cooks Company Library is now held at Guildhall Library; the Company formed a Golfing Society in 1928; in 1953 it adopted the 625 Light Anti-Aircraft Regt, Royal Artillery, which held its last parade two years later.

Today the Company administers its ancient trusts, arranges an annual prize giving for its numerous prizes and awards to City and Guilds of London catering students, and those of the

Army Catering Corps and catering branches of both the Royal Navy and the RAF, and to prizewinners at Hotel Olympia, Salon Culinaire and other cookery exhibitions. The Company is a Patron of the Cookery and Food Association. The prizes are principally Caithness glass goblets and bowls, and in 1977 the Company instigated the Silver Jubilee Competition for a silver statuette of a chef, to be held by a technical college in the London area winning an annual cookery competition.

The Coopers. First recorded in 1298 when Coopers were fined by the Lord Mayor and eleven Aldermen for unknown reasons, the fraternity of Coopers obtained ordinances with powers of search, and laid down standards preventing the use of old oil or soap barrels, or poor materials in 1396. In 1420 they were required to brand their products with a registered mark. In 1422 they were governed by two wardens, and in 1440 the Guild was officially recognised. In 1464, sixty below-standard containers were burnt at the water conduit in Cheapside. In 1490 John Baker, Cooper, left the Guild his property in Basinghall Street, with a life interest to his widow, on condition that the Coopers obtained a charter, within ten years of her death.

In 1501 the Company was incorporated. The first Master was Hew Crompe and the Company numbered eight. In 1509, it secured a Grant of Arms with the motto 'Gaude Maria Virgo' (changed to 'Love as Brethren' after the Reformation). In 1522 the Company took possession of Baker's bequest — The Swan. By 1547 a Hall had been built. During the 16th century, the Coopers, whose prosperity increased with the growth of the Navy and the need for storage of commodities on board ship, secured legislation which empowered them to inspect and measure casks for ale, beer and soap, charging a farthing apiece. The Company sealed each vessel with its branding iron. Their powers of search and control of outsiders extended two miles outside the City.

The final effective charter was that of 1661, a year before the present Beadle's staff was presented to the Company. The Company lost its Hall in the 1666 conflagration, and rebuilt four years later. Somewhat large and expensive, that building was demolished, and in 1867 part of the site sold to the Corporation. In 1868 a third Hall was completed on the remaining land, but this was destroyed by enemy action in 1940. The remaining site was sold to the Corporation after the war. In 1958 the Company bought 13, Devonshire Square, Bishopsgate, an 18th century building, converting part for use as a Hall.

Since the first World War the Company has maintained a Register of Coopers who have satisfactorily completed their apprenticeships. It also administers numerous charities. These include William Alexander Cooper's Liverymen Fund and the Ratcliff Pension Charity for poor Liverymen and their dependants and poor residents of the London Borough of Tower Hamlets; Strode's Egham Pension and Eleemosynary Charity helps the poor of Egham and the Harold Griffin Gift Fund, which assists members of the Company, and the poor people of Battersea. In addition, the Company operates the Coopers' Company Benevolent Fund, which awards scholarships to pupils of the Coopers' Company and Coborn School, Upminster, opened in 1974 as the successor to schools at Bow, founded in 1563 and 1701. The Company appoints a Foundation Governor to Strode's College, Egham, the original foundation by Henry Strode, who was Master in 1703-4. The Company maintains close links with the London Division, Royal Naval Reserve.

Tylers and Bricklayers. Available records of the Company are sparse, but a Guild existed for some centuries before the somewhat late incorporation of 1568, which gave it rights of search and regulation of the trade up to fifteen miles outside London. The original charter has been lost. Ordinances were laid down in 1572, three years after the Company's Grant of Arms. Arguably the most famous bricklayer, Ben Jonson became a freeman c1593 and worked in his craft before turning to stage and letters. In 1598 he killed actor Gabriel Spenser in a duel in Hodgsden Fields — where 200 years later Tyler and Bricklayer William Rhodes had his brickworks.

The Company already occupied a Hall in the 16th century in Leadenhall Street — its second. The first was in Wormwood Street. Let as a synagogue around 1760, the second Hall was partly rebuilt in the early 19th century but sold off during the first World War. In 1660 the Company acquired a Beadle's mace, presented by Peter Mills, Master, and City Bricklayer. After the 1666 Fire he was appointed one of the Surveyors who superintended London's rebuilding. In 1783 Sir William Plomer was both Master and Lord Mayor. Twenty two years earlier Sir Samuel Fludyer, another Tyler and Bricklayer, was Lord Mayor. He died worth £900,000.

In 1825 William Rhodes was Master. He was a builder with brickfields at Rhodes Farm, Dalston, and in Hoxton. His grandson was Cecil Rhodes. In 1832 the Company built almshouses 'for decayed Liverymen and their widows' at a cost of £5,000 in King Henry's Walk, Balls Pond Road, designed by William Grellier. The almshouses have since been demolished, but the boundary wall survives, with the Company's name inscribed. In 1820 three brothers, George, Stephen and William Bird were elected to the Livery. This one family has provided forty five Liverymen, twenty Masters and three Clerks. Stephen Bird at one time was Chairman of the West London Railway.

In the 19th century the Bricklayers' Trade Union 'borrowed' the Company's arms. A reproduction of those arms was presented to HMS *Anson* in 1945 and returned when the ship went out of commission in 1950. The Company for many years awarded lead wall plaques and gold medals to outstanding buildings and their architects. In 1963 new awards were instituted for tiling and brickwork, with similar plaques and medals.

The Bowyers. The motto of the Company is 'Crecy Poitiers Agincourt'. It reflects the great victories of Edward III's longbowmen over the superior numbers of the French. The weapon had a draw weight often exceeding 100lbs and it was made by the Bowyers. The Fletchers made the arrows. The two guilds were one until 1371, when the Bowyers successfully petitioned the Mayor and Aldermen for an ordinance that no bowyer should work by night as this led to inferior craftsmanship, and that the two trades should be practised separately.

The Stringers and Longbowstringmakers supplied the bow strings: both companies are extinct. The Guild obtained a Grant of Arms in 1488 and its incorporation in 1621 and a further charter in 1666. The trade diminished, but the Company survived. The Hall at the corner of Hart Street and Monkwell Street was destroyed by the Great Fire of 1666. That same year James Wood left his manor in Leicestershire to the Company, to facilitate scholarships to Cambridge University and to help deserving young men within the Company. He also made a condition — that the Company attend a service every other year at St Nicholas Cole Abbey, and this request is still observed on Master's Day. In 1856, Alderman and Bowyer Timms was the last Lord Mayor to process by water.

The Company administers charitable funds and sponsors archery events.

The Fletchers. In 1371 the Fletchers separated from the Bowyers, but were never incorporated, being a Company by prescription. Its Grant of Arms was obtained in 1467. The Fletchers fought long and hard against the threat of gunpowder but, unlike the Longstringbowmakers, who were recognised as a separate Guild in 1416, they have survived as a City Company. The Longstringbowmakers were a Guild of Freemen, without Livery, and faded away in the 19th century. Today the Company presents trophies for archery events and assists the disabled to buy archery equipment.

The Blacksmiths. Originally the Fraternity of St Loie, the Guild was first known as the Tooth-Drawers. In 1325 it was officially recognised, and in 1394 regulated by ordinance. In 1494 the Blacksmiths acquired the lease of a property in Lambeth Hill, and a list of its contents in 1496 survives. This included an image of St Loie, wall hangings, 'A gret cheste of elme', tablecloths and napkins, trenchers, trestle tables, forms and some small items of silver.

The Company's account books of the 16th century reflect the King's monetary demands, but strangely, not the religious upheavals of the time, except 'Paid unto My Lord Mayer to be toward the charges of the Sowdeers wich shuld aben sent into the Northe Contrey XXs' — a reference to the Pilgrimage of Grace. By the 1550s the Guild was living beyond its means, chiefly through feasting and drinking. In 1553 'The Dyner' for two years included bread, beer, ale, 'wyne both claret and Ffrenche', 'great Raysons', cloves, maice, saffron, 'Synamon', ginger, currants, prunes, 'byskytts and carraways', sugar, eggs, two dozen geese, three dozen rabbits, legs of veal, eight 'hinder quarters of moton', sirloin of beef, suet, sturgeon, two fresh salmon, ten capons, two bushels of meal, butter, salt, vinegar and mustard, and also for the services of a cook, 'mynstrelles', porter, two washer women, and the means to heat and light the Hall. Throughout the century the Guild furnished men and arms: 'Ffor the settynge fforthe of sodyers to go to the sea'. There were also disputes with the Armourers, at some cost to themselves.

In 1571 the 'Art and Mystery of the Blacksmiths-Spurriers' was incorporated by charter. The Clockmakers were then blacksmiths, as were the gunmakers; so were the anchorsmiths. There followed a period of relative prosperity but much dispute.

In 1605 the Court temporarily expelled Roger White and Thomas Wiltsheire who 'bothe confessed that they went to an Aleshouse or Bawdie House, and there supped and kept company with lewd women . . .'. The affair rumbled on with the pair welcomed and then dismissed, Wiltsheire rushing into the Court meeting, 'whereupon the Assistants being displeased thereat rose upp'. In 1607 the son of a knight, Sir Thomas Dorrell of Lillington of the Bucks militia was bound apprentice — a rare occurrence. In 1609 'William Harber brought a dagger for his proofe piece' indicating the careful regulation of the trade and the cross-over with other crafts, and in the same accounts we read 'Paied out ye 27 of Ffebruarie 1608 att a meeting among ye Gunmakers . . .'. In 1609 the White-Wiltsheire matter was settled, but 'Laied out and spent att divers meetings & for divers dynners in the tyme that the Woodmongers sued to have had William Stephens free of this Companye that goeth with a cart to have been translated unto them . . .' reflects a major dispute which cost over £26 in legal, eating and even perhaps bribery costs.

The Company subscribed to the Irish loan, and by that time spent a significant part of its income on benefactions to clergy and to the poor. 'Old Iron' was a forbidden cry in the City and the Blacksmiths were chartered to prosecute offenders. By 1623 the Company had repaired its Hall, dined well, helped many and had cash in hand. In 1632 occurred the first reference to educational grant — of 40s a year to John, son of John Hodges, freeman, a scholar at Trinity College, Oxford, for three years. In 1631 the Clockmakers seceded from the Company.

With the new charter of 1639, the Company faced multiple costs — the Gunmakers were restive and seeking their own charter; the Clockmakers were the subject of some disagreement. There was also trouble from Mathew Griffith, Vicar of St Mary Magdalene, who sought payment of tithes in respect of the Hall. He was sharp in his comments: 'I should have looked for better respecte from some of you who are zealous professors, but that I know you are all but Blacksmithes and show yor breedinge . . .'. The Blacksmiths understandably went to worship at St Anne, Blackfriars, where their protege, John Hodges was vicar. They also took over the property at the Old Bailey left them by Edward Preston in 1601. Until recently, a tablet marked the site.

The summer of 1657 saw the usual Feast with 'musicke' and substantial refreshment — 'a barrell of strong beere, a barrell of small beere, and a kilderkin of Ale', beef, and 'Paid the Cooke for fourteene messe of meat; Viz, Six boyled chickens in a dish, a giggett of mutton, a pattie of Mutton, a goose, a capon and a codling tart — and for fancies and dressing the same £24 4s 8d'. The beef was probably for the apprentices the next day.

In 1631 'Michaell Pym, gent, a clarke in ye Lord Mayor's Court in London' became Clerk to the Company. In 1655 he resigned in favour of his son, Christopher who celebrated his admission to office by presenting the Company with a silver cup — and thus assured himself a footnote in the annals of connoisseurs. The Blacksmiths Cup is a major example of baroque silvercraft, and has passed through a number of hands, with the Blacksmiths in spasmodic search of it ever since it passed from theirs. It surfaced in 1862 and again in 1902, 1915 and 1929. Eventually it came to belong to Lady Brabourne and in 1977 she passed it to the Company on permanent loan.

The Blacksmiths, who generally seem to have paid scant attention to affairs of state, nonetheless welcomed the Restoration of the monarchy with unaccustomed zeal — '26th July 1660, spent July 6th, being Quarter Day, and the day the King dined in the Citty £9 5s 5d Paid for Ribbands and Staves for the Whiflers (trumpeters) . . .'.

The Blacksmiths appear to have been relatively unscathed by the plague epidemic of 1665, though they paid for George Palmer to go to the pest house, burnt coal fires in the street and took no admissions nor held any dinners. In 1666 their good fortune changed. Fire consumed their Hall and all their leasehold properties, but they set to with a will and salvaged what they could, renting the Quest House at Cripplegate for their meetings. They had saved most of their goods before the fire reached the Hall, but scoured the site and dug out melted iron, and other articles, including copper and pewter: 'Spent att the time of the late dreadfull fire, and att digging up the iron and pewter 8s 4d'. The Quest House was demolished in 1905. The new Hall was ready by 1670, and having cost the Company dear, was let out for other Companies' use — the Tobaccopipe Makers, and in 1678, the Carmen.

In the closing years of the 17th century the quarrel with the Clockmakers flared, when the latter petitioned for greater powers and, in so doing, appeared to the Blacksmiths to threaten their own. The dispute was complex and rumbled on for many years, but essentially the Blacksmiths sought to restrain threats to their ancient powers, and the Clockmakers sought to control their by now extremely sophisticated craft. It was not until 1756 that they succeeded. At the start of the 18th century the Blacksmiths faced six years of litigation, threats to their monopoly and internal dissension. Times were changing.

By 1724 the number of liverymen had increased to 225, the Yeomanry had been organised and 'foreign' brethren recognised. Smiths were rapidly becoming too numerous for the nature of their Company.

In 1717 the journeymen complained to the Mayor and Aldermen, inconclusively. In 1748 the Company faced its problems. The Hall was a constant drain on resources, and there was other property to maintain — adjacent, at Puddle Dock, the Old Bailey, and at St Andrews Hill. By the 1760s there was widespread discontent within the Livery and by 1780 the Company decided to seek legal vindication of its rights to enforce payment of fines and quarterage. The Company rested its case on its charter; the lawyers were in serious doubt that this was justification for any restriction upon trade. Smiths had flooded in from outside the City and not taken up their freedom; effectively the medieval system was dead, but the Company would not lie down. The Company lost, and in 1785 determined to dispose of the lease of its Hall, and to sell its plate, investing the cash in pension funds, since it no longer needed a headquarters for a trade it no longer controlled.

Today the Blacksmiths make awards for craftsmanship and continue to administer their charitable funds. They also maintain another tradition, instituted in 1828, when Moses Kipling's *Blacksmith's Song* was first rendered at the George and Vulture tavern off Cornhill. Kipling was Prime Warden, the music written by his friend Frank Abernethy, and the Company approved and adopted the song. The Blacksmiths today stand and after each of the three verses, render the chorus in unison. It runs thus:

'To the mem'ry of Vulcan our voices we'll raise,
May he and his sons be revered thro' the land;
May they thrive, root and branch, and enjoy happy days,
For by Hammer and Hands all arts do stand.'

The Joiners and Ceilers. The Joiners and Carvers were associated with the Saddlers in Saxon times, as employees of that craft, making saddle bows. They were also known as Fusters — either experts in timber or in the extraction of sap for colouring purposes. In 1239 William le Joynier, Mayor 'Builded ye choire of ye Grey Friars Church of London', and in 1253 Jacob le Junctor worked on the 'alter screen' at Westminster Abbey. The Joiners and Fusters gained approval for their own ordinances in 1269 and in 1307 the Saddlers accused them of using green wood, cut at night and smuggled into their workshops, to be sold to dishonest Painter Stainers, who treated them so they could be sold as good saddle bows, which then collapsed to the discredit of the Saddlers. The Mayor and Aldermen instructed the Joiners to use only quarters (of the trunk) duly marked by their guild and not to deal in second hand saddle bows. In 1375 the Guild of St James Garlickhythe was formally recognised.

In 1514 'Richard Rydge, Joynour and Carver is payd 2s 6d each for cutting and carving 32 Lintells in Kings and Queens Badges' at Hampton Court Great Hall — 24 years ealier Will Heyward made 'stayes' (ribs) for the King's ship. Joiners Hall was built between 1518 and 1551; three years later a joiner, John Streete caused an affray and was 'incontinently taken, with dagger drawn, to Newgate Gaol, where he fayned himself mad'.

In 1571 Elizabeth I granted the company its first charter and in 1590 a custom started which still survives, of a July meeting on the feast of St James, a service and dinner. The Company's powers of search were extended in 1613 to cover coachmakers, trunkmakers, gunstock, flask and touchbox makers, cupboard and boxmakers and carvers, and to require those crafts to submit proof pieces. The Joiners contributed £164 to the Ulster colonisation programme. It experienced the general surrender and subsequent restoration of charters in the 1680s.

The Great Fire destroyed the Hall and it was rebuilt, and again burnt down in 1694. It was rebuilt in 1799.

In 1707 Richard Saunders, Joiner, carved the giants Gog and Magog for Guildhall for £70. In 1724 an act of Common Council compelled all joiners to join the Company; in 1731 the Master upset the Court by using poor box receipts to gamble on the state lottery — but he won £100 and was congratulated. In mid-century the Company ceased to use its powers of search. In 1800 such were the Company's finances that the Hall was let as a warehouse and the Hall contents sold for £203 8s 9d. It was burnt down yet again in 1811 and rebuilt as a warehouse. In 1940 the last Hall was destroyed in the blitz.

The Company associated itself with the establishment of the City and Guilds of London Institute in 1878 and also the Carpenters' School at Great Titchfield Street.

Two hundred years ago a Joiner wrote The Joiners' Song, updated in 1971. The chorus runs as follows:

> 'Let Brother Joiners hand in hand
> Their friendship never sever,
> But drink the toast "Our Brotherhood",
> And may it last for ever.'

The Weavers. Believed to be the oldest of the City's Companies, the Weavers are mentioned in the Pipe Roll of 1130: 'Robert son of Levstan renders account of £16 from the guild of weavers of London. He has paid it into the treasury. And he is quit'. The Guild's earliest charter was granted in 1155 and refers to its existence in the King's grandfather's time. The Guild's monopoly of the craft led to friction with the civic authorities and, in 1300, they forced the Weavers to acknowledge their jurisdiction. With the influx of Flemish weavers, there began two centuries of infighting between the guild and its rivals in the textile trade; they combined in 1497, but not before some aspects of the trade had separated, with the formation of such other guilds as those of the Mercers and the Drapers in the 14th century.

In the 17th and the 18th centuries, similar conflicts emerged with the arrival of the Huguenots, but these newcomers strengthened the craft and laid the basis for modern developments in manmade fibres. In 1666 the Company's original Hall in Basinghall Street was destroyed by the Great Fire and rebuilt on the same site. In 1856 this was again replaced by an office block, the site of which was sold in 1962.

The Weavers differ from the other Companies in that instead of a Master, they are headed by an Upper Bailiff and a Renter Bailiff drawn from the Court. The Upper Warden and Renter Warden are drawn from the body of the Livery.

Despite losing control of its trade with the development of the Industrial Revolution, the Company has maintained its links with textiles. It supports the Textile Institute with the Weavers' Company Technology Award, the Young Weaver of the Year Award, the Weavers' Company Craft Prize, the Weaver Company's Medal and Prize and the Weavers' Company Scholarships. In addition, the Company offers, through the Royal Society of Arts, a travelling bursary, and supports the RSA by contributions to relevant aspects of the Design Bursaries Competition. It also makes grants to students at the School of Textile Design at the Royal College of Art, and it awards prizes within the Bradford Textile Society Prize Scheme. It offers a Silver Medal Award for an outstanding student at Derby Lonsdale College of Higher Education, has supported conservation projects at the Courtauld Institute and the Victoria and Albert Museum, while encouraging hand weaving, such as by helping to establish the Crafts Study Centre at Bath.

The Company's Benevolent Fund, apart from 'casual' grants of some £6,000 a year, £1,000 a year to the Lord Mayor's Appeal and £500 for charities selected by the Upper Bailiff, concentrates its activities from a current income of some £90,000 per annum, on projects concerned with crime prevention and prisoner after-care. First consideration is given to youth work and helping young offenders, especially with schemes that are new, and without official support. The Company also administers its own almshouses at Wanstead which provide for forty elderly people.

The Woolmen. From time to time Packers, Woolmers, Winders, Shooters, Folders, Broggers and Woolmongers, the merchant guild of Woolmen finds its origins in 1180 as one of the eighteen adulterine guilds fined by Henry II for exercising monopoly of their crafts without licence. Yet in a strange way the Guild *was* recognised, since it was one of the five 'bridge guilds' charged with the upkeep of London Bridge, which was financed by a levy on wool.

In 1257 Woolmen were granted the right to nominate the weigher of the King's Great Beam on which wool was measured. In 1274 the Mayor sold an illegal charter to the guild for 40s — 'De paccatoribus Lond' xls.' but in 1327 the Packer's Guild was formally recognised, 14 years after the first compulsory enactment of the Staple, embracing Woolmen, and controlling the packing, sale and taxing of wool — our major export at that time. The Lord Chancellor's seat on the Woolsack derives from the sacks of wool on which sat those who oversaw minders and packers who were appointed by the guild and themselves, and who were tested by the guild's 'Tryer'.

Many are the phrases in common usage stemming from the Woolmen's trade: 'Dyed in the wool', 'Pull wool over his eyes', 'wool-gathering', to 'fleece' someone, and 'spinster'.

Other merchants traded in wool, and many were the conflicts between their guilds and the Woolmen, but foreign competition was scotched in 1337, when William de la Pole and Reginald Conduit, Woolmen, were granted a monopoly of wool export to the exclusion of the Italian bankers. In 1354 the Statute of Staples awarded the Guild the monopoly of licensing winders and packers, and in 1422 the woolpackers were recorded as an ancient company by prescription. The 1466 Act of the Retainer empowered the Company of the Staple to farm the whole of the Custom and subsidy on wool, for which it paid the garrison at Calais, the 'Staple' town; many Woolmen were Staplers. In 1473 the Guild was unsuccessfully forbidden to trade on behalf of 'foreign' merchants. In 1488 its ordinances were recognised, and in 1522 it was incorporated. Gradually the Woolmen developed their trade to include woolbroking, buying the farmer's product and selling to Flemish merchants, but the incidence of Flemish weavers and a ban on raw wool export reduced the Company's powers. In that one century exports dropped from 35,000 to 4,000 sacks of wool. Despite this, and successive bans, the Company continued to trade on behalf of foreign merchants. The Staplers' activities gradually reduced, though the Woolmen continued to broke wool.

The 1313 Le Stapled Hall, later Staple Inn at Holborn Bars, was originally a custom house, part let to the packers. It passed from the Staplers' hands until 1623, then again in 1884 and the later buildings today provide the Institute of Actuaries with their home. It is believed that Woolmen had a Hall near old Wool Wharf, at the foot of Bear Lane, destroyed in the 1666 Great Fire. The Company built premises, possibly a Hall, at Mark Lane some time after 1686 — the buildings were sold in 1827. After 1779, when the right to license winders and packers was confirmed, the Guild's connection with its trade diminished, and its activities almost ceased, until in 1823 the Company obtained a Grant of Livery.

Today the Company's members include many concerned with wool, and it supports major agricultural shows with medals and prizes; presents medals at Bradford University, to the Clothing Institute, and for Leeds University competitions, while aiding many City charities and those associated with wool.

The Scriveners. The origin of the Company lies in the Guild of Writers of Court and Text Letter, accepted as a professional class by 1357, when the then Mayor, Henry Pycard, and Aldermen ordered that they should not in future be summoned on inquisitions in the sheriff's courts between any parties pleading there. In 1373 the Writers of the Court Letter were granted ordinances — in 1403 they broke away and formed a guild with the Limners, from which the Stationers' Company developed. The 1373 ordinances show that the scrivener made wills and wrote charters and other deeds, and signed his name as evidence of his good faith. The Scriveners acted as conveyancers and, by 1477, the term was synonymous with the notary who today prepares and authenticates legal documents intended to take effect abroad.

In 1617 the Scriveners were incorporated, and their qualifications were further defined in the 18th and 19th centuries. Today their principal activity is the jurisdiction over notaries public practising in or within three miles' radius of the City. They do not possess property or extensive funds, though they support certain charities. Their 17th century hall was disposed of by 1703. They have recently revived a four hundred year old tradition of producing 'the Scriveners' play'.

The Fruiterers. The original fellowship existed before 1300, but the first reference to the Fruiterers occurred in 1416, when John Graunt and Geoffrey Whyt were sworn as Wardens of the Mystery. The Guild obtained ordinances in 1463, which regulated the sale and measure of fruit, upon which tolls were levied. The office of Fruit Meter was purchased of the City, highly prized, and at one time cost £3,960. It was abolished in 1902.

In 1606 the Company was incorporated, and in 1660 it was recorded that 'information had been lodged that several of His Majesty's goods at the Fruiterers' warehouse at the "Three Cranes" in Thames Street, which were kept there as the goods of Mrs Elizabeth Cromwell, wife of Oliver Cromwell, deceased, sometimes called "The Protector", and it not being very improbable that the said Mrs Cromwell might convey such goods, the Council ordered persons to view the same'. The Three Cranes was in Fruiterers' Alley, off Thames Street and the Company's Hall was in Worcester House, Thames Street, in 1754. Since 1748 the Company's books record charitable donations to members in need, their widows or children of deceased members — whenever there is a genuine case of need.

The Company also makes grants and awards for the development of fruit growing, and for service to fruit culture, under the auspices of its Fruit Culture Council. Since 1754 the annual presentation of fruit to the Lord Mayor, started in 1577 to settle a dispute over tolls levied by the City's Meterers, has acquired a ceremonial character, and is maintained annually at Mansion House.

The Plaisterers. An association of Plaisterers or Pargetors existed long before 1501 when the Company was incorporated — the first of five charters. In 1546 the Company achieved a Grant of Arms. That first charter referred to 'our Well beloved faithful and liege men of the mistery of art of "Gipsars" within our City of London comonly called Plasterers'. William Elder bequeathed the Company its first Hall in 1556, on the corner of Addle Street and Philip Lane. It was consumed by the Great Fire and rebuilt in 1669 to Sir Christopher Wren's design. A description survives: 'One Kitchen under the Great Hall, One Buttery — Two little Cellars — a Coal hole and one great Cellar under the Parlour and the Room going into the Garden — one little Parlour under the Lobby and one great Parlour even with the said little Parlour — One large Room or Chamber with a Closet lying over the said great Parlour — and one little Room or Chamber lying even with the said Great Room or Chamber — Five Chambers lying over the said Great Room or Chamber and little Room aforesaid and the Common Hall.'

This was destroyed by fire in 1882 and the land leased for building, but that building was in turn demolished by enemy action in 1940. The City acquired the site in 1956. In 1961 the Company acquired a new site at 1, London Wall and started building their present Hall in 1970; it was opened in 1972 and includes the City's largest Livery Hall; its decor is based on faithful reproductions of John Adam's 18th century designs — a fitting tribute to the Plaisterer's craft.

The Company was one of the twelve original founders of the City and Guilds of London Institute, and has supported it ever since. It also provides a Challenge Cup and prizes in the Guilds' examinations and maintains a register of skilled plasterers.

The Plaisterers' Song concludes:

'Hark to the strain of the Plaisterers Song
Sing it with fervour loud and long
Mark its refrain in a voice crystal clear
A message that ev'ry-one may hear
Thro' all the centuries proudly proclaim
The motto by which we all live steadfastly the same
By brotherly love we are bound one and all
And by that motto shall we ever stand or fall
Here's to the Livery, our ancient Guild
Root and Branch.'

The Stationers and Newspaper Makers. A stationer is known to have dealt in manuscripts in the early 13th century, and in 1262 Reginald was recorded as a stationer of Oxford; the term crops up again in 1275 at Cambridge, in 1319 at York and in 1311 in London when William de Southflete, 'stacionarius Londiniensis', was paid for making and binding Royal Wardrobe accounts. In 1480 Piers Bauduyn was paid for binding and guilding Edward IV's books. John de Grafton of St Paul's Churchyard was described as a *parchmener,* then as a stationer in 1366 and Roger Horslee, warden of the lymners' guild, was described as a *scriptor,* though in his will he was termed *stacionarius.* Gradually the term stationer came to mean one who dealt from a fixed place of work in books and writing materials. By 1357 the Scriveners and lymners had formed a guild; by 1373 Scriveners, who copied legal documents, formed a separate organisation; the lymners and text writers maintained separate guilds.

Then, in 1403, textwriters, lymners and 'other good folks, citizens of London, who were wont to bind and sell books' were designated Stationers. The name varied until it became finally accepted by 1441. With the introduction of printing in 1476, manuscript books continued to be produced, but printers gradually joined the Guild. In 1557 the Company was incorporated. It was granted powers of search and seizure, and authorised to burn prohibited books — the Crown used the Companies' officers to censor seditious and heretical material, as no printer could function unless he joined the Company. In 1559 the Company achieved a Grant of Arms, and a livery.

It is believed that the original Guild had its own Hall, but the first evidence is of purchase of Peter's College c1554, east of the Deanery of St Paul's. By 1606 this was too small, and the Stationers took over Abergavenny House for £3,500. The Company's charter protected it from competition, but it had to settle internal disputes over ownership of texts, which grew into copyright. By 1565 the Company was formulating rules that required every book not covered by Royal grant to be presented to the Wardens, and claims could be settled by entry in the register books. The first folio of Shakespeare's works was so registered in 1623.

Inevitably, certain stationers held monopolies in certain categories of work, but opposition to this led in 1603 to a Royal grant to the Company 'for the benefit of the poore of the same' to print books of private prayer, primers, psalters and psalms, almanacks and prognostications. This became known as the English Stock, run from Stationers' Hall. In 1609 the Company was involved in the colonisation of Virginia, contributing £125: in 1614, £520 was found for a share in the Plantation of Londonderry.

Hall expenses bore heavily on the Company, and in 1656 the rights in Foxe's *Book of Martyrs* were sold to fund repairs. By 1664 the Hall was no longer in a fit state, and the fire of 1666 provided a necessary stimulus to rebuild by 1673. Most of the cost of £5,000 was raised from Stock profits. The English Stock strengthened the Company, and it prospered where other Companies gradually lost their trade associations in the 17th and 18th centuries. Nonetheless, the almanack monopoly was successfully challenged in 1774 by Thomas Carnan; after his death in 1788 the Company bought his interests for £1,500, profiting greatly from Francis Moore's *Vox Stellarum,* better known as *Old Moore.* The Hall was refronted in 1800 and subsequently improved in the 19th century more than once.

The 19th century enquiries into Livery Companies found the Stationers Company retained their trade links and, in 1884, the Royal Commission noted that apprentices were still bound at the Hall. In 1861 the Stationers' Company School opened in Bolt and Johnson's Courts. In 1894 it moved to Hornsey, becoming first a grammar school, and in 1967 a Voluntary Controlled Comprehensive. In 1937 the newly formed Newspaper Makers Company joined the Stationers.

The Hall was damaged in 1940, but restored. Earlier, in 1927, the Company sold its rights to *Old Moore,* as no longer befitting the Company's dignity or reputation. In 1961 the English Stock was wound up. After 1911 it was no longer necessary to register with the Company to establish copyright: a new voluntary register for unpublished material was set up in 1924.

The modern Register is widely used.

Today the Company maintains its charity funds, which date back to 1567, and are mostly geared to the needy within the trades of the Guild. A special training board deals with technical education; the Company has a library of books about books and also houses the library of the Bibliographical Society. The Company restricts admission, other than by patrimony, to those engaged in its trades. The Company is among the seven that still retain their archives on their premises. The others are all deposited at Guildhall.

The Broderers. English embroidery — the art or mystery of 'broderie' — was world famed from Anglo-Saxon times, as represented by the AD915 stole and maniple, parts of which were found in St Cuthbert's tomb at Durham and now kept in the Cathedral library. They were made for Friedestan, Bishop of Winchester, at the instance of Queen Aelfflaeda. It is generally accepted that English Broderers made the Bayeux Tapestry. Most of the work was done in professional workshops in the City, by qualified craftsmen, who had served a seven year apprenticeship. Nonetheless, there was competition, both from great private households and, before the Reformation, from nuns. 13th century records describe some of the broderers' work — 'to Adam de Basing 20 Marks for 6 . . . by the King's order and offered to St Paul's Church London . . . and 22

Marks for an embroidered chasuble bought to the King's order . . .'. The 13th and 14th centuries saw the craft at its peak. In 1376 the Guild was mentioned in a Corporation Letter Book. Thereafter the standard of workmanship declined.

In 1561 the Company was incorporated. It had by then acquired its own Hall, on what transpired to be an originally Roman site, later part of a monastery, and at 36, Gutter (Gundruns) Lane. A plaque on the Carey Lane face of Abacus House commemorates the building. In 1558 a Grant of Arms was obtained. The Reformation saw the end of the old craft, and a new tradition of 'fashion' embroidery emerged in the Elizabethan and Stuart periods. The Broderers participated in the Ulster scheme, maintaining a link with the Mercers for 300 years, rejuvenated in 1948 with that Company's interest in Southern Rhodesia, in which the Broderers again participated. Their Hall was let and then destroyed in 1940.

Today the Embroiderers Guild and Royal School of Needlework maintain the craft tradition; the Company helps financially, and keeps its own unique tradition of the Master's Song, led by the Master on all festive occasions in response to the toast of the Company; The chorus runs as follows:

> 'Oh! give us your plain dealing fellows,
> Who never from honesty shrink,
> Not thinking of all they shall tell us,
> But telling us all that they think.'

The Upholders. Variously known as Upheldere, Uphouldesterr and for long known as Fripperers, the Upholders were principally concerned with upholstery, though their dealings ranged from feather beds to shoe horns, furniture warehousing to second-hand clothes and chattels, and even to undertaking. Some became pawnbrokers and others costumiers and wardrobe dealers. Clearly the Guild's members were engaged in a variety of commerce, and one in 1356 dealt in armour, pickaxes and pitchforks. In 1360 the Upholders were formally recognised. In 1494 the guild promoted legislation to regulate those stuffs to be used in bedding, forbidding 'Fenn-down, Deers-hair and Goats-hair'. In 1465 it obtained a Grant of Arms.

Forty years earlier, the members of the mistery were charged as habitual receivers of stolen goods. They certainly dealt in cast-off clothes and hired out garments. In 1495, new ordinances extended the Upholders' powers. At one time associated with the Skinners, they nonetheless retained their independent status. The Company was incorporated in 1626. Its original hall was subsequently sold. In 1856 its powers were repealed, some time after they had ceased to be effective. The use of proper filling materials is now safeguarded through legislation and government control.

Today the Upholders administer a charitable trust for needy brethren, and, since 1980, have awarded their gold and silver medals for bedding and upholstery design at the International Furniture Show.

The Musicians. Minstrelsy has existed since the days of Homer, and musicians existed in the City from earliest times. Waits, who were watchmen and musicians, were well established by 1334 when Musicians were recorded as in the City's employ. They had formed more than one guild when the Guild of Minstrels was granted ordinances in 1350, solely concerned with charitable purposes. They were regarded as the City's Minstrels, as distinct from the King's Minstrels, with whom they were later in dispute. Perhaps due to the Royal musicians, also known as the King's Musick, their activities at that time, and indeed their continued existence, is in some doubt. During the middle ages there were three classes of musician — those in service of the King, Corporation, Church or nobility; itinerants often classed with rogues and vagabonds, who moved from house to house, and part-timers principally engaged in other trades.

The itinerants and part-timers were a continuing threat to the 'professionals' and in the middle of the 15th century these last complained of 'rude husbandmen and artificers . . . feigning to be minstrels and some of them wearing the King's livery and so pretending to be the King's Minstrels . . .'. In 1469 they obtained a charter as the Brotherhood of the King's Minstrels. The charter appears to have been a qualified failure, since in 1500 the City recognised the Fellowship of Minstrels (of London) who expressly dissociated themselves from their Royal equivalent. Initially, the new organisation concentrated its attention on the City, ignoring other such guilds in other towns, and avoiding conflict with the Royal musicians. Principally, the fellowship was concerned to stop unfair competition from 'foreigners'. It then set about excercising control over the City Waits, employed by the Corporation, successfully petitioning for the Waits to be admitted to, and thereby controlled by the Fellowship.

However, the City's aquiescence did not actually compel the Waits to join. All were freemen, generally through other Guilds, and they only numbered six or eight. In 1518 an act of Common Council strengthened the Fellowship's ordinances, among other matters requiring that 'It shall not be liefull to eny Mynstrell ffreman of the said ffeliship to supplate hire or gete out another mynstrell ffreman of the same ffeliship beying hire or spoken to ffor to sue (ie: *serve*) at eny Tryumphes Ffeests Dyns Sowps Mariags Gilds or Brotherhede or eny such other doynge whereby eny such mynstrell shuld have perte of his lyvying under the payn to eny such Supplanter . . . of XLs'. In 1554 the Minstrels sought more powers to stop outside competition — obviously an increasing nuisance. Another act of Common Council in 1574 tried to deal with the same problem, finding the Fellowship 'brought into contempt and hatryd by occasion of sondry disorders and inormities vsed by psonnes excercising that arte beinge not subjiecte to the good laws and ordinauncs . . .'. but still allowed any freeman of the City to exercise the art of music.

Then in 1604 the Company was incorporated, as the 'Art or Science of the Musicians of London', and given powers over musicians in and within three miles of the City. With the new security of this charter, the Company started reforming the profession and controlling outsiders. But thirty years later this enthusiasm brought the Musicians into confrontation with the King's Musick, for Whitehall lay within the three mile limit of the Company's rule and the King's men determined to destroy the Company. They proposed that, relying on their own original charter of Edward IV, the City Company had obtained its powers by fraud. In 1633 the King's men won, and obtained a revocation of the City Company's 1604 charter. In 1635 they obtained their own new charter and almost countrywide control over all musicians.

The City Company, without legal existence, now sought protection from the City and without immediate success. It eventually obtained new ordinances in 1638. Then the Civil War intervened but, after the Restoration, trouble flared again, with the Westminster Company (The King's men), obtaining confirmation of their charter and seeking a meeting with 'the musique of the cittie of London' for discussions, which simply led to more conflict.

The outcome of the ensuing law suit by the Westminster Company and the City Fellowship's backing by the Corporation has not survived, but the City Company was still in being two years after the Westminster Company last met in 1677. Unfortunately, there followed the King's overriding anti-City actions but, in 1688, the restoration of all the City Companies' charters included that of the Musicians. In 1694 they obtained further powers from the Corporation and set about consolidating their new found freedom from competition and Royal interference. In 1699, they strengthened their hand yet again, with a new act of Common Council.

In one century the Company's numbers rose from nineteen to 264, but the next century saw a commensurate decline in activity and membership. It was the election to the Court in 1870 of William Chappell which sowed the seeds of revival. In 1889 the Company established a silver medal competition and in 1893 the Composition Prize at the Guildhall School of Music. Exhibitions and lectures were organised, and the Livery Club inaugurated in 1902. Many forgotten works were revived through its medium. Between the wars the Cobbett Medal and the Collard Fellowship were instituted. The post-war period has been one of revival; in 1947 Sir Felix Cassel established Cassel

Prizes for Service Schools of Music; in 1948 the Evelyn Broadwood Scholarships were established; a new charter was granted in 1950, and the Prendergast Gift established at the Royal Academy of Music; in 1951 the Cassel Prize Fund was extended, and the Mary Naomi Wallace medal instituted for the best instrumentalist in the Womens' Royal Army Corps Staff Band; in 1954 a silver medal for the best member of the National Youth Orchestra was first awarded; in 1955 the Company started the Opera Singing Scholarship.

In 1959 the Percival Hart Fund was created and the Company's Foundation Fund began. Over these years, recitals were organised, and new works commissioned. In 1964 the Opera Singing Scholarship became the John Christie Award at Glyndebourne, and a fund was donated for prizes for the Household Brigade Junior Musicians Wing. In 1966 HM Queen Elizabeth the Queen Mother accepted the Honorary Freedom of the Company. The Company, during this time, helped to fund various music festivals. In 1969 the Maisie Lewis Young Artists' Fund was funded by Sir Edward Lewis and in the early 1970s the Company's charitable interests started to benefit from the Allcard Fund, the largest gift so far received by the Company.

The Turners. The Pipe Roll of 1179-80 listing the adulterine guilds included 'The gild of strangers of which Walter le Turner is elderman . . .'. In 1295 the *Liber Albus* recorded rules for measures and their marks, and in 1310, six turners were sworn before the Mayor and Aldermen not to make any measures except gallons, 'potells' (two quarts), and quarts, not to make false measures such as 'chopyns' (pint) or 'gylles' (half a pint) and to act against false measures. In 1310-11 the Turners were granted limited powers. As the makers of wooden vessels, commonly used for drinking, they were naturally involved in the making of measures. In 1347 all Turnours were summoned to mark their measures and make them from dry wood (as otherwise the measure would vary with the moisture content) and they were granted the virtual monopoly of the sale of measures.

The Turners feature in a list of guilds of 1422 and in 1435 Wardens John White and John Hendon successfully petitioned the authorities for powers of search and supervision, to ensure measures were not made of green wood but well 'clonge' (shrunk) and dry. In 1479 they were granted ordinances. Restrictive trade practices are not new; in 1558-9 the 'whole Fellowship and Company of Turners' was accused of infringing John Benbowe's licence to supply turnery ware to Queen Mary; they undertook to match his quality and prices.

In 1591 the Guild acquired a 'substantial mansion in Philpot Lane' on a lease from Sir George Philpot for forty years. It built and let houses on the adjoining land, which connected with Eastcheap by way of Turners' Alley. The Company was incorporated in 1604. This cost £64 17s 8d, including 'given to the King's Attorney 2 pairs of brasell bowlles and bagges 8/-'. John Turner was the first Master. Powers of search were augmented by powers of siezure.

Turnery mentioned included shovels, scoops, bushelltrees (measures), washing bowls, chairs, wheels, pails, trays, truggers and all kinds of wooden measures. Proof pieces were required and the craft restricted to the Company. Turned articles for the Navy were specifically mentioned: blocks, sheaves, deadmens eyes, ribs, trundles for barrel pumps, pump boxes, rammers, sponge heads, fire trunks, and the timber to be used for them was laid down: ash, elm, beech, maple, hornbeam for blocks; lignum vitae, elm, beech, maple or hornbeam for sheaves. That Turners were a rumbustious company is evidenced by the unusually full court record of Richard Titlow's 'moste wild speeches' against the then Master: 'a nytty breeched fellowe, a round thinge like a footeball, and that he could finde in his hart to give him a kick in the breech and tumble him up and downe the street like a footeball'. He was fined 33s 4d. That they were also chivalrous is clear from the 1609 entry that '. . . the mistery of arte de lez Turnors London did perform and make a dynner for the Master Wardens Assistants and Lyvery of the Company and their wyves according to the ordinanes in that behalf', also clearly showing that such a practice was built into the rules.

In 1606 the Hall lease was renewed, and John Bland leased an adjacent tenement from the Company. Thirty years later Mistress Bland refused to leave, though the lease expired with John's death. In 1639 her daughter was offered £5 to 'avoid' (vacate) the house. She refused. In 1640 she was offered 30s yearly for life. She went. In 1629 the Company 'is verie smale' and consisted of 'hardy tradesmen'. In 1634 it received its Grant of Arms.

Company inventories have survived, and that of 1661 includes 'a great booke called *Stowes Survey of London*' and 'three bookes of *Martyrs*'. A draft inventory of 1666 lists the Company's possessions and is frequently annotated with the dread word 'burnt' — in 1666 the Hall and most of its contents were destroyed in 'the dreadful fire'. In 1670 the Hall was rebuilt. Unhappily, the Philpots parted with their freehold to John Tyssen, who was bankrupted by the South Sea Bubble catastrophe in 1726. After litigation, they lost their tenure and in 1736 bought a mansion in College Hill. It was sold thirty years later.

By mid-18th century the Turners' fortunes were in decline, perhaps due to changing furniture fashions: turned chairs were out, cabriole legs and shaped backs were in.

In 1612 the Turners initially contributed £68 to the Irish estates through the Haberdashers, and topped this up later to £102. In 1686 they sold out to the latter for a profit, but retained a share of fisheries and ferries which they released for £50 in 1731. In 1739 the Company made a somewhat last ditch attempt to reinforce its powers of search, and by 1794 the trade connection was all but gone, and worse, the Company was hard put to run its affairs and to collect its dues. In 1800, for the first time mention was made of 'annual bounty' to poor widows. By 1850 the Company was, as Roland Champness says 'dying on its feet'.

The conditions may be said to make the man, and in 1873 John Jones brought life and controversy to the Court and Company; starting with Income Tax, he spent seventy of his 94 years channelling reforms and raising issues through the Company, with many successes and, without doubt, he stimulated the Company to turn its attention back to its ancient craft. In 1854 he instigated an apprentice prize scheme.

In 1870 the Company awarded its first silver medal for turnery, extending the scheme over five years, to take in numerous materials as well as wood, and promoting exhibitions. Potting, diamond engraving, glass blowing, cutting and engraving increased the repertoire. In 1913 the distribution of some 63 lathes to industrial and other schools was funded, leading to an exhibition of the resultant work and to further medals and other prizes.

In 1931 the Company learnt from the Press that Richard Gardner Williams, a relatively unknown liveryman, had left the majority of his estate to the Company, subject to a familial life interest, and in 1948 the Company received over £40,000 — transforming its centuries of comparative penury overnight.

Apart from the commemoration dinner requested in the benefactor's will, the income from this windfall has permitted the Turners to enlarge their award scheme, in consultation with the City and Guilds of London Institute, and the Society of Ornamental Turners, and to continue their occasional exhibitions and awards for practical turnery.

The Basketmakers. Basketwork predated pottery; provided buildings, containers and shields, was used as scaffolding, and was perhaps the first Celtic export to the Romans — before their conquest. The Basketmakers own one piece of coiled basketry which is nearly six thousand years old. Their own guild is first mentioned in 1422, and forty three years later, they were restricted to Blanche Appleton within the City — a manor which Stowe records as standing at the NE corner of Mart or Mark Lane, long since gone. By 1517 Dutch wares were imported and 'foreigners' were practising the trade; in 1569 the Basketmakers sought to remedy these infringements of their rights.

By the sixteenth century basketmakers lived in St Margaret Pattens and St Andrew Hubbard parishes. Pudding Lane in particular was dominated by them, the Butchers and the Turners. Clearly Basketmakers were often free of the other two guilds. In 1538, on 27 May, there 'was a great fyre in St Margarett Pattynsparishe amonge the baskett makers, where were burnt and perished in three houres a dossin howses and 9 persons of men, women, and children, cleane burnt to death, which was a pyteous sight'. Fire was an occupational hazard, but the City was worried, and they were ordered out. In 1539 they agreed not to imperil the City by fire and their expulsion was stayed.

With their ordinances of 1569 the Butchers amicably released Basketmakers free of their company: '. . . well contentyd and pleased to depte wt all the baskettmakers being ffree of there sayd company so that they . . . be hereafter erected unyted . . .' though the Turners were hesitant — 'the matter betweene the Tournors and Basketmakers' coming before the Mayor and Aldermen. The new ordinances conferred powers of search and imposed quality control. They defined '. . . all manner of basketts, fflasketts, Scrynes, Mawndes . . .', and put foreign basketmakers and sellers under the Guild's control: '. . . such fforeigns, Alyens, and strangers, baskettmakers . . . tollerated and suffred . . . to occupie the same Crafte or occupacion . . . within the said Cittie . . . shalbe alwaies under the search and government of the said Wardens of the said Crafte . . . And shall paye quarteridge . . .'. Shortly after, freemen of the Butchers, the Weavers, and the Carpenters transferred to the Basketmakers.

The Basketmakers appear not to have had their own Hall, but they seem to have supported their guild church of St Margaret Pattens from the late fifteenth century, when vestry minutes record 'an nodr Awter cloth of byrds eyen werke wt a crosse in the mydds And writt undr neith of the gyft of Bowenpersons wyff baskett maker'. In 1494 William Johnson, basketmaker, left £10 to the church. Charity was restricted by the Guild's comparative penury, but nonetheless it was evident in 17th century gifts to the poorer still, such as 'Given Mr Harper's son that is blind . . . 00 05 00' in 1693 and two years later 'Expended at the buriall of old Rymes . . . 00 06 06'.

First steps to a Royal Charter were taken in 1664; perhaps the Great Fire intervened, for application was made to the Crown, (without reference to the City authorities) in 1682, energetically and with the backing of the cane-chair makers. Nothing came of it, and the two bodies combined forces a year later, again without success. They tried once more in 1685 and spent a great deal of time, effort and money: 'Spent foure dayes waiteing at Whitehall and on ye Secretary . . . 00 17 00', and 'Spent waiteing on the Secretary ten dayes . . . 01 18 06'. They paid their lawyer some £6 14s and passed 'ten ginneys' to the Attorney Generall (sic), went to Windsor, Whitehall and Hampton Court — a total of some thirty days of attendance on various officials and £84 0s 10d expenditure over two years — all for nothing. Despite several more attempts, they gave up in 1691, when the Corporation instructed lawyers 'to prepare reasons against the said Baskett-makers and Caners being incorporated . . .'. There was one later reconsideration but it was not pursued. The last entry on the Company's records was for £6 10s 'for writings and attendance in the Charter business' from which we sense the frustration and also the finality of this affair. (The Company was finally incorporated in 1937).

Despite this failure, the Guild maintained its powers by ordinance and disciplined Jerome Benton in 1610 for buying from 'a foreyner' — he was a constant thorn in their side and in 1624 attacked Upper Warden Richard Bingham, drawing blood. He apologised and was fined. In 1661 the guild siezed '10,000 of twigg at Bull Wharfe' as below standard, seized 'skreene basketts' in 1667, prosecuted hucksters in that year and deposited faulty wares at Guildhall in 1676: 'Wares by them Discovered to be Defective and not well made . . .'. Next year they were to 'obteine an order . . . for burneing' at Smithfield 'badd and defective ware'. Their powers increased with useage into the 18th century, and they used the right to fine frequently.

By then the Guild owned some properties on mortgage, but from the mid-18th century its powers waned, despite attempts at enforcement right into the 19th century. In 1799 'a poor Frenchman who sold baskets was ejected from the City'. This was the last reference to such action and in 1828 the Guild accepted that it could no longer impose its will on the trade.

The raw material for basketmaking was the osier — immature willow. Osier plantations were known as holts, and existed at Kew, Kingston, Barnes and Molesey from the 14th and 15th centuries until 1859. In 1747 T. Waller's *A General Description of all Trades* described basketmaking as 'an inferior hidden Sort of a Handicraft Business' though 'not without its Niceties' requiring 'not much else besides Strength and Application' in the growing and harvesting of osiers but 'more Invention and Nicety' for 'the White Work' and added 'They are a Company by prescription only'.

In 1825 the Basketmakers obtained a Grant of Livery, first sought in 1775. Their arms were in use by 1672, but not formally granted until 1931. The Company's motto is 'Let us love one another'. It was modestly involved in financing the Virginia Company in 1609 and contributed £32 to the Irish estates that same year.

Today the Company numbers over 400, including freewomen, and encourages its apprentices to study the industry, taking a particular interest in blind basketmakers. In 1981, £2,260 was raised towards restoration of its guild church of St Margaret Pattens. It administers general charitable funds, which are currently under review, while its own benevolent fund and the Snelling Fund are devoted to the needy of the Company and its trade. In 1945 HMS *Anson* was adopted; in 1981 the Company formalised an association with 289 Commando Battery Royal Artillery Volunteers. It also supports the Basketmakers Association.

The Glaziers, (and Painters of Glass). The original Guild was first recorded on its reorganisation in 1328, when John Husbonde was Master and Alan Gille the Warden. In 1368 'This day came the glaziers (Vitrarii) before the Mayor and Aldermen and presented Harry Stannerne and William Papelwyk, glaziers, to the wardens of their mistery'. The only record (in 1373) for the next hundred and six years referred to John de Brampton and John Geddynagge as Masters. In 1474 the glaziers petitioned the authorities against 'Foreyn persons as well as Etrangers' and in 1541 a similar complaint was voiced by 'the poore wardens and cityzens of ye Craft of Glaziers' against those from outside the City who practised the trade and undercut the freemen. At the same time the Guild sought to fix imported glass prices at 'iiij the foot'.

By 1588 it had achieved a Grant of Arms — interestingly, an error in the grant has been compounded, with the current use of the term 'glazing' iron, which was earlier 'grazing' and should have been 'grozing'. (A grozing-iron was a tool in the form of clippers for cutting glass).

The 17th century Royal practice of licensing manufacture and sale rights to specific individuals pushed glass beyond the reach of all but the wealthy. Isaac Bungard and John Dynes led a cartel to corner the market, and Sir Robert Mansell obtained a patent for glass manufacture. In his case, the product was 'dear, bad, scarce, and want full of size' and the Glaziers launched a series of petitions to the Crown against such monopolists. These led to their incorporation in 1638, when they promptly impeached Mansell and his collaborators, and admitted Bungard and Dynes to the Livery. Meanwhile, by 1601, the Glaziers had their own Hall, in Five (Fye) Foot Lane, between Old Fish (Victoria) Street and Thames Street, its frontage on Old Fish Street Hill. This was leased from the Fishmongers.

Further adjacent leases were also acquired. The 1666 Fire destroyed the Hall, and thereafter the Glaziers met variously at Loriners' Hall, the Queen's Arms Tavern, St Paul's Churchyard, the Baptist Head Coffee House in Aldermanbury and the Half Moon Tavern in Cheapside among other places. In 1749, new bye laws supplemented the charters of the 17th century, but, by 1845, the Company had little remaining control of its trade.

Thenceforth, it devoted its attention to promoting the use in particular of stained glass and leaded lights. Until 1917 it met in Cannon Street Hotel, and then in Painter-Stainers' Hall. In the '20s the Company ran classes for craftsmen in cooperation with the Carpenters, and exhibitions, medals and awards were instituted. In 1929 a scheme for a new Hall was launched; nine years later a Hall Building Committee was formed. Funds were donated in the post-war period, and in 1956 a supplemental Royal Charter was granted. Ten years later, the Glaziers' charities were augmented by the Glaziers Trust Fund for the restoration of stained glass in churches.

In 1968 the Sir Arthur Evans Travelling Scholarship for students in stained glass was inaugurated; in 1974 an annual prize competition for practical glaziers was started, in concert with Wandsworth School of Building. That same year the new Hall project was launched, and in 1975 the first reception was held there. The Hall is on a 150 year lease within Hibernia Chambers, London Bridge. The Company supports and encourages the use of stained, painted and engraved glass, with a design competition, and has recently formed a repository for good glass from redundant churches, with the ILEA and Church Commissioners, for subsequent re-use in new or existing churches, and secular buildings.

The Horners. Processors of raw horn and makers of horn goods, the Horners were first recorded when their ordinances were corrected in 1284 — probably not long after their first organisation as a Guild. In 1391 'the pour men of the litell crafte of Horneris' obtained new ordinances 'to distroye the dissentis grevawnas and unable werkis with inne the forseide Crafte And by cause to eschewe Anoyawnce and grevaunce to their neybouris and straingeris that hath be doon by cause of the gret noys that thei maken doyng her Craft . . .'. In 1455 these were augmented, principally to stop outsiders encroaching on the trade and to regulate the 'grete and corrupt stenche' involved when the Horners 'kutte eny hornes . . . in eny of the bocheries' — by banishing the initial processes to the suburbs. The Horners then congregated in Petticoat Lane. In 1465 the Guild's powers of search were extended to a 24 mile radius and to the fairs at Ely and Stourbridge.

Horn rather than glass was then used for glazing lanthorns and windows — when suitably heated, flattened, split and polished, it is transparent. It is also less fragile, and was then a good deal more cost-effective. Complete horns were used for drinking and blowing, and pressed horn was used for inkhorns, combs, spoons and other goods in general use. Horn was also sold at the Great Charlton Horn Fair, near Greenwich.

Following the Peasants' Revolt of 1381, landlord and Alderman John of Northampton set about challenging the hold of the ruling group in Common Council, with the support of smaller tradesmen, among them Horners. Walter Gerard and William Milward were two who joined the temporarily changed Council and backed Mayor John's reforms. Their elevation lasted two years, when John lost power and the old system returned. In 1391 they obtained new ordinances.

In 1368 the Bottlemakers, who worked in leather, had joined with the Horners; in 1373 they obtained separate powers. By the last quarter of the 15th century, both crafts were in dire straits — principally due to the increasing use of glass. They successfully petitioned for amalgamation. The merger worked well enough for fifty years but, by 1567, there was only one (leather) bottlemaker left in the City, outsiders were blatantly practising as Horners, and even the wardens quarrelled among themselves. By 1562 they were exempted from any contribution to poor relief after 'plainly declaring their small number and poverty', and in 1565 the Horners demanded 'that they myght clerely be severyd and dyschargid from the companye of botell-makers and remayne and be a sole compayne of themselfes'. The authorities refused to throw the Bottlemakers out but compromised, by the rare allowance that outsiders could be taken into the freedom by redemption — an effort to strengthen the dying trade. None came forward. The Horners pointed out: 'all the persons . . . that were skilled in botell makinge . . . are now utterly decayed and dead, save onely one'. They got no change out of the City, but time resolved the issue, for no Bottlemakers ever again emerged.

The 17th century brought a return to prosperity — for reasons peculiar to the Company. Most guilds had by then lost control of their sources of supply and were monopolised by the merchant classes. The Horners were ever craftsmen and, as small producers, never lost control of their corporate organisation to a ruling clique. They enforced the 1465 law that effectively forbade the export of raw horn from the City. In 1550 two merchants challenged this monopoly, which until then had left the control and profits of surplus horn in the Horners' hands, but the Guild won the day. In 1604 expansionist City merchants obtained the repeal of the 1465 Act. The Horners complained: '. . . Dealers . . . daylie buy up . . . the greate and cheif (sic) Stuffe of English Hornes . . .

carrie them beyond the Seas, and there make them into divers Workes, whereby . . . the Companie is growne soe poore and decayed as in short tyme, if remedie be not provided, they and theires shalbee utterlie undone . . .'. In 1610 Parliament virtually re-enacted the statute. Pressure remained, since the trade was enjoying a revival. 17th century lanterns used horn; snuff- and tobacco-boxes were increasingly popular, and the thinnest horn leaves found a new use — the glazing of 'horn books' for a growing educational demand.

In 1628 the Guild obtained Letters Patent empowering them to search ships or houses; in 1638 they were incorporated. Meanwhile, the trade faced another problem — wealthier members were buying up the increasingly scarce raw material before it reached the market. The Horners created a cooperative system which succeeded where other crafts had failed, and refined this with new ordinances in 1600, which prevented abuses and frauds within their own ranks. In 1604 they obtained premises to warehouse their bulk supplies and which doubled as a Hall, in what was later Wentworth Street. The Horners dealt with case after case of infringement, until in 1674 they had to go to law to maintain their buyers' control. They won on that score, but lost their export powers, since it was held that as a City body they could not claim powers beyond its limits.

The Charlton Fair had, by the 18th century become somewhat of a nuisance. Defoe wrote of 'the yearly collected rabble of mad people at Horn-Fair; the rudeness of which I cannot but think, is such as aught to be suppress'd . . . The mob indeed . . . take all kinds of liberties, and the women are especially impudent . . . giving themselves a loose to all manner of indecency and immodesty . . .'. Until 1745 the Company upheld its rights, but then the rot set in. Sheffield took over the horn trade; in 1770 cooperative buying was abandoned; in 1780 apprentices were few and far between; in 1789 the Hall was leased and the plate sold. For the next hundred years the Horners simply met twice a year, elected their officers, spent their Hall rent, and dined. Unlike other Companies, they had no Livery, so could not involve themselves in City politics.

In 1846 they obtained a Grant of Livery. Recovery was slow. The Clerk, George Henderson, was against any increase in the Livery up to the permitted sixty. In 1879 the Hall was sold. Then the tide turned with a horn exhibition in 1882, which attracted 7,000 and was supported by the Queen. In 1929 a charitable fund was established. The Livery was increased by several steps to 450.

Today the Company has a close association with the plastics industry and with the British Plastics Federation, presents an annual Horners Award for design and two scholarships, and an annual Plastics Address is given under its auspices.

The Farriers. The farrier *(ferrier)* is traditionally a shoeing smith and one who treats the ailments of horses. In 1356 the Fellowship of Farriers was first formally recognised, when two 'the most sufficient men and best knowing' were given powers to oversee and govern the trade. In 1674 the Guild of Farriers was incorporated as the Worshipful Company of Farriers and required to increase the number of skilled and expert farriers within the City and Westminster and a seven mile radius. It was given the responsibility 'of preserving of horses and preventing their destruction'.

The Farriers Registration Act of 1975, sponsored by the Company, gave it the statutory duty of securing adequate standards of those engaged in shoeing of horses, and of promoting the art and science of farriery and of making appropriate educational provision. Today its interests are countrywide.

Under the Company's Farriery Apprenticeship Scheme, over 250 youngsters have learnt the craft, and for eighty years the Company has organised examinations. In 1980 a Young Liveryman section was inaugurated. The Company administers its own Poor Fund and maintains the Farriers' Golfing Society. It supports the Farriers' Registration Council, and operates a Craft Committee. There are currently 125 apprentices training within the Farriery Apprenticeship Scheme, now administered by CoSIRA. The Company last year awarded some sixteen medals for horse shoeing competition winners. A Farriery Department at Herefordshire Technical College has the Company's support, and it has financed research by the Equine Research Station of the Animal

Health Trust. It makes grants to apprentices, and receives donations from various horse and show jumping organisations and the Horse Race Betting Levy Board.

The Paviors. Rammers have been used to consolidate roads since Roman times: *pavire* means to ram or beat, hence the term Pavior. Even today lightweight rammers are used to tamp pavement slabs. References dating back to 1302 mentioned 'old' ordinances for the craft of paving, and in that year four Paviors of London, John de Brimmesgrave, Robert de Harewe, Walter Stedeman and Nicholas de Brackele were 'sworn to make the pavement throughout the streets and places of the City only in the manner most commodious for the public . . .' but their office was no sinecure. Pigs and dogs wandered the streets and there was no proper drainage. In 1315-16 the King issued a writ requiring the authorities to repair the pavements, clean the streets and eliminate vagrant pigs.

In 1479 ordinances were obtained and a coat of arms was in use by 1483, though no Grant of Arms survives. In 1643 a lawsuit highlighted conflict between Paviors and Goldsmiths, since some London Paviors were freemen of the latter Company. By 1672, the Paviors included 35 Goldsmiths in their ranks. A year later the Company was incorporated by Royal charter, but the corporation was opposed to its implementation and a further attempt in 1724 met with a similar response.

London's streets were supposed to be made with stone bound with sand from the Thames, but often sand was taken from the Fleet at Bridewell, resulting in slimy surfaces in the wet, and dusty ones in the dry. Open drains carried surface water and sewage. After the Great Fire, little was done to improve matters until, a century later, granite setts formed the basis of a better road surface. After another century, asphalt made its appearance. Gradually the maintenance of the City's streets came under the Corporation's control and, by the mid-19th century, the Guild's influence had virtually ceased.

In 1889 the Guild turned the corner, and incorporation and successive grants of livery since 1900 have taken its numbers to 225. Six Paviors have held the office of Lord Mayor, three while Master. In 1928 the Company established an Educational Trust to advance education in highway engineering. A Chair was established in the subject at the Imperial College of Science and Technology in the University of London. This was discontinued in 1939, but in 1951 the surviving Trust provided a bursary for travel study. In 1955 a summer school was established by the Civil Engineering Dept of Birmingham University, and the Company supported the course and subsequently a lectureship — the Paviors' Lecture in Highway and Traffic Engineering. This has since become a Chair.

With the translation of the Northampton College to City University, the Trust became associated with highway education through the Civil Engineering Dept, funded study travel for the staff, and post-graduate bursaries. In 1975 the first Paviors' lecture was given at the University. These continue. The Company supports a Golfing Society, and has also been associated with units of the Territorials. It has recently adopted 'D' Company, 6/7th (Volunteer) Battalion, The Queen's Regiment.

ABOVE LEFT: the Founders' Arms and
RIGHT: Founder Richard Weoley's glass
goblet. (FR) BELOW LEFT: the Poulters' Arms
(PR) and RIGHT: those of the Coopers. (C)

GOD THE ONLY FOUNDER

REMEMBER YOUR OATH

LOVE AS BRETHREN

ABOVE LEFT: the Cooks' Arms. CENTRE: presentation Cup to the Army Catering Corps. RIGHT: the Cooks' Trophy. CENTRE LEFT: Chaucer's The Cook of London. BELOW LEFT: Caithness goblet presented to a student prizewinner by the Cooks and RIGHT: Cooks' Hall in 1739. (CK)

ABOVE LEFT: the Bowyers' Master's badge. (BY) RIGHT: Chorus of the Blacksmiths' Song. BELOW LEFT: the ancient Quest House and RIGHT: Lady Brabourne hands over the Blacksmiths' Cup on loan to the Company. (BS)

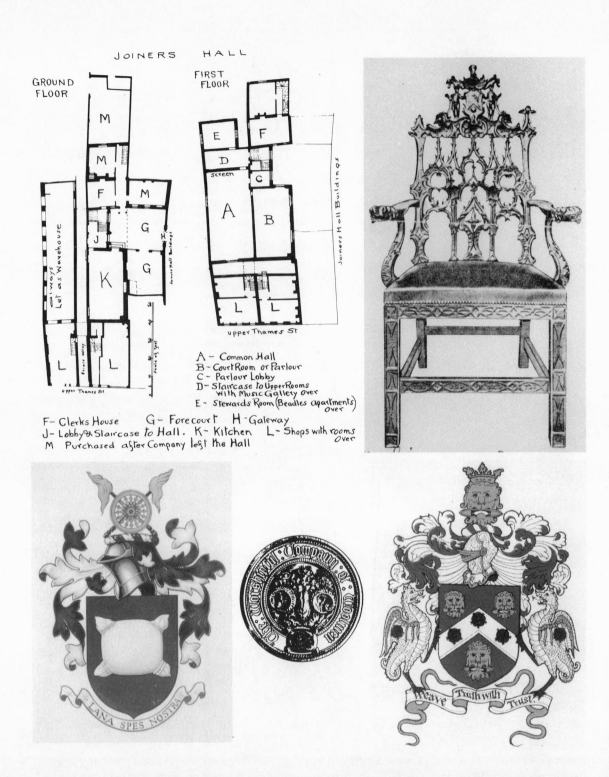

JOINERS HALL

GROUND FLOOR

FIRST FLOOR

Upper Thames St

A — Common Hall
B — Court Room or Parlour
C — Parlour Lobby
D — Staircase to Upper Rooms with Music Gallery Over
E — Stewards Room (Beadles apartments) Over
F — Clerks House   G — Forecourt   H — Gateway
J — Lobby & Staircase to Hall. K — Kitchen   L — Shops with rooms Over
M Purchased after Company left the Hall

ABOVE LEFT: the 18th century Joiners' Hall. RIGHT: 1754 Master's Chair, Joiners' Company. (J) BELOW LEFT: the Woolmen's Arms and CENTRE: their medal. (WM) RIGHT: the Weavers' Arms. (WV)

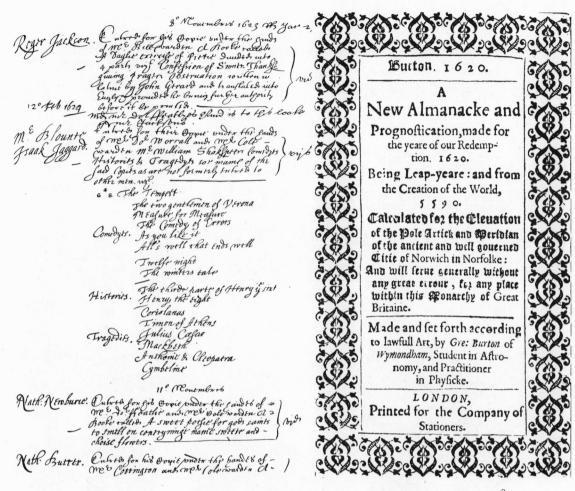

Burton. 1620.

A
New Almanacke and
Prognostication, made for
the yeare of our Redemp-
tion. 1620.

Being Leap-yeare : and from
the Creation of the World,
5590.

Calculated for the Eleuation
of the Pole Artick and Meridian
of the ancient and well gouerned
Citie of Norwich in Norfolke :
And will serue generally without
any great errour, for any place
within this Monarchy of Great
Britaine.

Made and set forth according
to lawfull Art, by *Gre: Burton* of
Wymondham, Student in Astronomy, and Practitioner
in Physicke.

LONDON,
Printed for the Company of
Stationers.

 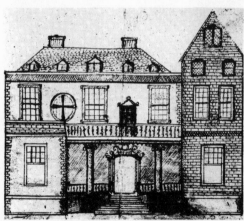 

ABOVE LEFT: Shakespeare's first folio registered with the Stationers and RIGHT: a 1620 Almanac. (SN)
BELOW LEFT: the Fruiterers' Arms. (FR) CENTRE: 18th century Turners' Hall, (TR) and RIGHT: the
Musicians' Arms. (MU)

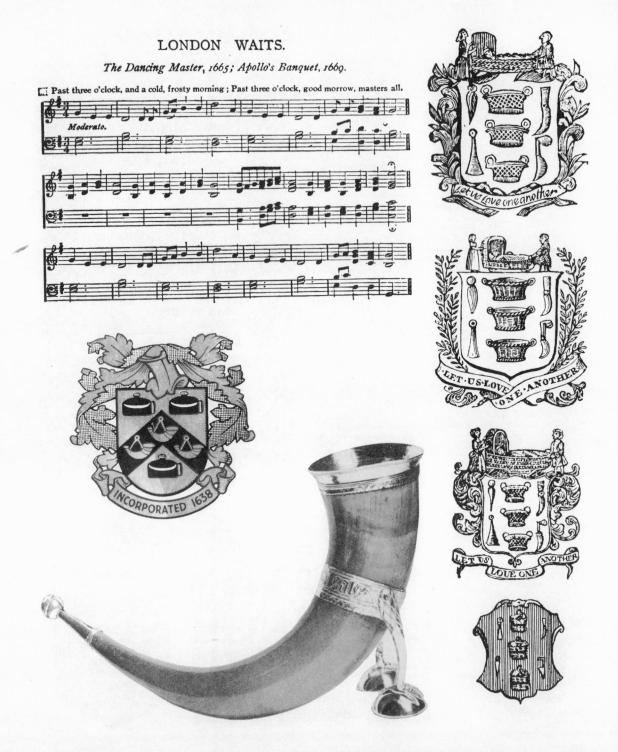

LONDON WAITS.

The Dancing Master, 1665; Apollo's Banquet, 1669.

Past three o'clock, and a cold, frosty morning; Past three o'clock, good morrow, masters all.

Moderato.

INCORPORATED 1638

Let us love one another

LET · US · LOVE · ONE · ANOTHER

LET US LOVE ONE ANOTHER

ABOVE LEFT: London Waits, 1665. (MU) RIGHT: Old Arms of the Basketmakers — top to bottom: 1721, 1827, 1772, 1750. (BT) LEFT: Horners' Arms and BELOW: a medieval drinking horn. (HR)

ABOVE LEFT: Farriers' ordinances of the 16th century, RIGHT: their arms. (FA) BELOW LEFT: 17th century Apothecary's shop, (AP) and RIGHT: the Shipwrights' Arms. (SH)

The Loriners. The business of a Loriner is to make bits, spurs, stirrups and the minor accessories of a horse's harness. In 1261 the *Liber Custumarum* records the Guild's first ordinances 'for the improvement and relief of the Mistery and the honour of the City and the abatement of all frauds and deceits'. In 1511 the Guild complained to the authorities that French bits were being imported 'whereby great hurt and destruction groweth' and again in 1570, an order was made, following a further complaint, regulating 'bits and other foreign wares touching that occupation'. Arms were granted in 1588. The Guild had a hall 'time out of mind' according to its later charter. It was in Postern Street, adjoining London Wall. The Company was incorporated in 1711 and met for the last time at its Hall in 1759 when the lease expired, though the building survived to 1792.

The Company administers a number of charitable trusts to the benefit of the aged and poor, and the Loriners Charitable Trust assists causes such as riding for the disabled. Each year the Company awards a bursary to the first-placed student in examinations in bitting, through the Rural Saddlers' Course at Cordwainers Technical College. Through the Pony Club it also awards the Loriners Equestrian Scholarship, which enables the winner to attend a Pony Club Riding Instructor's Course.

Today the trade is exclusively centred at Walsall. A bridle is presented annually to the winner of the King's Cup at the International Horse Show at Wembley and the Loriners Cup is to be reintroduced at the Combined Services Equitation Association annual Horse Show. A Trade Liaison Committee is maintained. The Company traditionally presents a bridle and bit to members of the Royal Family on their coming of age.

The Apothecaries. The Apothecaries originated within the Grocers' Company. The medical profession emerged slowly. The priest-physician was the historic medical man. In 1518 the Physicians were incorporated by Henry VIII as a College. The surgeons were then merely craftsmen of the knife, incorporated in 1540. The Spicer or Pepperer, later *Apothecarius*, administered drugs, spices, perfumes and sweetmeats in Royal palace or great household. He would dispense to the physician's order. The Apothecaries, seeking regulation of their interests, joined the Grocers, who imported and sold their drugs, spices and compounds. The grocer-apothecary became a special case within that guild. In 1525 they were recorded as a separate body, and two years earlier, Henry VIII decreed 'th'apothecaryes maye be swore and upon a payne commaunded that they shall not serve any byll (prescription) of any physicians not examyned and approved by the College'. They obtained powers of search in 1540 jointly with the College. In 1607 they were recognised as separate but within the Grocers, and in 1614, led by Dr Gideon de Laune, they petitioned for a charter. The following year, with Sir Francis Bacon's support, James I saying 'Grocers are but merchants, but the business of an Apothecary is a Mistery, wherefore I think it fitting that they be a Corporation of themselves' they seemed set to succeed. But some of their number preferred the status of the great Grocers' Company, and they had to wait until 1617 to achieve their incorporation. Though recorded for a century as a Company, they were chartered, as they remain to this day, The Society of Apothecaries.

Officially the guardians of the quality of drugs, the Apothecaries invevitably found themselves treating the poor, 'unable or unwilling to fee a leech or a physician', and this led to conflict with the College.

In 1634 Nicholas Culpepper was apprenticed to the Master of the Company. He set up as a physician without further qualification and pioneered popular 'self-help' medicine, with his famous *Culpepper's Complete Herbal*. He infuriated the physicians. They and the authorities successfully restricted the Apothecaries' activities, and the dispute continued until the Privy Council investigated the Apothecaries' charter. The two bodies compromised in 1635; 'to bring ourselves againe into the goode opinion of the College of Physicians upon whome wee doe depend'. The City then asked the King to revoke the charter, but he declined.

In 1632 the Society acquired Cobham House and adjoining property, including Blackfriars

Theatre in Playhouse Yard, paying £1,800 in two instalments. The Hall was consumed in 1666 but rebuilt by 1671. Meanwhile, in 1630 a Grant of Livery was achieved. Their coat of arms had been granted in 1617. In 1673 the Society rented four acres at Chelsea for a physic garden in which to grow indigenous and imported plants for their medical properties and to supply their laboratory established in 1623 and subsequently joined by another, to research and manufacture chemical drugs — originally the products of alchemy. These laboratories laid the foundation of the later great commercial houses, such as Allen and Hanbury and Savory and Moore. From the mid-18th century the Society was able to form and purchase shares in 'Navy Stock', due to its Royal monopoly of medicinal requirements for the Navy. This and the laboratory output provided finance and attracted entrepreneurs, which stood the Society in good stead. The laboratory stayed in production until 1922.

The Society's first gardener, John Watts, may have initiated the English greenhouse. In 1722 its landlord, Sir Hans Sloane, agreed a nominal rent and lease in perpetuity in return for a guarantee that annually, fifty plants would be grown and given to the Royal Society until 2,000 varieties had been achieved. The garden flourishes still under a charitable trust. Sloane introduced Philip Miller as gardener, and he authored *The Gardener's Dictionary,* hosted Linnaeus the botanist, and exported cotton seeds to Georgia, thus fathering the US cotton plantations which led to slavery and the American Civil War. Another gardener, Robert Fortune, subsequently introduced Chinese tea plants to India, thus starting the international tea trade.

Meanwhile, the conflict with the Physicians flared again in the reign of Charles I, when the Physicians sought to restrict Apothecaries from dispensing drugs other than by their prescription. The Civil War intervened, the Physicians mostly fleeing London, while the Apothecaries remained and embraced the Parliamentarian cause. By the Restoration, they were more influential and more affluent. The Society now suggested that its members should practise medicine at night or when physicians were unavailable. The Physicians sought to abolish their monopoly to dispense drugs. They compromised, and then the Plague struck. Again the Physicians largely left the City, and the following year, the Great Fire forced both groups to flee.

In the aftermath, the Apothecaries rebuilt their Hall and consolidated, but the Physicians found themselves in financial difficulties. A pamphlet war erupted. The dispute continued until Richard Mead and other Fellows of the College started the practice of coffee-house consultations with the Apothecaries, thus shaping the future of modern medical practice. In 1695, the College established a dispensary for the sick poor which lasted until 1725. Thereafter the Apothecaries provided a special shop in each of the newly founded voluntary hospitals in the City.

In 1701 William Rose, Apothecary, was successfully sued for treating a butcher called Seale, without the intervention of a Physician. The House of Lords reversed the decision in 1703, holding that it was against custom and the public interest to prevent advice and treatment by Apothecaries. Thus was the College monopoly at last broken. The qualified Apothecary could now practise medicine and dispense remedies, though a century would elapse before he could charge for the former. Thus arose the dispensing doctor of today — the product of an historic City Livery Company.

The pharmaceutical Apothecaries remained the majority within the Society until 1748, when the original monopoly of compounding prescriptions and selling drugs was lost. Unqualified chemists and druggists emerged, and in 1774 the Society limited its membership to medical practitioners. In 1841 the chemists, druggists and pharmaceutical apothecaries formed the Pharmaceutical Society of Great Britain. After the Apothecaries' Act of 1815 the Society and the College worked in harmony. With the Medical Act of 1858, the Apothecaries left their shops and became 'proper doctors'. By 1873 the Society had encouraged the formation of forty-three medical schools in provincial hospitals, effectively extending medical practice across the Nation.

In 1865, Elizabeth Garrett-Anderson qualified through the Society — the first woman doctor and later the joint founder of the Royal Free Medical School and Hospital for Women. In 1947 the

Society first admitted women doctors as freemen. The Society was, from 1815 the first, and for fifty years the only professional body to evolve an organised system of education and qualification. The Act of 1858 established the General Medical Council, which took over the Society's disciplinary function. The Society then established a certificate in dispensing, since the formation of the NHS known as Technician in Pharmacy. Diplomas for post-graduates, scholarships, endowed lectureships and gold medals for scientific advances followed. The Society organises symposia, is represented on the principal medical bodies, and in 1959 founded the Faculty of the History of Medicine and Pharmacy. Among famous Apothecaries was John Keats, the poet, who only practised for one year after qualifying.

The Society's Hall remains largely as it was rebuilt after 1666, virtually escaping the air raids of the last war. Today the Society is unique among City Companies as within Medical Corporations. It remains a craft guild but is dedicated to a learned profession. It continues to license medical practitioners and dispensers. Its toast reflects its purpose: 'The Worshipful Society of Apothecaries of London; may it flourish root and branch bringing help and health to all, till time ceases'.

The Shipwrights. The Brotherhood or Fraternity of St Simon and St Jude was established in the 13th century beside the Thames below London Bridge. In 1387 it first appeared in the Roll of Apprentices as the Free Shipwrights, and obtained ordinances in 1428 and again in 1483, with powers of search and supervision and the obligation to use good timber and to be workmanlike. In 1380 the hamlet of Ratcliff was the home of seamen, and John Philpot, a former Mayor, proposed to erect towers on the river banks to protect the King's ships and the City. Common Council acquired London Field (south of Stepney Station), and Ratcliff became the gateway to the Port of London. Ratcliff prospered, and Stow recorded in 1598 'that of late years Shipwrights, and, for the most part, other marine men have built many large and strong houses for themselves . . .'. Here the Shipwrights established their first Hall, on the east side of Butcher's Row, Ratcliff Cross.

As the sixteenth century drew to a close, another community of Shipwrights emerged at Redriff (Rotherhithe) on the Surrey riverside, who were not free of the existing guild, and it petitioned the Queen in 1578 for a charter of incorporation within the liberty of the Thames and adjoining area. The Free Shipwrights were then a Company by prescription and without incorporation. In 1612 the 'foreigners' succeeded — James I chartered them as The Art or Mystery of Shipwrights of Redriff, and thus started a bitter feud between the rival companies, as the upstarts tried to absorb the older body. The City supported the Free Shipwrights and granted new ordinances in 1620. Meanwhile, the citizens continually complained of the noise made by shipbuilders, and the risk of fire due to the substantial timber stocks held in the congested area below London Bridge. Gradually the Free Shipwrights took their business to Ratcliff, and by 1606 their Hall there was recorded in the will of a Deptford shipwright called John Addey. The claims of the two rival bodies persisted, with Samuel Pepys supporting the Redriff contingent, until 1684, when their charter was surrendered and cancelled.

In 1782 the Free Shipwrights obtained a Grant of Livery and, two years later, they took over the 'foreign' Shipwrights' coat of arms, together with its motto, 'Within the Ark Safe for Ever'. That same year the City authorities confirmed and ratified the acts, ordinances, bye laws and constitution of the 'Commonalty of the Ancient Fraternity or Brotherhood of Free Shipwrights of London'. In 1794 the Hall was destroyed by fire. Its site is now incorporated in the public gardens adjoining St James' Church, Ratcliff.

In 1808, Common Council required all Shipwrights to be freemen, and in 1830 the livery was enlarged. In 1877 the Company held an exhibition at Fishmongers' Hall of 285 model ships, and again in 1882, with 400 models. In 1888 it established classes in naval architecture at the Bow and Bromley Institute, to match similar facilities already in virtually every shipbuilding port except London. In 1920 the Royal Warrant formalised the Company's coat of arms, and in 1932 HM George VI was installed as Permanent Master — that office is now held by HRH The Prince Philip.

In 1927, with the then Board of Education and the Institution of Naval Architects, the Company helped inaugurate National Certificates in Naval Architecture, which are today awarded to successful students at technical colleges at both Ordinary and Higher Levels: outstanding students receive prizes from the Billmeir Shipwrights Educational Trust Fund administered by the Company. In 1947 the third model exhibition was held, at the RHS Halls at Westminster, with several thousand models. In 1952 HM The Queen became Patron of the Company.

For many years the Company has awarded grants to shipyard apprentices countrywide; the premier award-holder receives a silver medal presented by HM The Queen — they are known as Queen's Silver Medallists. With 500 Liverymen, the Shipwrights are one of the largest Livery Companies, and they limit their membership to those from the maritime industries — ship owners, builders, brokers, Naval personnel. Charitable interests include the Sea Cadets, the Royal National Lifeboat Institution and projects such as the ss *Great Britain*, Operation Drake and the Outward Bound Trust.

The Company has, since 1913, conferred its Honorary Freedom on the wives of Past Prime Wardens. It maintains standards of workmanship and design, through its contribution to the training of naval architects and shipwrights, and significantly, provides an impartial forum for all maritime interests, both traditional and contemporary.

The Spectacle Makers. The origin of spectacles is a matter of dispute, but the basic modern article had emerged in England in the 13th century; Chaucer refers to spectacles in *The Wyf of Bathe*. The poem, London Lyckpenny, c1400 also mentions them:
>'(In Westmynster Hall) neither rich nor yett poore
>Wold do for me ought, although I shold dye.
>Which seeing, I gat me out of the doore,
>Where Flemynges began on me for to cry,
>"Master, what will you copen or buy?
>Fyne felt hattes, or spectacles to reed?
>Lay down your sylver, and here you may speede".'

In 1422 no craft guild was listed, but some opticians were numbered within the ranks of the Brewers. A pair of riveted spectacles c1440 were recently recovered during excavations at Trig Lane of a medieval refuse dump. They were possibly imported from the Low Countries, or even perhaps made here by a Dutch craftsman. Paul van (de) Bessen of Suthwerk (sic) was active in 1458-9. The French had an organised guild by 1465, and Caxton's introduction of printing in 1476 must have stimulated a market in spectacles. The Haberdashers sold them in the City in the 15th century. German, Venetian and Spanish craftsmen organised themselves in the 16th and early 17th centuries.

In 1563 Thomas Newbery wrote for children:
>'All makers of Combs and forgers of lies,
>All Spectacle makers for dim sighted eyes'

in his list of important trades, and later added the line
>'I have spectacles made of fine burral glass'

In 1628, Robert Alt, Brewer, and fifteen other Spectacle Makers, twelve of them Brewers, petitioned successfully for a charter and in 1633 the new Company was incorporated, with powers throughout the Kingdom. Though the ordinances ratified in 1634 referred to a Hall, there is no independent evidence that one ever existed. The ordinances also ruled that frames should not be sold without glass or vice versa, and otherwise regulated the craft and trade. The Spectacle Makers survived the Stuart threat to their charter.

Innovators within the Company included Richard Reeves, who refined the compound microscope and John Marshall, who invented the modern method of working several lenses by one tool, which put London opticians ahead of their foreign counterparts. James Ayscough invented folding side pieces, and John Dolland and his son Peter pioneered optical instruments, while Peter may have made bifocal spectacles before Benjamin Franklin is reputed to have invented them.

Not all Spectacle Makers joined the Company; the 1666 fire dispersed the craft. The Master, John Turlington was patronised by Pepys, who recorded him as 'the great spectacle-maker'. Standards were diligently upheld. In 1671, for example, 'Mrs Elizabeth Bagnall Widdow, a wholesale Habre in her shop were found two and twenty of English Spectacles, these being all very badd both in the glasse and frames not fitt to be put to sale' and 'They are all seized . . . Condemned to be broken defaced and spoyled both glasse and frames the wch Judgement was executed accordingly in Canning Street on the remayninge parte of London Stone where the same were with a hammer broken all in pieces'. In 1679 William Boyce claimed to be expert in artificial eyes that turned in the socket — usually regarded as a much later development. In the early 18th century the Company faced considerable outside competition. Clockmakers made optical and mathematical instruments and also sold spectacles; others ground watch glasses, traditionally the preserve of the Company's craftsmen.

Spectacle makers in the 17th and 18th centuries were not slow to advertise. George III prohibited their projecting signs, and many of them advertised extensively in the papers of the time, often in robustly competitive terms: 'John Yarwell . . . who makes the famed true spectacles . . .' and '. . . Wildey and Brandeth . . . neither have, nor can make a telescope of two foot long, which will do as much as one of four foot, as they pretend'.

In 1756 John Berge was apprenticed to Peter Dolland, optician — the first recorded use of the term. It was his father, John Dolland, who pioneered the achromatic object glass, which removed the discoloration of images seen through optical glass at its edges, though Chester Moor Hall, a barrister, was the actual inventor. Peter Dolland won a lawsuit for infringement of the relevant patent after his father's death, because the judge ruled 'it was not the person who locked up his invention in his scrutoire that ought to profit by a patent . . . but he who brought it forth for the benefit of the public'. It was the same Dollond and his brother John who introduced brass draw tubes into their telescopes, thus making the hitherto fixed apparatus portable, and incidentally introducing the more general use of the term into the language..

By the end of the 18th century the spectacle maker had become an optician, and the skills involved had fragmented the original craft. In 1809 the Company achieved a Grant of Livery. From 1739 the Company, without a grant of arms, had used a seal in the form of a heraldic device, which was replaced in 1810. In 1813 the Company found itself in dispute with the Clockmakers again, over the admission of a mathematical instrument maker. The Clockmakers claimed Robert Bretel Bate for their Guild; he wanted to join the Spectacle Makers. The dispute rumbled on for over three years, when Bate was allowed to join the Company, became Master and invented the spring folding lorgnette.

The original charitable bequest of John Yarwell was augmented in 1862 by that of Sir William Tite. In 1873 the Company made its first educational grant to the Society of Fine Arts. In 1898 the first award of optical apparatus to a deserving institution was made. With the independent founding in 1895 of the British Optical Association, in 1897 the first professional examinations were inaugurated. These led to acrimonious dispute with the BOA, finally settled by 1907. Henceforth opticians qualified through one or other of the two bodies. Research grants followed. In 1958 legislation established a statutory register of opticians and a General Optical Council — the Company was recognised as one of the bodies whose examinations qualified for registration. In 1949 the Company finally achieved a Grant of Arms.

By 1981 the Company, the BOA and the Scottish Association of Opticians combined to form a single examining body — The British College of Ophthalmic Opticians, and the Company has jointly sponsored the Faculty of Dispensing Opticians. A technicians' course is run under the aegis of the Company at the City and East London College. The Company is now the only organisation that provides common ground for all the differing interests within the optical world, for its 4,000

Freemen include ophthalmic and dispensing opticians, contact lens practitioners, academics, frame and lens manufacturers and ophthalmologists. An Optical Liaison Committee has been formed to reinforce this special situation, and all Freemen also belong to the Spectacle Makers' Society, which has taken over the social side of the Company's activities. The Company also administers its modest charitable funds for City, optical profession and industry and for needy members and their families.

The Clockmakers. Hourglass and sundial preceded the mechanical clock, the first of which appeared at the end of the 13th century, though the Chinese had astronomical water-driven clocks of wood, c725. Watchmaking originated in Europe in the early 16th century, becoming a native craft here towards the end of that century. In 1600 clockmaking was the preserve of the Blacksmith. Thereafter English watchmaking led the world. In 1622 there were sixteen clock and watchmakers in London, and their living was under pressure from Huguenot refugees. In 1627, the clockmaker freemen of the Blacksmiths tried unsuccessfully to persuade their Guild to oppose the French incomers. The Clockmakers then sought their own charter. In 1631 they succeeded, gaining powers to control 'the horological trade in the City of London and within ten miles thereof...' but without the privilege of obliging clock and watchmaking freemen of other companies to join theirs. In 1696 they petitioned the authorities to force apprentices to join, once they had served their time. The Blacksmiths strenuously opposed the move as diminishing their authority.

The Blacksmiths contended it was 'well knowne that they were the original and proper makers of clocks . . . and that no clockmaker can finish any clock without the distinct and peculiar workmanship of ye Smith . . .', but the Clockmakers pointed out that their bye laws of 1632 gave them sole responsibility for 'trading in clocks, watches, alarums, sun-dials, case making, graving and mathematical instrument making in any nature of material whatsoever...'. Both Companies agreed that 'great Church Clockmakers of Iron' were the preserve of the Blacksmiths. The Blacksmiths won the day, until 1765, when Common Council ruled that all clockmakers should take the Freedom of their own Company.

In 1813 the Clockmakers were in dispute with the Spectacle Makers over mathematical instrument making, resolved by a compromise ruling by the authorities. In 1671 the Company achieved a Grant of Arms. These were redrawn in 1967. The Company's motto is 'Tempus rerum imperator' — 'Time is the ruler of all things'.

In 1954 the Company instituted the Tompion Gold Medal for outstanding horological achievement, in memory of Thomas Tompion, the father of English clock and watchmaking, who was Master in 1704. Recipients have been W.H. Shortt in 1954 for inventing the Shortt Free-pendulum clock, (in 1925) for thirty years the standard observatory time-keeper; in 1955, W.A. Marrison for work in the development of the quartz-crystal clock; Dr Louis Essen in 1957 for development of the Essen Ring-Quartz-crystal oscillator and the first atomic clock of high precision, and in 1963, Max Hetzel for development of the tuning-fork as a time standard for the wristwatch.

In 1813 the Company founded a horological library and a collection of timepieces and in 1873 these were deposited with Guildhall. They include John Smith's *Horological Dialogues,* 1675, the first English book on clocks and watches; Micheli's *Della Dichiaratione de l'horologio di Mantova,* 1574, the first printed book devoted to a clock; Mary, Queen of Scots' silver skull watch; a star-shaped watch made by the Company's first Master, David Ramsay, watchmaker to James I; 18th century manuscripts of James and John Harrison, carpenters of Barrow-on-Humber, the most important pioneers of precision time-keeping in the world, and books, clocks and watches representing every facet of the science and art of timekeeping to the present day.

The Glovers. In 1349 the existing guild of Glovers was formally recognised, when ordinances laid down that no glover should sell his wares by candlelight on pain of forfeiting the wares, 'seeing that folks cannot have such good knowledge by candlelight as by daylight, whether the wares are made of good leather or of bad, or whether they are well and lawfully, or falsely, made'. In 1498 the Glovers and Pursers sought amalgamation for economic reasons and, in 1502, the Glovers-Pursers were merged with the Leathersellers. They regained their independence in 1639, when they achieved a charter of incorporation and a common seal. They then obtained power to purchase property as a Hall, and were at the same time obliged to pay the Crown forty shillings annually in perpetuity 'for the aforesaid incorporation — at the Feast of the Annunciation of the Blessed Virgin Marie', an unusual obligation, and one which still stands.

Queen Victoria confirmed and ratified the original charter by an Inspeximus Charter, in 1898 — the only one of its kind granted during her reign. In 1882 the Hall in Beech Lane, Cripplegate, was beyond the Company's means and was relinquished, and the Company itself came within an ace of surrendering its independence.

Queen Victoria accepted a pair of gloves on her coronation, and the custom has continued to the present day, while gloves have also been presented to Royal brides. Since the 13th century, an embroidered glove has been presented to the Sovereign at the Coronation ceremony, a right previously held by the Manor of Farnham Royal, Bucks, and then, that of Worksop, Notts. This privilege was transferred to the Company in 1953.

Today, a third of the Company is active in the gloving industry. This takes in all processes from raw material and production to design, wholesaling and retailing, covering all gloves, whether fashion, industrial or special purpose. 'Charity through gloves' includes collecting 2,000 single gloves annually for distribution to single-handed people through the Department of Health; researching the ideal glove for use with wheelchairs; annual awards of framed gloves at Stoke Mandeville Stadium for the Disabled to the fencing and relay teams; presentation and maintenance of boxing gloves for the twenty seven Regional Final Boxing Bouts of the National Association of Boys' Clubs; prizes to the trade for marketing and display; long service certificates; exhibiting the Company's Spence Collection of gloves from the 15th to 19th centuries; adoption of the 21st SAS Regiment (Artists), to whom is presented canoes for the Devizes-Westminster race, and gymnastic equipment. The first Golden Glove award was made to Sir Derek Ezra of the National Coal Board for high performance in buying British gloves. There are also a number of working committees covering aspects of the trade and Company activities. The Company's motto is 'True hearts and warm hands'.

The Feltmakers. The Hatters and Furriers united with the Haberdashers in 1501, and the Feltmakers were effectively among those original Hatters, whose origins perhaps stem from the Hurrers and Milinars (milliners), whose interests were served when the Haberdashers separated from the Mercers in 1488. In 1576 the Feltmakers sought their independence, but the Haberdashers opposed the move. In 1604 the Feltmakers achieved incorporation, were re-incorporated in 1667, chartered again in 1669, and in 1772.

In 1650 the Feltmakers were admitted a Free Company of the City and in 1733 obtained a Grant of Livery. From 1730 to 1802 they met at Pewterers' Hall, Lime Street and at Guildhall thereafter, until 1917. They currently meet at Tallow Chandlers' Hall. The Livery was increased from 60 to 120 in 1787, and more recently to 350.

The felt trade largely comprises hatters, a currently reduced industry, due to modern fashion trends against headgear. Its two principal centres are Luton and Stockport. The Master of the Company wears a tricorn hat of 18th century design, and annually presents the Lord Mayor with his ceremonial hat.

The Company has in modern times maintained more than one longstanding family link with its past. Sir Hugh Wontner, Master 1962 and 1973 is the descendant of Thomas, a hatter in the

Minories in 1771; in 1792 hatter Miller Christie was elected Master: Lt Col John Christie-Miller's family is still in the trade, and he and Sir Hugh met for the first time when admitted to the Company, to find their ancestors had served as consecutive Masters. The grandfather of J.L. Bowler, Master in 1982, gave his name to the hard hat.

The Company gives an annual research medal for the best paper about the felt trade, and encourages arts and crafts in feltwork. It also administers several charitable funds, such as Macham's, King's Gift and the Mills McKay Memorial Fund, for the poor and elderly. Recent bequests or gifts include that of Alfred John Healey, Master 1946-7, and of Arthur E. Hemens, from whose gift of retail property in Consett, income funds the Feltmakers Charitable Foundation. Past Master Edward George Walpole-Brown left funds to be reinvested and accumulated for ten years. The Millinery Trade Benevolent Association supports the Feltmakers Charitable Foundation, and raises funds to support former millinery workers in need.

The Framework Knitters. The Guild's origin is unusual. An Elizabethan Master of Arts of St John's College, Cambridge called Lee fell in love with a country maiden, who seemed more interested in knitting her hose than courtship. Lee set about making knitting needles redundant by inventing the first frame for mechanical knitting. Whether this solved his romantic problem is not known. Oxford University disputes the story, and claims the invention for an Oxonian, who made his frame to enhance his wife's knitting output. The Cambridge tale is generally the accepted version, but Lee unsuccessfully sought Queen Elizabeth's interest, and turned instead to Henry IV of France. That monarch invited him to exploit his looms at Rouen, but the King's assassination left Lee without support, and he died in penury in Paris. His descendants and their associates established framework knitting in London, Godalming and Nottingham.

Good Queen Bess did, however, acquire a pair of silk stockings. These were presented by a framework knitter called Mrs Montague, in the presence of Burleigh and Leicester, and she assured her Queen they were as good as cloth hose. Leicester, flatteringly, said '. . . they are as fit for the fairies to wear and your gracious Majesty is all beautiful, in fact a fairy queen wanting but this gossamer wear to perfect fairy attire'. Burleigh suggested the Queen should stick to cloth hose, especially as she had passed sumptuary laws forbidding extravagant dress. He also suggested 'these things could not by any possibility fit'. The Queen tried the stockings successfully, enjoining secrecy; but the story of her stockings soon spread.

By the middle of the 17th century the industry was so well organised that Cromwell in 1657 granted a charter of incorporation — one of two in that period. The petitioners attributed the method of knitting 'silk stockings or other work in an engine or frame' to William Lee of Calveton, Nottingham. On the Restoration, Charles II ignored the Cromwellian charter and created 'The Society of the Art or Mistery of Framework Knitters of the Cities of London and Westminster and the Kingdom of England and Dominion of Wales' — their second charter. The new charter conferred nationwide powers of search and supervision. Subsidiary Courts were established at Nottingham and at Leicester, where the Company's powers were enforced by deputies. The Company prospered for a century, until Parliament challenged its regulations as restraining trade. In 1809, a lawsuit restricted the Company's control to its own members, and allowed outsiders to engage in the industry without interference. In 1821 the Company's Red Cross Street Hall was sold and in 1861 its plate went the same way, to support its almshouses, established long since.

In 1906 the almshouses were sold, land purchased and the Cottage Homes built at Oadby, near Leicester. There are now twenty four homes and the Corah Hall for the residents' entertainment.

Most of the Livery of 225 is actively involved in the industry; annual gold and silver medals are awarded to students in the examinations of the City and Guilds of London Institute, in the manufacture of hosiery and knitted goods.

The Needlemakers. The needle dates back to the Stone Age, and was made of bone splinters from the reindeer horn. Initially a well pointed awl, there evolved first the hook, then the eye. Most needles of modern type were evolved in the Bronze Age, and the modern needle finally developed in the Iron Age. In the Middle Ages, monasteries fashioned needles for their immediate areas but, on the Tudor dissolution, a needlemaking community emerged in London.

During the Protectorate, the Needlemakers gained their incorporation — with the Framework Knitters, the only Companies to do so. With the Restoration they were chartered afresh in 1664. Their powers included condemnation of needles not 'made and wrought of good studd and materials without fraud or deception' and rights of search within a ten mile radius of the City. No woman except a Master's widow was permitted to follow the craft. The industry was then centred on London Bridge, and the Company's Hall believed to be on the Bank of England corner of Three Needles (Threadneedle) Street. In 1758 the houses on London Bridge were demolished and the industry gradually moved, first to Long Crendon, Bucks and thence to Redditch, Worcs, where it is currently concentrated.

This promoted a serious decline in the Company's prosperity and activities until, in 1873, it was all but extinct. Revival in 1874 saw an increase in the Livery, and again a year later. In 1929 it was further increased to 250. In 1876 the Company set about establishing new links with its old trade. Prizes were awarded for inventions, specimen tools and needles. Now proficiency certificates are issued, and medals and prizes awarded to apprentices for needle tool-making or machine construction, on the recommendation of the Needlemakers' Association.

The Master in 1896-7 was The Duke of Teck and in 1919 the future George VI was elected to the Company. The Company's charitable funds are modest, but it has established an Endowment Fund, and it actively supports the City and Guilds of London Institute and the City University, while making donations to charities and schools controlled by the Corporation.

The Gardeners. In 1345 the Gardeners were first recognised as a Guild, permitted to sell produce 'where they have been wont in times of old in front of the Church of St Austin at the side of the gate in St Paul's Churchyard' (St Augustine's, Watling Street). In 1605 the Guild was incorporated by charter, and two years later its ordinances were approved and a Grant of Livery achieved. In 1616 a further charter conferred powers of search within six miles of the City. In 1617 the Company sought admission to the Freedom — without success. In 1632 and 1634 the Gardeners' rights were reinforced. In 1649 they had large markets outside the City, and employed 1,500 men, women and children, apart from 400 apprentices. In 1659, the Company was admitted to the Freedom, and leased its standing in the Herb Market in St Paul's Churchyard, but the markets were moved to Aldersgate Street the following year. In 1675 the Company was allotted sixty stations in the Gracechurch Street Market. In 1891 the Court of Aldermen at last recognised the Grant of Livery. A year later the first scholarship was instituted. In 1895 the first pension was endowed.

In 1903 the Company's Charitable Fund was inaugurated, and in 1905 the Company's arms were recognised by Royal warrant. In 1908 the Company presented flowers and garden produce to the Lord Mayor — an annual presentation, maintained ever since, and in 1911 the Company first visited Holland to study the economics of horticulture. That year, Queen Mary accepted a coronation bouquet. In 1913 the Company visited Belgium, and a year later, France. In 1915 the livery was increased to 160. In 1918 a member of the Court was appointed to the Council of the Chamber of Horticulture, and a year later, following a visit to Belgium, the Company raised £3,000 to offset the devastation caused there by the first World War.

In 1920 the Livery was again raised to 250, which led to a question in the Lords concerning the 'manufacture of fagot-votes'. A tradition of presenting Royal wedding bouquets was perpetuated on the marriage of the then Lady Elizabeth Bowes-Lyon (now HM Queen Elizabeth the Queen Mother) and this has continued since. Visits continued to other countries, and in 1933 the

Honorary Freedom was conferred on Princess Mary. In 1937 the Company presented the Royal bouquet to HM the Queen (now the Queen Mother) and thereafter, as with Queen Mary, the Company has made an annual presentation on the anniversary of the coronation.

In 1942 the Company, together with the National Allotments Society, set up a circulating library managed by the Society which, within two years, comprised over 500 books. In 1949 a City Window Box and Gardens Competition was inaugurated and a year later, the Company paid an official visit to Holland, when Queen Juliana accepted the Honorary Freedom. From 1950 to 1962 the Company awarded competition cups to local horticultural societies within six miles of St Paul's, with grants to their prize funds. In 1951 the Company presented three bronze heads for the fountains in the Corporation's newly created St Paul's Garden, and gave two cups to the National Association of Almshouses, for competition among almshouse gardens.

In 1952 a bouquet was presented to HM Queen Elizabeth II which she carried in the coronation procession in Westminster Abbey and anniversary bouquets have been presented ever since. In 1954 Her Majesty accepted a bouquet for a state drive to the Mansion House. The London Non-Teaching Hospitals Gardens Competition was inaugurated in 1955, and the Company founded a £100 scholarship at Wye College. In 1959 the London Church Gardens Competition was started. In 1962 King Baudouin was made an Honorary Freeman; the following year HRH the Duke and Duchess of Gloucester accepted the Honorary Livery and Honorary Freedom respectively.

In 1971 the then President of Portugal became an Honorary Freeman, and that same year the Company planted the first official garden of the Company in the City in modern times — the Southern Garden of St Dunstan in the East. King Gustav VI Adolf of Sweden became an Honorary Freeman.

From time to time the Company has continued to pay official visits to foreign countries, being received by Royal Heads of State, and also on numerous occasions entertaining Royalty on their visits to this country. Members of the Royal Family have received the Master, Wardens and Clerk on several occasions, and have attended their functions, particularly in 1977 when HM the Queen received a replica of her wedding bouquet on her 25th wedding anniversary, and when HM Queen Elizabeth the Queen Mother attended the spring Court Dinner that year. In 1974 the Company resolved to accept the admission of ladies to the Livery; HRH Princess Alice, Duchess of Gloucester, became the first lady Liveryman of the Company.

In 1975 Queen Fabiola of Belgium accepted the Honorary Freedom. In 1976 the Company entertained delegates to the International Rose Conference on their centenary meeting — a reflection of the long-standing practice of associating the Company with such international organisations. In 1977, the Master planted a magnolia in the garden of Clarence House, to commemorate the Silver Jubilee.

The Tin Plate Workers (alias Wire Workers). The craft of wireworking was first recorded in 1451, when the Wireworkers and Pinners joined the Girdlers' Company 'forasmuch as they would not otherwise be able to maintain their charges in the City'. Stow records 'that in Edward IV's reign, all basketmakers, wiredrawers, and other Foreigners were permitted to have shops only in the Manor of Blanch Apleton at the eastern end of what is now known as Fenchurch Street' adjoining the (old) Hall of the Ironmongers. In 1639 the Pinners seceded. Under the Girdlers' charter, the wireworkers and plateworkers regulated their trades, though these ordinances were not implemented until 1682. Wireworking and plateworking meanwhile extended westwards to the Crooked Lane area, to the north of London Bridge, and adjoining Fishmongers' Hall. Many Plateworkers joined the Fishmongers. The Crooked Lane men were known as 'tinmen' and, because domestic tinware was cheaper than pewterware, found themselves in constant dispute with the Girdlers and Pewterers. Many Plateworkers and Wireworkers were free of other companies.

As the craft developed and became more prosperous, led by Thomas Aris, Ironmonger, its exponents decided in 1668 to form a trade society of Plateworkers and Wireworkers, plate for the first time taking precedence over wire. In 1670 they petitioned for approval of their ordinances: 'The humble Petition of the Tyne Plate Workers, alias Wyre Workers within our Citty of London, and the parts nere adjacent, that for the better ordering and government of ourselves and others using the Trade, arte or mistery in the Cittys of London and Westminster, Burrough of Southwarke, and fyve myles compasse thereof, being now increased to a great number, and for the better reforming and suppressing of the falsityes and deceipts now commonly used and practiced in the saide arte, trade or mistery to common abuse and damage of our subjects'.

The Company was incorporated by Letters Patent that year, with City approval, and the following year was made free of the City: 'body politic and corporate, in deed and name with continuance perpetual succession for ever . . . of the art and mistery of Tynne Plate Workers, al's Wyre Workers . . .'. Standards of workmanship, materials and design were defined and enforced. Price lists were issued, that of 1760 including lamp and candle holders, with 'Lamps, large, three spout 6/- per doz'. The arms first appeared in 1679, featuring three spout lamps without lids, and a lanthorn, demonstrating the Company's association with the Horners, who glazed the lamps, and with the Tallow Chandlers, who supplied the candles. In 1690 the three companies supplied the lighting for Cornhill. In 1707 the Company petitioned Parliament for relief from an increase of 700% in the tariff on 'single and double plates'.

In the 1870s, the Company's Master, George Offor, a leading figure in the electrical trade, advocated street lighting by electricity, and this was introduced in Sydenham in 1878 — the foundation of the Company's association with the electrical industry. Today about half the Livery come from the London area, for since the 17th century, when its Freemen practised the craft in Worcester, Northampton and York, the Company's trade has been nationwide.

This century, the Company has promoted technical education, and training of apprentices in the tinplate, wireworking and electrical industries. It sponsors an annual competition for production of an original example of tinplate craft and makes an annual award of £1,000 to the City of London Freemen's School, to enable the Headmaster to help needy parents of deserving pupils. Liverymen today represent the wire and steel industries as well as electrics and electronics.

The Wheelwrights. The origin of the wheel goes back to prehistoric times, and the earliest known example is of 5000 BC. Spoked wheels evolved by 2000 BC, and Homer referred to wheelwrights in 1000 BC. Their work often extended beyond the wheel to shafts and axles, and even entire vehicles. In 1277 the City ruled that 'no cart serving the City, bringing water, wood, stones, etc. be shod with iron' but in 1485 Common Council ordered that all cartwheels should be shod 'with flat nails' to protect the pavements. In 1630 the Wheelwrights and Coachmakers together petitioned the authorities for incorporation. The Court of Aldermen were in no hurry to comply, and in their report of 1631 they mentioned 'many frauds and deceits are daily used . . . much young and unseasoned timber . . . And we find also that many green wheels are vended by Bargemen . . . they may have power given them to make reasonable ordinances . . . provided that the Blacksmiths be not restrained to sett on strakes and other iron works upon the wheels . . .'. Another committee sat in 1632 to 'hear and consider of the said petition' but nothing came of this until a petition submitted independently of the Coachmakers was accepted, and the Wheelwrights were chartered in 1670. The City endorsed the new charter, but without Grant of Livery.

Women were admitted from the start, some of them contributing to the £300 needed for the costs of incorporation. Apprentices were bound, to learn other trades as well as that of the wheelwright. The first bye laws were approved in 1670 and, in 1671, the Company conducted its first searches. In 1681 it was decided that 'Every Cart from henceforth to be made for the said use, shall be in bodie of the same Cart between the staves thereof four feet of Assise and in lengths from the fore end of the shaft to the outside of the hinder Earebred thirteen foot four inches and noo more' and '. . . noe Axletree of any such Cart exceed three foot nine Inches in length under the bodies of the said Carts'. Other rules specified wheel design, and in 1688 Thomas Girlder was fined 10s 'for his rotten wheels'.

Even Past Masters were not exempt from the rigours of the Company's searches: in 1692 four of them were fined '2s. a peece' for 'dishing' their wheels beyond the allowed tolerances. In 1679 the Company accused its own officers of operating a price cartel.

By the 18th century the Company was actively involved in charity, revenue from the Poor Box coming from admission contributions and voluntary payments. In 1771 Samuel King pleaded 'extream low condition' and was granted a guinea and told 'not to apply again'. In 1773 the Company achieved a Grant of Livery, which was increased to 150 in 1792. The Company's freemen then numbered 'upwards of nine hundred'.

During the French Wars, the Company, already determined to economise, resolved in 1798 'that during the War all Dinners except that of the Master in October be discontinued and that £100 be paid yearly into the Bank for the Defence of the Country against Invasion'. The dinner of 1780 for 26 at the Paul's Head cost 4s, but the Summer Feast came to £21 1s overall, including 'Cold Tongue Bread Beer . . . Ham & Dressing . . . Haunch Venison . . . 6 Fowls & Dressing &c . . . 2 Geese & Dressing &c . . . 2 Ducks & do . . . Beans Peas & French Beans Butter &c . . . 3 Cooling Tarts Cream'd 1 do. plain . . . 2 Rasberry Tarts . . . Custard . . . Greens Carrots &c . . . Bread & Beer . . . Apricots Rasberries Cherrys Currants . . . Porter & Ale . . . Tea & Coffee . . . Brandy & Water . . . Cyder . . . Arrack Punch . . . 5 Bottles Madeira . . . 9 Bottles Old Port . . . Lisbon & Mountain . . . Brandy Punch . . . Red port & Madeira Made to Negus . . . Lemon & Sugar . . . Tobbacco . . . Wax Lights . . .' and 10s 6d for the servants.

Costs continued to rise and, when income tax arrived in 1799, the Company tightened up on arrears of quarterage, while seeking new sources of income. One was to charge Liverymen who wished to be translated to other Companies. In 1794 Past Master David Davidson had to find £100 for the Poor Box to move across to the Fishmongers, and freemen were admitted from well outside the City, such as Ralph Wedgewood, son of Thomas Wedgewood, Potter, late of Burslem, Stafford, Joel Cadbury of Exeter, John Ogle Ogle (sic) of Yorkshire and Original Hayward, son of Original Hayward of Great Ealing, Middlesex.

Industrial unrest surfaced in 1724 when members of the ten-year-old Journeyman's Club were prohibited from serving on the Court. Ten years later some of the City's Journeymen Coach Wheelwrights demanded shorter hours and more pay. The Court refused, and took legal advice, whereupon the men went on strike, and the Company sought and obtained an indictment for conspiracy. In 1781 trouble flared again and all the journeymen went on strike. The Company imported labour to break the strike, prosecuted, and the men were convicted in 1782. The Company had determined 'THAT the present wages is sufficient to enable an industrious workman to provide for himself and Family' and 'THAT the profitts of the Trade will not allow of givin the advanced wages required'. In 1787 those who worked without serving their apprenticeship were also prosecuted and convicted — the last time the Company used the law to enforce its rights.

In 1773 the General Turnpike Act (the Broad Wheels Act) sought to reduce the ruts that heavy vehicles caused in the unmade roads of the time. The Act laid down detailed specifications and defined tolls for vehicle types. Broad-wheeled vehicles benefitted; the carriage trade was exempted. The Wheelwrights were thus more affected than the Coachmakers, and in addition, wagoners found the new wheel regulations ruined their horses. Experts proliferated, and in the early 1800s a Parliamentary Committee considered the traditional dished wheel, originally designed to take the strain of sideways motion of the horses' action, against the proposed flat, cylindrical wheel.

The controversy rumbled on without conclusion, until the railways and the parallel decline of road transport intervened.

In 1817 the Livery was increased to 250; of 27 proposed new Liverymen, none were practising Wheelwrights. In 1838 the last Freewoman was admitted by patrimony — Jeannette Stoffel. By 1849 the Company's perpetually embarrassed finances showed a surplus of expenditure over £300 income of £15. Economies were pursued and stock sold. In 1843 the Wheelwrights were the first of sixteen Companies to oppose proposals to alter the basis of City voting rights.

On 11 January 1855 the Court heard 'with feelings of the deepest horror and regret' of the assassination of their Upper Warden, George Moore, on December 8, 1854. Moore was a soda-water manufacturer, of 73, Warren Street. He received Emmannuel Barthelemy, a political exile from France, and a mysterious veiled woman whom Barthelemy later claimed was illegitimate and supported by Moore, in his back parlour. Barthelemy had repaired equipment for him. Moore's servant heard a scuffle and the cry 'Murder', and found her master and Barthelemy struggling. Barthelemy shot Moore and, trying to escape, ran into his next door neighbour, greengrocer Charles Collard, whom he also shot. The murderer was pursued and captured, found by police to have two pistols, a dagger, and a ticket for Hamburg, and was brought to trial for Collard's murder where he maintained a 'rigid silence' throughout. He was hanged at Newgate Gaol, having told the chaplain that he visited Moore simply to help the veiled woman, who was never found, and that this had led to the quarrel. Barthelemy had been convicted of manslaughter in 1853, following a duel.

In 1881 the Company contributed £210 to the City and Guilds of London Institute and, in 1894, appointed a Technical Education Committee. This arranged classes for wheelwrights at the Carpenters' School. In 1897 prizes were instituted. In 1904 a course of lectures was started 'on the elementary work of the motor-car'. In 1918 the Court collectively cleared the Company's £200 overdraft. Thereafter late 19th century legacies yielded useful income.

In 1945 the Livery was increased to 300. In 1965 the Company achieved a Grant of Arms. By then the trade had virtually ceased to exist, but the Company still supports technical education and in 1966 instituted medals and awards. The Company maintains the tradition of the Poor Box.

The Distillers. In 1638 the Company was incorporated by Royal charter with extensive powers and duties in the regulation of the trade of distillers and vinegar makers, and of those making artificial and strong waters, and of making 'Beeregar and Alegar', in London and Westminster, the suburbs and liberties thereof and a radius of 21 miles. The Company's jurisdiction was extended a further ten miles by the further Royal charter of 1688 and the bye laws were regulated in 1689. A Grant of Livery was obtained in 1672 and, in 1774, an Act of Common Council imposed penalties on anyone practising the trade in the City who was not free of the Company, ruling that no such person could be free of any Company other than the Distillers. In 1638 the Company achieved its Grant of Arms, with the motto 'Droppe as Raine, distill as Dewe'. The Company does not restrict membership entirely to its trade, though those in the trade are preferred.

The Pattenmakers. The patten was a type of undershoe comprising a metal ring, to which was fastened by metal uprights a wooden platform, or sole. The ordinary shoe was fastened on top of this with a leather strap. Pattens performed the same function as the later galoshes, allowing the wearer to walk through the City's mud relatively clean-shod. The 'mistery of Patynmakers' was first recorded in 1379, but already existed as an unincorporated guild. The trade was centred on Rood Lane, where St Margaret Pattens now stands — the only City Guild church named after a City Company.

In 1670 the Company was incorporated and achieved a Grant of Livery. In the last century, the Company's procession coincided with that of the Lord Mayor. Travelling from tavern to tavern, it constantly merged with its Mayoral counterpart, so it was decided over a century ago to grant the Company the right to take part with its own coach in the Lord Mayor's procession every third year. It is the only Company which has this honour.

As the City's streets became better paved, the pattenmaker's trade died out, and the Company's raison d'etre with it. Nonetheless, the Pattenmakers continued to meet, dine and administer their charities. In the post-war period, they sought new links with the shoe trade, and increasingly supported Young Enterprise. This movement, to educate and train young people in industrial and commercial private enterprise, was developed by two Past Masters of the Company, Walter Salomon and Frank Taylor. The Company also grants bursaries at the City of London School and funds maintenance at St Margaret Pattens.

In 1967, a conference at Windsor Castle led the Company to create a forum within its ranks for the fragmented footwear industry - a continuing process. Charitable activities have been extended to the shoe trade, and many leading members of that trade have been admitted to the Livery. In 1981 the Company was granted a third Royal charter, which conferred additional powers, including that of appointing an additional Warden, known as Warden to the Trade, whose duties are to advise the Court on, and liaise on behalf of the trade. The charter also enabled the Company to appoint a Patron, the first of whom is HRH The Duke of Gloucester.

The Glass Sellers. Originally makers and sellers of looking glass or mirrors, and sellers only of drinking or table glass, bottles, stoneware pots and other stoneware goods, the Glass Sellers dealt in English glass and pottery, and imported decorative glass from Venice. In 1549 Edward VI licensed individual Venetians to manufacture glass for the English market; in 1575 Verzelini secured a 21-year patent for making drinking glasses 'as good cheap, or rather better cheap than the imported article'. Licences such as his prohibited general glass manufacture without the licensee's consent. In 1589 George Longe petitioned for a patent to make glass in Ireland, indicating that an existing patent was not being properly implemented, but its privileges exercised by unlicensed manufacturers, 'by which means besides the great spoile of tymber and woods Her Majestie hath lost the custome of all the glasse made . . . (which) would in short tyme increase both the price of tymber and glasse'. He suggested that fewer than the then 14 or 15 glasshouses would protect the timber stock essential to the process involved. Indigenous glass sellers continued to protest and the legitimate trade not only faced the high prices of the licensed monopolies, but also the unregulated competition of chapmen and pedlars, who hawked inferior glass at cut price, bought from illegal glasshouses.

In 1615 James I prohibited the use of wood in glass manufacture, and also glass imports. That year Sir Robert Mansell was granted a patent to make glass, using coal. In 1635 the Glass Sellers drew up a charter of incorporation, which they finally obtained in 1664 and which was enrolled in the City within the year.

The new Company faced numerous problems: the itinerant glass sellers, the licensed monopolists, the greedy wholesale merchants within their own ranks, imported glass, and the costs of incorporation. They pursued the hawkers mercilessly. In 1666 each Assistant contributed 20s towards the costs of prosecuting one William Wyatt at the Old Bailey, having two years earlier instructed their Beadle 'to endeavour to discover any Pedlars or Hawkers who wander up and down to sell glasses and find out where they dwell and where they sell or offer to sell such glasses in order to their prosecution'. In 1667, the officers lent the Company £5 each to pay off the collective debt. In 1670 the Court authorised five Assistants to 'treat with all the White Glassmakers about London and to agree upon what terms and prices they will furnish the Company . . . and other customers . . . for the prohibiting of all sorts of foreign drinking glasses . . .'. Thomas Wyatt was prosecuted in 1670 'for selling drinking glasses at the Boar's Head' and Samuel Browne likewise 'at the King's Head in "Herculis his pillars Ally"'.

In 1674 the Company concluded an agreement with George Ravenscroft to forestall imports and raise standards. In great secrecy they set him up at a glass house in Henley-on-Thames, after he took out a patent to produce 'fine Chrystaline Glasses in resemblance of Rock Christoll', at his glass house at the Savoy in the Strand — the introduction of lead crystal glass. The Company took his production and he agreed not to produce any more than they required, the first of a number of similar agreements with glass makers, and potmakers. The second agreement with Ravenscroft, of 1677, required that 'a Raven's head shall be made or set in all glasses to distinguish the same from all others that shall be made in resemblance of the said glasses' — a necessary protective device for the new process 'not heretofore being made for public use in this nation'.

In 1691 the Glass Sellers documented the problem of hawkers in connection with a bill before Parliament, which enacted that 'all such persons as shall wander up and down to sell glasses shall be treated as rogues and vagabonds and dealt with accordingly'. During those early years the Company faced multiple difficulties, such as opposing the Pottmakers' attempts to gain a charter, these having obtained an order in Council prohibiting the import of glazed earthenware. They had to treat with George Villiers, Duke of Buckingham, since he held the patent for making Venetian glass at his Greenwich glassworks. Between 1667 and 1672, Glass Seller John Greene shipped glass from Alessio Morelli of Venice, instructing his supplier how to evade customs dues by 'factories' (false invoices) and shrewd packing. Their correspondence, with design and specification, has survived, to demonstrate the variety of glassware, speckled, enamelled, clouded and for very many purposes.

In 1707 'the glass trade was improving greatly and the Company being increased in number and quality', the Glass Sellers sought an increase in their Livery to sixty. In 1698 the Company paid 'to Old Mitton and Mr Farlow's daughter each 2/6 apiece' — the first record of the Poor Box. In 1703 they quashed an attempt by the glass grinders to achieve a separate charter. In 1825 the Livery was increased to 120.

Gradually the control of their trade diminished and, in 1874, the Company instituted medals for competition among workers in glass. The Court was not happy about the reaction to their efforts to support an exhibition of Technical Art at Alexandra Palace. In 1876 they recorded 'their deep regret at the cold and indifferent manner in which' a 'good deal of time and much money' had been received. In 1882 they inaugurated prizes for essays on glass manufacture and earlier, in 1875, to artizans in glass. That year, Master John Abbott founded the Abbott Scholarship at the City of London School.

The Company substantially supported the first Glass Department in the world — at Sheffield University. Until recently, the Company made a substantial award to encourage post-graduate research, and is currently engaged in a scheme to recognise outstanding technical and artistic achievement. In 1947 the Livery was increased to 180, and in 1955 funds were advanced to the Restoration Fund of St James' Church, Garlickhythe. By 1965 the augmented Hayes legacy for the poor yielded £1,500 annually. Today the Company maintains close links with the glass manufacturing industry, continues to support technical education and to administer its charitable funds. Over a quarter of the Livery are directly involved in the the glass industry.

The Coachmakers and Coach Harness Makers. One of the earliest recorded uses of a coach was when Richard III's mother rode in a 'whirlicote' in 1381; Henry VIII entered London after his Bosworth Field victory in a horse drawn contraption; Mary Tudor rode through the City in a chariot in 1553 and Walter Rippon supplied the Earl of Rutland with the first English coach in 1555. A Stuart coach could cost some £35, its horses £11-£12. By 1625, the cast-off coaches of the rich plied for hire as hackney coaches. Sedans rivalled these early cabs, but the river was still London's principal highway. Waterman John Taylor wrote:

> 'Carroaches, coaches, jades and Flanders mares
> Doe rob us of our shares, our wares, our fares,
> Against the ground we stand and knock our heels,
> Whilst all our profit runs away on wheels.'

In 1631 the Coachmakers and Wheelwrights sought to form a Guild. The authorities prevaricated, the Civil War intervened, and the stage coach emerged. About 1650 coach building took off. By 1662 there were regular stage coaches on main routes. In 1677 the Coachmakers received their long-desired Royal charter, and obtained their ordinances. Its powers of search extended to 20 miles outside London. The Company suffered the common Stuart charter 'frauds'. By 1694 there were 700 coaches in London.

In 1703 the Company bought the Scriveners' Hall in Noble Street for £1,600. An additional £616 was spent on refurbishing. Certain lets were agreed, and 109 members contributed cash sums, yet still the Clerk had to lend the Company money to defray the balance of cost. In 1700 journeymen caused trouble by not paying their quarterage; other freemen broke the other rules, and outsiders unlawfully practised the craft. In 1721 the journeymen combined to raise wages, setting 'a very ill example to journeymen in all other trades'. In 1724 they rioted at the Hall, wounding the watchman, who later died. Charity began and ended at home — in 1768 Past Master John Westley was 'in distressed circumstances', and received an annual £12 pension. Apprentices were protected, as when Wm Wright complained he 'had no victuals nor work' from his master, Edward Wootton, and the Court transferred him to another.

In the Company's early days, to overcome the onerous responsibility for taking on apprentices within their original, pre-charter guilds as well as their own, the Coachmakers made William Watson a freeman by redemption, and he acted as 'a nominal person', binding apprentices, and turning them over to other trades. Unfortunately he died before all his apprentices had served their terms, or been admitted. The problem evaporated as the prosperity of the 18th century enabled Coachmakers to bind more apprentices, who came increasingly from other traders' families. The buy-in cost for putting one's son to a trade varied from £10 to £80 in 1765; in 1787 Coachmaker John Browne, of Fish Street Hill, obtained £200 for an indenture; in 1791 he secured £500, and later that year, another £500. But he improved his reputation by also taking Henry Trollop 'late one of the boys of the Foundling Hospital' free.

The Company was rigorous in applying the proper standards and prosecuting offenders. In 1679 Mr Awbry was summoned 'to shew cause why he should not be fined for putting an old Carriage to the Queen's body Coach . . .' and again 'A carriage at Mr Polehamptons — rotten cross-bars, old pearch, knotty standards, & 2 old plates belonging to Mr Obediah Bentley; on voate fined for the same 40s'. By 1757 the Court suspended its searches not least to avoid clashes with the Saddlers as competitors in the harness trade. In 1714 Robert Fawdery's will showed a Coachmaker's worth: £1,136 6s 3d, with debtors and creditors pretty well in balance, except for some accounts 'esteemed desperate'.

In 1754 the Company unsuccessfully charged wheelwright John Miles of Camomile Street with six offences against their rights of monopoly, for 'being a very avaritious Person . . . took it into his head to set up the Trade of a Coachmaker and Coach Harness Maker . . . without any the least knowledge . . . for his own Lucre and Benefit . . .'.

The year before, the Company viewed its journeymen with a jaundiced eye: '. . . the best hands . . . have risen to such an intollerable, insufferable, insupportable height of self sufficiency and disobedience . . . very many of them refusing to work by the day . . .' requiring '. . . unusual and unwarrantable wages, loosing the time of their said masters by frequent and almost continued Rioting, Drunkenness, and Debauchery, . . . so that is impossible for the said Masters to get a reasonable support . . . unless they in like manner raise their prices upon their Customers . . .'. In 1789 a committee was set up to consider prices paid to the workforce; three years later the two sides agreed a book of prices. In 1777 a new coach cost Rev John Drake £104 3s 6d: 'To a new Coach neatly run with raised beads, painted dark green with Arms & Crests, the Leather japan'd and brass beads all round it, lined with fine light colour'd Cloth, trim'd with Velvet Lace the same Colour, the Seat cloth with one row of fringe, plate glasses to slide separately in front. Plate glasses & Mahogany Shutters in the doors, wainscott Trunks under the Seats, a Carpet to the bottom, hung on a light strong Carriage, with iron Axletrees, a new Boot, the Carriage Coach-box to take off the Carriage, & Wheels painted the colour of the Body'; the cost was £88. The remainder was equipage, mostly harness.

Coachmakers' Hall was unhappily involved in 1780 in the Gordon 'No Popery' Riots. The

177

Protestant Association, with Lord George Gordon, met at the Hall, and decided to process some days later to Parliament with a petition. Over 60,000 rioted for six days, culminating in 285 deaths and 173 wounded, when the army restored order.

Towards the end of the century, with better roads, vehicle design improved. First came the phaeton — a high-bodied, tall-wheeled carriage. Then followed the Italian curricle, a two-wheeler drawn by two horses, and the French one-horse cabriolet. Then there were gigs, a workaday vehicle which Coachmakers hired out to escape the tax on new carriages, which became the height of fashion, a hooded version known as a buggy. Of the many cars and carts, the best known was the dog-cart, c1800; at the other end of the scale was the private drag — a four-in-hand; in 1822 the German landau was introduced, a convertible with foldaway hood(s). The barouche, a sporting vehicle, was also German, and in 1823 David Davies of Albany Street introduced the first hackney cabriolet, or 'cab'. The brougham emerged in 1838, and the Company owns the original vehicle, now at the Science Museum, Kensington. It was made for Lord Brougham by Robinson & Cook of Mount Street, Grosvenor Square. In 1842, Amersham Coachmaker Lovell made the first wagonette. Hansom invented the cab in 1834 which, much modified by John Chapman, became the two wheeler of Victorian memory; the four-wheel equivalent, known as the 'growler' is said to have been introduced in 1842 by Laurie & Marner of Oxford Street. It was also known as the clarence. My grandfather (his grandfather hired carriages out in 1832), left a curious note, worth quoting: 'I have no doubt the 4-wheeled cab was called Clarence after him (William IV) during George IV's reign. I think that, in all probability, the 4-horse cab was before the Hansom (2-wheel). When I entered the business (Dec 18th — 1885) all our 2-wheeled cabs had in black letters over the windows HANSOMS PATENT SAFETY . . .'.

In 1804 a new bye law removed any numerical restrictions on apprenticeships. The Company's powers were now unenforceable and out of date. By 1867 George Hooper commented, it was a 'worn out and effete Guild which had drifted into a wretched state of mismanagement'. Quarterage was so far in areaars that one case was 80 years old. Hooper and others set about restoring the Company's efficiency and repute. Meanwhile the Company's Hall had been rebuilt in 1842, and rebuilt again 28 years later, for £3,854 — £3,000 of it borrowed money. Adjacent property was developed and injected much-needed finance. In 1917 a German bomb slightly damaged the roof, and twenty years later the building was modernised. It was engulfed by fire in the incendiary raid of 29 December 1940. Shelley House now occupies the site.

In 1865 the Company rekindled its trade links, with the Operative Coachmakeis' Industrial Exhibition and medal awards, generating a new tradition of awards and prizes covering every aspect of the trade. In 1873 the Duke of Edinburgh was admitted to the freedom and livery. That same year Disraeli also joined. In 1874 there were 432,000 carriages in use. Three Georges — Thrupp, Hooper and Maberly, working coachmakers, formed the Institute of British Carriage Manufacturers in 1883. Masters in that era included Baxter and Pearce, Birch, Berry, Holland, two Hoopers and Thorn. Lionel Lukin (Master in 1793) pioneered the lifeboat with his 'unsubmergible boat'. Four members of the Windus family were Masters, and the Peters family gave five Masters to the Company. Appropriately, the Masters family provided six! In 1895, a farsighted Master, John Philipson, had this to say of the new 'automobile' — 'the development . . . will assuredly grow to extraordinary proportions . . .' and a year later the Company was actively involved in an exhibition at Crystal Palace which included 17 horseless carriages. By the following year the Company awarded a prize for a 'self-propelled light motor carriage'. Unhappily there were only two entries and neither was judged of sufficient merit.

For five years the motor was ignored. In 1897, Alexander Henderson, a Coachmaker, opined '. . . however perfect the motor may eventually become, . . . most people will still prefer, for private use, the life-like, animated appearance of well-appointed horse traction to any dead mechanism . . .'. In 1898 the Company helped to found the Polytechnic Day School of Carriage Building and from 1903 the car prize was resuscitated. Meanwhile the motor trade made its own bodies, and the carriage trade gradually diminished. Coachmakers like Hoopers offered custom built bodies

178

for cars. Firms like Mulliners and Alford and Alder joined this lucrative trade. Even so, other firms like Birch Bros Ltd continued to build their own bodies for 'bus, coach, and van, up to the '39 war, the commercial vehicle sector perpetuating the separation of chassis and body, where the car industry manufactured the total package. Park Ward was founded in 1919. But the standard Bentley model of 1946 was the death knell of the independent coachbuilder. In 1927 the Company formally recognised motorcar manufacture as bona fide coachmaking. In 1931 the motor industry in turn took an increasing interest in the Company, and the Livery base widened beyond manufacture to the trade at large, the oilmen and the aircraft industry. In the post-war years, the Company drew great strength from aviation, following the lead established in 1943 by Master, Sir Frederick Handley Page.

In 1972 the Company inaugurated the Coachmakers Awards to Industry — for technological advance in aerospace and motoring. The Company in 1974 adopted HMS *Hermes,* following the withdrawal of HMS *Centaur* which had been adopted in 1955; in 1961 it had adopted No 216 Squadron of No 46 Group, Strike Command, replaced on disbandment in 1975 by No 10 Squadron RAF. In 1974 the third arm of the military was drawn in with the adoption of the 4th/7th Royal Dragoon Guards. The Coachmakers also support the British Driving Society, which has regenerated national interest in the horse-drawn carriage, and on the harness making side, now enjoying renewed prosperity, the name Connolly stands out as leather dressers for a century and as members and Masters of the Company. So today the Coachmakers embrace the traditional craft of their forbears, and the modern age of transport.

The Gunmakers. While the Chinese are credited with inventing gunpowder, its practical application to warfare dates to the 14th century. It was used, largely for effect rather than execution, at Crecy in 1346, and developed mainly for use in sieges, to demolish defences. The first handgun record dates to 1418, using a firing wire; the slowmatch appeared in the 15th century — manual application of a length of treated cord — and was superseded by the serpentine (lever) which automated the application of match to powder: the matchlock. In the early 16th century the wheellock produced ignition by means of rubbing a lump of pyrites; soon this gave way to the snaphaunce lock, using flint and a spring-loaded cock, or striker, which led inevitably to the simpler flintlock. By 1720 the musket was the principal infantry weapon. The blunderbuss was popular in the 17th century as a domestic weapon, and sporting flintlocks developed, some double barrelled, while pistols evolved during the same period, becoming lighter as coach travel and urban crime increased. Gunmakers developed expertise in various branches of the craft, including duelling pistols. The flintlock, in all its applications, reached its zenith in the early 19th century. The percussion cap appeared in 1805, leading to repeating weapons and, by the 1860s, cartridges that included their own source of ignition were increasingly used, leading ultimately to the sophisticated weapons of our times.

Initially gunmakers were armourers who included the first crude guns as a minor part of their craft. Gradually specialised gunsmiths emerged, working by hand supplemented by water power, and they employed other craftsmen for ornamentation. London was the main centre, concentrated in the Minories, with Birmingham as a secondary source, overtaking the capital in the 19th century. Some sixteen craftsmen might be involved in the different production phases for one gun.

By the 17th century the London Gunmakers were spread through numerous other Guilds, principally the Armourers or Blacksmiths. It was an established trade, developing fast and in need of its own organisation. In 1637 the Gunmakers sought recognition, stating 'how for many years the Gunmakers of the City of London had practiced and upheld the manufacture of making all sorts of hand-guns for Horse and Foot for the King's Special Service and supply of Stores as well as for the occasions of Sport . . . and had obtained a more exquisite skill in that Mistery than in former times and now divers Blacksmiths and others inexpert in the Art had taken it upon themselves to make, try and prove guns after their unskilled way, damnifying the Gunmakers in their particular trade and causing much harm and danger through much unskilfulness to the King's loyal subjects'. The charter was granted.

Sixty two gunmakers formed the new Company, which secured rights of search, view, gauge, proof, trial and marking of all hand-guns, great and small, dags (heavy pistols) and pistols within the City and ten miles radius. Imported weapons were to be proved and apprentices, after serving their seven years, were required to furnish a proof piece. The Gunmakers' mark — 'GP' crowned — was approved and is still in use. The Company was formally recognised by the City authorities in 1656.

The Company's proof house was established in Goodman's Fields, Whitechapel, where the later 1757 building still stands, much rebuilt in 1826 and 1952. The Hall was built adjoining in 1872, but sold in 1927. The existence of the proof house outside the City limits appears to have saved the Company from the depredations of the Reformation, Great Fire and the Ulster imposts. With the ordinances of 1670 came a Grant of Livery and monopolies were curbed, restricting single sales to 150 hand-guns, and controlling outsiders 'working in holes and corners', and hawkers selling 'false, deceitful and unproved' weapons. Gunmakers were enjoined to submit their own marks for the Company's approval, and all imported guns were to be proved by the Company. The individual marks were stamped on the Company's Copper Plate, which survives. Ten years later, the Gunmakers failed to persuade Parliament to ban imported guns.

In 1710 the Government owed the Company the astounding sum of £30,000 and was asked to pay up, against which the Gunmakers would supply 30,000 arms every half year. The petition was ignored and the money remains outstanding to this day. In 1892 a supplemental charter conveniently moved the Company's election day out of August to October, thus avoiding conflict with the grouse season. Earlier Acts of 1855 and 1868 protected the public from unsound guns and upheld the Company's rights. The Gun Barrel Proof Act of 1868 was amended in 1950, and in 1954 the Company updated the Rules of Proof, which were enshrined in law the following year. In 1952 the Proof House was renovated and modernised. A modern Grant of Arms permitted the inclusion of two Royal insignia; the motto is 'Probis Civibus Canones Probentur' or 'May guns continue to be Proved for Loyal and True citizens'. The Gun Barrel Proof Act of 1978 enabled the Company to establish a Branch Proof House in Manchester in 1979. Today, therefore, the Gunmakers, who number some 200, are specifically involved in precisely the same craft in the same way as when they were formed over three hundred years ago.

The Gold and Silver Wyre Drawers. The craft goes back at least 4,000 years and the earliest 'wire' was made by gilding skins with gold foil, cutting it into strips and winding it round thread. In the 14th century the principles of the modern product were established. Essentially, silver was coated with gold, and then drawn through smaller and smaller holes in a die to become fine wire. To make gold thread, the wire is then flattened and spun onto the silk (or today, man-made fibre). Today the wire is drawn down to 1,500 yards to the ounce. It can also be woven straight into lace, and when silver and gold wire and thread are combined, this is known as orris lace. In embroidery the wire is fashioned into patterns, such as purls, or coiled springs; spangles, or pearl purl, such as is used for borders to badges. Modern methods are sophisticated and, while automated, still require highly skilled operatives, but the craft is essentially the same as in the past. The Preston works of Stephen Simpson is the only surviving English manufacturer of gold and silver wire. Cloth of gold is essentially material woven from gold wire.

The trade in the finished wire probably started in Britain by the 7th century. London workshops financed by merchants exported much of their output by the 13th century, though foreign merchants were permitted here by an Act of 1378. The Broderers in 1423 obtained government support for the prohibition of copper in wire for embroidery and in 1489 against the unacceptable quality of some imported work. In the 16th century much of the wire was imported, principally from Venice. By the 1570s the craft was flourishing and practised by both indigenous and immigrant workers. There were few master craftsmen, mostly in the Broderers, Mercers and Goldsmiths, controlling a large number of outworkers, mostly women and children. The trade was a luxury one, serving the needs of the monarch, nobility, wealthy City companies and the export trade. Control was vested in a minority through the Tudor and Stuart practice of granting monopolies by licence. In the 17th century, belief in gold and silver as the foundation of a sound economy dictated conservation of bullion and restriction on the outflow of gold and silver products abroad. Prohibition of the manufacture of gold and silver thread followed.

In the early 17th century Charles I appointed Thomas Violet, a convicted dealer in gold and silver on the European market, as surveyor of gold and silver wire making, in return for £1,500. He instituted assay and craftsmen's marks and rigorously controlled standards of manufacture. He fell from grace with the Civil War. Meanwhile, in 1623, a year after the Royal prohibition, a charter was issued to the Gold and Silver Wyre Drawers, with rights subject to the Assay Masters of the Mint and the Goldsmiths, and office subject to the Crown. With Violet as Assay Master, the charter proved ineffective.

In 1662 John Garill was granted a patent for a new process, and sole rights to manufacture. His competitors predictably reacted with fury, meeting in Gutter Lane at the house of Simon Urlin. But the trade remained disorganised, and it was not until 1693 that at last the craft obtained formal recognition and powers, by charter of incorporation. Powers of search extended 30 miles outside London and provided for the multiplicity of outworkers beyond those limits. Women were allowed the freedom by apprenticeship and patrimony, as well as by a husband's death. From the beginning, the journeymen bargained for representation on the ruling Court and for acceptable pay and apprenticeships. Standards were laid down for wire manufacture, and strictly enforced. In 1698 the Company instigated legislation reinforcing such standards. It was not a wealthy Company, since most of its members perforce invested their money in their high cost raw material.

In the 18th century the Company absorbed the effects of mechanisation and welcomed skilled foreigners and in 1764 it provided inspectors of foreign lace for the Customs authorities. By now the French had replaced the Venetians. Earlier, in 1742 the Company had promoted further legislation. Domestic difficulties centred on the need to maintain funds, especially with the exorbitant costs of encouraging Parliamentary support, and on pay negotiations with the journeymen, increasingly restive as industrialisation developed. New prices were agreed in 1789 and attempts to employ foreigners successfully resisted. During the 18th century the Company adopted a coat of arms, without Grant, and received benefactions for charitable purposes. In 1780 a Grant of Livery was achieved.

As the century closed, fashions changed and, with the exception of the military, gold and silver wire diminished rapidly in use. The trade declined, and the Company abandoned most of its powers and its parliamentary activities. Much of the trade moved out of London. As the 19th century unfolded, the Company turned more to a concern for its City role, though displaying its craft at numerous exhibitions. At the height of Empire, the trade itself prospered, centred in London and Coventry. But Stephen Simpson was established in Preston in 1829, while David Kenning was in Coventry; he was taken over by Toye's — today Toye, Kenning and Spencer Ltd are pre-eminent in many related products.

Gradually the progressive Lancashire manufacturers, readily assimilating the advances in the textile industry, gained at the expense of the more conservative London firms. But they also benefitted from the good labour relations that the craft had so assiduously fostered through its Company from its beginnings. This was in stark contrast to the apalling conditions and pay in the lace industry. Much of this was due to the fact that they were largely family concerns. Simpsons survived by a policy of diversification, and gradually absorbed other firms, their skilled employees and their equipment.

The Company itself revived in the 1920s, administering its small charitable bequests and properties, and mounting exhibitions. In 1943 the Livery was increased to 250, and in 1956 to 350. In the post-war years a Hall was envisaged, but the scheme was finally abandoned in 1966, though investment was made in property. A Grant of Arms was at last achieved in 1975. In 1969 a new trust fund was set up for charitable purposes, which supports the London Homes for the Elderly. The Company has contributed to the upkeep of several City churches. In 1969 HMS *Olympus* was adopted. The Company also supports the City and Guilds of London Institute financially and with prizes for design and workmanship in its ancient craft; similarly the Royal College of Arts, and the Royal School of Needlework. In 1961 the Company, with others, saved the School from closure. Its motto is 'Amicitiam trahit Amor' — 'Love draws forth friendship'.

The Makers of Playing Cards. The charter of 1628 records 'the Art and Trade of making of Playing Cards . . . which had been used and put in practice for divers years last past', witnessing that cards were played well before that time. The trade was virtually confined to London and its environs, and suffered from imports and cheap indigenous manufacture, when the card makers previously petitioned James I, who was 'graciously inclined by making them a Corporation . . .' but failed to do so. In 1615, the import duty realised five shillings a gross of packs for the Crown.

Charles I's charter expressly forbade all imports, requiring Customs officers to seize them on pain of losing their office, provided for the Company's control of apprentices, and powers of search and siezure, up to ten miles outside the City. To offset the Crown's sacrifice of its import levy, the Company covenanted to pay two shillings on every gross of playing cards to the Crown and one shilling to the appointed officer for 'labour, pains, charges and attendance' in sealing them and accepting the duty payment. He was known as the King's Receiver of Composition Monies, made a freeman of the Company and charged with applying the Company's seal 'for the better preventing of such frauds . . . (and) . . . cosinages wherewith all Our loving subjects have been heretofore often abused and cheated by the frequent use of false cards'. No cards could be sold without the seal. The Officer appointed deputies for other towns, and the Company was required to peg its prices at the level previously obtaining for foreign cards over seven years. Only those cards bearing the maker's approved stamp would be sealed, the maker's mark being 'entered, filed and enrolled' with the Officer and the Company.

Two years later, orders and bye laws were confirmed which compelled paste board makers to pay 2d a ream for paper. In 1792 the Company achieved a Grant of Livery. By 1925 the 'duty' had risen to 3d, an Inland Revenue wrapper replacing the King's Seal. In 1882 the Company inaugurated an annual practice, still maintained, of creating a specially designed pack of playing cards for presentation to the Livery. In 1897 the H. D. Phillips Prize was instituted for the design of the Company's cards, to mark the 52 years' service of Past Master Henry Phillips, who in 1907 presented the Company with his collection of old playing cards. These are held at Guildhall Library. During the first World War the Company issued 20,000 packs of specially designed cards to war hospitals. In the second War, a similar proposal to sell cards, against the established practice, was of limited success but income was raised and went to war charities.

In 1943 the Company established a Trust Fund for the relief of hardship and sickness among workers in the industry and their dependants. The major manufacturers contributed and the fund was called the Cutler Trust, after the then Master, Lindsay Cutler. In 1960 the excise duty on cards was abolished, since the £50,000 raised was more than absorbed by the cost of collecting it.

To celebrate its 350th anniversary, the Company held a playing card design competition in 1978 — and coincidentally, 350 entries resulted. The winning design was used for the anniversary pack. In 1978 the Cutler Trust's terms of reference were widened to enable the Company to further its charitable work. Since 1977 the Company's cards have, with the exception of the anniversary pack, featured ladies — HM the Queen in 1977, the first woman Premier in 1979 and HM the Queen Mother in 1981.

The Fan Makers. Fans may have originated in China several thousand years BC, were in use in Egypt from 1350 BC and extensively used by both Greeks and Romans. They were variously employed as a Royal emblem, to protect sacramental vessels as the ecclesiastical *flabellum,* and as a symbol of chastity. The Japanese invented the folding variety in the 7th century AD and Vasco da Gama introduced it to Europeans in the 16th. Elizabeth I collected fans — in 1603 she had thirty one. In England the folding fan was used for ornament and fashion, and the long plumed variety for ceremonial occasions. After the 1914-18 War its use virtually ceased.

Until 1685 most English fans were imported, though a few native fan craftsmen worked in London. That year brought a major influx of fanmakers from France and Italy, fleeing religious persecution, and it became necessary to regulate the trade, protect its craftsmen and stem the flood of imported wares. In 1709 the Fan Makers were chartered — the last to be so incorporated, and therefore the youngest of the old Guilds. In 1710 well over two hundred had joined the new Company, many of them French fan makers who had settled, bound apprentices and taught the trade to others.

The Company was much exercised by imports, warning traders of the penalties: 'Selling any foreign fan embellished with gold, silver or any other metal, is £200, with full costs of suit'. An advertisement in the *Daily Advertiser* of 1752 recorded '. . . the poor unfortunate artificers in the . . . fan trade, whose number is nearly 1000, returning thanks to the Company of Fan Makers petitioning the East India directors to discontinue the importation of Fans . . . home made fans are in every way preferable to foreign . . .'. In 1741 the Company's bye laws were authorised, and again in 1787, when the first were lost.

In 1806 the Company faced a decline in the trade and its own affairs, largely due to foreign competition. It made the last of several petitions to government, without success. In 1809 a Grant of Livery was allowed of sixty. By 1877 total membership was down to thirty one. Led by Sir Homewood Crawford, the Company's fortunes revived and, in 1879, the livery was increased to 200. (In 1966 this was further increased to 250). From then until 1910 a number of fan exhibitions were successfully mounted and competitions held. In 1861 the original bye laws were rediscovered. In 1928 the Company inaugurated a silver medal competition and prize for the best thesis from a student of the Fan Engineering Section of the National College of Heating, Ventilating, Refrigeration and Fan Engineering. In 1934 it started the Latchford Prize Competition for the best design for a painted fan through the City and Guilds of London Institute, and later also through the Royal Academy. In 1941 it started its now considerable fan collection. In 1948 HRH the (then) Duchess of Gloucester became a Freewoman — HRH the Princess Mary had set the precedent in 1926. In 1975 HRH the Duchess of Gloucester followed in her mother-in-law's footsteps. Fans have been presented for Royal weddings and coronations since 1911 and also annually to the Lady Mayoress.

In 1951 the Poor Fund was instituted and some of the Company's old records turned up at Guildhall in an old chest. The following year the Company acquired the use of the Church House of St Botolph in Bishopsgate as its Hall, having raised over £10,000 for refurbishment. In 1973 the Poor Fund and the 1917 Cook Fund were merged into the new Fan Makers Charitable Trust. In 1953/4 the Company adopted the City of London Territorial Unit, 56 London Armoured Division, Signals Regt, TA, City of London Signals.

Following its disbandment, the 79th (City of London) Company, WRCA, TA, was adopted in 1962. Perhaps the most unusual possession of the Company is the Royal Autograph Fan, which bears the signatures of all those members of the Royal family who have received fans, or otherwise taken an interest in the Company. Since 1953 two annual prizes have been awarded within the aerospace industry through the Cranfield Institute of Technology.

ABOVE LEFT: The Spectacle Makers' Arms and CENTRE: the Trig Lane 15th century spectacles; (SP) RIGHT: the Clockmakers' redrawn Arms; BELOW: the Clockmakers' original charter. (CL)

ABOVE LEFT TO RIGHT: The Arms of the Framework Knitters (FK), the Neeldemakers, (N) and the Gardeners. (GD) BELOW: The wheelwrights' shop at Birch Bros Ltd of Kentish Town in 1885. (CB)

ABOVE LEFT and RIGHT: Both sides of a Tin Plate Worker's apprentice badge; (TW) CENTRE: the Glass Sellers' Arms (GS) and BELOW: a Hansom. (CB)

A Courte holden on Thursday the 8th day of December 1664

Where at was present

William Carter Master

Humphrey Kilby Warden

Michaell Moses	John Strawn
John Lemster	Robert Ward
Richard Sadler	Hugh Bolter
William Sadler	John Hudgboat
John Greene	Dauniell Ditty

Assistants

Hugh Bolter, John Strawn, Dauniell Ditty, William Sadler sworne asistants

At this Cort Hugh Bolter John Strawn Dauniell Ditty and William Sadler fower of the Assistants named by his Ma[jes]tie in his said Lres Pattents of Incorporation before menconed did before the said Master William Carter and the said Warden Humphrey Kilby and the Maior pt of the Assistants that is to say Michaell Moses John Lemster Richard Sadler John Greene Robert Ward John Hudgboat and Dauniell Ditty according to the power and Authority given unto them as aforsaid Administer and give unto the said Hugh Bolter John Strawn Dauniell Ditty and William Sadler the oath Contayned in the said Booke of Orders for the due execution of the said office of & by all things apperteyninge to the said office of Assistants

Willm Pennenden sworne first Beadle

Allso at this Cort William Pennenden being elected and Chosen Beadle for the said Company of Glassellers did likewise take his oath before the said Master and wardens and Cort of Assistants for the due execution of the said office of Beadle according to the oath contained in the said Booke of Orders

Ordered yt ye Subscribers yt promised to pay 5li towards the charge of ye shippe should pay it on Thursday next to ye Master

Whereas sev[er]all p[er]sons of this Society did subscribe to contribute each of them a c[er]taine summe of money towards the charges of the shipp for this Corporation and whereas allso it was agreed since the said Subscription of the xxth of ... aforesaid that the sev[er]all p[er]sons that had soe subscribed should advance the same summe to the summe of five pound a peece it is this present day Ordered by the Cort abovesaid that all those p[er]sons that are in arreares of their sev[er]all summe of five pound or any pt thereof shall betwixt this and Thursday next bringe and pay or cause to be paid to the Master of this Company their said arrearages

Master to buy a chest

And allso it is Ordered by the Cort abovesaid that Mr Carter Master of this Company shall buy a fitt and convenient Chest for the use of this Company that shall have three locks and keys to it for to keepe their By lawes and Charter and other writings belonging to this Company

Master & Warden shall provide a chest

And it is likewise agreed upon at the Cort abovesaid that the Master and Wardens of this Company shall provide a Convenient and decent feast for the Cort of Assistants and such other of the Society as shall be invited to the same upon Thursday next

oath to be printed

And it is further Ordered by the Cort aboves[ai]d that the oath contained in the Booke of Orders appoynted to be taken by such p[er]sons as shall be made free of this Company be forthwith printed

The Glass Sellers' 1664 charter. (GS)

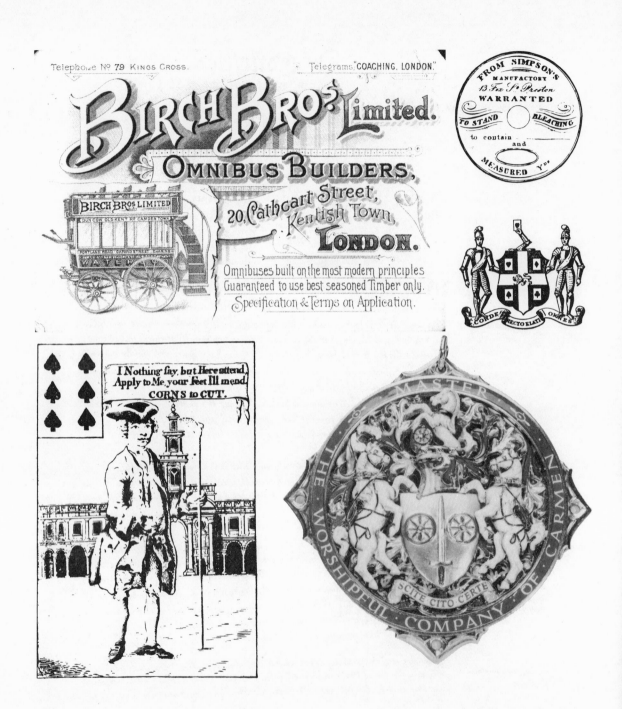

ABOVE LEFT: A coachmaker's 1880 advertisement card, (CB) RIGHT: the bobbin label of a Gold and Silver Wyre-Drawer, c1831, (GW) with BELOW: the Arms of the Makers of Playing Cards. (MPC) BELOW LEFT: John Kirk of St Paul's Churchyard issued, c1754, a pack of 52 London Cries — this one shows the Royal Exchange, (GL) and RIGHT: the Carmen's Master's badge. (CC)

The Carmen's Royal charter of 1605 incorporating the Woodmongers and Carmen. (BL)

ABOVE LEFT: The Carmen's Remonstrance of 1649, (GL) RIGHT: Carmen's Past Master, the late Raymond Birch CBE, conducts the ancient cart hiring ceremony in Dowgate Hill in 1961, the cart belonging to A. Jacobs & Sons Ltd, formerly Tingle and Jacobs; (CB) BELOW LEFT: the Master Mariners' sloop *Wellington* and RIGHT: their Badge. (MM)

The Carmen. It is traditionally held that a fellowship of Carmen existed in the 13th century — unsurprisingly since transport is the lifeline of all commerce. Yet cars and carters were from earliest times regulated by the City authorities, as evidenced by the 1277 and 1391 rulings on iron-shod wheels. In 1300, four cart brokers tried to circumvent the Royal prerogative of requisition by hiring carts from non-freemen outside the City and rehiring them at a profit. They went to prison. In 1479 the Carmen, in a row with inhabitants of Lower Thames Street, were derided thus: 'their employment requires stout bodyes and naturally renders their minds unthinking and unheeding, rough and sturdy, untractable and ungovernable by themselves or by one another, or without great difficulty by their superiours'.

Royal transport was regulated by the City, usually using suburban carriers; when they were also required to 'carye oute in their seid Carts . . . such Rubbush ordure dung or other fylthe as lyeth in the Streets . . .' the Carmen of London offered a solution. In 1517, Thomas Newman, Innholder and others contracted 'to provyde horses and cartes able and sufficient to serve the kyng . . . to clense, purge and kepe clene all the Streets . . . to carie and convey frome all manner of wharffe and other places within the seid Citie . . . all manner of fewell . . .' and they were granted the right to 'use themselves as brethren of oone ffeliship and ffraternyte to contynew to the honor of God and seynt kateryne . . .' with sole rights of cartage, except that any other freeman might 'occupye oon carre for the cariage oonly of his own stuffe and marchaundises'.

Those that joined were promised exemption from Royal requisition. Unlike other guilds, the Carmen were given no rights of regulation and no specific qualifications. Significantly, outsiders were not disallowed from the freedom. As a result the Fraternity could not stop excessive charging, provide sufficient Royal carts or handle the City's food transport. In 1528 new regulations were authorised, and the Fraternity was incorporated. These laid down the obligation to hold a cart in readiness for Royal use, required wood-wharf owners, rakers of refuse and carriers of building materials to join the Fraternity, and that 'noo carre be admytted nor marked without it be entred as well yn the yeldehall . . .'.

Despite an attempt to abolish the carroom, (the place or stand on which a car stood for hire), the boom in transport encouraged the authorities in 1528 to award grants of carrooms to allcomers, which weakened the Guild's new powers. Many Woodmongers were free of the Company, and they outnumbered Carmen. In 1546 the authorities ruled that Woodmongers should have one cart for their fuel carriage and one for 'eny kynde of wares', which totally undermined the Fraternity. This effectively promoted a competitive Guild of Woodmongers. By 1548 these obtained ordinances 'that all carremen be under the governannce of the . . . company of Woodmongers'. So the Fraternity of St Katherine ceased to exist.

Three Carmen, Robert Shardlowe, William Cornewall and Edward Drane then approached Christ's Hospital, which was in need of income, and struck a deal whereby 'Christe Hospital shall . . have the rule charge oversyght and government of all the Carts Carres and Carmen . . . as the Companye of the Woodmongers . . . heartofore have had and enjoyed, all which benefytt comodyte and profits rysynge or comynge . . . to be employed oneleye to the relyefe of the pore children within the same Hospitall'. Christ's Hospital sealed the cars annually, for which the Carmen paid 1d, and received all fines for breaches of the rules plus a quarterly rental of 6s 8d from every carman, carter or woodmonger. The Woodmongers protested in vain. In 1586 an Act of Common Council reinforced the new regulations comprehensively, and introduced apprenticeships.

Traffic control, pedestrian safety and noise control were all built into the new order. Congestion was strictly controlled, with specified standings for carts in given streets and penalties of imprisonment and vehicle confiscation for infringement. Carmen and Hospital worked well together. In 1600, times were harder and the Carmen joined the Woodmongers in resisting the Hospital's rule. It reacted against 'that uncivell and disordered Companie of Carmen' when they won a law suit, but the authorities were chary of challenging common law and, in 1605, the Carmen again came under the Woodmongers' control.

In that year the Company of Woodmongers was incorporated by Letters Patent and, although the Carmen were in the majority, they were prohibited from office. The Carmen petitioned the Privy Council, but the Lord Mayor dismissed this as 'manifest untruthes impudently suggested' so they went to law in Star Chamber, suing the clerk to the Woodmongers for fooling them into signing the ordinances. The Woodmongers counter claimed, accusing the Carmen of attempting to overthrow their rule. Both suits were dismissed. In 1617 the City authorities implemented one way streets 'for that the Carremen meetinge one another in narrowe streetes and places, are so churlishe one to another as that they will not make waye, one for another'. New stands were appointed to handle riverside commerce, and it was ordered that 'all Carrs beyond the number of 400 be suppressed' including wharfingers' carts. Carmen and Woodmongers combined against this iniquity, taking the battle to the Lord Mayor, Common Council, King's Bench, Privy Council, House of Commons and Star Chamber. In the end the 400 rule was upheld, but the wharfingers were allocated most of them. Worst of all, the right to carrooms was restricted to a life interest for Carmen's widows, thus at a blow reducing their capital value. The coal merchants now controlled the Woodmongers and the Carmen were effectively squeezed out, for coal carriage from the wharves was the principal business.

In 1641 the Carmen went to Parliament to retrieve their rights of disposal over carrooms and to obtain office in the Woodmongers. They failed. The carmen's widows then sued the Company and the Company went into print with 'The Carmens remonstrance or a Reply to the falfe and fcurrilous Papers of the Woodmongers'. In 1650 a Committee of the House of Commons found in their favour, but the contemporary disruption of Parliament prevented legislation. The same thing happened in 1653. They tried with Cromwell in 1656 without success. In 1664 the Woodmongers were in trouble for abusing their monopoly of the coal trade, and in 1665 the authorities returned the government of cars to Christ's Hospital.

In 1667 matters came to a head and the Woodmongers lost their charter, more for their own sins than to favour the Carmen. In 1668 the Carmen drew up a 'Booke of Orders' which was ratified by the Lord Mayor and Aldermen — but it left their renewed Fraternity virtually powerless, and still under the ultimate control of Christ's Hospital.

In 1668 Carmen's Hall was established on the east side of Harp Lane, but in 1670 they moved on. Meanwhile the Woodmongers continued to operate illegally as fuellers, backed by their considerable wealth and influence. The wrangling proliferated, the Carmen petitioning for incorporation and Christ's Hospital opposing them, stating 'They are labourers, their business is not a Trade'. In 1697 the Woodmongers and Carmen started negotiations to see if together they could win where separately they had failed to achieve incorporation, but their inherent distrust of one another bedevilled matters and by 1746 the Woodmongers were recorded for the last time.

For the next century the Carmen's main concern was to suppress competition from traders using their own carts, and they prospered overall. Many owned a number of carrooms, worth £150 apiece. In 1803 the Company offered 420 carts and 1,000 horses for the war against Napoleon. In 1811, years of combatting the loss of business occasioned by the rise of the Port of London ended with modest compensation payments. That year the Carmen wished to present a child annually to Christ's Hospital, pointing out they had paid £50,000 since their incorporation. They were rebuffed. There followed a major tussle over the licensing of carrooms.

In 1835, an Act of Common Council reformed the Company's constitution. In 1838 a further Act removed Christ's Hospital's power to license carts, to Guildhall.

A Grant of Livery was achieved in 1848 but, by the 1860s, the Company was in a sorry state. In 1899 it was proposed to abolish licensed stands for Carmen, but this was successfully resisted. In the first decade of the 20th century the Carmen started to revive their ancient fellowship with a prize to the Cart Horse Parade Society, a petition against LCC tramline proposals and regularisation of their domestic affairs, including the binding of an apprentice. After 1918, led by Past Master E.E. Coxhead, the Company grew in strength and in 1920 Past Master James Roll became Lord Mayor — the first of six. In 1929 a Grant of Arms was achieved, with the motto 'Scite, Cito, Certe' — 'Skilfully,

Quickly, Surely'. The Livery was increased to 150, and again in 1935, 1944 and in 1952 to the present 450.

In 1943 a mobile first aid unit was presented to the City; earlier, in 1934, the Benevolent Fund was started, and in 1946 the Company was granted incorporation by Royal charter. In 1956 Master Reginald Bezzant inaugurated the Viva Shield for transport innovation. That same year the ancient custom of standing and hiring a marked cart on a carroom was revived in Dowgate Hill. In 1965 the Company successfully resisted the Town Clerk's attempts to drop the ancient car marking ceremony. The Company in 1958 increased its support (since 1878) for the City and Guilds of London Institute. In 1961, Master Raymond Birch caused The Carmen's Whistle of 1612 to be adopted as the Carman's Musick. In 1964 the Herbert Crow Memorial Prize was instituted, for award to the highest marked candidate in the RSA Road Transport (Goods) Diploma. The Raymond Birch Award similarly recognises the passenger side.

Two families stand out for their record of service: Gordon Sunderland was Clerk for thirty one years until his death in 1966; his son Oliver served as Clerk for three years and is an Assistant on the Court. E.E. Coxhead and his son, Past Master Lt Col F.E. Coxhead, the present Hon Almoner, together have given 42 years' service. The tercentenary of 1968 launched a major appeal which enlarged the Company's Benevolent Fund. In 1974 it paid £2,000 for a Donation Governorship of Christ's Hospital and Alderman Christopher Leaver was nominated. In 1975 articles of association were agreed with the Royal Corps of Transport, and each year the Company presents a ceremonial sword to the top cadet candidate of the Corps. That same year the London Cartage Fund and Benevolent Fund resources were amalgamated under the Chairmanship of Past Master G.W. Quick-Smith, and today the fund approaches £200,000. Many and varied are the Company's charitable works, primarily for education, through the City and Guilds Institute, Christ's Hospital, City University and the City of London Freeman's School. The Company's Guild church at St Michael Paternoster Royal also provides a meeting place, the Whittington Hall.

In 1980 there came an echo of old battles when the Society of Coal Merchants proposed to petition for the Livery of the Company of Woodmongers and Fuel Sellers. After courteous consultations, it was agreed that the Carmen held succession to the Woodmongers and the Company of Fuellers has applied for the Livery. In 1981 the Carmen furnished the City with their sixth Lord Mayor, Sir Christopher Leaver GBE DMus.

The Master Mariners. At the annual Shipmasters' dinner in Liverpool in 1921, Sir Robert Burton-Chadwick suggested the formation of a Guild or Company of Shipmasters. In 1926 the Company of Master Mariners was formed, and in 1928 HRH The Prince of Wales became the first Master. In 1930 the new Company received its Royal Charter and in 1932 a Grant of Livery. That such a Company was not formed before was undoubtedly due to the nature of its members' calling — continually on the move, mariners had little opportunity to form a Guild.

The Company was originally formed by a Foundation Council of 100 and within 18 months achieved its total membership of 500. Nowadays there is a waiting list, and membership is restricted to any British Master Mariner holding a Certificate of Competency as Master of a foreign-going ship, or a comparable Certificate held for a minimum of five years.

The Company's objects are to provide a central body representative of the Merchant Navy's senior officers, to develop and promote the traditions and efficiency of the service; to encourage and maintain standards of ability and conduct; to promote cooperation with the Royal Navy; to provide a statistical service; to furnish advice and expertise; to offer a forum for discussion; to help those in need within the Service.

Apprentices are bound and when one has held his Master's qualification for five years, he may be admitted. The Honourable Company publishes a quarterly *Journal*. In 1947 it bought the sloop *Wellington* from the Admiralty and, after conversion at Chatham, this appropriately floating 'Hall' has been moored at Temple Stairs. Charitable work comprises two funds for needy Masters and

Navigating Officers and an Education Fund which provides nautical literature and funds prizes for the Nautical Colleges.

The Solicitors. In 1908 four members of the Solicitors Dining Society formulated the idea of a City Company. They were H.F. Eve, P.C.C. Francis, J.C. Holmes and Laming Worthington Evans. Later that year 26 members of the Society circulated the proposal, and called a meeting of members of the profession, stressing there was no intended conflict of interest with the Law Society. In 1909, The City of London Solicitors Company was registered as a Company limited by guarantee. Membership was limited to 200 (increased subsequently to 500) of whom 60 might be life members, and restricted to those practising within three quarters of a mile of the Bank of England. At their first dinner at Mansion House, a cheque for 70 guineas was presented to the Mansion House Earthquake Fund.

One of the first considerations was to form a Library, resulting in the then arrangement with the Law Notes Library. Lectures were inaugurated in 1911. A number of specialist committees were formed, one failing to find sufficient support, which wanted to pursue compulsory membership of the Law Society, members' giving £1,000 security on admission; a bottom age limit of 25; sole trustee-ship only above 30, and undertakings to keep separate trust monies accounts. One Committee discussed Counsel's fees and again the matter was not pursued. Among other matters the Company opposed the Solicitors (Admission of Women) Bill, and favoured special juries in commercial cases.

In 1920 the Company supported a move to standardise dividend warrant forms and protested at the appointments of two barristers as Solicitor and Assistant Solicitor to the Ministry of Labour, which the Lord Chancellor deprecated. The idea of a Ministry of Justice was supported and concern was expressed about the rising rents in the City. In 1921 it was felt that Law Court congestion might be relieved by reducing the vacations.

In 1923 counsel's fees cropped up again and the Company succeeded in obtaining an amendment to the pending Law of Property legislation. The rule that those joining the Company must be members of the Law Society was formalised but not now maintained. In 1924 the Company started its 20 years' pressure to eventually remove the ceiling on City land conveyancing fees. In 1926 the Company was pressing five distinct matters and obtained a Grant of Arms.

In 1927 the City of London Solicitors' Company Prize was inaugurated, and in 1930 the Company proposed a number of amendments adopted within the Finance Bill affecting solicitor-client relationships, and in 1935 the Grotius Prize was founded. In 1939 the Law Society agreed that the Company could form itself into a competent local Law Society, though this did not in effect happen, though it is now treated as such. The Alfred Syrett Prize was founded. In 1942 City firms were circularised on post war problems, and one result was the success of L.C. Bullock's battle over conveyancing charges, which had hitherto failed to reflect the scale of property transactions in the City. In 1944 the Company achieved a Grant of Livery, and adopted as its motto 'Lex Libertatis Origo'; in 1957 it was incorporated by Royal Charter.

From an original Livery of 250 the figure has risen to today's 450. Since the Grant of Livery the Company has actively considered and promoted among others, matters affecting conveyancing charges, legal aid, house price controls, landlord and tenant acts, the obscure drafting of statutes, and retrospective legislation. In 1965 the Company set up a Charitable Fund.

The Farmers. There was a Guild of Corn Chandlers in the 14th century, and agriculture clearly touched the lives of Londoners in a multiplicity of ways from earliest times. Predictably, there was no specifically agricultural guild since farming by definition lay outside the City limits. With the changes in membership and purpose of so many of the old craft and trade guilds, the rapid development of agricultural methods and the modern interface between City institutions, finance and property, it is perhaps less obvious why no agricultural organisation emerged until 1946.

Today farming is one of the nation's fastest growth industries, despite the rapid decline in farmland, with an enviable productivity record. In 1939 the Lord Mayor instigated the Agriculture Fund to raise money for the Duke of Gloucester's Red Cross and St John Appeal. Built up by Sir Richard Haddon, with the help of its Secretary, Alec Robertson, the Fund raised £8,500,000 by the time it closed down in 1946 — more money than any single industry's previous charitable achievement. In Windsor Great Park, five red oaks were planted by the King, the Queen, Princess Elizabeth, Princess Margaret and the Duke of Norfolk as a permanent memorial to the Fund when it reached £5,000,000. When it closed, the King caused four more trees to be planted, forming a cross, with a plaque bearing these lines, selected by him:

'Through God's good grace, through strength of English oak,
We have preserved our faith, our throne, our land;
Now with our freedom saved from tyrant's yoke
We plant these trees. Remember why they stand.'

The Fund comprised not only spokesmen for farmers, landowners and farm workers, but also representatives of some forty ancillary trades and industries, the first such comprehensively representative body. The Chairman of the Fund's Horticultural Committee was Walter Brett, and he suggested the formation of an Association of Agriculture, which was later successfully established.

When the Fund was wound up, it was obvious that the cooperative effort involved should be maintained in peacetime. A Chairman's Committee was set up and a scheme formulated for training ex-servicemen in agriculture; due to a coincidental Government project, this was dropped. Sir Cleveland Fyfe then suggested the formation of a City Livery Company. In 1946 the Company of Agriculturists was established, later changed to the Company of Farmers in deference to City opinion, in many ways reflecting the ideas of Walter Brett. A petition for Grant of Livery was submitted in 1947; a second petition was successful in 1951, on one condition among others, that the majority of the Court should be in the farming industry. The number of the Livery was set at 250.

In 1953 the Company was incorporated by Royal charter and in 1964 the Livery increased to 300. In 1962 advanced courses in farm business management were initiated through Wye College, University of London. These were increased, their scope gradually widened and farmers from the Common Market invited to participate. The Company contributes to the Nuffield Foundation Travelling Fellowships which enable researchers and students to visit overseas farming communities.

In 1975 HRH The Prince of Wales, HRH The Princess Anne and Captain Mark Phillips were elected Honorary Liverymen. Today the Company funds scholarships and grants to agricultural colleges and research; helps rural arts and crafts, and promotes communication between farming and other industries. It administers the Philip Henman Trust and has plans for an eventual Hall, while its motto is 'Give us our daily bread'.

The Air Pilots and Air Navigators. In the 1920s the status of the aviator was precarious and his future uncertain. A small group of commercial pilots, deciding to remedy this unsatisfactory situation, in 1929 together formed a Guild, much along the lines of the traditional City craft guilds. It is today known as The Guild of Air Pilots and Air Navigators. From its inception it has been entirely non-political, and precluded from any form of activity of a trade union nature. From 1932 the Guild's Panel of Examiners was for thirty six years the sole competent authority examining instructors in flying. In 1968 the Government assumed this responsibility as an extension of its control and supervision of flying training establishments, but the Guild has maintained its involvement with the standards of training at these colleges. All students training for professional pilot or navigator licences are encouraged to enter the Guild's cadet scheme.

In 1938 HRH The Duke of Kent became Grand Master, a position today held by HRH The

Prince Philip. HM The Queen has been Patron of the Guild since 1947, before which Her Majesty was Grand Master. In 1956 the Guild achieved a Grant of Livery. The Livery is conferred on Freemen as a mark of distinction; the Guild's membership is otherwise divided between Upper Freemen, Freemen and Cadets. Upper Freemen must have five years' professionally qualified experience within the past ten years, be licensed, have full instructor rating or be a test pilot recognised by the Guild. In appropriate circumstances, flying experience in HM Forces is accepted. Freemen include those who do not yet have five years' experience; private pilot licence holders of five years' standing; pilots and navigators of three years' experience in HM Forces; highly qualified glider pilots. In both categories there is allowance for those with other distinguished service to aviation. Cadets must be under 25 and engaged in fulltime training.

In 1976 the Guild acted as the catalyst in bringing together over twenty disparate societies, associations, airline operators and manufacturers to form the British Civil Aviation Standing Conference, a recognised body which liaises between the industry and the Civil Aviation Authority.

The Guild's main objects are the pursuit of the highest standards of air safety, the enhancement of the status of air pilots and air navigators and liaison with all authorities connected with licensing, training and legislation affecting pilot and navigator, whether professional, private or military.

Uniquely among City Companies, the Guild has an active branch in Australia, and local groups in Hong Kong and in Scotland. These and the Guild's freemen overseas provide a world-wide network of advice and information, and it is undoubtedly the one single body which maintains liaision with Ministers, Members of Parliament, commercial interests, educational institutions and learned societies on all matters affecting the pilot and navigator. It issues Master Air Pilot and Master Air Navigator certificates, and awards trophies for feats of aerial navigation, transport operation, experimental flying, consistency and reliability, and other outstanding achievements.

The Guild is represented on the Airworthiness Requirements Board, Flight Time Limitations Board, the Flight Safety Committee, the General Aviation Safety Committee, and the National Air Traffic Management Advisory Committee, as well as the Aviation Training Committee. Its own Technical Committee makes recommendations to the Civil Aviation Authority and Department of Trade. The Guild acts as a consultative body on legislative proposals, and provides legal aid to members at Courts of Inquiry; it persuaded the Government to hold tribunals to review evidence and findings of inspectors' accident reports to avoid injustice to licence holders.

The Benevolent Fund, in association with the RAF Benevolent Fund, BALPA, and British Airways Benevolent Fund helps disabled pilots, their widows and children, and allied causes. It funds a donation governorship at Christ's Hospital and helps the elderly through the Crossways Trust.

The Guild's trophies include the Johnston Memorial Trophy (which commemorates the navigator of the ill-fated R101 airship) for outstanding navigation or navigational development; the Cumberbatch Trophy for air safety; the Brackley Memorial Trophy, originally for flying boat operation, now for outstanding flying, contributing to operational development or new techniques in air transport; the Derry and Richards Memorial Medal for experimental flying achievement; the Pike Trophy for contribution to flying instruction; the Award of Merit for Guild members; the Grand Master's Medal for the best cadet each year at the College of Air Training, Hamble; the Guild Sword of Honour for outstanding contribution to general aviation outside scheduled airlines; the Guild Medal for exceptional contribution to aviation. The Guild also administers the Sir Alan Cobham Memorial Award for the most meritorious student pilot from the three major Civil Air Training Establishments and the Sir James Martin Award for original, outstanding and practical contribution to safety, whether operationally or in the survival of aircrew and passengers, or for an act of valour which leads to greater safety and enhanced survival.

The Tobacco Pipe Makers and Tobacco Blenders. In the 16th century, English sailors acquired the habit of smoking cigars and pipes from Spanish, Portuguese and French contemporaries. In 1586 Sir Francis Drake introduced the tobacco plant, and Sir Walter Raleigh found a method of curing it, popularising smoking among Elizabethan courtiers, who became known as 'reeking gallants'. In 1604 James I published his famous 'Counterblast to Tobacco', which held that it was 'a custom lothsome to the eye, hatefull to the nose, harmefull to the braine, dangerous to the Lungs, and in the blacke stinking fume thereof, nearest resembling the horrible Stigian smoke of the pit that is bottomelesse'. In 1613 there were 'upward of 7,000 houses that doth live by that trade'.

In 1602 the Port of London imported 16,128 pounds of tobacco, and in 1608 the King ordered the duty raised from 2d to 6s 10d a pound. This encouraged smuggling and indiginous tobacco growing. In 1619 the Crown forbade the latter, and restricted all imports to London. In that year the Tobacco Pipe Makers of Westminster in the County of Middlesex were incorporated by Royal Charter — not a City Company. This followed the granting of a monopoly in pipe clay the year before to Philip Foote and others.

In 1634 these monopolists persuaded the Company that its charter did not conform to the Statute of Monopolies of 1624 and to covenant with the Crown to burn only coals, a new process of clay firing, and pay an annual rent of £100 a year. The monopolists undertook to cover the rent and incorporation expenses in return for the Company's agreement to buy all its clay from them. The original charter was duly surrendered and a second one obtained by the Tobacco Pipe Makers of London and Westminster and England and Wales in 1634. In 1638 the Company complained to the Privy Council that the monopoly created high fixed prices and a year later it was ended. By 1663 the Company had 'long since' forfeited its charter for non-payment of the Crown rent.

In 1663 Charles II granted a new charter to the Tobacco Pipe Makers in the Cities of London and Westminster and the Kingdom of England and the Dominion of Wales, for a yearly rent of £1 6s 8d. Despite its grandiose title, the powers of the new Company appear to have been limited in scope and area, for there were thriving pipe makers in Bristol and elsewhere. In 1663 the Court of Aldermen granted City Company status without Livery. Meanwhile, in 1639, the Tobacco-workers of Westminster had unsuccessfully sought a charter, and in 1690 the Grocers were empowered to bring tobacconists and tobacco-cutters within their control.

The new Company suffered the disadvantage that many of its freemen were free of other companies and their apprentices' dues therefore went elsewhere. Most of the Company's freemen lived on the outskirts or without the City, possibly due to the citizens' dislike of the manufacturing processes and its effects. Having no Livery, and no power to compel practitioners of the craft to take up its freedom, the Company remained small and penurious, and clearly could not afford a Hall. In the 18th century, snuff supplanted pipe smoking in the fashionable reaches of society, and cigars and cigarettes created even more serious competition in the next century.

Bye laws made in 1738 were repealed and replaced in 1805 and again in 1821, making allowance for a Livery which was not granted. In 1823 the Company launched the first of a series of expensive law suits designed to reinforce control of its trade, but which crippled it financially. The final action was in 1851, the last enrolment of an apprentice in 1852 and, in 1868, the Clerk died and the last admission of a freeman of the Company to the freedom of the City took place. In 1903 it was said that the Company had been extinct for at least 30 years.

In 1954, when Alan L. Adler heard the old Company mentioned on the radio, he suggested a revival. Under the Chairmanship of Alfred H. Dunhill, the briar pipe and tobacco trade formed the Company of Tobacco Pipe Makers and Tobacco Blenders. Its early success was largely due to the Clerk, W.M. Wilson. In 1956 a Grant of Arms was achieved, with the motto 'Product Terra' and in 1961, a Grant of Livery.

In 1959 an appeal to members generated £3,000 towards charitable funds; in 1961 the Benevolent Fund was created and, by 1969, £50,000 had been raised. In 1963 Sevenoaks School was selected for special support initially by way of three scholarships; in 1964 the Company furnished a Governor. By 1975, £11,000 had been provided to equip language and biology laboratories. In addition the Company has endowed scholarships and bursaries at the Guildhall School of Music and the Sail Training Association and made grants to the London Federation of Boys' Clubs.

The Furniture Makers. In medieval times, furniture principally comprised chairs or simple case work of nailed board and iron strapped construction. The Turners controlled the former, and the Carpenters and Blacksmiths the latter, while the Cofferers oversaw chests, coffers and upholstered chairs. Numerous other crafts were also involved, such as those of the Clothworkers, Cordwainers, Curriers, Weavers, Woolmen and Broderers. Even the Basketmakers were concerned — with cradles. From the 15th century, furniture became a specialised branch of joinery, and the Upholders grew in importance and influence. With the Restoration, and the return from exile of courtiers used to continental fashions and cabinet-work, furniture changed in style and technique. Most of the cabinet-makers were immigrants. The 1666 Fire accelerated demand, and, by the 18th century, the Upholders had become the arbiters of taste, skills, prices and the principal stockholders of finished wares. Thomas Chippendale was an Upholder.

During the 19th century, the retail and manufacturing aspects of furniture making separated, and in our own time, the industry has polarised between retail, manufacturing and labour organisations. For these reasons no specific furniture makers' guild ever existed or needed to exist until, in 1949, George Hensher suggested the time was ripe. Seymour Plummer was the first Clerk of the Guild formed in 1952, and the first Court included men like H. Stanley Wharton, Master, Sir Herman Lebus CBE, Senior Warden, and Junior Warden, Alderman Ralph E. Perring; Lucian Ercolani, Anthony Heal, Frank Lupton, Sir Giles Gilbert Scott OM and Edward H. Pinto. The Guild was primarily formed for charitable purposes. Membership was and is largely drawn from the trade, its unions, the Royal College of Arts, Royal Institution of British Architects, Council of Industrial Design, Furniture Development Council and Society of Industrial Artists.

By 1955 funds raised generated scholarships of £400 out of annual income. By 1963 the figure was £3,000 and it is currently £17,500. In 1958 the Guild inaugurated the Guild Mark Scheme for pieces of outstanding British made furniture. In 1963 a Grant of Livery was achieved. Appropriately, the Lord Mayor that year was Sir Ralph Perring, a member of the furniture industry, and Founder Member and Past Master of the Guild.

In 1981, manufacturing awards were made to twelve individuals, ranging from the £100 A.H. Mackintosh Award to the £700 Schreiber, Alston and Bowen Awards. Five design awards were made, two to students of the Ravensbourne College of Art and Design, one to a student of Carlowe Technical College, another to a Leeds Polytechnic student and another to a student of the Royal College of Art. Four retail awards were made, worth altogether £2,100.

The awards fall within the following categories: The Master's Prize of £1,000; business prizes and awards totalling £2,500; manufacturing scholarships worth £8,000; design awards worth £3,250, and retail scholarships to the value of £2,750. The Master's Prize is awarded for a thesis promoting original thought and research, of wide benefit to the industry.

The Company has recently completed a Royal College of Art research project with the Painter-Stainers on new techniques for the decoration of composition board for internal cladding for furniture, by supporting research fellows working on lasers, colour and staining, instant inlay and other techniques.

The Scientific Instrument Makers. Instrument makers have been active in the City for some three centuries and, in fact, one firm, W. Ottway & Co was founded near the Royal Exchange in 1640 and has been handed down from father to son to the present day. Originally the Blacksmiths controlled the craft until the Clockmakers broke away in 1631, with powers over watchmaking and mathematical instrument making. In 1677 several instrument makers were made free of the Company. The case of Robert Bate in the 19th century stimulated existing contention between the Clockmakers and Spectacle Makers, resolved by the authorities determining that Bate should become free of both Companies or cease trading in mathematical instruments 'which in their construction peculiarly or particularly belonged to Clock Making'. Henceforth instrument making apparently ceased to be recognised as a separate craft, and was virtually eliminated from both guilds.

In 1955 C.E.T. Cridland, then President of the Scientific Instrument Makers Association, called a meeting at which it was agreed to form a City Guild to foster scientific instrument making and promote goodwill in the craft or science. In 1964 the Guild was constituted a Company, with a Grant of Livery of 200.

The Chartered Surveyors. Incorporated with a Grant of Livery in 1977, the Company was the first of nine new Companies to be formed from modern professions and trades in the past six years. Membership is restricted to chartered surveyors, therefore members also of the Royal Institution of Chartered Surveyors. The Livery is limited to 300. Its ordinances require it to raise funds for charity and foster relations between all branches of the profession through the RICS.

In 1979 the Company adopted 135 Field Survey Squadron RE(V) and annually presents a silver salver and personally engraved pewter tankard, its Endeavour Award, to the member of the Squadron who has done the most to promote its activities. Its charitable Trust administers the Sydney A. Smith Fund to help students finish further education courses when in financial difficulty. It also runs two annual award schemes to the top students in their final year of the Land Economy Tripos at Cambridge, and second year of the similar courses at Reading, Aberdeen and the Royal Agricultural College, Cirencester.

In 1979 the Robert Steel Award was launched to commemorate his sponsored walk, which raised £71,000 for the RCIS Benevolent Fund: it goes to the branch of RCIS which contributes most in cash or kind to that Fund. The Trust also provides holiday awards each year to those in need and makes general charitable donations.

In 1981 the Company sponsored, jointly with the City University Business School, a week's seminar 'Focus on the Commercial Activities of the City of London', to introduce younger senior surveyors to aspects not normally met in their work. This was repeated in 1982.

The Chartered Accountants. The idea for the Company had been mooted before, but it was in 1975 that a Guild Committee was formed, following discussion between leading accoutants and the Corporation. The Committee included (later Sir) Kenneth Cork, James Keith CBE, a former Chief Commoner who became the first Master, and Oliver Sunderland as Clerk. In 1976 the Company was formed and in 1977 it was incorporated by Letters Patent. In 1978 the Lord Mayor was Sir Kenneth Cork — an undoubted stimulus to the newborn Company. The Livery is limited to 350.

One of the advantages enjoyed by the new Company, whose members are *ipso facto* also members of the Institute of Chartered Accountants in England and Wales, is the use of Chartered Accountants' Hall — the headquarters of the Institute.

With primarily charitable aims, the Company immediately formed a Trust, to give help to the needy and support City and other charities, but also to emphasise educational benefactions. The first scheme launched was an annual prize of £250 to the qualifying student with the best overall performance in the two professional exams.

In 1980 the Company launched its second scheme — The Commonwealth Project, to help the development of the accounting profession in member countries. This will take the form of finance to fill gaps in the funding of schemes initiated by indigenous bodies, such as for lecturers' travel expenses; seeking support from appropriate bodies in the Commonwealth where the Trust's funds are insufficient, and finding people to help.

The Company marks its close links with the Institute by the presentation annually of a Past President's badge, and it has also created a 'new' tradition for itself: the adoption of a livery jacket in velvet, which replaces evening dress on formal occasions.

The Chartered Secretaries and Administrators. The third professional body to secure incorporation and Grant of Livery in 1977 was that of the Chartered Secretaries and Administrators, whose petition reasoned 'as an encouragement to a profession that is essential in providing to the community a class of person well qualified to be employed in responsible and difficult duties . . .'. Membership is restricted to the profession. The Company's objects include the accumulation of funds for the relief of needy members and their dependants, and for educational research and awards, the acquisition of a City Hall, or other premises, and to work closely with the Institute and other relevant associations.

A Charitable Trust has been established, and has granted a bursary at the City University to a member of the Institute, for study for a Master's degree. Prizes have been awarded through various polytechnics and colleges throughout the country to outstanding students in the fields of business studies, law, economics, accounting and finance.

In 1980 the Company signed Letters of Association with the Royal Army Pay Corps.

The Builders Merchants. The desirability of enhancing the status of the industry and of developing charitable and educational work was first mooted in 1958. The first meeting to discuss ordinances was held in 1961 and that year the Company was formed, with 60 Founder Members. It sponsored the formation of the Institution of Builders' Merchants in conjunction with the National Federation of Builders' and Plumbers' Merchants, primarily for educational reasons, and continues to support the Institute.

In 1972, recognition as a City Company without Livery was achieved, and in 1975 the Company obtained a Grant of Arms. Two years later it achieved its Grant of Livery. It subscribes annually to the main charity of its industry, the Metal Trades Benevolent Society, and to other City Charities.

The Launderers. The formation of the new Company was first discussed in 1955 and 1956; a committee was appointed the following year. In 1960 an inaugural meeting in Tallow Chandlers Hall was attended by 32. Its declared objects included the provision of a City organisation for consultation and cooperation within the craft and between it and kindred trades, and the furtherance of technical education and research, as well as the provision of funds for the needy. Membership is restricted to Launderers and those in associated occupations.

In 1964 the Company's mace was carved by a Portsmouth craftsman in the form of a wooden laundering dolly, and the Company adopted the *March of the Launderers* based on the tune of the *Irish Washerwoman.* It also established a Charitable and Educational Trust. In the first year, grants totalling £2,650 were made to three post graduate students, working respectively at Battersea College of Technology on measurement and control of moisture during drying, at London University on computer programmes within the industry and at the University of Nottingham on the economics of the industry. The Company has also provided £4,125 towards the administration of the Guild of Cleaners and Launderers Examination Board, and new technology text books. A Grant of Arms was achieved, with the motto 'Cleanliness is Next to Godliness'.

In 1965 the Company introduced an apprenticeship scheme and in 1970, it arranged an exhibition at Baker's Hall and published a book, *The Craft of Laundering*. In 1975 the Company was formally recognised, and instituted a silver medal for the outstanding student of the year completing the Derby Lonsdale College of Art and Technology diploma course in drycleaning and laundry technology. In 1976 the Company endowed an annual berth in the Sail Training Association's schooner, *Sir Winston Churchill,* and received the Barrett Collection of Antique Laundry Equipment, which, in 1977, was given on permanent loan for display at the Museum of London. That same year a Grant of Livery was achieved. In 1979 the Company accepted continuing responsibility for a stall at the Red Cross Market. In 1980 it decided to sponsor a trainee on an Outward Bound course on an experimental basis.

In 1981 the Company was invited to invest in non-voting shares against a single day's right of use of Court Room and Hall in Glaziers' Hall, which also carried the sole use of a permanent office for the Clerk, and the right to refer to the building as Launderers' Hall, and maintain the Company's possessions there. The Launderers applied for six shares, to enable them to use the facilities six times a year for 75 years.

Benevolence has included an annual grant to a member's widow, funds to City churches, schools, HMS *Belfast* Trust, medical charities, and the industry's Training Committee.

The Marketors. The word marketor encompasses the entire spectrum of marketing — research, development, advertising, promotion, distribution, selling and support services. It is held to indicate total responsiblity for making the right product or service available to the consumer at the right time in the right place at the right price; the last syllable of the term emphasises the professional nature of the Company, which is restricted to members and fellows of the Institute of Marketing and those exceptionally distinguished in marketing or the City. In the early 1970s Fellows of the Institute laid plans for the formation of the Company and in 1975 the Guild was inaugurated, HRH The Duke of Edinburgh consenting to be the first Honorary Freeman.

The Guild's objects were and remain the wellbeing and success of Freemen and those associated with them, and the understanding and acceptance of marketing as a major force for economic good and consumer benefit. A Charitable Trust was established with charitable and educational aims. In 1977 a Grant of Livery was achieved; Founder Master of both Guild and Livery Company was W.R. Bowden. The first lady Liveryman was elected in 1981. Initially, the Charitable Trust's funds are small, but it has supported a number of causes, and supports the College of Marketing through the Institute and makes other awards in marketing and business studies. The Livery is limited to 200. The Company's motto is 'Mercatura Adiuvat Omnes' — 'Commercial activities benefit everyone'.

The Actuaries. In 1693 Edmund Halley of comet fame constructed a life table in London — the life table is the foundation of actuarial calculations. Scientific life assurance began with the establishment of the Equitable Assurance Society in the City in 1762 and the profession of actuary was formalised in 1884 with the establishment of the Institute of Actuaries, with its headquarters at Staple Inn. An Actuary was first defined in 1553 as a registrar or notary who recorded the acts of a court, but came to mean one who compiles tables of mortality, calculates premia and solves monetary problems depending on interest and probability, in connection with life, fire and accident.

In 1979 the Company of Actuaries was formed and incorporated, with a Grant of Livery. Membership is restricted to Fellows or Associates of the Institute of Actuaries or Fellows of the Faculty of Actuaries. The principal objects are to promote the expertise and skills of Actuaries and their application to other professions and industry, and to relieve poverty of Actuaries and other professions, advance professional education, fund research, award exhibitions, prizes, and grants.

The Insurers. The first attempt to establish a City insurance guild was made unsuccessfully in 1974; the second attempt started in 1978 and in 1979 the Guild was incorporated, within three months receiving its Grant of Livery — probably a record. The Livery is limited to 300 and the objects are to foster insurance, mutual information, funds for charitable purposes and aid other insurance bodies. In 1980 the Company achieved a Grant of Arms, with the motto 'Omnium Defensor' — 'Protects All'. The Clerk has his office in the Hall of the Chartered Insurance Insitute. A Charitable Trust has been formed.

The Arbitrators. The latest of the modern professions to achieve incorporation and Grant of Livery for a City Company was that of the Arbitrators, in 1981. London arbitration is a term that has been used in international contracts for many years, and it was in the City in 1892 that one of the oldest arbitration bodies in the world was inaugurated — the London Court of Arbitration. It operates under the general direction of a Joint Committee of Management culled from the Corporation, the Chartered Institute of Arbitrators and the London Chamber of Commerce and Industry. The Institute administers its arbitration activities. The Court is based at the International Arbitration Centre as is the associated London Panel of International Arbitrators.

The Institute was founded in 1915 and granted a Royal charter in 1979. It is a multi-disciplinary body drawn from law, shipping, building, engineering, banking, insurance, accountancy, commodity markets and so on. Its membership of some 4,500 is spread across 72 countries. The Panel was formed in 1976. The Court was first envisaged by Common Council in 1883 and in 1975 its work merged with that of the Institute. Arbitration is a second profession, and intending members must complete the Institute's training programme, or have extensive arbitration experience; the Institution's exams can be taken overseas as well as at home. The Institute's Panels cover thirty eight fields.

Only members of the Institute may be free of the new Company, which is run from the Institute's International Arbitration Centre in Cannon Street. The Livery numbers 300 at its maximum, and 180 have so far joined.

An immediate purpose of the new Company is to establish a Charitable Trust Fund for needy members and education; application has been made for a Grant of Arms.

It is perhaps appropriate that this new City Company should be formed little short of a century after the City conceived the need for the Court that has made it the centre of international arbitration, and some might see a certain piquancy in the actual Court centenary of that conception falling just a twelvemonth short of Orwell's arbitrary year of human bondage. By definition, arbitration presumes choice, and considered choice protects freedom with responsibility, so that the final Livery granted, prior to this record of the City's Companies, provides an appropriate punctuation mark to the City's living past.

Companies without Livery, and under consideration. There are three Companies without Livery, and at least two new companies under consideration. Of these last, it is too soon to comment on one, and the other echoes an ancient Guild, the Company of Woodmongers, now itself regarded as embraced implicitly within the Company of Carmen. The Woodmongers surrendered their charter in 1667, but remained responsible for the collection of coal tax and dues — it is said that five sixths of the cost of rebuilding St Paul's Cathedral was met from coal taxes, which passed through the Guild's hands. In 1730 the Society of Owners of Coal Craft took on the Guild's duties, and in 1836 became the Society of Coal Merchants of London. Coal factors by 1761 formed the Society of Coal Factors, and in 1831 the two combined to set up the Coal Meter Committee to weigh coals entering the Port of London. These three bodies ran the Coal Exchange until its demolition in 1959, and the funds then realised were devoted to charity. In 1981 this trio formed the Company of Fuellers which, in October, took the first steps towards incorporation, when the Mayor and Court of Aldermen recommended that its petition be granted and its ordinances enrolled.

The Parish Clerks. In the early Church, the reader was probably the only literate member of the community; with the institution of the parish system, he became the chief or parish clerk, in minor orders. Until the Reformation, he was concerned with parish worship and sometimes its children's education. Thereafter the office was held by laymen, whose duties included leading the singing and responses, and in the modern world, most of his responsibilities have been taken over by church officials or local administration. Today the Parish Clerks are appointed by the parochial or guild church council of existing churches or parishes within which ancient parishes have been amalgamated, and they are eligible for admission as brethren of the Company. Those ancient parishes in 1639 originally numbered 129. Ninety seven were within the City's walls and, of those without, four were in Southwark. By 1824 twenty one more parishes were added so that today there are 150 brethren.

In 1274 the Fraternity of St Nicholas was first recorded, with property near Bishopsgate, on a site now named Clarks Place; their Hall, confiscated in 1547 with the suppression of chantries, was demolished in 1553. Clerkenwell takes its name from the well where the Clerks assembled to 'play some history of holy scripture'. Stow records two such masques of 1390 and at Skinners Wells in 1409, a custom revived in recent City of London Festivals. In 1442 the Chief or Parish Clerks of the City of London were recognised by Royal charter of Henry VI and, seven centuries later, they still share in Holy Communion and meet in common hall to mark the Feast of St Nicholas referred to in that charter. The Company confers neither freedom nor Livery on its brethren, since originally the distinction of the surplice was considered preferable to the wearing of a livery.

Between 1449 and 1521 an illuminated obituary roll of deceased brethren and of 'any willing in a devout spirit to carry out the Fraternity's objects' was inscribed and survives, and the tradition it represents is kept alive in corporate worship and a silent toast at Company meetings to monarchs, benefactors and 'to all brethren departed this life'. Two of these benefactors in 1568 were William Roper, son-in-law of Sir Thomas More (who approved the 1530 ordinances), and Richard Hust, parish clerk of St George, Southwark, in the time of Dickens' *Little Dorrit,* and the man principally behind the foundation in 1826 of the Company's former Camberwell almshouses, built in 1832. Another reminder is the Elizabethan funeral pall cloth.

In 1582 the Company achieved a second Grant of Arms, reflecting musical responsibilities. (The Company's motto is 'Unitas Societatis Stabilitas'.) The crest is an open prick-song book and these are repeated in the arms, with supporters of angels with trumpets; the Company's third (1671) Wood Street hall contained an organ — the second Hall (1562) was in Vintry ward and destroyed in the Great Fire. In 1601 two embroidered head-dresses were provided for the crowning of the two then joint Masters; replicas are now worn by the retiring Master and the Master-elect at the July installation ceremony.

The presently operative Charter was granted in 1639 to the 'Parish Clerks of the Parish Churches of the City and Suburbs of London and the Liberties thereof, the City of Westminster, the Borough of Southwark and the fifteen out-parishes adjacent'. At that time, the Parish Clerks kept the church registers and (from 1546) the Bills of Mortality for the City authorities, printing the latter on their own press, installed in 1625.

The Company's third hall and its contents were lost in 1940 through enemy action. Their Patron today is the Archbishop of Canterbury and the Company's Visitor is the Bishop of London. At the annual Michaelmas service at St Lawrence Jewry, preceding the Lord Mayor's election at Guildhall, the Master acts as crucifer.

The Company's pension funds aid widows of members, their daughters, sons, widows of parochial or chapel clerks of the Church of England, Parish and Vestry Clerks, secretaries of Parochial Church Councils and their widows and their dependants, in that order of priority.

The Watermen and Lightermen of the River Thames. The river gave birth to the City and for centuries remained its main highway. The Company is the child of statute. In 1514 Parliament regulated Thames fares but the watermen went their own way, so in 1555 Parliament appointed rulers of all watermen and wherrymen working between Gravesend and Windsor, requiring one year apprenticeships, and the Company was born. The Company obtained a Grant of Arms in 1585, with the motto 'At Commandment of our Superiors'. By the end of the century the Watermen had their own Hall — the Mansion of Cold Harbour, east of today's Cannon Street Station. Stow, in 1598, recorded no less than forty thousand river workers. In 1603 a further act extended the apprenticeship term to seven years.

The ordinances of 1626 recorded weekly pensions of 8d for 'poor and impotent freemen' though the Watermen and Lightermen are not free of the City and have never been granted a Livery, though their historic objects remain to maintain navigational standards of Watermen (passenger carriers) and Lightermen (goods carriers) on the Thames: annually, boys are bound and examined at Watermen's Hall.

In 1666 the Hall went up in flames and was rebuilt in 1670 on the same site. In 1700 the Lightermen, previously within the Woodmongers' Company, were admitted by statute into the Watermen's Company, gradually outnumbering the original Watermen, as road transport improved in the City and Westminster. That same year, regular payments from the Poors Fund were also authorised. The Rulers could licence freemen to work on Sundays, and the surplus, after wages, went to the Poors Box. Other income derived from government grants when the Thames was frozen over, internal fines and compensation for ferries lost when bridges were built.

In 1715 Thomas Doggett, an Irish comedian, founded the annual Doggett's Coat and Badge sculling race, to celebrate the anniversary of the accession of the House of Hanover to the Throne. It is only open to freemen within the twelve months following completion of apprenticeship. The course, from London Bridge to Chelsea, is a furlong short of five miles, and the winner receives the orange-red coat and silver badge. The first to win was the water poet, John Taylor, who was apprenticed to a Westminster waterman and pressganged into the Navy on seven different occasions. He supported the Watermen against the removal of theatres from south to north bank, and against the introduction of sedan chairs and hackney carriages in the City, keeping them out for 35 years, unless their journies ended at least two miles from the Thames. Another winner in 1730 was Jack Broughton who, four years later, became champion prize fighter of England, introducing gloves and science to the sport, his code being the forerunner to the Queensberry Rules.

In 1721 the Company again rebuilt its Hall, moving to the present Hall at St Mary-at-Hill in 1780. Among its treasures is the 1695 Batchelors Bowl, used for 135 years by elderly widows of freemen, who filled it with ale and gave each young freeman a draught as he left the Hall, against 1s payment. Towards the close of the 18th century, reflecting the immemorial tradition of furnishing literally hundreds of men for Naval service, the Corp of River Fencibles was formed at Watermen's Hall, paving the way for the abolition of impressment, in 1859.

In 1827 the Company was incorporated by statute and gained its independence, the further Act of 1859 consolidating and extending its powers. It fixed fares and appointed plying places, measured and registered boats and barges, and regulated Watermen and Lightermen. In 1857, the Thames Conservancy Act restricted its sphere of operation to eastwards of Teddington Lock.

In 1839 John Dudin Brown, Master Waterman, gave the Company land at Penge, and funds were raised to build forty eight cottages (which survive today) for freemen redundant due to the growth of docks and tugs, and to house those returning from the Napoleonic wars. In 1888

William Vokins built twelve further surviving almshouses at Ditchling, Sussex. In 1908 the birth of the Port of London Authority and the following Act of 1920 removed the Company's duties and authority, except for apprenticeships, freedom and charitable works.

In the last war the Hall sustained some damage, was restored in 1951 and improved in 1961. That year Philip Henman endowed after-school education for port transport workers, which has also facilitated help for the Apprentices Training School and three berths in the Sail Training Association's schooner, *Sir Winston Churchill.*

For four centuries, son has followed father as freemen of the Company, thus ensuring a surely unique family loyalty to this ancient Company without Livery.

The Builders. Restricted to chartered architects, engineers, surveyors, builders, town planners and academics in building and civil engineering, the Company of Builders was formed in 1976, by senior officers of the Faculty of Building. Within a year, the membership of three hundred was taken up, and the waiting list numbers over two hundred.

A Charitable Trust was formed, now with substantial funds, which supports universities and children's charities. The Builders were among the first to admit ladies to their Company. Their plate includes nine loving cups, each dedicated to a different profession within building and civil engineering, and the Dusseldorf Plate, reflecting links with the guilds of that city. Much of the silver is kept in hand-crafted chests, the finest being a hand carved replica of St Paul's Cathedral.

The Company is dedicated to aiding training in building and civil engineering, intends to petition for a Grant of Arms and in due course, for a charter of incorporation.

Commander John Young of the space shuttle *Columbia* receives the Air Pilots and Air Navigators' Brackley Memorial Trophy from Capt Hugh Dibley. (AP)

The Livery Hall of the Armourers and Brasiers. (AB)

ABOVE LEFT: The Owl Pot of the Armourers and Brasiers, (AB) CENTRE: the Arms of the Accountants, (AC) and RIGHT: of the Furniture Makers. (FM) BELOW: The modern Grant of Arms of the Surveyors. (SS)

TO ALL AND SINGULAR that shall hear or see these presents We Peter Beckford Rutgers Vanneck Knight Grand Cross of the Most Excellent Order of the British Empire Companion of the Most Honourable Order of the Bath holder of the Air Force Cross and holder of the Air Efficiency Award Lord Mayor and the Aldermen of the City of London send GREETING – BE IT KNOWN that on the eighteenth day of October in the twenty-sixth year of the Reign of our Sovereign Lady Queen Elizabeth the Second a Petition of the good men of the Guild of Marketors was read in the Court of Mayor and Aldermen before Robin Danvers Penrose Gillett Baronet Knight Grand Cross of the Most Excellent Order of the British Empire holder of the Reserve Decoration Lord Mayor in the Inner Chamber of the Guildhall Praying that the said Lord Mayor and Aldermen might constitute their Guild a Livery Company of the City of London in such manner as to the Lord Mayor and Aldermen might seem fitting And that the said Court did refer the said Petition to the Worshipful the Committee of the Whole Court of Aldermen for General Purposes to consider and report thereon Which Committee did consider with the counsel of certain of its Officers the objects constitutions and ordinances of the said Guild And FORASMUCH as the good men of the said Guild did approve certain constitutions and ordinances for the future regulation of their Guild as a Livery Company in conformity with the law and custom of the City of London which constitutions and ordinances were considered approved and accepted by the Worshipful the Committee of the Whole Court for General Purposes on the second day of December in the said year the said Committee on the thirteenth day of December following did report to the Court of Mayor and Aldermen and did recommend that the Prayer of the Petition be complied with on condition THAT the number of the Livery should not exceed 200 THAT the Fine for admission to the Livery should be 200 pounds and THAT no person should be admitted to the Livery unless he first produce the copy of his Freedom of the City of London WHICH REPORT was well liked and approved by the said Court of Mayor and Aldermen THEREUPON the Lord Mayor and Aldermen on the said thirteenth day of December in the said year did Grant Confirm and Ratify unto the good men of the Guild of Marketors that they be a Livery Company of the City of London by the name of the Worshipful Company of Marketors and subject to the aforesaid constitutions and ordinances and did Order that the Chamberlain of London admit their freemen to the Freedom of the City and enrol their apprentices in accordance with the Custom of London that the Constitutions and Ordinances of the said Company be enrolled among the records of the Court and that the Grant of Livery be embodied in Letters Patent under the Mayoralty Seal

GIVEN under the Seal of our Office of Mayoralty of the City aforesaid the Fourteenth day of the month of April in the twenty-seventh year of the reign of our Sovereign Lady Queen Elizabeth the Second

Clayton
G. W. Gillet
Clerk of the Seal

LEFT: Sir Kenneth Cork, as Lord Mayor, presents the mace to the Accountants, (AC) RIGHT: the Launderers' Arms, (LR) and BELOW: the Marketors' Letters Patent. (MK) OPPOSITE ABOVE LEFT: The Actuaries' Arms, (AT) RIGHT: the Parish Clerks' Elizabethan funeral pall; BELOW LEFT: the Beadle's staff and CENTRE: their Crowns in use. (PC) BELOW: One of the Builders' loving cups. (BR)

The Rt Hon the Lord Mayor(1981-2), Sir Christopher Leaver GBE DMus. (UPPA)

My Lord Mayor, Sheriffs, Aldermen

The Lord Mayor is the symbol of the independence of the City — an independence which is much valued by those who still regard London as the financial centre of the world.

The Lord Mayor is elected by the liverymen of the City who nominate two candidates, both of whom must be aldermen who have served as sheriffs, at a ceremony in Guildhall every Michaelmas Day (29 September). The full description of the gathering is 'The Meeting or Assembly of the Mayor, Aldermen and Liverymen of the several Companies of the City of London in Common Hall assembled'. At the Hustings (a word of Saxon origin meaning a house-court as distinct from one in the open air but now referring to the raised dais at the east end of Guildhall), the Recorder reads to Common Hall: 'The Court of Aldermen are now electing a Lord Mayor from the two names selected by you, the liverymen of the City. They and you will be exercising "your undoubted right" in selecting a person to fill the highest office in a system of government that is unique in this country'. The liverymen then nominate the two candidates who are presented to the Court of Aldermen, who make the final choice. At the election of Lord Mayor all Aldermen who have served the office of Sheriff are in nomination.

Before a citizen can attain the office of Lord Mayor he must submit himself for election on three occasions and finally to scrutiny by the Court of Aldermen: first by voters of the Ward for which he is a candidate for the office of Alderman, secondly, by the liverymen in Common Hall assembled, on election as Sheriff, thirdly, by the liverymen in Common Hall, on nomination for Lord Mayor, and finally, by the Court of Aldermen, who select one of the two nominated by the Livery. Both as Sheriff and Lord Mayor the election requires the approval of the Sovereign.

When the Lord Mayor-Elect is later presented for the Sovereign's approval, as required by King John's Charter, he goes accompanied by the Recorder to the Palace of Westminster to receive the approval through the Lord Chancellor. On the Friday before the second Saturday in November the Lord Mayor-Elect makes his declaration of office in Guildhall, and the following day (Lord Mayor's Day) he goes in state to the Law Courts where he is presented by the Recorder to the judges of the Queen's Bench Division for the statutory and final declaration. It is this journey which is called the Lord Mayor's Show, and it is intended to *show* the Lord Mayor to the people.

On the day before the Lord Mayor's Show, the Lord Mayor receives the Lord Mayor-Elect at Mansion House, and there is a luncheon in the Egyptian Hall. Afterwards, they go by car, with the ensign flying, to Guildhall for the ceremony of the Silent Change, where the Sceptre, Seal and Purse are handed in absolute silence by the City Chamberlain to the outgoing Lord Mayor, who delivers them to his successor. The rest of the regalia is then presented to the new Lord Mayor, and is taken back to its respective custodians. The outgoing Lord Mayor then delivers the keys of the City and Hospital Seals to the new Lord Mayor. And at last, vocally, the Aldermen, Sheriffs and City officers offer their congratulations. Trumpets sound, and the procession then leaves Guildhall, led by the Lord Mayor, the outgoing Lord Mayor walking on his left.

Nowadays the Lord Mayor's Show takes place on the Saturday, the Silent Change the day before. Then on the Monday following, the Lord Mayor's Banquet — an annual event now for over four centuries — is held at Guildhall. The Prime Minister is among the honoured guests and speakers.

Samuel Pepys records that in the seventeenth century the cost of the Banquet's ten sumptuous courses, eaten off common wooden platters, and choicest wines served in plain earthenware beakers, was between £600 and £700. To-day's Banquet works out at considerably more than that.

As First Citizen of the City and head of the Corporation of London the Lord Mayor presides over many of its meetings, including that of the Court of Common Council and the Court of Aldermen. He is also the Chief Magistrate of the City, and the head of the City Lieutenancy. Like the two Sheriffs, the Lord Mayor has ceremonial duties in connection with the Central Criminal Court — popularly known as 'The Old Bailey'. He also sits weekly if possible at the Mansion House Justice Room.

During his year of office, the Lord Mayor lives at Mansion House and often makes three or four speeches a day at official functions in London and elsewhere. At Mansion House or Guildhall he may receive visiting Heads of State and several hundred other distinguished visitors. The Corporation's City Cash gives the Lord Mayor an allowance to help him carry out his engagements which can range from State receptions for members of the Royal Family to travelling to any part of the world on missions of goodwill, arranged in consultation with the Foreign Office. But even so, the Lord Mayor usually has to draw considerably on his own resources, and none of the expense of the Mayoralty falls upon the rate or tax payers.

The Lord Mayor is held in high esteem. His duties and his role are of national as well as local significance. He is more in the public eye than the Mayors of other large towns, and appears to us as the embodiment of civic success. It is important, however, to remember that the Lord Mayor is only mayor of the City *proper,* and not the whole area of London. Other parts of London are governed by their own Borough Councils, each with their own Mayor. (Westminster has a Lord Mayor.)

The Lord Mayor can also arouse and direct the Nation's pity. When disasters such as floods and earthquakes occur, both at home and abroad, it is often the Lord Mayor who opens Funds for the relief of victims. Thus he constitutes a permanent reminder of the Christian duty of the better off to care for the poor.

The area of which the Lord Mayor is the civic head lies at the heart of the British Commonwealth. It includes great trading and financial bodies such as Lloyds, the Bank of England, the Stock Exchange, the Baltic Exchange, the London Commodity Exchange — for cocoa, coffee, hides and skins, ivory, rubber and tea, etc — the Wool Exchange and the Markets for diamonds, gold, silver and furs. Many other Banks and insurance companies have their headquarters in the City. There is also the new residential centre at the Barbican.

The Lord Mayor, in the City, has precedence over every subject and takes his place immediately after the Sovereign. His status was indicated in 1379 when he was assessed as an Earl. In 1415 it was decided that the Mayor had precedence, within the City, of the Archbishops and the brothers of the Sovereign, and should sit at the head of the table with the Bishops on his right and the Dukes on his left. When on State occasions, the Sovereign desires to enter the City the Lord Mayor awaits at the City boundary. On ceremonial occasions the Lord Mayor surrenders the Pearl Sword point downwards, and on receiving it back bears it erect in procession before the Sovereign. A Charter of 1354 confirms the right of the Mayor's sergeants to carry gilt or silver maces, and the office of Swordbearer is mentioned as far back as 1419. Prior to 1520 the Mayor used his own sword or was presented with a ceremonial sword by his Livery Company. In 1520, however, the City purchased Sir James Yerford's sword and thereafter it was maintained as the Mayoralty Sword.

The collar of SS forms part of the Lord Mayor's official clothing — he has five different robes for differing occasions. The collar was bequeathed by Sir John Allen, a Mercer who was Lord Mayor in 1525-6; it is richly designed in gold throughout, and the principal feature of the insignia are the red rose and the portcullis. The original jewel or pendant was given by Sir Martin Bowes, a Goldsmith who was Lord Mayor in 1545-6, and was a gold cross inlaid with gems and pearls. This pendant ceased to be used in 1607, when it was replaced by another which was in turn replaced in 1802 by the present one, emblazoned with the City Arms within a garter bearing the motto *'Domine dirige nos'* — meaning 'O Lord, Guide us'. This was not always the City motto. The first appears to have been 'Cease not Thomas, to guard me who brought thee forth', the words being the original reverse of the old common seal of 1225 (which was destroyed in 1539) in the following form 'Me que te peperi ne cessa Thoma tueri'. The Thomas mentioned was Thomas Becket. Henry VIII caused all images and pictures of Becket to be destroyed. Accordingly a new motto was adopted: 'Londoni defende tuos Deus optime cives' (Most Gracious God defend thy citizens of London). No instances of the use of this motto other than that on the seal have been met with. In 1633 a new motto made its appearance — 'Domine dirige nos', and this motto, which in fewer words expresses the same sentiment as that contained in the motto of 1539, has continued in general use up the present day.

The Lord Mayor for 1981-2, Sir Christopher Leaver, is the 654th elected holder of this office. In former times many Mayors held office for more than one year, and on fifteen occasions during the thirteenth and fourteenth centuries the Mayor was replaced by a Warden or Custodian appointed by the Sovereign. Sir Christopher Leaver, at 43 years of age, is one of the youngest Lord Mayors to occupy the Mansion House and certainly one of the few to bring with him a family of a six-month old baby daughter and her sister of nearly four years to that historic building.

Until recently the office of Lord Mayor was open to a person of any age, but as the mayoralty also carries with it the title of Chief Magistrate of the City of London, the holder must be a Justice of the Peace and so retire at the age of 70; this should encourage younger men to join the City Corporation and strive for this high position.

The Mansion House is the Lord Mayor's official residence, and is the only private house in the country which contains a Magistrates' Court. The main part of the building, designed by George Dance, was completed in 1752.

The Corinthian portico facing north and looking out onto the circus, into which Threadneedle Street, Princes Street, Cornhill, Cheapside, Queen Victoria Street and Lombard Street lead, provides a vantage point for the Lord Mayor to view processions or take the salute. A mass of pageantry has passed this building over the centuries, only a small portion of which is recorded in old prints and photographs; films and television have, however, in recent years, added their quota for future generations to enjoy.

The Mansion House includes residential and ceremonial apartments and a Justice Room where the Lord Mayor sits regularly as magistrate. The principal ceremonial apartments are the Egyptian Hall, the Saloon, the old Ballroom, drawing room and reception rooms, all richly decorated. It is extensively used for entertaining by the Lord Mayor, Livery Companies, commercial firms and organisations, charities etc.

It was built on a platform sunk into a marsh, a factor, it is said, which contributed to its coming through the Second World War comparatively unscathed, because of the blast resistance this lent to it.

The ceremonial officers who attend the Lord Mayor are the Swordbearer, the Common Cryer and Sergeant-at-arms, and the City Marshall. They also have considerable duties in the Mansion House helping to organise the Lord Mayor's activities.

The appointment of a Swordbearer is first recorded in 1419, and his chief duty, in addition to carrying the Sword before the Lord Mayor on ceremonial occasions is issuing the summons to the Aldermen and members of the Court of Common Council to attend the various Courts and Meetings. The Swordbearer wears the fur cap on all occasions, even in the presence of the Sovereign.

The office of Common Cryer and Sergeant-at-Arms is one of the most ancient of the Lord

Mayor's household, dating back to the fourteenth century. Nowadays he carries the Mace before the Lord Mayor and reads Royal Proclamations from the steps of the Royal Exchange.

The first City Marshall was appointed as far back as 1595. On Lord Mayor's Day and in other carriage processions he rides before the Lord Mayor on horseback. On State occasions indoors he precedes the Lord Mayor on foot. The Private Secretary is an indispensable executive in the Lord Mayor's household.

At each of the meetings of Common Hall it is the duty of the Beadles of the respective Livery companies, stationed at the entrance to Guildhall, to see that none but liverymen attend. The members of each company enter by a particular wicket guarded by their Beadle, and the Common Cryer opens the proceedings by proclaiming 'Silence. Be uncovered in the Hall. All ye that are not liverymen depart this Hall on pain of imprisonment'. On Michaelmas Day this adjuration is followed by a Proclamation by the Common Cryer in the following terms: 'Oyez, Oyez, Oyez.

'You good men of the livery of the several companies of this City, summoned to appear here this day for the election of a fit and able person to be Lord Mayor for the year ensuing, draw near and give your attendance God Save the Queen'.

The office of Sheriff is the oldest in the City. Until 1191 when the office of Mayor was instituted, the Sheriffs were the leading officials. Under Royal charters, the citizens elected the Sheriffs of London and Middlesex, who held office jointly, but since the Local Government Act of 1888, the two Sheriffs have been elected for the City alone. In order to perform adequately the duties appertaining to his office, each Sheriff must be prepared to expend a considerable sum of money from his own estate.

Like the Lord Mayor, the Sheriffs are elected by the Liverymen in Common Hall; the election takes place on Midsummer Day in Guildhall. Besides the Sheriffs, the Liverymen also elect the Bridgemasters and certain minor officers. (Before 1979, the Chamberlain was appointed by Common Hall; since then he has been appointed by Common Council, as are the Remembrancer, the Comptroller, the City Solicitor and the Town Clerk.) The names of the persons who have been nominated for office are read out by the Common Sergeant, and the Liverymen give assent by a show of hands or, if necessary a poll is taken. The Sheriffs make the declaration on Michaelmas Eve (28 September) before the Lord Mayor, the Aldermen, and the Courts of the Livery Companies of which they are members. The year of office begins the same day; at the end of the term, the Sheriff who is neither an Alderman nor a Councilman retires from the Corporation as well as from office.

The Sheriffs have many duties to perform. They are expected to attend the Lord Mayor in the discharge of many of his official functions and to join with him in works of charity and occasions of hospitality. They are present at the Court of Aldermen and the meetings of the Common Council unless officially engaged elsewhere, and occupy an indispensable place in assemblies in Common Hall and the Court of Husting. The presentation of petitions from the City to Parliament is made by the Sheriffs, attended by the Remembrancer, at the bar of the House of Commons, a duty last exercised in 1948, against the clause in the Representation of the People Bill of that year which annulled the representation of the City as a separate constituency. The passing of that Bill into law and the amalgamation of the Cities of London and Westminster as a single constituency ended the continuous representation since the reign of Edward I. The Sheriffs are the Execution Officers of the Central Criminal Court and they, or the Secondary or Under Sheriff, must be in constant attendance to discharge any directions given by the Judges. They must give personal attendance each day of the Sessions to see the Judges into Court, and upon the first day to accompany the Lord Mayor and Recorder. During the day the Sheriffs take turns — one on duty at the Old Bailey while the other accompanies the Lord Mayor on official engagements. Generally, both Sheriffs are present when the King's Bench Judge makes his first appearance and on other ceremonial occasions.

It is the duty of the Sheriffs to wait upon the Sovereign by direction of the Corporation, to ascertain the Royal will and pleasure as to the reception of addresses from either the Court of Aldermen or the Court of Common Council.

An Alderman is chosen by the electors of the Ward over which he is to preside and is not appointed by the Common Council. The Common Council is organised throughout on a Ward basis. Matters within its jurisdiction are largely delegated for consideration and report to Committees usually composed of two Aldermen and representatives from every Ward, appointed thereto by the Common Council on the recommendation of the Ward members, standing orders ensuring an equitable distribution of committees among such members. Each committee elects its chairman by secret ballot, no interference from outside being tolerated. This system distinguishes the Corporation of London from all other municipalities, and particularly from those elected on political lines, where some or all chairmen of committees are appointed in proportions corresponding to the strength of the political parties; the distinction is also reflected in the proceedings of the Court of Common Council, where voting is free, individual, and unfettered and is not directed by party organisations. These differences, combined with the practice of annual elections, the rendering of an account in the annual Wardmote, and the opportunity given to the electors there to bring by resolution their own particular grievances and recommendations directly to the notice of the Council, appear to justify the claim that the Common Council of London is more truly democratic than any other municipal body in the kingdom.

The Court of Common Council meets at Guildhall every third Thursday. The foundation of the present Hall, as seen in the Crypt, was commenced about the year 1411.

The building was damaged during the Fire of London in 1666 and again in the blitz of 1940, but on each occasion it survived the conflagrations and was restored. The present North block was built soon after the Second World War, to replace the war-damaged offices. The new West Wing houses not only the committee and conference rooms and departmental offices, and the Court of Aldermen, but also the Guildhall Library and the Clock Museum; it was opened in 1974.

Guildhall is the headquarters of the Corporation and the meeting place of its committees and Courts. It is situated in the heart of the City on a site which has been the centre of City government for possibly more than a thousand years. It has a library and art gallery and the famous Great Hall where the Lord Mayor's Banquet is held each year under the eyes of the carved figures of Gog and Magog, or Gogmagog and Corineus. The original papiermache effigies, on wicker frames, were carried in the early Lord Mayor's Shows; they were, however, lost in the Great Fire in 1666 and replaced in 1708 by fresh carvings. These were lost in the blitz in 1940, and replaced by the present effigies.

The Aldermen of the City of London have a Court of their own, with its own functions quite distinct from those of the Court of Common Council of which, nevertheless, the Aldermen are members. The Court of Aldermen is, in effect, the 'Upper House' of a two-tier system of City government. The Aldermen are divided into Senior and Junior Aldermen according to whether or not they have served in the office of Lord Mayor. Except in certain matters, decisions are taken by the whole body of Aldermen and Councilmen under the title of 'The Mayor, Aldermen and Commons of the City of London in Common Council assembled'.

The Court of Aldermen is presided over by the Lord Mayor, who is responsible for summoning it. Its meetings, about fifteen each year, are held in public, and twelve aldermen as well as the Lord Mayor must be present.

One of the important functions of the Court of Aldermen is making the final choice between the two candidates presented by the Liverymen for the office of Lord Mayor. The Court has the power to confirm or reject persons elected by the Wards as Aldermen. Any elector, too, can petition the Court against the return of a Common Councilman or any Ward officer elected in Wardmote.

The Livery Companies come under the authority of the Court of Aldermen, which gives sanction to new Companies wishing to adopt a livery, has power to limit the number of liverymen and to set the amount of the livery fine. The Court also has the right to approve Charters of

Incorporation of Livery Companies before they are submitted to Her Majesty in Council.

The Court of Common Council is presided over by the Lord Mayor, and is constituted by the attendance of forty members, one of whom must be the Lord Mayor or his *locum tenens* (who must be an Alderman who has already been Lord Mayor) and two of whom must be Aldermen. The Lord Mayor summons the Court, its business is considered and discussed under his control, and he has power to dissolve the Court. Aldermen occupy seats on the dais. There are seats for the Sheriffs on the right and left of the Aldermen, but a Sheriff who is not an Alderman takes his seat on the dais only at the invitation of the Court.

Commoners take seats in the body of the Court, the front rows each side of the aisle being allotted to the Chairmen of Committees. The officers sit at the table on the dais in front of the Aldermen. At the first Common Council in the Mayoralty the Members are gowned, the Lord Mayor, Aldermen and Sheriffs wearing scarlet gowns and the Commoners mazarine blue gowns.

The business is conducted by the Town Clerk on behalf of the Lord Mayor, referring to each item of the Agenda in turn and obtaining the directions of the Court. These items include questions of Members, motions, letters, lettings of Corporation property, applications for admission to the Freedom of the City, and reports of the Corporation's Committees, which occupy most of the agenda. By its decisions on these reports the Common Council carries out its work as local authority for the City.

The Court of Common Council is the policy-making body of the Corporation and is organised throughout on a Ward basis. The Common Councilmen of the 25 Wards of the City are elected annually on 17 December at the Wardmote which is held within each Ward. The number of Common Councilmen ranges from four to twelve according to the size of the Ward. The number of candidates in any Ward for election is not limited, and may exceed the number of vacancies in any Ward. If the election is contested and a poll demanded, the same will take place at a time and place notified by the Ward Clerk.

The Court meets in the Great Hall at Guildhall every third Thursday except during the Christmas and Summer recesses, and receives recommendations from, and gives instructions to some thirty working committees which deal with the day-to-day running of the Corporation. The major spending committees have sub-committees to deal with the specialist topics, but the budget for all the Corporation's work is controlled by the Coal, Corn and Rates Finance Committee. The Finance Committee has this unusual name because it was given powers to levy a toll on coal and corn entering the City to finance rebuilding after the Great Fire in 1666. This committee prepares the estimate of spending for all Corporation activities and recommends a rate to the Court of Common Council. It also prepares estimates for expenditure which will be met from the City's separate funds — City's Cash and Bridge House Estates.

Other Committees are the Policy and Resources Committee, the Planning and Communication Committee, Port and City of London Health Committee, the committees which control the management of the Barbican; other committees deal with Open Spaces, the City Markets, Education, the Guildhall School of Music and Drama, Housing etc and the establishment at Guildhall.

The Corporation's control extends also beyond the boundaries of the Square Mile to the great open spaces of Epping Forest and Burnham Beeches. These are owned and maintained by the Corporation, which for more than a century has shewn its sense of responsibility and appreciation of the need for open spaces in and around London by preserving parks and woodlands and has, in fact, often prevented their being used for building development, and by their foresight and generosity saved these areas for the free enjoyment of the public.

The local government authority of the Corporation of London is based largely on prescriptive rights, confirmed subsequently by Charter and later amended by Statute.

The Corporation, however, performs various duties carried out elsewhere in the country by a county council. Under the provisions of the local Government Act 1888, many functions which had formerly been exercised by some department of the Corporation were vested in the Court of Common Council instead of the new County Authority, in order to secure the continuity of administration.

For some purposes the City has the status of a county within a county, ie for the administration of justice, and for others, certain Statutes confer on it the powers of a county borough.

The London Government Act 1939 contained provisions enabling the Corporation and the London County Council to agree to transfer functions where desirable by changes in circumstances. Most of the County functions were exercised by the Corporation through a committee known as the County Purposes Committee, which was first appointed immediately following the passing of the Local Government Act, 1888. The Committee consisted of four Aldermen and twenty-nine Commoners, together with such members of the Common Council who had seats in Parliament, the London County Council or the Metropolitan Water Board. The powers of public control, regulation, inspection, licence, and registration are exercised under numerous Acts of Parliament. However, the County Purposes Committee ceased to exist in 1956 and its functions were transferred to the Port and City of London Health Committee.

The title and office of Chief Commoner is not well known or understood. In rural England a Commoner is a person who has joint rights with others in the common lands of a manor, and for many centuries the Commonalty of London has enjoyed similar rights in the land in and around the City.

A Charter of Henry VI (1444) confirmed to the citizens, that is, to the Commoners, all Commons soils and waste lands and the soil of streets and watercourses, thus recognising the City's Estate, and the management of this common estate was entrusted by the citizens to their elected representatives in Common Council, who subsequently delegated much of their authority to the City Lands Committee.

The Chairman of the City Lands Committee presides as a trustee for the Citizens, and should ensure that the common estate of the Citizens is not wasted but preserved for the enjoyment of generations of the Commoners to come. There is thus a certain aptness in attaching the title of Chief Commoner to the Chairman of the City Lands Committee, who is Chief Commoner in deed as well as in name. By reason of its antiquity and the importance of its work, the City Lands Committee has always been considered the premier Committee of the Corporation; it has charge of the Corporation's main assets and, through this control of the source of revenue, it has always exercised a great influence on the policy and activities of the Corporation.

Over the course of the last hundred years or more, controversy has arisen in the Court of Common Council as to whether or not the *Office* of Chief Commoner should be created; there were many divisions of opinion, and on 22 November 1905, it was even suggested by one member of the Court, that the Chief Commoner should wear a gown on all Court days and at civic functions, with an official chain or badge of office, that he should be chairman of all Reception and similar Committees and that a sufficient allowance should be made to him. The discussions in the Court of Common Council continued over the years and also the differences of opinion, and one report of the City Press commented that the proceedings detracted from the dignity of the Court and anyway were only of interest to a few ambitious men.

The title, however, received official recognition in 1918 when Mr T.F. Rider, of Cripplegate Ward Within, the Chief Commoner, was appointed Chairman of the Special (Royal Reception) Committee. He received the MVO and it is said that the letter from Buckingham Palace announcing the honour referred to him as 'Chief Commoner'. The citation in the *London Gazette* of 23 July 1918 referred to the title of Chief Commoner, but the resolution of the Court, congratulating Mr Rider on his honour, referred to him simply as Chairman of the City Lands Committee; yet the Minutes of the following December record that he was presented to the President of the United States of America as *Chief Commoner*. This precedent of presentation at

Freedoms under the title and status of Chief Commoner has been followed on all subsequent occasions, whether or not the reference in the Court has been moved by the Chairman of the City Lands Committee. It appears, therefore, that although the Court has twice refused either to confer or acknowledge the title, it has in fact been used on many occasions in the official minutes, and as the passage of time strengthens the custom, the term has passed into general use, and it is now accepted in the Court of Common Council as the alternative title of the Chairman of the City Lands Committee.

The Freemen are the citizens of the City of London. Until the middle of the 19th century it was necessary to be a Freeman to trade in the City or to work as a craftsman. The Freedom also carried certain privileges, among which were immunity from toll at markets and fairs, freedom from impressment into the armed forces and the right to vote at Ward and Parliamentary elections. Today there are few remaining privileges or immunities and the ranks of Freemen are filled by men and women who like to be identified with the City. The remaining privileges include the right of admission to a Corporation Almshouse and the free education of orphans of Freemen at the City of London Freemen's School in Surrey.

The Freedom is obtained in four ways. The highest honour the City can bestow is to present the Honorary Freedom; this it does to statesmen or other individuals for exceptional service to the nation or to humanity. The Honorary Freedom has been presented to such figures as Nelson, Disraeli, HM The Queen (as Princess Elizabeth), the Duke of Edinburgh, Lord Montgomery, Nehru and the Prince of Wales. The other ways of obtaining the Freedom are through servitude (apprenticeship to a Freeman), by right of patrimony (being the son or daughter of a freeman born after the admission of the freeman) or by Redemption. Although Redemption is officially described as 'purchase with the approval of the Courts of Aldermen or Common Council', the fee is no more than a contribution towards administrative expenses. Freedom by Redemption is the most usual form, as Servitude and Patrimony are seldom appropriate, and the Honorary Freedom is rarely bestowed.

To become a Freeman by Redemption with the approval of the Court of Common Council, one must be a British subject or Commonwealth Citizen and be nominated by two people who are either Aldermen, Common Councilmen or Liverymen. The name is then submitted to the Court of Common Council for approval. A copy of the Freedom is later given to the successful applicant by the Chamberlain of London when the applicant makes the declaration of a Freeman which includes allegiance to the Sovereign and the City.

The Freedom can also be obtained through the intervention of a livery company. In this case, the application is considered by the Court of Aldermen.

There are two organisations for Freemen; the Guild of Freemen and the Society of Young Freemen. The Guild was founded in 1908 and has now become the largest company of its kind in the City of London with a membership of more than 3,000. It is an association for charitable purposes. The Young Freemen was founded in 1976, and promotes interest in the City among young people.

Several members of the Royal Family have been invited by the Corporation to claim their right to be admitted to the Freedom of the City and have been admitted with ceremony in Guildhall.

In summary, the City franchise is constituted as follows — *Parliamentary:* British Nationals who reside within the City, aged 18 or over, and who are not subject to any legal disability are entitled to vote for the Member of Parliament to represent the constituency of the City of London and Westminster South.

City Corporation Wards; All persons who qualify for the Parliamentary franchise by residence, and those other persons who occupy premises within the City as tenants or owners (British national aged 18 and suffering no legal disability) are entitled to the Ward franchise and may vote, in their appropriate *Wards;* for the election of the Aldermen and Common Councilmen for the Corporation of the City of London.

For the purposes of the Ward Franchise, premises may be any land or buildings or some definable portion of a building capable of occupation, and having a gross rateable value of not less than £10 per occupier.

The non-residential franchise (ie for the occupation of business premises) requires that a person shall (a) be aged 18 or over on or before the date of expiry of the Ward List (b) be a British Subject or a Citizen of the Republic of Eire (c) suffer no legal disability and (d) occupy premises of gross annual value exceeding £10, as owner or tenant. A tenancy agreement in writing is essential.

Local Government (GLC): The franchise to elect Councillors is the same as that for Parliament.

Companies incorporated by Charter, Statute or under the Companies Act are legal entities separate from the individual persons who comprise them and they, in consequence, have no franchise for Ward Elections.

Common Hall: All Liverymen of at least one year's standing of the City Guilds, irrespective of their address or residence, may vote in Common Hall for the election of the Lord Mayor, the Sheriffs and certain other Officers. To acquire the Livery, application must be made direct to one of the Livery Companies for admission.

The Lists are compiled by means of annual house-to-house visits to discover all persons entitled to the franchise upon the qualifying date for Parliamentary, Local Government and Ward purposes. For Ward purposes this is done in June and for the remainder it is carried out in October.

Prior to 1617 the trained bands of the City were under the control of a Committee of the Court of Common Council called the Committee for Martial Causes.

The earliest Commission of Lieutenancy of which there is any record was issued in 1617 by James I to the Lord Mayor, Sir John Leman, eight Aldermen and the Recorder.

During the troublous times of the reign of Charles I, the administration of the Lieutenancy of the Kingdom, and of the City trained bands or militia in particular, was one of the questions in dispute between the King and Parliament. These questions were settled by Act of Parliament in 1662 during the reign of Charles II, which may be taken as the foundation of the Lieutenancy of the City of London and its duties, as it and they exist to-day.

Until the late 19th century the Lieutenancy had the power of appointing, issuing and signing commissions to officers of the auxiliary forces, but an Order in Council in 1872 provided that the jurisdiction powers, and duties, command and privileges of, or in relation to the auxiliary forces vested in, or exercisable by Lieutenants of Counties (including the Lieutenancy of the City of London) should be exercisable by the Crown, and the officers' commissions were thereafter to be issued in the manner of those in the Regular Army, ie through the Sovereign.

Her Majesty's Lieutenants for the City of London have the privilege by custom of being received, upon presenting any Address, by the Sovereign upon the throne. This privilege was questioned during the reign of Edward VIII but was ultimately admitted and exercised on the accession of George VI, the Lord Mayor, as head of the Commission, presenting the Address, supported by a representative deputation of Commissioners.

The Lieutenancy and the Commissioners have similar powers to those vested in the Lord Lieutenant within his county, so far as relates to the Reserve Forces. The Lord Mayor is named first in the Commission and the Senior Aldermen are among a number of *ex-officio* members. Each Lord Mayor may recommend for approval to the Secretary of State one eminent citizen for inclusion on the Court. These must have rendered worthy service in an active or civil capacity to the Armed Forces of the Crown.

Members are not, as sometimes described, Deputy Lieutenants, but Her Majesty's Lieutenants, forming together the Lieutenancy of the City of London.

ABOVE: The Lord Mayor's Coach 1981, and BELOW: the present Lord Mayor's mother company, the Carmen's coach, 1981, with the Beadle on the left and (left to right) Lt Col Geoffrey Pearce, Clerk; Frederick Bird, Junior Warden; John Peters Wells, Master, and Anthony Hart, Senior Warden and a Past Sheriff. OPPOSITE ABOVE: The Silent Change in the 1960s, and BELOW: the Wilson Banquet in the Egyptian Hall, Mansion House, 1839. (GL)

LEFT: Gog and RIGHT: Magog, in Guildhall. (GL) BELOW: Queen Mary and George V entering the City in 1935. (GL)

ABOVE: HM the Queen (as Princess Elizabeth) receiving the Freedom of the City in 1947, and BELOW: Sir Winston Churchill accepting the Freedom in 1943. (GL)

ABOVE: The Old Bailey in the 1920s and BELOW: the City of London Police in 1955. (GL)

The Square Mile

The City is, in fact, slightly larger than a square mile. It covers an area of 677 acres and is 1½ miles by seven-eighths of a mile at its widest points.

Roman London, within the walls, however, covered only 325 acres. The suburbs and liberties without the walls, originally claimed for grazing and similar purposes, were incorporated during the Saxon period. The boundaries of the City of London have not altered materially since the Norman Conquest, and legislative changes have not greatly affected its government; no other municipal body shares the traditions and peculiar dignity of the Corporation.

The daytime population is about 302,000 and there are between 7,000 and 7,500 residents, and 5,893 residential electors. The night-time population has increased with the completion of the Barbican residential scheme which houses 4,000 people. Other centres of population in the City are in Queenhithe in the south, the Temples on the western side, and the Middlesex Street estate and the Katherine Dock areas on the eastern side of the City.

Until 1969 the Lord Mayor and other Aldermen were sole Justices of the Peace within the City but the Bench has since been widened to include magistrates appointed by the Lord Chancellor. Should an Alderman retire, be dismissed or discharged, his authority as a Justice ceases forthwith.

The Central Criminal Court is under the management of the City Lands Committee of the Corporation of London. It stands on the site of the famous Newgate Prison, which was first used in the eleventh century and was demolished in 1902. The Court was orginally called 'Justice Hall in the Olde Bailee'.

The Mayor's and City of London Court forms part of the County Court system of England and Wales. It is the County Court for the City of London and its two courtrooms are presided over by a Judge and a Registrar respectively.

There are two Magistrates' Courts in the City, one being the Justice Room at Mansion House and the other the Justice Room at Guildhall. The title of Justice Rooms is of long standing and has been recognised in Acts of Parliament since 1848.

The Lord Mayor and Aldermen were exercising functions as Justices and Keepers of the Peace long before any Charter confirmed their jurisdictions, and there is evidence that the Aldermen performed such duties as early as 1298, when they were described as Justices and Keepers of their Wards.

The Crown has no direct power to discharge the Aldermen from the position of Justice of the Peace as is exercisable in the case of other Justices. No disadvantage, however, results from this, because experience has shewn that, when necessary, the opinion of the Court of Aldermen has always operated to impress on any defaulting or undesirable Alderman the propriety of resigning his gown.

The City of London Police are an independent force, although there is of course the closest co-operation with the Metropolitan Police. The City Police is maintained by the Corporation, and officers are distinguished from their Metropolitan colleagues by their Roman-style helmets, brass buttons and gold sergeant's stripes. The authorised strength of the force is around 1,000 men, and it is unusual in that a high proportion of its officers are more than six feet tall, the minimum height for a man being 5ft 11in, and 5ft 6in for a woman.

The Corporation of London's Health Department is responsible for a range of duties which is not excelled by any other local authority in the country.

The Corporation is also the Port of London Health Authority, and the Medical Officer of the Health of the City holds that office in the Port of London. The Port Health Authority is responsible for the maintenance of health services over some 90 miles of the river Thames and its estuary and over all the enclosed waters of the various dock groups of the Port.

To prevent the entry of infectious diseases into the country a quarantine service is maintained on a 24 hour a day, seven day a week basis. The Quarantine Section is staffed by doctors, one of whom is on watch at all times.

The Medical Officer of Health is the chief officer of the Health Department and has the ultimate responsibility. To assist him he has a number of sections dealing with their own specialised work, such as the Chief Port Health Inspector, whose job it is to examine imported foodstuffs, to follow up cases of infectious diseases, supervise water supplies to ships, inspect ships' quarters etc, and act as district health inspector to the people who live in houseboats on the river, and the Chief Public Health Inspector, whose functions include the Environmental health in the City and the responsibility for the very careful supervision of the food hygiene of catering establishments, registration and inspection of the many office premises, maintenance of the Clean Air programme, and following-up infectious diseases both among City residents and workers. The Corporation has a long tradition of care in the matters of the health and welfare of citizens and workers.

Under the City of London (Various Powers) Act 1954 which became effective from 2 October 1955, the Corporation of London became the first local authority in Europe and the Commonwealth to designate its whole area a smokeless zone. The effects of this Act soon became apparent in the cleaner air over the City, which benefitted not only the City but adjoining areas. In 1973 the Corporation received one of the Arnold Marsh Clean Air Awards presented by the National Society for Clean Air. The City's powers under its own legislation were supplemented by powers under the Clean Air Act 1956 to take action in respect of smoke from railway engines, which had been excluded from the Act of 1954. Further advances were made by Clean Air Act 1968, which extended and adapted a number of the provisions of the Clean Air Act 1956, which attacked sulphur pollution by reducing ground level concentration by control of the height of chimneys.

The personal health services in the City are similar to those in other local health authorities and include dental services, child health facilities, sale of welfare goods, recuperative holidays and health education. The Medical Officer of Health of the City is also the Director of Social Services, which provides residential accommodation for elderly people, meals on wheels and care for homeless families, and is available to provide services in the event of any disaster occurring during peacetime.

A number of Charities are administered by the Corporation under the control respectively, of the Lord Mayor and Aldermen, and the Recorder of London, and the Chamberlain of London. Among these are The Emanuel Hospital, founded in the year 1600 under the Will of Lady Anne Dacre (dated in 1594), which included a provision to purchase land at Westminster on which to build a hospital to be named 'The Poor of Emanuel Hospital'. The educational branch of the Foundation grew and eventually became the most important part of the Charity, and was severed from the Hospital branch and allied to other schools in Westminster under the title 'the United Westminster Schools'. In 1889, in consequence of economic conditions, the Almshouses were sold and the proceeds of sale utilised in the payment of pensions to selected inhabitants in Westminster, Chelsea and Hayes. The City of London Freemen's Houses was founded after the passing of the first Reform Bill of 1832. These Almshouses, built at Brixton for the benefit of householders Free of the City, came under the control of the Corporation in 1848. The Gresham Almshouses in the Parish of St Peter-le-Poor in Broad Street Ward (within the boundaries of which is the Dutch Church in Austin Friars) were erected under the provisions of the will of Sir Thomas Gresham. Later, however, in 1883, they were demolished and rebuilt at Brixton. Roger's Almshouses were built in Hart Street, Cripplegate, in pursuance of a bequest under the Will of Robert Rogers. The date of the erection is not known, but in 1856 the Court of Common Council, with the sanction of the Charity Commissioners, demolished them and erected others in lieu thereof on land belonging to the Corporation at Brixton, adjoining the London Freemen's Almshouses. Morden College was founded by Sir John Morden at Blackheath in 1695, during his lifetime, and endowed by his Will of 15 October 1702. Modern conditions require that the beneficiaries shall be widowers or bachelors of the age of 60 years at the least who must have been principals in a wholesale merchanting or manufacturing business of at least ten years' standing, and who, from misfortune or accident, have become materially reduced in circumstances.

A Royal Commission was appointed in 1878 to report on the Parochial Charities of the City of London as it had become apparent, by reason of the decrease in the resident population of the City, that some extension of the area and objects of the charities formerly confined to the small City Parishes was both necessary and advantageous. After the passing of the City of London Parochial Charities Act 1883, a scheme was made which provided that the five largest parishes of the City, viz St Andrew, Holborn; St Botolph, Aldgate; St Botolph, Bishopsgate; St Bride, Fleet Street, and St Giles, Cripplegate, should retain the management of their own charitable endowments, but that the charities of the remaining 107 parishes should be administered by a Corporate Body to be called the Trustees of the London Parochial Charities. The Trustees, as the Central Governing Body, are nominated as to five by the Crown, four by the Corporation, four by the London County Council, two by the Ecclesiastical Commissioners, and one each by several other authorities.

The Scheme divided the charities into two groups, providing a Central Fund and a City Church Fund, and such Funds are administered as separate Trusts under one management. From the Church Fund certain payments are made to individual Churches, mainly for maintenance, and the surplus is paid to the Ecclesiastical Commissioners. From the Central Fund grants are made to Polytechnics and kindred institutions, and also for such purposes as Open Spaces, Libraries, Museums and Art Galleries, Old People's Homes, and other schemes for the improvement of social and moral conditions of the less fortunate inhabitants of the Metropolis. The Charity, now generally known as the 'City Parochial Foundation' has made possible by its support a great deal of pioneer work in social service.

Samuel Wilson's Loan Charity is administered by the Chamberlain of London; its object is to grant loans at a nominal rate of interest to young tradesmen carrying on business in the City of London or the Counties of Middlesex, Surrey, Kent, Sussex, Buckinghamshire, Hertfordshire, and Essex. The loans are granted for a period not exceeding five years. The charity was founded by one Samuel Wilson, who by his will dated 27 October 1706 bequeathed a sum of £20,000. Management and control is vested in the Lord Mayor, the two senior Aldermen, the Recorder and the Chamberlain, as Trustees.

Although the Corporation is not a statutory authority under the various Education Acts it runs three schools. Within the City are the City of London School for Boys, and the City of London School for Girls. The City of London Freemen's School, founded for the orphans of freemen, and still fulfilling that purpose as a day and boarding school, has been in Ashtead, Surrey, since 1926.

The Corporation also administers the Guildhall School of Music and Drama — an internationally acclaimed conservatoire of the musical and dramatic arts in a new building in the Barbican Arts and Conference Centre.

In addition to the educational establishments belonging to and under the direct control of the Corporation, there exist in the City several schools to which Managers are appointed by the Court of Common Council.

When the school branch of Emanuel Hospital was separated from the almshouse branch of that Foundation, the United Westminster Schools were all placed under the control of a new body, consisting of (inter alios) the Lord Mayor, the Recorder, and the Master of the Clothworkers' Company. In 1910 the Free Grammar School of William Lambe, in the Parish of Sutton Valance, Kent (of which the Master and Wardens of the Clothworkers' Company had been Governors since its foundation) was also transferred to the United Westminster Schools.

In 1877 the Livery Companies invited the Corporation to co-operate in the City and Guilds of London Institute — a project for the furtherance of technical education, and the Court of Common Council on 18 July 1878 approved in principle the draft Scheme submitted by a committee of the companies.

On 12 December 1878 the Court agreed to appoint the Lord Mayor, six Aldermen, the Recorder and twelve Common Councilmen to serve on the Board of Governors with representatives of the livery companies.

Grants amounting to many thousands of pounds have been made by the Corporation towards the expenses of the Institute since its foundation.

The ancient connection of the Aldermen with the governorship of the Royal hospitals of St Bartholomew, St Thomas and Bethlem was severed by the National Health Service Act 1946. Until 1942 it was usual for the Lord Mayor to be elected President of Bridewell and Bethlem Hospitals, but the Governors of those three hospitals are now appointed in accordance with the constitution established by Part III of the Third Schedule of the National Health Service Act 1946. Since the year 1890 Christ's Hospital has been subject to a scheme drawn up by the Charity Commissioners, the purpose of which was to extend the educational scope of the foundation. This came about in 1552 through the problems posed by the increasing swarms of the sick and poor in London. Bishop Ridley's sermon was among many which drew attention to their plight, and the boy King Edward VI was moved to found three hospitals, St Thomas, for the 'sore and sicke', Bridewell for the 'idell vagabondes' and Christ's Hospital for the 'education of children'. His genuine personal concern led to a speedy launching of the project. The then Lord Mayor, Sir Richard Dobbs, was persuaded to gather together a Committee of thirty to raise money as quickly as possible. £2,476 was donated in a year, and some benefactors were moved even to grant gifts of an immediate practical nature. One of the 'thirty' gave '500 Featherbeds and 500 padds of Straew'. The earliest chronicler of the school remarked in 1582 'God in secreate broughte great things to passe in advancement of this foundation'. So efficient were the organisers that 380 boys and girls (surely a very early co-educational foundation) entered the Old Greyfriars monastery, granted for the purpose, in November of that year.

The school soon blossomed and began to acquire its reputation for scholarship, which it has retained to this day. In the 1560s the first scholars gained places at Oxford and Cambridge. Others, like Camden the historian, and George Peele the poet, were later to make names for themselves. The Great Plague of 1665 claimed 32 of the children, and the following year the Great Fire destroyed at least half of the buildings. The children were sent off to inns at Islington and Clerkenwell, to return 14 months later. The rebuilding of the hospital was not completed until the end of the century, the school gaining some fine buildings — Wren and Hawksmoor were among the architects. It was the dogged pursuit by Samuel Pepys of his ideal of a highly professional navy that caused him to be chiefly instrumental in the foundation of the Royal Mathematical School within the walls of Christ's Hospital, and it was largely through his efforts that Charles II was moved to release £7,000 and grant a second Royal Charter in August 1673 providing 'that a Nursery . . . be erected for children to be educated in Mathematics for the particular use and practice of navigation'. By November of that year, a master had been appointed, and forty 14-year-old boys were chosen from within the school who had 'reached a reasonable degree of skill in Grammar and Arithmatic'. Two years later the first boys were examined successfully by Trinity House, prior to their seven year apprenticeships to ships' masters.

For a visitor to Christ's Hospital, one of its most distinctive features is the School's uniform. Substantially unaltered since Tudor times, it must have a strong claim to being the oldest school uniform in existence. The entire school was removed to West Horsham on 29 May 1902. In the building of the new school, the architects, Sir Aston Webb and Ingress Bell not only embodied some of the features of the London buildings in their Horsham plans, but designed both the Old Science School and the Chapel very much along the lines of some of the abandoned London buildings. Soon the people of Horsham became familiar with the long blue coats and yellow stockings of the pupils. The girls' school remained at Hertford, and both the boys' and the girls' schools have their own administration.

The musical tradition in Christ's Hospital has for a long time been one of the school's strongest. In addition to singing, the small band which was formed in 1868 is now one of the school's best known institutions.

The Lord Mayor and Aldermen and twelve members of the Common Council are Governors of the school, but only the Lord Mayor has any right of presentation. The Lord Mayor is also *ex-officio* Almoner, and the Court of Aldermen has the power of recommending for appointment by the Governors six Nominative Almoners to act on the Council of Almoners. The presentation to be made by the Lord Mayor is limited to either one boy or girl, as determined by the Council of Almoners. The twelve Common Council Governors of Christ's Hospital are appointed for a term of six years by the Wards in rotation. For the other hospitals, the Ward rotation of Common Council Governors, who were appointed for life, was regulated by a scheme approved by the Common Council on 24 February 1870 and 19 March 1891.

Sir Thomas Gresham, by his Will, devised one moiety of the Royal Exchange to the Corporation of London and the other to the Mercers' Company upon various trusts, one of which was that the Corporation should pay £50 a year to each of four lecturers in divinity, astronomy, music and geometry, and that the Mercers' Company should make similar payments to three lecturers in law, physics, and rhetoric. He further devised his mansion house in Bishopsgate Street to the Corporation and the company on trust to permit the lecturers to occupy the same and read their lectures there. The house became a centre of learning and was soon re-named Gresham College. From this association of learned men grew the Royal Society. The collegiate character of the Gresham foundation was terminated by Act of Parliament in 1768, but a new Gresham College was erected at the corner of Gresham Street and Basinghall Street in 1842 and was rebuilt on an enlarged site in 1913.

The Corporation and the Mercers' Company respectively appoint committees to control and carry out the provisions of the will, which consist of twelve members who sit together as the Grand Gresham Committee and appoint and pay the lecturers, each of whom deliver four lectures a year in one week of each of three terms, twelve lectures in all.

The City University is in Bunhill Row, just off Chiswell Street, within a stone's throw of the Barbican Centre, the City of London Girls' School and the Guildhall School of Music and Drama, and another seat of learning, the City of London College.

That the Lord Mayor for the time being is the Chancellor of The City University is an outward indication of the uniqueness of the City's own University. Its degree-giving ceremonies take place in the medieval Guildhall, but the University is a modern, outgoing university whose motto is 'To Serve Mankind'. Its links are not only with the City civic but also with the City commercial, the Business School having made its mark in banking, insurance, commerce and management. The physical presence of the University in the City of London is Gresham College, the headquarters of the Business School.

Founded in 1891 under a scheme of the City Parochial Foundation that redirected ancient charity funds to modern purposes, the forerunner of The City University was known as the Northampton Institute after the Marquess of Northampton, the donor of the site. The foundation stone of the first building was laid in 1894 and additional buildings were provided in 1932 and

1956, with an impressive range of modern buildings added in the late sixties and seventies.

A major feature of the original foundation was the requirement to serve both the educational and social needs of the Finsbury locality. Thus a gymnasium, swimming pool and concert hall were provided and, in the past, many north Londoners who could not afford to go to university gained qualifications by evening class study.

The greatest contribution of The City University is that it has remained dedicated to the practical approach to education that has been followed within its walls continuously since 1904, the sandwich course system. This meets the needs of British industry and commerce by producing graduates who have had their lectures, laboratory work and book learning fully integrated with periods in the workplace. This concept has been adapted into courses in new subject areas.

Thus the granting of the Charter to The City University in 1966 was an accolade to an existing College of high standing, mainly in engineering, but with a young and vigorous business school, having all the advantages of location in, and close by the City of London.

Great care has been exercised over many centuries to preserve a record of the Corporation's administration, and the accumulation of archives in the City of London Records Office, covering a period of almost nine hundred years, are considered, in view of their antiquity, continuity and wide range, to be the most complete and valuable series of municipal records in existence. The long series of City Charters and Letters Patent begins with the famous Charter of William the Conqueror. Among the archives are the now well-known Letter-Books, comprising details of the Minutes of the administrative assemblies commencing in the year 1275, and continuing to the present day in the Journals of the Court of Common Council and the Repertories of the Court of Aldermen. In addition are the Husting Deeds and Wills and Plea Rolls from the year 1252, and the rolls and files of the Mayor's and Sheriff's Court commencing in the thirteenth century. Sessions Records of Proceedings at the Old Bailey can be seen there as well as numerous records relating to sociology, genealogy, and other interesting historical data.

The Town Clerk, being the Keeper of the Records, now performs the duties through a Deputy Keeper who is appointed by the Library Committee.

Among the valuable documents in his care is the most famous of all custumals, *Liber Albus,* compiled by John Carpenter, Town Clerk of the fifteenth century. There is also *Liber Dunthorn,* named after another fifteenth century Town Clerk, William Dunthorn. Another cherished record is *Liber de Antiquis Legibus,* compiled in the late thirteenth century. Andrew Horn, a fourteenth century City Chamberlain, is another who deserves the gratitude of posterity by reason of his *Liber Horn,* a further record of the City's history. There are countless others covering a wide range of historical interest and Calendars of many ancient records have been published by the Corporation. Every facility is offered for research by students, historians, and others interested in the annals of London and its citizens.

The first mention of a Library at the Guildhall is contained in the records of the Corporation, 27 September 1425. The Library was attached to the ancient College of Guildhall, which had a Custos and four priests, one of whom was Keeper of the Library. John Clipstone, priest, was the earliest librarian of whom records exist.

The Library was set up by John Carpenter and John Coventry, under the terms of the will of Richard Whittington and by the executors of the will of William Bury. The foundation came to an end in 1550 and no other library was established at Guildhall until the early nineteenth century. In 1828 a small library was set up for the Court of Common Council.

In 1873, the building in the north-west part of Guildhall abutting on Basinghall Street, which housed the Library until it was moved to its present position, was opened to the public. It provides an unrivalled collection of material on the history of London, printed, manuscript and graphic; it includes records of the City Livery companies and City parishes, and an extensive collection of prints, drawings, maps and books, and records covering most fields of knowledge as well as those relating to the City. Other Libraries in the City are Bishopsgate Institute, the City Business Library, St Bride's Institute and the St Bride Printing Library, all offering a great range of books and information.

The Museum of London, opened in 1976, tells the story of London and the Londoner, and more than 7,500 objects on display contribute to that story, from pre-history, Roman, Saxon and Medieval London, Tudor and Early Stuart, Late Stuart London, Georgian, early nineteenth century and early twentieth century London. Among the ceremonial items on display are the Lord Mayor's coach, together with all the harness, standing ready for its annual outing in the Lord Mayor's Show. There are two archaeological units, and a separate education wing with classrooms, refectory and craftrooms. This Museum is an amalgam of the old London Museum, Guildhall Museum, and various other small museums and art galleries. The separate Guildhall Clock Museum tells the story of horology over five hundred years. More than 700 exhibits of clocks and watches are on display. This fascinating collection belongs to the Worshipful Company of Clockmakers and is deposited on loan to the Corporation.

The beginnings of the City's art collection date from 1667, when, after the Great Fire, the Corporation commissioned the portraits of the Judges who had settled the various fire-claims. The official establishment of the Guildhall Art Gallery begins with the recommendation of the Library Committee on 23 July 1885 that the vacated Court of Queen's Bench (on the corner of Basinghall Street and Guildhall Buildings) be appropriated for the purpose of providing an Art Gallery with a view to forming a permanent home for the Corporation's pictures, which up to that time had been housed in the various Guildhall offices and other Corporation buildings. The Gallery was opened in 1886, and enlarged in 1890; it was destroyed by enemy action in 1941, but only a small number of unimportant paintings were there, the remainder having been sent into the country for safe custody. A temporary building was erected on the site in 1946 and used as a reception room for Guildhall functions, and also for exhibitions of selected pictures from the Collection. The permanent collection of Guildhall Art Gallery will not be transferred to the Art Gallery forming part of the Barbican Development but will remain at Guildhall; it is always possible that some items may be lent to the Barbican Gallery for display. The Guildhall Art Gallery may be used for exhibitions by outside bodies; a new Art Gallery may be built within the next ten or twenty years.

The Barbican Scheme was designed to encourage people to live in the City and to ensure that it is 'alive' at all times and not just during office hours. The 35 acre site, at the heart of which is the Barbican Centre for Arts and Conferences, is a magnificent achievement, and without doubt the largest complex of its kind in Western Europe. It is the home of two world-famous performing companies; it houses internationally important exhibitions of paintings and sculpture, and acts as host to national and international conferences and meetings. The 2,000-seat Barbican Hall is London's newest concert hall and the first permanent home of the London Symphony Orchestra, and the Royal Shakespeare Company is resident in the Barbican Theatre which has been custom-built to the company's requirements. Members of both resident companies work closely with students of the adjacent Guildhall School of Music and Drama, one of the country's leading schools of the performing arts. The Barbican includes some 2,000 flats and houses which have brought back 4,000 people to live in the heart of the City.

The City of London Churches are administered by the Bishop of London, assisted by the Archdeacon of London and the Rural Dean.

Immediately before the beginning of the Second World War there were 47 churches in the City — that is, churches of the Church of England; there were, of course, the two churches in the Tower of London, and the Temple Church, but they were outside the boundaries of the City, and the Dutch Church. Of these 47, forty-six were parish churches, and one, St Benet, Paul's Wharf in Queen Victoria Street, was a chapel of ease to serve the interests of the Welsh.

Since the 1920s the authorities of the Diocese of London had considered schemes for making fuller use of City churches, and their future was next considered by the Merriman Commission, which reported in 1946. Finally, these and other deliberations resulted in the London (Guild Churches) Act 1952 which enabled the Bishop of London to designate sixteen as Guild Churches, to serve the non-resident day-time population of the City, and associate them with the civic life of the City Wards and other organisations, each Guild Church being appointed to one of the Wards of the City.

Guild Churches are non-parochial in the sense that they are free from the jurisdiction of the incumbent of the parish church. Normally, the freehold of the churches was held by the incumbent but this was not to be so in respect of the Guild Churches; the freehold of each was vested in the Bishop of London. There was, however, one exception — St Lawrence Jewry, vested in the Corporation of the City of London. This was designed to strengthen the long term ties between the Church of England and the various organisations of the City, and in particular the Corporation of London itself. The Lord Mayor has his special pew at St Lawrence Jewry Church and it is here that he and the Corporation repair on special civic occasions. Guild Churches have a rest for the Lord Mayor's sword when he attends in his official capacity of Lord Mayor with the Sword Bearer, the Mace Bearer, the Sheriffs, etc.

In 1952 the resident population of the City was just over 5,000; there were still 47 churches — an average of 100 residents per church. It was therefore decided to experiment. Of the 47, 24 were to be parish churches and 16 guild churches. Three of the damaged ones were not restored; they were St Mildred, Bread Street, St Stephen, Coleman Street and St Alban, Wood Street. Two of the others were designated for other ecclesiastical purposes, one as a choir school and one as a diocesan office. Of the two remaining, St Stephen and St Swithin, Walbrook, was subsequently used by the Samaritans, and St Anne and St Agnes, Gresham Street, was rebuilt. Forty-six churches were still considered too many for this population while special spiritual provision was needed for the large daytime population of the City, then about 500,000.

This required clergy with special preaching and other gifts, and the churches required special facilities to enable such clergy to exercise their new role; it was therefore proposed that these clergy would not work full-time as parish priests, but would be specially qualified for service in the general work of the Church, and in particular, selected for their preaching capacities. Economic change has proved this impractical. Previously, on death or retirement, another priest was appointed but nowadays, one of the existing priests is often appointed to the vacant living as 'priest-in-charge' and is responsible for this and his own church.

One of the 16 Guild Churches, St Nicholas Cole Abbey in Queen Victoria Street, has been leased to the Free Church of Scotland, but it is still used annually or biennially by Queenhithe Ward Club and the Worshipful Company of Bowyers.

The Ward Clubs, of which there are nineteen, usually hold their annual Ward Services at their Ward Churches.

St. Paul's Cathedral, however, is the centre of religious worship in the City and, perhaps the Nation, and has been so many centuries, and it is the focus of such City occasions as the United Guilds Service.

The Second World War was responsible for great damage to the Cathedral but when, in the early hours of 12 September 1940, one bomb, eight feet in length and weighing a ton, missed the clock tower at the south-west of the Cathedral by a few feet, it buried itself more than 27 feet into the subsoil; when the bomb was exploded on Hackney Marshes it made a crater 100 feet in diameter.

The City Livery Club was founded in 1914 to provide a centre where the members of the several Guilds of the City of London could meet; its membership is restricted solely to Liverymen.

Primarily, its objects are to uphold and strengthen the immemorial traditions and privileges of the Corporation of London and its ancient Guilds; to encourage the Livery to exercise their undoubted right to elect their own Sheriffs of the City, and nominate Aldermen for the Office of Lord Mayor of London, and to foster an active participation in civic life as well as a sense of good citizenship generally.

There are 25 Wards but only nineteen Ward Clubs; this is because some of the Wards are too small to warrant a separate Ward Club, Vintry and Dowgate being an example. However, size is not necessarily relevant, as Vintry and Dowgate Ward Club is one of the most active Ward Clubs in the City. The object of the Ward Clubs is to encourage members to take an active interest in civic affairs, particularly in the City of London, to watch and promote concern for their Wards and to promote neighbourly and friendly relationships therein. Most of the Ward Clubs entertain the Lord Mayor at least once during the year's mayoralty; the occasion is either a dinner or a luncheon.

To be eligible for membership, a candidate must be a person belonging to, interested in or employed within the Ward, who shall have been proposed and seconded at a duly constituted meeting of the Committee of the Club. Rules vary from Club to Club as to candidature.

The United Wards Club of the City of London was instituted a few years ago to promote and further the spirit of citizenship, to maintain the traditions and prestige of all civic affairs and to encourage and foster the Ward Clubs within the City, and maintain contact with, and make representations to the Lord Mayor, the Corporation of London, Members of Parliament, Government Departments, the City Livery Club, the Guild of Freemen, and other bodies and individuals on matters of general or special concern to the Club and its members.

The Thames is London's river and its historic highway. This great river offers a profusion of impressions: small-town wharves between Southwark Bridge and Blackfriars, the promenade on Victoria Embankment, the busy commercial port in the Pool of London, and pleasure boats. Thames-side is a fascinating phenomenon, best seen by riverboat, with a waterman as guide.

Whenever the Queen and/or the Royal Family visit or perform duties on or around the river, a Guard of Honour is often selected from the Watermen; the Guard comprises a Barge Master and 24 Watermen (known as The Crew).

The prime duty is the escorting of the Crown Jewels and articles of State to the Palace of Westminster for the State Opening of Parliament; this goes back to the time when the Crown Jewels were kept in the Tower and were transported by water to the Palace of Westminster.

All the four bridges that connect the City with the southern bank of the Thames are owned and maintained by the Corporation. Expenditure on building, rebuilding, maintenance, watching, and cleansing is met, not from the rates, but by income from property known as the Bridge House Estates.

London Bridge has been famous throughout history, legend and nursery rhyme. In 1831, after numerous fires and bad weather, it was replaced; it was the facing of this later bridge which was removed stone by stone to Lake Havasu City, Arizona, USA in 1967, after it was sold by the Corporation for £1 million. The new London Bridge is 100 feet wide and 850 feet long, and carries six lanes of traffic.

Blackfriars Bridge, built between 1760 and 1769, was the first supplement to London Bridge within the City. At first to be known as Pitt Bridge, it was re-named Blackfriars Bridge even before its completion. In spite of £105,000 spent on repairs in 1833 it became unsafe and was pulled down in 1860. The present Blackfriars Bridge was opened by Queen Victoria on 7 November 1869, having cost £401,131.

Southwark Bridge, originally erected in 1815 by a private company, was purchased by the Corporation in 1868 for £218,868. Widening and improving was interrupted by the First World War, but the reconstructed bridge was opened by King George V on 6 June 1921. Tramways were laid in 1925 but later removed. The present bridge was designed by Sir Ernest George, is 55 feet wide and 708½ feet long.

In 1884 the Corporation, acceding to public demand, promoted a Bill in Parliament for powers to construct a bridge near Irongate Stairs, immediately beyond the eastern boundary of the City. Sir John Wolfe Barry was commissioned to deal with the engineering work and Sir Horace Jones, the City Surveyor and Architect, was responsible for the Gothic architecture; the cost was £1,184,000. Tower Bridge is probably the best known and most photographed bridge in London. It was opened by the Prince of Wales, later Edward VII. Its two central bascules were raised originally by steam pumping engines, but have now been replaced by modern electro-hydraulic machinery.

The two highwalks, which have been closed to the public since 1909, and the engine rooms, are now open to visitors, and a permanent exhibition and Museum under the south approach to the Tower of the bridge opens this summer (1982).

The income of the Bridge House Trust is now applied to the maintenance of the four bridges.

The Thames provides London's access to the high seas. The Corporation of Trinity House, with its headquarters on Tower Hill, is a unique maritime organisation which, throughout its long and distinguished history, has had as its prime objective, the safety of shipping and the welfare of sailors.

The service provided by Trinity House can be divided into three main functions. It is the General Lighthouse Authority of England, Wales, the Channel Islands, and Gibraltar, and as such is responsible for providing such aids to navigation as lighthouses, light vessels, buoys and beacons; the Principal Pilotage Authority in the United Kingdom with responsibility for London and 40 other districts, including such ports as Southampton and Falmouth; a charitable organisation for the relief of mariners and their dependants who are in financial distress, with purpose built homes at Walmer in Kent.

The day-to-day affairs of Trinity House are controlled by a Board of ten members who have had long experience of command in either the Merchant or Royal Navies, and the Secretary, who is the Chief Administrative Officer. The Board is assisted by administrative, engineering and technical staff.

As a corporate body, Trinity House still retains its traditional titles which are as venerable as those of the Livery Companies and Guilds of the City of London, although they are now reserved mainly for ceremonial occasions. The Members of the Corporation are divided into two main categories: 'Elder and Younger Brethren'.

The 'Younger Brethren', who number approximately 300, are Master Mariners or Senior Naval Officers of high professional distinction. It is from this pool of nautical expertise that the Board members are appointed, with the life title of Elder Brother. In addition there are a number of honorary Elder Brethren selected by invitation, in recognition of their distinguished services.

The 'head' of the Corporation is the Master, a title dating back to the original charter of 1514. By charter of James I provision was made for the appointment of a Master's Deputy, a title which to-day is reserved for the Chairman of the Board. The present Master is HRH The Prince Philip, Duke of Edinburgh.

The Corporation licenses the pilots, who are self-employed. The service, like the Lighthouse Service, is entirely self-supporting and receives no government funds. Its income is derived from a levy on pilots' earnings, dues paid by vessels for shipping and landing pilots, and from licence fees. There are about 670 Trinity House Pilots, of whom about 450 are in the London District. To qualify, a London pilot must be physically fit, possess a Foreign-going Master Mariner's certificate and have had five years' experience as a watch-keeping officer and be under the age of 35. For the first three or four years of service London pilots are restricted to piloting small vessels.

The Corporation owns and operates a fleet of pilot cutters, fast launches and pilot boats in the London and Isle of Wight Districts, and also owns vessels stationed at Falmouth and at Districts which it administers in the West Country and on the North West Coast.

In addition to the homes for former officers of the Merchant Services and their dependants at Walmer, the Corporation is responsible for a number of legacies left by former Elder Brethren and other benefactors of the Corporation.

On 18 July 1555 the former house of the Earls of Derby, between St Paul's and the river Thames, was assigned to the Heralds by Charter of King Philip and Queen Mary 'to the end that the officers of the College might be enabled to assemble together and consult and agree amongst themselves, for the good of their faculty, and that the Records and Rolls might be more safely and conveniently deposited'. The present College of Arms or Heralds' College stands on this site, and here the Heralds have their chambers and keep their records.

Kings of Arms and Heralds were members of the Royal Household from the 13th century and pursuivants from the 14th century. From 1420 these Officers of Arms used a Common Seal and, in 1484, were incorporated by a Charter of King Richard III, which conveyed to them the mansion of Coldharbour or Pulteney's Inn in Thames Street (now Lower Thames Street). This they lost, however, until Richard's death at Bosworth the following year, 1485.

The present building was built shortly after the house was destroyed in the Great Fire in 1666. The south range was pulled down in the middle of the last century to make way for Queen Victoria Street, and the present magnificent gates were given to the College by an American benefactor in 1956.

The present establishment of the College consists, under the Earl Marshall (the Duke of Norfolk, who is not himself a member of the corporation), of three Kings of Arms — Garter, Clarenceux, the Norry and Ulster; six Heralds — Lancaster, Somerset, Chester, Richmond, Windsor and York — and four Pursuivants, namely, Rouge Dragon, Rouge Croix, Portcullis and Bluemantle.

The kings, heralds and pursuivants of arms, generically called the Officers of Arms, are appointed for life by Letters Patent of the Sovereign. Only kings of arms are empowered to grant arms, but all the officers may act as agents for prospective grantees. Their work, apart from organising and appearing at State ceremonies, consists of tracing and recording pedigrees, establishing rights to arms, and similar matters.

In the north range of the building is the courtroom where the High Court of Chivalry may be held for correcting infringements of the laws of arms. The hereditary judge in this court is the Earl Marshall. The Court of Chivalry was abolished by Oliver Cromwell and restored under Charles II in 1660, but the cases brought before it were not serious, and as many of the defendants in these cases objected to its jurisdiction, it ceased to function. However, Blackstone, the great English legal commentator, stated in his 18th century *Commentaries upon the Laws of England* that the Court existed and had jurisdiction in matters armorial. The only case brought to the High Court of Chivalry since then was in 1954, which was held in the Lord Chief Justice's Court at the Royal Court of Justice in the test case *The Mayor, Aldermen and Citizens of the City of Manchester v. the Manchester Palace of Varieties Ltd.*

Barely half a mile from the Bank of England is the Finsbury Barracks and Headquarters of the Honourable Artillery Company who, in 1937, celebrated the 400th anniversary of their incorporation by Royal Charter of Henry VIII.

The Honourable Artillery Company was originally a band of citizen archers known as the Guild of Saint George, which was incorporated by Henry VIII in 1537 as the Brethren or Guild of Artillery of Longbows, Crossbows and Handguns 'for the better increase of the defence of this our realm.'

It originally consisted entirely of infantry, the word 'artillery' being used in its absolute sense, meaning 'missile weapons'; and its artillery division was not added until 1781, when the City presented two brass guns in reward for services during the Gordon Riots.

The primary function of the Company for two and a half centuries was to provide and train officers for the Trained Bands of London, and long before the formation of the Regular Army it was the recognized 'School of War' for the whole Kingdom. In 1908 it was converted by special Act of Parliament into a Territorial Unit, taking precedence of all others by virtue of its ancient standing.

Its privileges are many. It is one of the few regiments entitled to march through the City with fixed bayonets; it also has the privilege of providing all guards of honour when Royalty visit the City.

Young men of suitable qualifications wishing to join the Honourable Artillery Company must be proposed and seconded by members, or produce satisfactory credentials. On admission they sign the Vellum Roll, a list of members in unbroken sequence since 1611, which bears the signatures of almost every King of England since Charles II. Among other signatures are those of Prince Rupert, James, Duke of Monmouth, Samuel Pepys, and the great Duke of Marlborough.

On 11 June 1685, King James II authorised Lord Dartmouth, who was Master-General of Ordnance and Constable of the Tower of London, to raise a regiment from two independent companies which had for a long time formed the Garrison of the Tower, and from ten companies drawn from the Trained Bands of the City. This new regiment, the 7th of the Line, was to be raised as an Ordnance Regiment, its duties being the protection of the guns of the Artillery. It was to be armed with the new type of flint-lock musket known as a 'fuzil', and as the regiment was the first of its kind in the English service, the King named it 'Our Royal Regiment of Fuzileers'.

Until the end of Queen Anne's reign (1714) all guns had stamped on them the Royal badge of the Union Rose surmounted by the Crown, and this was the first badge of the Royal Fusiliers. In 1751 the Union Rose was incorporated within the Garter, and this, with the Crown over it, has been the badge of the Regiment ever since.

In 1881 the additional name City of London Regiment was given to the Royal Fusiliers, and the Regiment still draws the majority of its recruits from the City and neighbourhood of London. The Regiment has the privilege of marching through the City with bayonets fixed and Colours flying.

The Regiment of Royal London Militia, directly descended from the old City Trained Bands, came to an end as such with the Territorial and Reserve Forces Act 1907, which converted the various battalions of the militia into units of the Army Reserve, and the Royal London Militia became thereafter the 7th Battalion Royal Fusiliers. The headquarters of the regiment provided by the Lieutenancy, under the provisions of 1 Geo. IV c.100, continued to be used by the regiment in its new form, and Finsbury Barracks is still maintained by the Court of Lieutenancy.

The Tower of London, which houses the Regimental Headquarters and Museum of the Royal Fusiliers, was the birthplace of the Regiment. A large number of Service Battalions were raised during the 1914-18 War and the Second World War and the Colours of many of them are displayed in the Museum.

On St George's Day, 23 April 1968, the four Fusilier Regiments of England, already grouped together as the Fusilier Brigade, united to form the Royal Regiment of Fusiliers. They had served continuously for almost 300 years in the British Army, had frequently fought together in war, and equally served together in peace; thus the four regiments were old comrades in arms. They were: The Royal Northumberland Fusiliers, 5th Foot The Royal Warwickshire Fusiliers, 6th Foot The Royal Fusiliers (City of London Regiment), 7th Foot The Lancashire Fusiliers, 20th Foot.

Of the Exchanges and Markets within the City, the most important is the Stock Exchange. The two main functions of the Stock Exchange are to provide a free market in stocks and shares and to provide capital for new enterprises. It is controlled by a Council of 36 members, and membership is on a strictly yearly basis. One third of the Council members retire each year and, in addition to its administrative responsibilities, the Council regulates the conduct of members' business, authorises official quotations for stocks and shares and in many ways safeguards its members and investors generally. It is a vast market, and its influence can be felt round the world.

The Baltic Mercantile and Shipping Exchange which is in St Mary Axe, between Leadenhall Street and Houndsditch, deals in four classes of business: ships are chartered to carry all kinds of goods to and from all parts of the world; aircraft and aircraft space for passengers and cargoes are chartered; grains, including maize and barley, are purchased and sold and seeds and vegetable oils are bought and sold.

Ships are chartered by agents representing merchanting organisations of all kinds on the one hand and by shipbrokers representing shipowners from all over the world on the other.

The London Commodity Exchange, a merger of the former Commercial Sale Rooms and the Rubber Exchange, is in Mincing Lane. Trades represented in its Plantation House headquarters include cocoa, coffee, copra, oil seeds, essential oils, pepper and spices, ivory, jute, hemp, rubber and shellac. Until 1971 the tea market was held there, but in that year the Tea Trade and London Tea Auctions moved to Sir John Lyon House, in Queenhithe Ward. The London Tea Auctions are the only auctions in the world where tea from all parts of the world is sold. If, however, the proposed purchase by the London and Edinburgh Investment Trust and S. & W. Berisford Ltd of the old Billingsgate Market building is confirmed and completed, the London Commodity Exchange may be housed there.

There is a large number of associations which have developed to represent the various trade interests, each with its own rules and internal organisation, though many are grouped for secretarial purposes. They usually represent the producing, shipping and marketing sections dealing with a particular commodity, but not usually the manufacturing interests. The associations also act as representatives of their trades in negotiations with the Bank of England when the necessity arises.

The City is, in fact, a market-place — a market-place for the whole world, where the surpluses of every nation are exchanged for the goods they require. Without London's services to world trade of banking, shipping, insurance and merchanting and the half-million people who make their way into the Square Mile between London Bridge and Temple Bar (and pour out again every night at around 5.30) the rest of London and the nation would be the poorer.

It is said that some sixty per cent of the trade of the world is now done direclty, or indirectly, in sterling, and most of this is one way or another related to the City, which certainly accounts for the bulk of our invisible exports. The value is difficult to ascertain, but after deducting what we pay out to other nations, it must represent about one-third of our gross earnings of foreign exchange.

As a result of two world wars it would not have been surprising if the City markets had died out. In fact, many did die; but slowly, and sometimes painfully. Since about 1945 they have been reborn, and many more have arisen. The Fur Market was one of the first to come back to life after the Second World War. London has always been a fur centre, and while Queenhithe was a Saxon Port, furs, amongst many other commodities, were landed in vast quantities at that Dock. From the landings of these cargoes Matilda, Queen of Henry I, and thereafter a series of queens and favoured ladies received the dues and profits of the Dock. Together, Queenhithe includes two fur auction companies and a large number of brokers, merchants and manufacturers. In fact, the Corporation of London has erected a building, predominantly for those following the ancient craft, and named it 'Fur Trade House' — a permanent reminder that it is a vital part of the City's fabric. Corn also was for long the principal import of the Hythe.

The Corn Exchange, in Mincing Lane, is the most important cereal market in the United Kingdom, nearly 200 firms having stands on the floor. The Exchange is concerned with the distribution within this country and, in some cases, to overseas countries, of imported and home-grown cereals, pulses, flour, oats, barley, wheat and rye products, agricultural seeds, animal feedstuffs, oil seeds, fertilisers, hay and straw, etc.

At the southern end of London Bridge is the London Provision Exchange, whose members include most of the importers and distributors of Commonwealth and foreign provisions, namely, bacon, butter, cheese, hams and lard, and many importers and distributors of canned meats, supplying London and the fifteen surrounding counties.

The London Commodity Markets, which provide an essential service and play a vital part in the economic welfare of the world, can be divided into two main areas: metals and soft commodities. The non-ferrous metal markets in copper, tin, lead, zinc, silver, aluminium and nickel operate on the London Metal Exchange, Plantation House, in the heart of the City, while most of the soft commodity markets such as cocoa, gas oil, sugar, vegetable oils, wool and rubber are situated at the Corn Exchange Building in Mark Lane.

In the early 19th century, when metal merchants met in coffee houses in the City to buy and sell, trading was mainly a domestic affair and quoted prices remained unchanged for long periods. Technical changes and industrial growth during the 19th century, together with the opening of the Suez Canal in 1869, changed all this and, from a surplus metal exporter, the UK became a nett importer. The import of large tonnages from overseas at irregular intervals meant that prices fluctuated sharply, causing serious concern to both merchants and consumers. With the introduction of telegraphic communications, news of cargoes preceded the arrival of the ships and merchants were able to sell their metal forward for establishing delivery dates, thereby protecting themselves against a fall in price during the period of shipment. However, buyers at satisfactory prices could not always be found when they were needed, so a new metal 'futures' market began to evolve in the Jerusalem Coffee House in the City. This eventually became a continuous market and, when the Lombard Exchange and News Room was opened, the metal merchants and brokers made it their headquarters, until the inconvenience caused by the presence of members of other trades drove them to find their own premises.

In 1876 a group of metal merchants subscribed the capital for the London Metal Exchange Company. A room was rented in Lombard Court, telegraphic links were set up, and the first company secretary was engaged at a salary of £150 per annum. Membership rapidly increased until it reached the impressive total of more than three hundred. In 1882 the Exchange moved to Whittington Avenue, where it remained for 98 years, until increasing business and lack of space for expansion caused it to move to new premises in Plantation House in September 1980.

The London Wool Exchange, for nearly a hundred years situated in Coleman Street, was transferred early in 1963 to a new address in Brushfield Street, Spitalfields.

The Wool Exchange is Europe's spot market for raw wool from Australia, New Zealand and South Africa, and sometimes English wool as well as consignments from Kenya, the Falklands and South America are also available. Buyers represent all sections of the wool textile industries of Great Britain and Western Europe. The United States, Russia and Eastern Europe are also often represented.

The running of four Markets, namely Billingsgate, Leadenhall, London Central Market, Smithfield and Spitalfields Markets, is the Corporation's responsibility, and administered by the following Ward Committees: Central Markets Committee, Billingsgate and Leadenhall Markets Committee and Spitalfields Market Committee. Members are appointed to these committees for a period of four years, and are often appointed for a further term. No member is allowed to serve on the committee which administers the market in which he may be interested as a tenant or trader Each market has a Superintendent who presents written reports at every calendar meeting as to the business of the market and on all matters of detail.

Billingsgate is the most ancient of the markets belonging to the Corporation, and was one of the havens where the King's tolls and customs were collected as early as the reign of Ethelred (AD 979-1016). Originally, Billingsgate was a general market for corn, coal, iron, wine, spices, fish and many other goods. For many centuries Queenhithe was the main fish-market, and Billingsgate did not become an established fish market until the end of the seventeenth century. The first Act of Parliament relating to the market was passed in 1699 under which it became 'a free and open Market for all sorts of Fish whatsoever'; several subsequent Acts consolidated and amended the various statutes relating to the market, and improvements have been made from time to time. Finally, the market was moved to new premises at the Isle of Dogs in January 1982, and it has been proposed that the site of the old Market may be used for the London Commodity Exchange.

Leadenhall is a retail Market dealing in meat, poultry, game and provisions.

In early records the site of the London Central Market, Smithfield, is described as 'Smoothfield', when it was a plain, grassy space, several acres in extent, just outside the City walls, and remained as such until 1615. It was the play, archery and tournament field of the citizens of London, and a recognised place for public executions. During the reign of Mary I the site became infamous for the burning of Protestant martyrs. In the four years ended 1558, 200 people perished in the flames.

The first definite mention of Smithfield as a market appears in 1174 when, in the writings of Fitzstephen, clerk to Thomas Becket, it was described as 'a smooth field where every Friday there is a celebrated rendezvous of fine horses to be sold, and in another quarter are placed vendibles of the peasant, swine with their deep flanks, cows and oxen of immense bulk'.

The Statute of Smithfield consisted of certain ancient ordinances which were proclaimed yearly in the City about Michaelmas, and were concerned to provide for cash transactions in the Markets. The Royal Charter of 1638 confirmed to the Corporation of London a cattle market on the site.

The Cattle Market, its shambles and meat shops in adjacent streets, Newgate Street Market in particular, survived until June 1855. Long before then it had become an intolerable nuisance to the public, and Parliament was frequently petitioned for its removal. Eventually Parliament intervened and the Cattle Market was removed to a specially laid out market and system of slaughterhouses at Islington, some two miles north of Smithfield. This market and abattoir, known as the Metropolitan Cattle Market, opened in 1855, was owned and controlled by the Corporation of London, until its closure in 1964. It was on the Market Square at Islington that the famous Pedlars' Market known as the 'Caledonian Market' was held until the outbreak of war in 1939. This Pedlars' Market was the successor to a similar type of Market known as 'Bartholomew Fair', previously held at Smithfield for hundreds of years.

The Hay Market which had existed from the earliest times side by side with the Cattle Market, continued to function in West Smithfield for 50 years after the removal of the Cattle Market to Islington.

The London Central Markets, known throughout the world as 'Smithfield', are owned and controlled by the Corporation of the City of London presided over by the Lord Mayor, and managed by a Committee of Members of the Court of Common Council, while the many interests of the trade are in the capable hands of the Smithfield Market Tenants' Association.

The first two sections of the present market were opened for trade in December 1868, and meat sales shops and the chief business of Newgate Street Market were transferred to the present market. With the growth of business, additional sections were added and opened in 1875, 1889, 1898 and 1899. Parts of the markets were destroyed by enemy action in 1945 and by a fire in 1958 and have been rebuilt.

The London Fruit Exchange (Spitalfields), includes a fruit and flower Market and a Fruit Exchange.

Although just outside the City boundary, near Liverpool Street Station, the Fruit Exchange is part of the City's immense trading system. It occupies two floors of offices, an auction room, ground-floor showrooms and warehouses. This large enclosed area facilitates speedy transport to and from loading bays, and gives the exporter a valuable opportunity of selling his produce quickly.

One of the better known and least understood aspects of the City is its role as the banking centre of the modern world. Money-lenders had become extremely unpopular because of their power and the exorbitant interest rates which they charged. Their place was taken by goldsmiths and silversmiths from the Lombardy region of Italy who were granted land in London in 1318 — including the site of to-day's Lombard Street. The Italians flourished as pawnbrokers and money-lenders. In Lombardy they had always done business in market-places on simple wooden benches and that was why the Italian word for bench, 'banco' became 'bank'. The word 'bankrupt' came from the old Italian 'banca rotta', indicating the bench is broken. However, the concept of investing money was then unknown. Wealth was hoarded — often as jewels, brooches or furs. People tended to carry it around, often in the form of gold chains, which is not unknown even to this day. Treasure was often hidden in mattresses and various other places, and wills often gave directions to find it.

Trade routes were then being pioneered and, with international commerce starting to develop, merchants needed financial help which was beyond the capabilities of the money-lending goldsmiths of Lombard Street. The scene was set for the birth of a more modern approach to banking. Sir Thomas Gresham, having accumulated a fortune as a pioneer trader with the East Indies, became one of the first goldsmith bankers. The business he founded in Lombard Street eventually became part of Barclays. Gresham adopted his family crest, a grasshopper, coloured green on the coat of arms, as his trading sign, but displayed in gold outside his business premises to indicate that he dealt in that commodity. Signs were necessary for shop-keepers in those days, as few people could read.

The Royal Mint, which has now been moved to Llantrisant, near Cardiff, into the new Royal Mint building opened there in 1975, was until then housed in a building just north-east of the Tower of London built in 1808-11 by James Johnson and Sir Robert Smirke, but after the Royal Mint 'theft' shock of 1640, the men of Lombard Street began entrusting their treasure to the goldsmith-bankers, realising that they were guarding gold which they could lend at interest. They also offered to pay interest on gold left with them, which increased the amounts being deposited.

The growth in the use of cheques as a means of payment led in about 1770 to the setting up of a clearing system in London; this eventually became known as the London Bankers' Clearing House which has been situated at Post Office Court, Lombard Street since 1833. The member banks became known as clearing banks, a description still in use to-day.

The direct history of Barclays can be traced back to a goldsmith-banker called John Freame. In 1728 he bought the Black Spread Eagle in Lombard Street and moved his office there. It later became the site of Barclays' Head Office, and the Spread Eagle, of course, has become internationally recognised as the symbol of Barclays.

In 1896 a dozen or more private banks joined together to form Barclay & Company Limited, but expansion had started some thirty years earlier when it amalgamated with Spooner, Attwood & Company in 1863 and Ranson, Bouverie & Company in 1888; nineteen other small banks joined the amalgamation in 1896. Barclay & Company, now called a joint-stock Bank, expanded its interests in 1897, which accelerated growth. In 1917 the name was changed to Barclays Bank Limited. In 1918 merging with the London, Provincial and South Western Bank made Barclays one of the 'Big Five'. More than thirty banks later became part of Barclays, and in 1968 they acquired Martins, the sixth largest in the country, and its 700 branches. In 1980 Barclays had more offices world-wide than any other British bank, and employed more than 120,000 people in over 75 countries.

A partnership between Sampson Lloyd, ironfounder, and John Taylor, button and metal box manufacturer, in Birmingham in 1765 began Lloyds Bank; they opened their books at Dale End, Birmingham that year. There were four partners — Sampson Lloyd, John Taylor and their respective sons. The two junior partners, with Osgood Hanbury, opened a bank in Lombard Street in 1771, under the name of Hanbury, Taylor, Lloyd and Bowman. In 1864, this London house merged with Barnetts Hoares, who traded under the sign of the Black Horse, and the horse became Lloyds' own symbol.

Although the formation of joint-stock banks was permitted by the Government from 1826, it was not until 1865 that Lloyds became a joint stock company under the title of Lloyds Banking Company Limited. The years after 1865 were marked by surging expansion and a process of amalgamation. These completely transformed Lloyds' position; at the beginning of the half-century, it was still essentially a local bank. By the end it had become a national financial institution. The years after the First World War were a period of consolidation which gave Lloyds a chance to digest the acquisitions of the pre-war era and to extend its business in those parts of Britain where it was less strong. The Depression years of 1929-32 put a damper on further expansion but the years after the Second World War saw the transformation of Lloyds from a national financial institution into an international banking group. It had had an interest on the

Continent of Europe since 1911, when it formed a subsidiary to handle the Parisian business of one of the small banks which it had taken over. This offshoot eventually changed its name to Lloyds Bank Europe and set up either branches or subsidiaries in France, Belgium, Holland, Switzerland, Jersey and Monaco, making Lloyds pre-eminent among British banks in terms of direct representation in Western Europe. Lloyds has built up strong interest in Latin America since the nineteenth century, and after the 1939-45 war expanded its business into the Caribbean. Its involvement in the United States since 1965 expanded still further after buying out the Mellon National Bank of Pittsburgh in 1973. The following year First Western Bank and Trust Company, a major Californian bank, was purchased, and the company's name was changed to Lloyds Bank International, with headquarters in Los Angeles and 94 branches throughout the State. This acquisition — since renamed Lloyds Bank California — gave a substantially increased presence in the fast-moving trading area of the Pacific Basin, which include the National Bank of New Zealand with its 208 branches which it purchased in 1966. Then in the early 1970s LBI opened offices in Tokyo, Manila, Hong Kong and Singapore as part of a rapid expansion of its international interests. Offices have since been set up in Russia, Egypt, Australia, Malaysia, South Korea, Iran and Canada.

The history of the National Westminster Bank is bound up, to a large extent, with that of its six main constituent firms — Smiths Bank, which was established in Nottingham c1658, the National Provincial Bank of England, founded in 1833, the Manchester and Liverpool District Banking Company, founded in 1829, the London and Westminster Bank, which opened for business in London on 10 March 1834, the London and County Bank, established in 1836, and Parr's Bank which, commencing in 1782 as a private bank under the style of Parr, Lyon & Co. It became a joint stock bank in 1865, with its head office at Warrington.

Each of these firms had in previous years amalgamated with other smaller banks, and in 1918 Smiths amalgamated with the National Provincial Bank of England (whose directors opened an office in London, 1866) and in 1924 became the National Provincial Bank.

The policy of expansion by opening new branches and by amalgamation continued, and at the turn of the century the National Provincial had a network of 200 branches, by 1914 increased to 450. In 1920 it acquired the capital of Coutts and Company and in 1961 took over the Isle of Man Bank, and the District Bank in 1962.

The London and County Bank opened a City office at 38 Throgmorton Street, and another in the West End, on 10 March 1834, thereby achieving the distinction of being the first joint stock bank to be opened in London. The London and Westminster absorbed a number of small London banks in 1864 one of which was Jones, Loyd & Co of Lothbury, and in 1909 amalgamated with the London and County Bank. In 1909 the London and County Bank amalgamated with the London and Westminster Bank to form the London County and Westminster Bank, embracing almost 300 branches. Nine years later, in 1918, it amalgamated with Parr's Bank to form the London County Westminster and Parr's Bank. In 1865 the firm became a joint stock bank under the style 'Parr's Banking Company Limited', and instituted a policy of rapid expansion, taking over smaller banking businesses and amalgamating with others. A further change of name followed these transactions, and the title was shortened to Westminster Bank. In 1968 the Westminster and National Provincial Banks merged to form the National Westminster Bank. Thus the combined institution had a network of 3630 branches, and group deposits amounting to £3,031.1 million.

To-day's Midland Bank began in Birmingham in 1836. It was founded by Charles Geach, a Cornishman from St Austell, working as a clerk in the Birmingham branch of the Bank of England. Geach was dissatisfied with his salary and his promotion prospects. At the age of 28, he encouraged a group of local businessmen to form their own bank. This, the Birmingham Town and District Bank, came into being early in 1836, but Geach was not made the manager. Undeterred, he set to work again, and the Birmingham and Midland, opened seven weeks after its rival, with Charles Geach as manager. This grew into to-day's Midland Bank. Under Geach's talented management it prospered, and survived the difficult times of the 1840-1870s when there were many bank failures. There followed a number of amalgamations until 1891 when an amalgamation was arranged with the Central Bank of London, a joint stock bank established in 1863 with a number of branches throughout London. One of the provisions was that the Head Office should be in London; the Bank was known as the London and Midland Bank. More amalgamations and takeovers followed, including one with the City Bank, with its excellent London business and a spacious head office in Threadneedle Street. Now known as the London City and Midland Bank, its business extended into Scotland in 1920 and 1924, and into Eire in 1965.

The outstanding figure responsible for its success during the critical period of 1891-1918 was Sir Robert Holden. When he joined the Birmingham and Midland in 1881 it was a small and unremarkable organisation. When he died in 1919, it was the largest bank in the world. The Midland Bank Group now has a total of over 2,500 branches in England, Wales and the offshore islands.

The rapid growth of its business placed a great strain on the Threadneedle Street headquarters. The London Joint Stock Bank, with whom it had amalgamated, however, had also acquired property behind Princes Street, including the old Poultry Chapel, and this additional property gave the Bank frontages to Poultry as well as Princes Street. The Poultry frontage was eventually extended by acquisition to give the bank the entire area between St Mildred's Court and Grocer's Hall Court. The site, despite its complexity, offered the advantages of a central location close to the Bank of England, the Mansion House and other prominent institutions. Soon after the amalgamation, the Midland Bank's directors adopted it for the site of their new head office.

In over 100 countries, British insurance companies provide financial protection to homes and motor-cars, factories and growing crops, air-liners and ships. The British market provides re-insurance facilities for the larger risks which are beyond the capacity of local insurance markets, for example nuclear reactors, new construction projects and engineering works, the values of which run into many millions of pounds. Insurance is one of the City's most important invisible exports which, together with the services provided by the financial institutions linked to the City of London, and derived in the main from London's predominance as an international financial centre, accounts for hundreds of millions of net foreign currency earnings. Without these vast contributions, we should be unable to maintain our present standard of living. Earnings from financial services and investments have exceeded the deficit on visible trade by thousands of millions of pounds over many decades; in this way we have, throughout our history, covered the international payments of this small island, so dependent on imported resources. But these earnings are still not enough to provide for the Nation's overseas expenditure, and we can only afford to live in Britain at our present standard if the earnings from visible trade, financial services and investments exceed imports from all other overseas commitments. The financial institutions linked to the City of London have always supported and will continue to support the efforts being made by industry to increase visible exports, and this source of earned income is not as well-known as it should be.

It was in the City that fire insurance was founded and life assurance developed; it was British insurers who first assessed the risks of underwriting nuclear reactors. But the earliest form of insurance transacted in London is believed to have been marine, brought here by Lombard merchants in the 14th and 15th centuries.

After the Great Fire had destroyed £10m worth of property in London, Nicholas Barbon set up the first fire insurance company and enjoyed immediate success. His, too, was the first fire brigade. Individual fire brigades lasted in London until 1833, when a single brigade was formed, which eventually passed into the control of the London County Council.

Insurance companies have taken a prominent part in post-war rebuilding in the City and many of the new office blocks either contain the head offices of companies or are owned by companies as an investment. The insurance industry has a fitting headquarters in Aldermary House, on the corner of Queen Street and Watling Street, where the various insurance associations are housed. Part of the building occupies the site of the old London Fire Establishment, the City's first central fire-fighting organisation, made up of several company brigades, which operated between 1832 and 1865. After that, fire-fighting became the responsibility of the municipal authorities. At the corner of Aldersgate Street and Long Lane is the present headquarters of the London Salvage Corps, formed in 1866 to attend fires and limit the damage to property.

Like many of the City's commercial and financial enterprises, Lloyds began in a coffee house in the second half of the 17th century and early 18th century. Lloyds coffee house, from being a meeting place for City merchants who backed insurance policies, became a centre of marine intelligence and insurance. Today, Lloyd's is the largest marine and other insurance market in the world. Lloyds deals in all forms of insurance except long-term life and financial guarantee. The Corporation itself accepts no insurance risks, but only provides the premises in which individual representatives of underwriters' syndicates, each one a member of Lloyds, conduct their business.

The Underwriting Room houses the Lutine bell, which is rung for silence for the announcement of important news, and here, too, is the Casualty Book in which is written the names of vessels which have or are likely to become total losses.

Fleet Street is the centre of Britain's newspaper industry and takes its name from the River Fleet which used to run down Farringdon Street to the Thames at Blackfriars. It is said 'Fleet Street never sleeps' — even when they 'put the papers to bed'.

With the exception of the *Times, Guardian* and *Observer,* the major daily newspapers are there. Many of the larger provincial newspapers have a London office in 'the Street'.

In Shoe Lane, just off Fleet Street, is the International Press Centre, founded by a group of journalists for the use of the international press and media organisations; the 17-storey building was opened in 1974 and has an adjoining conference and banqueting centre, as well as the Press Club, within the building. Off Fleet Street are a number of small courts. Crane Court, on the Street, witnessed the first meeting of the Royal Society; Gough Square, gained from Johnson's Court, marks the house where Dr Johnson lived from 1748 to 1759, and where he toiled over his great *Dictionary,* and other works. In Wine Office Court is the celebrated Old Cheshire Cheese, traditionally associated with Johnson and Goldsmith. Contemporary names have been perpetuated by new office blocks nearby — Johnson House, Boswell House, Gough House. With a frontage to Fleet Street and a longer one to Salisbury Court is the building occupied by the Press Association and Reuters.

To the east, and somewhat dwarfed by the building, is St Bride's Church, though the beautiful spire of this famous church rises to a height of 226 feet. Badly damaged during the war, but now superbly restored, it was rebuilt by Christopher Wren in 1680. Adjoining the church and south of Salisbury Court is Salisbury Square, not only the site of the town house of the Earls of Salisbury, but also of the printing works of Samuel Richardson, father of the English sentimental novel. In the crypt of the church are the remains of Wynken de Worde. Because of its literary and press associations the church has been called 'the Cathedral of Fleet Street'.

The City itself has had its own newspaper for 125 years. First, the *City Press* was launched in 1857 but ceased publication in May 1976. Then, in March 1976, the independent *City of London Recorder* started fortnightly publication and has now become required reading for all those interested in the City, here and overseas.

The site of Wren's Temple Bar (removed in 1878 to Theobald's Park, near Cheshunt) marks the boundary between the City and Westminster. Opposite are the Law Courts, erected in 1868; the architect was George E. Street. Most of the building is just outside the boundary of the City as is the famous Club 'The Wig and Pen'; it is one of the few buildings in the area which survived the Great Fire and, as the name suggests, is a popular haunt of lawyers and journalists. Another haunt is El Vino, the famous Wine Bar in Fleet Street. It has changed little since it was first opened about a hundred years ago; its rules of behaviour are also much as they were then. Men must wear coats and ties; ladies are not allowed to stand at the bar, but must sit down, either around the two tables near the door, or in the large back room. Further along Fleet Street from El Vino is Mitre Court, which gives directly on to the Temple and the courts of the Honourable Societies of the Inner and Middle Temple, two of the four Inns of Court. The Knights Templars moved in the twelfth century from their headquarters, near the top of what is now Chancery Lane, to the New Temple on the northern slopes of the Thames. Here they built a church — one of the four round churches in England. After the dissolution of their Order early in the fourteenth century, the property was transferred, in part at first, to the Knights Hospitallers. As the site was almost midway between the City and the Courts of Westminster, lawyers met in Inns and hostels near-by to discuss their business and eventually became tenants to the Hospitallers.

Change has ever been part of the City's progress, but the last war devastated great tracts while offering opportunities for reconstruction comparable to those of 1666. That reconstruction has been one of the City's major contemporary tasks, involving the Corporation in large-scale acquisition of land, and capital expenditure by private enterprise which has been measured in hundreds of millions of pounds.

Approximately one-third of City floor-space was lost; buildings destroyed included 20 churches, most of which were designed by Sir Christopher Wren, 18 livery halls, the main warehouses of the textile trade from Barbican to Upper Thames Street, and the traditional home of the book publishers north of St Paul's Cathedral. Miraculously, the Cathedral, although hit by several high explosive bombs, was saved from destruction by the volunteer Fire Guard organisation. The great Barbican development is now well-known to all who live and work in the City and to visitors.

Important views both to and from St Paul's Cathedral have been maintained; this was most carefully considered in relation to the buildings between the Deanery and the Cathedral and fronting Ludgate Hill, where the correct height and scale are critical to a full appreciation of the architectural drama which unfolds through movement towards the west front. Pleasant vistas north and east of St Paul's have also been preserved. South of the Cathedral, Fleet Street South and St Andrew's Hill are among the Conservation Areas of the City. St Bartholomew's, College Street, Finsbury Circus and Bow Lane are also in the list.

Cannon Street, Bucklersbury, Cornhill, Lombard Street, Austin Friars, Houndsditch and Aldgate have all been subject to post-war reconstruction by the City Planners, as have many other parts of the City. The reconstruction and additions to Guildhall, the rebuilding of Cannon Street Station, the new Billingsgate site area, the Nat-West building and other giant erections in Old Broad Street are all indications of the changing face of the City. Reconstruction is not yet completed; great changes are expected in the Bank area and in Cutler Street and the adjoining streets and lanes, and although a great deal of controversy exists in respect of Little Britain, no doubt we shall see more change there.

But the City is the child of change. It has always adapted to change and this is one of its strengths. More important, nowhere has there been such a concentration of excellence in so many spheres — commercial and charitable, professional and voluntary, educational and entrepreneurial and in civic administration. The city represents a unique matrix of tradition and innovation, and the citizens of London can justly claim that they lead the world and that they serve it well. Not for nothing is the City's motto 'O Lord, Guide us', for in all things the City exists to the glory of God through the service of men.

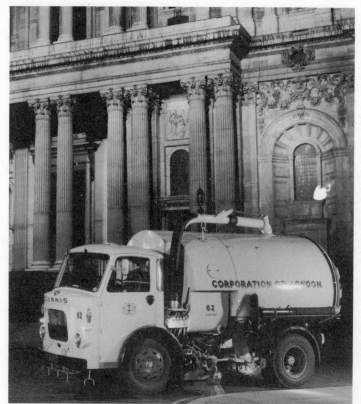

LEFT: A City cleansing vehicle at work outside St Paul's, (MOH) RIGHT: the modern City constabulary (POL) and BELOW: a Port Health duty inspector's launch. (MOH)

OPPOSITE ABOVE: The new Grammar and Mathematical Schools at Christ's Hospital, 1833, BELOW: Christ's Hospital pupils at Horsham today, and ABOVE: the Blue Coat School, Christ's Hospital, sketched from the tower of Christ's Church, Newgate Street in 1894; (CH) BELOW: the City of London Freeman's School at Ashtead. (GL)

247

ABOVE: The City of London School for Boys, RIGHT: Christopher Webb's window honouring Wren and his craftsmen, in St Lawrence Jewry-next-Guildhall, BELOW: part of Guildhall Library today, and OPPOSITE ABOVE: Guildhall Art Gallery. (GL) BELOW: the London Symphony Orchestra in their new home at the Barbican Hall. (PB)

ABOVE LEFT: St Lawrence Jewry-next-Guildhall in 1974, (GL) and RIGHT: St Nicholas Cole Abbey painted by Anthony Coombs, a sidesman. BELOW LEFT: St Botolph without Bishopsgate in 1728 (BWB) and RIGHT: St Mary Woolnoth, Lombard Street in 1812. (MW)

LEFT: St Ethelburga the Virgin, within Bishopsgate, drawn in 1954 by S.H. Joyce, (EV) and RIGHT: St Brigit, alias St Bride's Church, Fleet Street. (BFS)

LEFT: St Mary Somerset, Upper Thames Street, demolished 1875, the tower remaining and protected by act of Parliament, (MS) and RIGHT: St Michael Paternoster Royal in College Hill. (WD)
BELOW: St Paul's during the blitz. (GL)

ABOVE: Trinity House, CENTRE LEFT: replica of the *Loyal London,* Trinity House; (TH) RIGHT: mv *Naticia,* flagship of Catamaran Cruisers Ltd, a modern river craft; (CCL) BELOW LEFT: Pikemen and RIGHT: Musketeers of the Honourable Artillery Company. (JMH)

ABOVE: The Honourable Artillery Company at their Finsbury Barracks, 1893, and LEFT: the College of Arms. (GL) RIGHT: The Stock Exchange; OPPOSITE ABOVE LEFT: The 'floor' of the Stock Exchange. (SE) RIGHT: London Metal Exchange, 'ring' in Whittington Avenue before moving in 1977 and CENTRE LEFT: the Exchange in 1897. (ME) RIGHT: Hudson's Bay Company fur auction and BELOW: the 'auction by candlelight' at Garroway's Coffee House, Change Alley in 1672. (HBC)

OPPOSITE ABOVE: Old Queenhithe steps, 400 hundred years ago, (GL) BELOW: Smithfield Market as seen by Theodore Lane; ABOVE: invitation to the Inauguration Ceremony of the Metropolitan Meat and Poultry Markets, Smithfields, 1868. (MM) BELOW LEFT: The Old Lady of Threadneedle Street and RIGHT: the Bank of England. (BE)

ABOVE LEFT: Pay office of the London and Westminster Bank, (NWB) and RIGHT: Barclay's Bank head office in Lombard Street. (BB) BELOW LEFT: Aldermary House, Queen Street, home of the insurance world, (II) and RIGHT: the Lutine Bell. OPPOSITE ABOVE LEFT: The *City Recorder* office, 9-10 Little Britain, and RIGHT: the White Horse, Little Britain. (CR) BELOW LEFT: Commercial Union Assurance building in Leadenhall Street, (CUA) and RIGHT: the 1975 notice of a ward election.

NOTICE OF WARD ELECTION

CITY OF LONDON   WARD OF QUEENHITHE
ELECTION OF WARD OFFICERS

To the Electors of the Ward of Queenhithe

Notice is hereby given that by virtue of a precept from the Right Honourable The LORD MAYOR, a Wardmote will be held on Wednesday the 17th day of December, 1975, at 12 noon precisely at The Painters' Hall, 9 Little Trinity Lane, E.C.4 for the purpose of electing Ward Officers for the year ensuing.

Nomination papers must be delivered at Sandoz House, 23 Great Castle Street, London, WIN 8NQ, on any day after the date of this notice but not later than noon on the 1st day of December, 1975.

Forms of nomination may be obtained from me at Sandoz House, 23 Great Castle Street, London, WIN 8NQ.

In order that they may be effective for this election all applications to be treated as an absent voter and other applications and notices about postal or proxy voting must be received by the TOWN CLERK, Guildhall, London, E.C.2 by the last day for the delivery of nomination papers as shown above.

If the election is contested and a poll is demanded, the same will take place at Painters' Hall, 9 Little Trinity Lane, E.C.4 on Thursday the 18th day of December, 1974 between the hours of 8 a.m. and 8 p.m. or until such earlier hour as may be agreed upon by the candidates.

Dated this 15th day of November, 1975.

K. S. HARRISON, Ward Clerk

Note 1. The attention of candidates and electors is drawn to the provisions relating to the completion of nomination papers, the times and place for delivery thereof and the other provisions relating thereto contained in the Acts of Common Council made and passed on the 14th day of July 1960, the 23rd day of May 1968, the 9th day of April 1970 and the 17th day of February 1972.

Note 2. Every person guilty of a corrupt or illegal practice will on conviction be liable to the penalties imposed by the Representation of the People Act, 1949.

Note 3. Qualification of Candidates for the office of Common Councilman.

A person shall (unless disqualified by virtue of any enactment) be qualified for election to the Common Council as a Common Councilman if at the date of nomination and at the date of election he is a Freeman of the City and is of full age and a British subject or a citizen of the Republic of Ireland and (a) is registered in the list of persons entitled to vote at any Ward election ; OR (b) owns freehold or leasehold land in the City ; OR (c) has during the whole of the twelve months preceding the date of nomination, and has until the date of election resided in the City. (City of London (Various Powers) Acts, 1957 and 1967).

The changing face of the City: ABOVE: Barbican Arts and Conference Centre, (PB) and BELOW: the new buildings of the City cast their shadows on the old. (HP)

Bibliography

CHAPTERS 1-5

Primary Sources
Fitzstephen, William *A Description of London*
Holinshed, R. *Chronicles of England*
Ovatio Carolina, The Triumph of King Charles 1641
Stow, John *Survey of London,* Kingsford Edition
Taylor, John *England's comfort and London's Joy,* 1641
The Diary of Samuel Pepys
Treloar, Sir W. *A Lord Mayor's Diary 1906/7,* to which is added the diary of Lord Mayor Micajah Perry 1838/9

A collection of manuscript notes on the freedom and government of the City of London (J.F.V. Woodman)

Secondary Sources
Ashley, M. *England in the 17th century* 1952
Ashton, R. *The City and the Court* 1979
Baker, T. *Medieval London* 1970
Barron, C. *The Medieval Guildhall of London* 1974
Beaven, A.B. *The Aldermen of the City of London* 1908-1913
Besant, Sir Walter *London City* 1910
Birch, Walter de Gray *The Historical Charters and Constitutional Documents of the City of London,* 1887
Blackham, R.J. *London's Livery Companies* 1931
Borer, M.C. *The City of London: a history* 1977
Brooke, C. *The Shaping of a City. London 800-1216* 1975
Brett-James, N. *The Growth of Stuart London* 1935
Bryant, Sir Arthur *King Charles II* 1931
Clark, J. *Saxon and Norman London* 1980
Clarke, J.J. *A History of Local Government of the United Kingdom* 1955
Crawford, A. *History of the Vintners' Company* 1977
Davis, Mrs. D.*A History of Shopping* 1966
Eades, G.E. *Historic London* 1966
Fairholt, F.W. *Lord Mayor's Pageants* 1843-44
Ferris, P. *The City* 1960
Fisher, F.J. *The Development of London as a centre of conspicuous consumption* (transactions of the Royal Historical Society 1948)
Foster, F.F. *The Politics of Stability.* A Portrait of the Rulers in Elizabethan London 1977
Fraser, A. *Cromwell Our Chief of Men* 1973; *Charles II* 1979
George, M.D. *London Life in the Eighteenth Century* 1925
Glass, D.V. *London Within the Walls,* London Record Society 1968
Gray, R. *A History of London* 1978
Harben, H.A. *A Dictionary of London*
Hazlitt, W.C. *The Livery Companies of the City of London* 1892
Herbert, W. *The History of the 12 Great Livery Companies of London* 1836
Hibbert, C. *London The Biography of a city* 1969
Hill, C. *Reformation to Industrial Revolution* 1967
Holmes, M.J.R. *Elizabethan London* 1969
Jones, P.E. *The Butchers of London* 1976; *Some London Civic Institutions* 1946
Jackson, P. *London Bridge* 1971
Johnson's England ed. Turberville
Kahl, W.F. *The Development of London Livery Companies,* an historical essay and select bibliography 1960
Kellett, R.J. *The Breakdown of Guild and Corporation control over the handicraft and retail trade in London* (in *Economic History Review* April 1958)

Kent, W.R.G. *My Lord Mayor* 1947

Kenyon, J.P. *Stuart England* 1978

Knill, Lady *The Mansion House* 1937

Lang, J. *Pride Without Prejudice* 1975

Levin, Mrs J. *The Charter Controversy in the City of London* 1969

Marsden, R.V. *Roman London* 1980

Melling, J.K. *Discovering London's Guilds and Liveries*

Merrifield, R. *The Roman City of London* 1965; *Roman London* 1969

O'Brien, T. *The London Livery Companies and the Virginia Company* 1960

Outhwaite, R. *Inflation in Tudor and Stuart England* 1969

Pearl, V. *London and the outbreak of the Puritan Revolution* 1961; *Change and Stability in 17th century London* (in London Journal Vol 5 no 1); *London's Counter Revolution in 'The Interregnum'* ed G.E. Aylmer; *Social Policies in 17th century London in 'History and Imagination'* 1981

Paget, J.T. *The Pageantry of Britain* 1979

Perks, S. *History of the Mansion House* 1922

Pritchett, V.S. *London Perceived* 1962

Pevsner, N. *The Cities of London and Westminster* 1972

Rasmussen, S.E. *London: the unique city* 1935

Reynolds, S. *The Rulers of London in the 12th century* (in *History* 1972)

Robertson, A.G. *Tudor London* 1968

Robertson, D. *Chaucer's London* 1968

Robson, William *The Government and Misgovernment of London* 1939; *The Heart of Greater London* 1977

Robson, William *The Government and Misgovernment of London* 1939; *The Heart of Greater London* 1977 (TV conference background paper)

Round, J.H. *The Commune of London* 1899

Rowley, T. *The Lost Charters of the City of London* (address to Common Hall 1980)

Rowse, A.L. *The England of Elizabeth* 1950

Rude G., *Hanovarian London 1714-1808* 1971

Sharpe, R.R. *London and the Kingdom* 3 vols 1894-5

Sheppard, F. *London 1808-1870 The Infernal Wen* 1971

Smith, F.R.S. *The Irish Society* 1966

Spencer, B. *Chaucer's London* 1972

Stenton, F.M. *Norman London.* An essay. (Historical Association 1934; includes a translation of William Fitzstephen's description of London)

Sutherland, L.S. *The City of London and opposition to government 1768-1774* 1959

Summerson, J. *Georgian London* 1949

Tawney, R.H. *Religion and the Rise of Capitalism* 1948 ed; *Thomas Wilson. A discourse upon usury 1572*

Thomas, E.A.H. *Calendar of Plea and Memorial Rolls 1364-1381*

Thrupp, S. *The Merchant Class of Medieval London* 1948

Trease, G. *London. A Concise History* 1975

Unwin, G. *The Guilds and Companies of London* 4th ed. 1963

Welch, C. *A Modern History of the City of London* 1896

Webb, S.J. *The Reform of London* 1894

Wedgwood, C.V. *The King's Peace* 1966 ed; *The King's War* 1966 ed

Wheatley and Cunningham, *London Past and Present* 1891

Williams, G.A. *Medieval London from Commune to Capital*

Wrigley, E.A. *A simple model of London's importance in changing English society and economy 1650-1750* (in *Past and Present* 1967)

Archaeology of the City of London. Department of Urban Archaeology, Museum of London

Corporation of London Publications
The Livery of the City of London 1972
The Guildhall of the City of London
Mansion House, 1978
The City of London Official Guide

The Corporation of the City of London. Its origin, constitution, powers and duties 1950
Statement as to the origin, constitution, powers and functions of the Corporation of London 1974

CHAPTER 6

Primary Sources
Transcriptions of original Guild and Company records
John Stow's *Survey of London*
The Diary of Samuel Pepys (Robert Latham and William Matthews)
Papers of W.H. Birch Esq
Secondary Sources (general)
Akehurst, Richard *Antique Weapons* 1969
McCausland, Hugh *The English Carriage* 1948
Parker, James *A Glossary of Terms used in Heraldry* 1894 (reprinted 1970)
Sparkes, Ivan *Stagecoaches and Carriages* 1975
Trevelyan, G.M. *English Social History* 1942
Wilkinson, Frederick *Small Arms* 1965
Secondary Sources (Guilds and Companies)
Books
Adams, Arthur *The History of the Worshipful Company of Blacksmiths of London* 1951
Bennett, Eric *The Worshipful Company of Carmen* 1982; *The Worshipful Company of Wheelwrights in the City of London* 1970
Bobart, Henry Hodgkinson *Records of the Basketmakers' Company* 1911
Bone, George Allan *The Worshipful Company of Glass Sellers* 1966
Champness, Roland *The Worshipful Company of Turners of London* 1966
Copeman, Dr W.S.C. *Apothecaries* 1967
Crewdson, H.A.F. *The Worshipful Company of Musicians* 1966
Dumelow, John *The Wax Chandlers of London*
Fisher, F.J. *The Worshipful Company of Horners* 1936
Fowles, A.W. *The Revised History of the Worshipful Company of Fan Makers 1709-1975* 1976
Fox, Adam *A Brief Description of the Worshipful Company of Skinners* 1968
Girtin, Tom *The Triple Crowns* 1964
Glover, Elizabeth *The Gold and Silver Wyre Drawers* 1979
Hayton, Dudley *The Worshipful Company of Cutlers of London* 1956
Jones, Philip E. *The Butchers of London* 1976; *The Poulters of London* 1981
Lang, Jennifer *The Cordwainers of London* 1980
Law, Frank W. *The Worshipful Company of Spectacle Makers* 1978
Mayer, Edward *The Curriers and the City of London* 1968
Monier-Williams, Randall H. *A Brief Account of the Worshipful Company of Tallow Chandlers* 1978
Nockolds, Harold (ed) *The Coachmakers* 1977
Phillips, Frank Taverner *The Cooks' Company* 1966
Pinto, Edward H. *The Origins and History of the Worshipful Company of Furniture Makers* 1974
Prevett, H. *A Short Description of the Worshipful Company of Haberdashers* 1971
Ronald, Paul *The Basketmakers' Company* 1978
Steele, Arnold F. *The Worshipful Company of Solicitors in the City of London* 1962
Smith, Raymond *The Worshipful Company of Masons*
Taylor, Janet *The Brewers' Company*
Thrupp, Sylvia *A Short History of the Worshipful Company of Bakers of London*
Warner, Olive *A History of the Innholders Company* 1962
Anon, *The Coachmakers' Yearbook* 1977; *The Cooks' Company* (unpublished); *The Story of the Worshipful Company of Farmers* (unpublished); *Grocers Hall* 1980; *The Worshipful Company of Plaisterers of London* 1974; *The History and Work of the Worshipful Company of Shipwrights*

Pamphlets (abbr: WC = Worshipful Company)
Actuaries Granting of Letters Patent 1980, The WC of
Armourers and Brasiers, The WC of

Weavers, The WC of (Prize Scheme)
Woolmen's Company, A History of the

Articles
Accountants — Our Livery Company (Alan Hardcastle in *The London Accountant*)
Arbitrators, The WC of (J.F. Phillips)
Arbitrators, The WC of (anon)
Basketmakers, The WC of (Bernard Stroulger)
Bakers. History, The WC of (K. Mostyn)
Blacksmiths of London, The WC of (anon)
Builders' Merchants — A Brief History of the Company (anon)
Butchers, The WC of (anon)
Distillers, A Brief History of the WC of (anon)
Fletchers and Longstringbowmakers, The (James E. Oxley)
Framework Knitters, The WC of (anon)
Fuellers — Some Historical Notes (anon)
Grocers' Company, The (Doreen Crown in *Port of London* 1981)
Haberdashers — A Brief History of the Company (anon)
Innholders, The WC of (anon)
Insurers, The WC of (Jo Craig in the Chartered Insurance Institute *Journal)*
Ironmongers, The WC of (anon)
Launderers' Regalia, The Company of *(Power Laundry and Cleaning News* 1964)
Needlemakers — History of the Company (anon)
Pattenmakers, WC of (anon)
Paviors, The WC of (anon)
Pewterers, The WC of (anon)
Saddlers, A Brief History of the WC of (anon)
Salters, The WC of (anon)
Scriveners Company, The Rise of the (anon)
Shipwrights, The WC of *(Bank Line House Magazine,* 1979)
Spectacle Makers — A Short History of the Company (anon)
Stationers Company, The (Myles Glover)
Surveyors, The WC of Chartered (anon)
Tin Plate Workers and Wyre Drawers of the City of London, The WC of (D.L. Simmons)
Upholders, The (anon)
Wax Chandlers, The WC of (Eva Crane)
Weavers Celebrate 850th Anniversary (Lawrence Johnston in *City Recorder* 1980)

CHAPTERS 7 & 8

Bank of England, *Some Glimpses of the 'Old Lady's' History*
Barclays Bank Ltd, *A Story of Money and Banking*
Bede, *History of the English Church and People*
Brien Reidy & Associates Ltd, *History of the London Metal Exchange*
City Press, Editions of 29th March 1973 and 28th August 1975
City of London Directory, Guilds Guide and *Who's Who*
Corporation of London, *The City Franchise*
Corporation of London, *Conservation Areas*
Corporation of London, *The Year of the Livery*
Lloyds Bank Ltd, *Story of Lloyds Bank*
Loftie, W.J. *Historic Towns — London*
Masters, Betty R., BA, FSA *The City of London and Clean Air 1273 to 1973 AD*
Midland Bank Ltd, *Banking Handbook*
Midland Bank Ltd, *Buildings for Bankers*

National Westminster Bank Ltd, *History of National Westminster Bank*
Oman, Charles *History of England*
Page, William *London — its Origins and Early Development*
Pike, Maurice C. *The Corporation of London — its origins, constitution, powers and duties*
Plumley, N. in consultation with the Clerk of Christ's Hospital and the Headmaster, *A Pictorial History*
Port of London Authority, *Port of London and Development*
Riley, H.T. *Memorials of London and London Life*
Royal Regiment of Fusiliers, City of London Headquarters, *The Royal Regiment of Fusiliers*
Rudolph Woolf & Co Ltd, *A Brief History of the Company*
Sanderson, Peter A. *Catamaran Cruisers*
Torry, Gilbert *The Book of Queenhithe*
Trinity House, London, *Corporation of Trinity House*
Unwin, G.H. *The Guilds and Companies of London* (1908)
Walker, George Goold *Four Centuries of the Honourable Artillery Company*

Acknowledgements to Illustrations

BB	Barclays Bank Ltd
BE	Bank of England
BFS	St Bride's
BL	Bodleian Library
BM	British Museum
BWB	St Botolph-without-Bishopsgate
CB	Clive Birch
CCL	Catamaran Cruisers Ltd
CH	Christ's Hospital
CR	*City Recorder*
CUA	Commercial Union Assurance
EV	St Ethelburga the Virgin
GAG	Guildhall Art Gallery
GL	Guildhall Library
GR	Guildhall Records Office
HBC	Hudson's Bay Company
II	Insurance Institute
LME	London Metal Exchange
MC	Mansell Collection
ML	Museum of London
MOH	Ministry of Health
MS	St Mary Somerset
MW	St Mary Woolnoth
NWB	National Westminster Bank Ltd
POL	City of London Police
RJG	Rachel & John Grindall
SE	Stock Exchange
TH	Trinity House Service
WD	Rev William Down
VA	Victoria & Albert Museum

Livery Companies & Guilds

M	Mercers	BS	Blacksmiths
G	Grocers	J	Joiners
D	Drapers	WV	Weavers
F	Fishmongers	WM	Woolmen
MT	Merchant Taylors	FRR	Fruiterers
S	Skinners	SN	Stationers
H	Haberdashers	MU	Musicians
ST	Salters	TR	Turners
I	Ironmongers	BT	Basketmakers
V	Vintners	HR	Horners
DY	Dyers	FA	Farriers
B	Brewers	AP	Apothecaries
L	Leathersellers	SH	Shipwrights
P	Pewterers	SP	Spectacle Makers
C	Cutlers	CL	Clockmakers
BK	Bakers	FK	Framework Knitters
W	Wax Chandlers	N	Needlemakers
TC	Tallow Chandlers	GD	Gardeners
AB	Armourers & Brasiers	TW	Tin Plate Workers
BR	Butchers	GS	Glass Sellers
SD	Saddlers	GW	Gold & Silver Wyre Drawers
CP	Carpenters	MPC	Makers of Playing Cards
PS	Painter-Stainers	CC	Carmen
CR	Curriers	AP	Air Pilots
MN	Masons	FM	Furniture Makers
IN	Innholders	SS	Surveyors
FR	Founders	AC	Accountants
PR	Poulters	LR	Launderers
CK	Cooks	MK	Marketors
CO	Coopers	AT	Actuaries
BY	Bowyers	PC	Parish Clerks
	BR	Builders	

Photographs by

JA	John Armistead
HP	Handford Photography
JMH	Michael Hope
MJH	Mark Hope (maps)
PB	Peter Bloomfield
UPPA	Universal Pictorial Press & Agency Ltd
VFH	Valerie Hope

Index

Presentation Edition

I   Her Majesty The Queen
II   The Right Honourable The Lord Mayor, Sir Christopher Leaver, GBE, DMus
III   The Corporation of The City of London
VI   Guildhall Library

Subscribers

1 Valerie Hope BA
2 Clive Birch FSA FRSA
3 Gilbert Torry
4 Carolyn Birch
5 John P. List
6 Gerald Burton
7 N.S. Wass
8 J. A. Blott
9 Hugh M. Joseph CBE, F Inst PS
10 William R. Miller
11 R.I. Woods
12 Robert J. Sutton
13 F.S. Burton
14 The Hon Mrs Carole Lawson
15 Clifford S. Dennis
16 Robert Pooley
17 H. Richard Walduck JP, MA
18 G.E. Lapslie
19 J.F. Meade
20 Ronald Goodyear
21 R.J.A. Murray
22 John E. Mills
23 W. Oulton Wade
24 Peter Trower
25 H.J.W. Warrell
26 David R.W. Potter
27 R.L. Wakeham
28 Robert Pooley
29 A.N. Hollis
30 R. Alan Jones
31 J.F. Moultrie
32 Michael J. Bellis
33 Bell & Co (Westminster) Ltd
34 Mrs I.E. Shaw
35 C.V. Ridd
36 Peter Chard
37 B.S. Kiek
38 Malcolm Read
39 Victoria & Albert Museum
40 David Neil Parkes
41 Philip Lea
42 Michael H. Hinton
43 Harry T. Dennison
44 Eric R. Britt JP
45 Michael J.J. Collas

46 Dr. D.T. Hughes
47 Albert Hallam
48 P.J. Reeves
49 Richard Smart
50 Dennis Fisher
51 John N. Heyer
52 Robin W. Scott
53 Roger Pincham
54 Mrs M.W. Minshull-Fogg
55 Robert Gold
56 W.F.W. Southwood
57 Miss C.F. Gordon
58 G.T. Mandl
59 Sir John Ackroyd
60 A.J. Elliott
61 P.G. Warner
62 H.R. Vogt
63 N.G. Ellis
64 Sydney Mason
65 Alec L. James
66 Peter Trower
67 Michael H. Hinton
68 B.S. Glover
69 J.W. Hale
70 O.C.T.R. Normandale
71 F.F. Smith
72 M.B. Parry-Crooke
73 B.J.N. Vaizey
74 C.J.N. Miller MBE
75 F.B. Jackson
76 Sir Charles Hardie CBE
77 Major J.A. Henry
78 F.R.D. Holland
79 John E. Foister
80 E.A. Fairburn
81 Cynthia Bacon
82 Cdr James B. Livingston CBE DSC
83 Lt Col P. Halford-Thompson
84 G.H. Ratcliffe
85 C.H. Bowden
86 Henry C. Cottrell
87 Sir Kenneth Selby
88 Epsom Glass Industries Ltd
89 The Leathersellers Company
90 J.G. Thorpe

91 R.M. Simmonds
92 Mark A. Loveday
93 C.H. Beeby
94 F.F. Davy
95 R.T.D. Wilmot
96 George Sax
97 Maj Gen E.J. Younson
98 P.D. Northall-Laurie
99 T. Every
100 Johnny and Delma Geeves
101 Ralph and Gillian Harding
102 J.E.F. Hunt
103 C.G. Hamilton
104 A.C. Green
105 A.P. Oakley
106 D.C.W. Piercy
107 W.E.H. Brown
108 G.S. Simons
109 E.J.C. McDaniel FRICS
110 A.B. White
111 J.R. Rose
112 K.P.W. Stoneley
113
114 W.J. Farrelly KCSG
115 Dennis S. Pile
116 R.B. Tiley
117 R.W. Travis
118 Gordon H. Jones
119 John Hull
120 K.G. Pert
121 E. Wooster
122 Norman Bezzant
123 F.E.A. Taylor
124 Leslie Campbell Winterton
125 John Alfred Barker CC
126 K.J. Fuller
127 Tony Bellm
128 Dennis E. Dowse
129 E.H. Turner
130 H.V. Hodson
131 Arthur A. Carter
132 John W. Tompkins
133 J.R. Mahlich
134 John Stitt
135 D.J. Holborow

136 J.W. Maddern
137 Derek L. Kemp
138 H.J. Maddocks
139 T.A. Bailey
140 W.J. Dymott
141 R.H. Stubington
142 Edwin Lawrence
143 S.V.F. Leleux
144 Capt W. Ashby
145 John Drayton Hedges
146 Raymond Jayson
147 Andrew J. Wilson
148 Michael Bannister
149 S.F. Charles Brown
150 Dennis Fraser Hill
151 K.H. Mostyn
152 M.W.G. Wathen
153 George H. Coppen
154 Lavoy Moore
155 Norman Poultney
156 F.W. Gardiner
157 A.G. Cavan
158 L. St J. Tibbitts
159 L.H. Middleton
160 Dr R.G. Bird
161 Harold Gould JP, FCA
162
163 D.C. Spicer
164 G.R. Rose
165 Major B.G.N. Evelegh
166 Jonathan R. Kropman LLB
167 C.R. Lynam
168 D.G.M. Read
169 Howard Angus
170 Graham R. Young
171 Neville Rayner
172 John Barrett
173
174 A.M.C. Williams
175 G.M. Alston
176 W.N. Clarke AA DIPL, ARIBA, MSIAD
177 W. White
178 Arthur Garratt
179 D.F.A. Davidson
180 Robert Gibbins

181	Grp Capt L.E. Robins	238	E.S. Springate
182	Dr J. Freeborn	239	L.A. Taylor
183	Tom Hancock	240	Edward Kevin Sparks

181	Grp Capt L.E. Robins
182	Dr J. Freeborn
183	Tom Hancock
184	J.W. Stephens
185	John Bloxham
186	Robert Harding Davies
187	O.B. Gilbart-Smith
188	Keith Saxon Fullwood
189	Denis Weiner
190	Sir Peter Studd
191	Michael Hewison
192	John Guillaume
193	F.R. Hopkins
194	G.R. Kershaw
195	D.L. Barratt
196	L.A. Bains
197	Arthur A. Hammond OBE
198	M.H. Powell
199	Roy H. Hill
200	N.D. Green
201	Philip A. Girle
202	Roger Flemington
203	Harry Charles Burge
204	W. M. Mitchell
205	A.P.G. Borley
206	John D. Powell
207	Frank Austin Mines
208	F.C. Donaldson
209	Alderman Paul Newall
210	R.A. Crabb
211	J.N.A. Fletcher
212	W.S.R. Crabb
213	D.G. Milne
214	Maj H.H.H. James
215	Humphry M. Smith
216	G.J.R. Pannett
217	Lt Col F.E. Coxhead MBE
218	Victor Lucas
219	R.D.K. Edwards
220	Peter M. Gimson
221	L.C. Grainger
222	H.B. Laine
223	Edward Darlow
224	H.W.S. Horlock MA DEPUTY
225	J.E. Bartleet
226	J.T. Coggan
227	P.J. Miles
228	John Gedge
229	E.R. Britt
230	M.T.S. Matthews
231	D.D. Searle
232 / 233	A.D. Walker-Arnott
234	M.W. Chapman
235	Major C.A.A. Robertson
236	C.M. Wigan
237	Charles Peter Nichols

238	E.S. Springate
239	L.A. Taylor
240	Edward Kevin Sparks
241	Harry Johnson
242	Peter W. Barnes
243	P.H. Mack
244	Robert Spenser Ashby
245	B.M. Gilbart-Smith
246	T.L. Beagley
247	A.C. Feasey
248	J.G. Butlin
249	F.D. Wooldridge
250	W.R.T. Long
251	C.N. Packett
252	J.L. Bowler
253	Martin Macey
254	M.J. Maher
255	Bishopsgate Institute
256	W.T. McMahon
257	Arthur E. Stone
258	Peter Wiseman
259	K.W. Langley
260	Sir Robert Lawrence
261	Derek Fowler
262	Arthur Gold
263	T.D. Wilkin
264	P. James
265	Brigadier D.N. Locke
266	W.A. Honey
267	N.H. Collins
268	K.C.J. Hutton
269	John D. Haigh
270	B.H. & E.R. Adlam
271	Patrick J. Fisher
272	A.V. Vincent
273	John Cossins
274	A.S.D. Barrett
275	W.J.I. Ashley
276	
277	E. Gunner
278	
279	William R. Linton
280	V.L. Tucker Harvey
281	Earl of Lonsdale
282	Lt Col P.G. Jones
283	A.A. Best
284	Bernard Fisher
285	Edward J. Black
286	R.A. Hills
287	Paul David Herbage BSc, AHA, MRSH
288	D.A.J. Taylor
289	T.E.D. Mason
290	Cripplegate Foundation
291	A.R. Thornton
292	J.G. Mardon
293	Paul W. Gunn
294	G.T. Clark
295	A.J. Hart
296	James Eynon
297	B.P. Blount
298	John C. Wittich
299	C.M. Crapper

300	Geoffrey Heywood
301	G.S. Grantham
302	J.P. Williams
303	Julian Keyes
304	Keith Prosser
305	Val Brook
306	James Kennedy McKerrow
307	William R. Lee
308	C.C. Hanrott
309	Rev Dr. T.M. Parker
310	Vincent E. Emms
311	Worshipful Company of Bakers
312	Gordon Ellis Everard
313	R.E. Seeman
314	John A.J. How
315	David C. Marshall
316	Fraser A. Wilson
317	G.W. Quick Smith CBE
318	W.H. Dormor
319	H.C.M. Douglas
320	T.J.R. Gordon
321	J.M.Y. Oliver CC
322	K.B. Jacob
323	H.P. Kelway
324	Michael W. Turton
325	P.H.S. Pilcher FCIOB, FFB, MBIM, MIIM
326	R.N. Leppington
327	J. Gordon Bates
328	Thomas John Reed
329	P.R.C. May
330	J.B. Lightbown
331	Sir Ernest Goodale CBE, MC
332	Peter Styles
333	David Arthur
334	Cedric Jagger
335	H. Rudebeck
336	A.F. Shaw CBE
337	V.A.E. Pickett
388	E. Clive Rouse
339	Ivan F. Hanslip
340	David T. Young
341	A.H. Hamilton-Hopkins
342	Sir Hugh Wontner GBE, CVO
343	John H. Snaith
344	J.F.J. Faulkner
345	Gordon Edwards
346	E.E. Bulkeley
347	R.N. White
348	John G. Dawe
349	H. Bamford-Preston
350	J.J. Carnaby
351	
352	T.J.N. Duke
353	The Rt Hon Lord Swaythling OBE
354	David C. Butcher
355	J.A. Ridge
356	R.D. Cook

357	J.A. Clemence TD
358	Capt J.S. Stewart OBE
359	
360	H.O.H. Coulson
361	
362	T.G. Reeday
363	J. Carthew-Williams
364	F.S. Haigh
365	Denis Purcell
366	John A. Potter
367	R.J.D. Gardner
368	James T. Goddard
369	L.L. Allen OBE
370	Jack W. Whalley
371	D.A. Young
372	Philip Lea
373	A.G. Ingram
374	H.R. Harris
375	R.F.C. Mobbs
376	W.F.G. Crozier
377	T.G.S. Wilson
378	Herbert Pickering
379	G.S.T. Bamford
380	Lady Mairi Bury
381	Alexander Forsyth
382	Capt R.L. Jones
383	Joseph W. Hooke
384	Rev Alan Tanner
385	G.H. Ross Goobey
386	M.R. Liddiard
387	Dudley T. Dresch JP, FCIT
388	Capt R. Critchley MBE
389	Capt A.J.R. Tyrrell
390	R.W. Peart
391	C.W. Judge
392	David West
393	Barclays Bank Ltd
394	D.A.F. Rees
395	
396	John Briggs
397	Sir Desmond Heap LL.M, Hon LL.D
398	H.J. Loughran
399	P.T.H. Holloway
400	C.B. Sanders
401	R.S.G. Hewett
402	Robert G. Shillingford
403	Derek John Cole
404	John Edward Dove JP
405	Dr Charles Wickham-Jones
406	The Duke of Norfolk
407	David Chapman
408	D.K. Rowe-Ham
409	
410	J.H. Scott
411	
412	S.E.A. Spong
413	R. Dawnay
414	J.R. Davey
415	The Glaziers Company
416	Humphrey Whitbread

417	H.J.A. Bird	478	Major D.R. Baker
418	Michael C. Martin	479	H.M. Neal
419	David Reid FCA	480	L.W. Pratt
420	The Rt Hon Lord Mais of Walbrook	481	T.G. Castle
421	Harold K. King	482	Peter C. Osborne
422	C.G. Rickett	483	P.J. Attenborough
423	Keith Day	484	R.S.R. Sheldon
424	R.G. Wildash	485	Rear Admiral B.C. Durrant CB, PSO DSC
425	C.A. Gillot	486	L.F. Cambers
426		487	John Hovey
427	H.D. Newlyn	488	G.E.M. Norman
428	F.J. Burroughs	489	M.J. Hill
429	Keith Wells	490	H.H.W. Boulter
430	C.G.S. Sanders-Hewett	491	E.H. Rawlings
431	A.W.F. Castell	492	A.M. Graham
432	E. Jarman	493	D.J. Shepherd
433	J.G. Robinson	494	
434	C.D. Brewer	495	T.A. Donnelly
435	Jack Wolkind	496	Bell & Co (Westminster) Ltd
436	Jack Godfrey-Gilbert	497	Peter Whebby
437	J. Edward Garner	498	Stanley Blow
438	Roger Pincham	499	S.W. Howard
439	Donald Conway Davis	500	Wilfred C. Hammond MBE, JP, FCIS
440	Mary B. Strong	501	J. Kingsley White
441	P.C. Palmer	502	T.J.L. Milner
442	K.V. Douglass JP	503	N.D. Messum
443	John L. Moon	504	J. Cecil Bocks
444	D.L. Marshall	505	Michael E. Snow
445	G. Heywood Hill Ltd	506	Hyman Liss
446	R.H. Borradaile	507	M. Freedman
447	W.H. Sargeant	508	S.E. Matthews
448	Major D. Ide-Smith	509	Arthur Barrington
449	C.S.C. Bale	510	C. Keith Vartan
450	P.F. Herbage	511	
451	Frank Craven	512	David R.W. Potter
452	Bruce Humber	513	Michael H. Jensen
453	Edward Playne	516	
454	J.D. Watney	517	H.J. Osborne
455	R.A. Murray	518	C.J.R. Francis
456	Arthur H. Green O St J	519	Admiral Sir Anthony Morton GBE, KCB
457	B.H. Westcott	520	Derek Whiting
458	R.N. Godden	521	Geoffrey Crowther
459	T.C. Spicer	522	Jack Brookfield
460		523	Donald Best
461	J.E.O. Arnold	525	D. Geddes
462		525	B.H.K. Hern
463	N.C. Bramley	526	L.R. Springett
464	H.A. Rudebeck	527	D.C. Randell
465	H.T. Burchmore	528	Philip S. Palmer
466	M.I. Montague-Smith	529	D. Kemp
467	C. Herbert	530	Alan Pendergast
468	R.J. Kirby-Welch	531	Keith J. Hutton
469	R.R. Hitchins	532	F. Adams
470	Lt Col L.F. Gray ERD, TD	533	L.A.J. Holt
471	Miss M. Harris ACIS	534	A.G. Dudgeon CBE, DFC
472	S.J.S. Eley	535	James A. Allen
473	M.L. Sutcliffe	536	Rex Hudson
474	K.C. Jackson	537	Jane Hansford
475	Alan Essex-Crosby	538	N. Peter Dew OBE, FRSA
476	C.J.H. Wilson		
477	R.C. Baker		

539	H.J. Smith	601	J.S. Beach
540	D.C. Watney	602	Kenneth Rodgers
541	J.H. Berman	603	William O'Brien
542	Nigel Israel	604	W.M. Hattersley
543	Raymond P. St. G. Cazalet	605	J.L.G. Traice
544	Benson F. Catt JP	606	Thomas Lord
545	Keith C. Johnson	607	David Ireson
546	G.K. Todorovitch	608	John Eric Forrest
547	David H.S. Howard	609	Michael Cameron Brown
548	Leonard W. Power	610	John Heath
549	Norman J. Page OBE, MC	611	Peter Sharrard
550	Anthony Coleson	612	Arthur C. Langham
551	C.E. Keysell	613	N.M. Williamson
552	D.J. Simonds	614	Anthea Bird
553	David A. Collins	615	D.J. Parry-Crooke
554	Peter Marsh	616	Simon T. Gray
555	Capt L. Wallis	617	Peter J.M. Aston
556	K.C. Matthes	618	B.L. Morgan CBE, JP
557	Thomas Young	619	David J. Powell
558	Capt P.F. Mason CBE	620	A.G. Acton Pierce
559	D.O. Johnston	621	
560	H.A. Borradaile	622	City Livery Club
561	Capt D.T. Whitham	623	Michael Bird
562	Edwin Osborne	624	Major S.P. Barrow
563	Capt. G.G. Tennyson-d'Eyncourt	625	David B. Clerk
564		626	R.J.A. Smith
564		627	G.B. Thompson
565	K.S. Brunton-Reed	628	The Worshipful Company of Shipwrights
567		629	Godfrey Royle
568	H.L. Lassen	630	B.A. Holroyd
569	Anthony Ayers Hodges	631	K. Forster
570	P.A. Mann	632	C.E.M. Snagge
571		633	Douglas Tribe
572	A.P.W. Cane	634	Lt Col E.G. Heath
573	R.A. Jackson	635	Mrs M.E. Hagger
574	R.A. Pollitt	636	A.J. Bowker
575	Ernest A. Corp	637	C.J. Ball
576	C.E. Frappell	638	Robin Long
577	S.L. Lloyd	639	Rufus Ide
578	R.C. Hockey	640	Greville D. Spratt
579	F.R. Hamp OBE, TD	641	Bernard W. Ramsay
580	A.M. Elliott	642	Peter A. Sanderson
581	I. Hutchinson	643	Howard Watson
582	Rev E.H.W. Crusha	644	N.R.S. Bickham
583	C.A. Matthes	645	Dr Roger Pilkington
584	Richard A. Domb	646	J.R. Crickmay
585	C.E.I. Thornton	647	John P. Lefroy
586	E.W. Hughes	648	J.W. Mitchell
587	William R. Miller	649	F.A. Everard CBE
588	G.J. Matthews FRICS	650	Derek Glanvile Millard FIA, ASA
589	Peter Bicknell	651	G.M. Infield
590	Allan D. Thomson	652	Frederick A. Moody
591	B.E.E. Marshall	653	C.W. Lowe
592	Kenneth J. Burton	654	Peter Longley
593	Col J.F.E. Pye	655	R.J.R. Cousins
594	D.M. Shalit CC	656	J.R. Dalrymple
595	Dr John Scorey	657	D.J.R. Barttelot
596	D.S. Bridge	658	E.S. Palmer
597	Joan Mary Platford	659	M.H. Strelley
598	Francis J. Bergin	660	J.A. Murley ERD
599	Peter N. Lamprell-Jarrett	661	K.L. Vink
600	John Henry Dunn	662	Past Master — Cooks Company

663 E.J.E. Wood	718 Ft-Lieut Ben Morgan	778 F. Murphy	838 Peter Kershaw
664 Claud Potter	719 Frank R. Hazell	779 William J. Rowe	839 Dr Arthur Curtis
665 R. Martin Silber	720 E.A.G. Lewis	780	840 D.E. Stevens
666 Lt Cdr The Rev B.M. Palmer Finch	721 Dr R. Griffith-Jones	781 J.R. Shackley	841 P.S. Rollano
667 Alan Vincent Bramley	722 Ronald A. Frakes FRSA	782 K.C. Rees	842 A.B. Maitland
668 Antony Galdry	723 F.P. Tridgell	783 J.A. Perry	843 Katharine Evison
669 The Corporation of Sons of the Clergy	724 N.H. Harding CC	784 M.K. Gregory TD	844 A.L. Grant
	725 B.A. Lee	785 James R. Payne	845 Alderman Sir Peter Gadsden GBE, MA, DSc, FENG
670 HH Judge R.E. Hammerton	726 Dr F.C. Wells	786 W.A. Peplow	
	727 G.L. Littmoden	787 Howell's School	
671 Rev W.T. Armstrong OBE TD MA	728 Dr Donald Adamson	788 R.D. Jackson	846 Capt R.R.S. Pennefather RN
672 C.J. Pittard	729 J.F.O. Vaughan	789 Charterhouse	
673 Major J.E. Tye MBE, FCIS	730 C.A. Hicks	790 Patrick Bryans	847 Sydney D. Gifford
674 T.W. Fripp	731 Col R.M. Burton	791 A.E. Cast FAMU	848 R.O. Lightfoot
675 H.M. Threlfall	732 F.H. Cropp	792 G.C. Fox	849 V.P. Grant
675 Alec W. Thornhill	733 Terence Coombs	793 Geoffrey Heywood	850 John E. Haynes
677 V.W.L. Walker	734 A.R. Collinson	794 C.N. Candy	851 M.D. Miller
678 Francis Victor Kelly	735 The Earl of Erroll	795	852 L.C. Rolland
679 Bertie Mee	736 R. Smith	796 P.A.F. Chalk	853 Leslie G. Neville
680 Lt Col L. Stokes-Roberts	737 P. Morgan	797 J.W. Cridford	854 W.N.M. Lawrence
	738 G.T. Eagleton	798 John Hosier	855 J.R. Smith
681 C.J. Overton	739 Humphry M. Smith OBE	799 A.E. Hopper	856
682 Bryan A. Hitchings		800 E.J. Simmonds	857 Ronald Hooker
683 Sydney Frank Everson	740 G.V. Hodges	801 Michael H. Baylis	858 G.E. Villiers
684 Christopher St. J.H. Daniel	741 C.J. Elvy CDA	802 Anthony Perry	859 Graham Blacktop
	742 Ian Jackson	803 John R. Forward	860 R.D. Brown
685 Capt J.M. Downard	743 N.K.S. Wills	804 S. John Woldridge	861 Sir Leslie Bowes
686 Gerald J. Huber	744 C.J. Elvy CDA	805 Peter Boneham	862 E.N. Hurrell
687 A.H. Fewell	745 Geoffrey Segrove	806 Anthony C.B. Lister	863 G. Scott Graham
688 R.E. Gillman	746 P.J. Willoughby	807 D. Smith	864
689 F.D. Nugent	747	808 K.M. Leach	865 J.R. Moore
690 George Schruers	748 Donald C. Cann	809 Charles C. Mobbs	866 D.W. Gravell
691 David R. Harris	749 E.G. Trevor	810 Boris J. Eastwood	867 John G.M. Hart
692 Rt Hon Lord Murton of Lindisfarne	750 R.A.S. Brock	881 Lt Col T.R.L. Greenhalgh TD	868 M.J. Hughes
	751 C.J. Benson		869 J.A.C. Reynolds
693 Air Cdre W.I.C. Inness	752 John R. Lerche	812 William A. Garnett	870 J.H.A. Eames
	753 Charles Meisl	813 Charles Stephens	871 P.H. Swan
694 A.E. Pitcher	754 Capt Sir David Tibbits DSc, RN	814 Melvyn Raymond Luckham-Down	872 David Treharne Holloway
695 Brian G. Jenkins			
697	755 B.C. Briant	815 Edwin Raymond Luckham-Down	873 Peter How
698 Jack Wheeler	756 Maj General Sir John Bates		874 Mrs D. Tombleson
699 Donald P.H. Josephs		816 Bryan W.G. Wilmot FRICS	875 C.G. Mays
700 R.L. Newbury	757 Michael R. Katz		876 Cecil McFetrich OBE
701 W.J. Freeman	758 P.J. Foord	817 Keith Abrahams	877 D.M. Hughes
702	759 Francis Owens Hillman FICS	818 P.R. Moxom	878 J.B. Shaw
703 A.B. Harrison		819 I.F. Snelling	879 A.G. Coster
704 Colfe's School	760 Charles Allen Hart	820 F.A. Mercer	880 Andrew Agnew
705 J.R. Wells	761 A.T. Traill	821 Sir Frank Layfield	881 G.C.I. Gardiner
706 Ian A. Martin	762 Chas F. Golton	822 G.N. Metcalfe	882 Reg Ibison CBE
707 Donald C. Cox	763 J.C. Hayes	823 Sir H. Maguire	883 B.J. Styles FICS
708 A.M. Park	764 Tom E. Marris	824 P.J.E. Tyson-Woodcock	884 W.E. Catto
709 D.H. Hodson	765 H.J.R. French		885 R.F.C. Zamboni
710 Lt Col D. Russel Naylor MBE	766 J.E. French	825 V.C. Hender	886 J.K. Prentice
	767 Kurt Kreisky	826 D.W. Dunn	887 Wilfred D. Hart
711 George W. Odey	768 A. Cordory	827 Capt J.J. Guntrip	888 Miss E.H.D. Tranter
712 M.H.V. Jeans	769 W.J. Henderson	828 A.F. Bagley	889 C.A. Owens
713 John R. French	770 Prof H.E. Rose	829 B.G.L. Jackman	890 Lt Col G.T. Pearce MBE
714 Alan Littlewood	771 Robert Anderson	830	
715 Michael Kemp	772 J.S. Vine	831 Hon H.E. Boscawen	891 David C.H. Williams
716 Norman Searle	773 T.H. Seager Berry	832 Cyril Saper	892 Roger Heath
717	774 N.A. Maxwell-Lawford	833 J.F. Allen	893 Malcolm D. Beard
		834 Kenneth J. Slater	894 K.A. Bentley
	775 S.J. Midwinter	835	895 Clive Thomson JP
	776 D.W. Brewer	836 R.J.B. Heasman	896 R.M. Burton
	777 Raymond Mellor	837 Vernon C. Simmonds	897 Maj J.D.S. Olleson

898 Miss E.M. Candy
899
900 Cordwainers
    Technical College
901 J.A.L. Stacey
902 R.C. Beach
903 M.E. Appleby
904 C.B. Wells
905 W.H. Forsey
906 Vice Adml Sir Gerard
907 Mansfield KBE CVO
908 R.M. Willan
909 Clifford E.
    Harrington
910 Lt Col H. Errington
    Brewis
911 T.A. Sangster
912 Anthony Stocken
913 Donald Ellis Raley
914 Alan M. Dix
915 Andrew L. King
916 Stanley H. Burton
917 J.S. Cartwright
918 G.R. Browne
919 D.D. Dennis OBE
920 David B. Clement
921 W.D. Ewart
922 Capt G. Fowkes
923 The Rt Hon, The
    Earl of Inchcape
924 R.Y. Pritchard
925 Vernon Holding
926 Colin B. Wilson
927 A. Gilchrist
928 Lionel P. Altman
929 Capt G. Fowkes
930 Joseph J. Janssens
931 Alan A. Howell
932 R.E. Biscoe-Taylor
933 Edmund Vestey
934 W.J. Briggs
935 J.M. Donald
936 Michael Coates
937 R.M. Willan
938 Richard A. Bellamy
939 Wates Develop-
    ments Ltd
940 D.H. Barrett
941 W.C. Harris
942 G.E. Liardet
943 Paul Saper
944 Alan Parry
945 Norman Tribble
946 Luke Churchouse
947 K.P. Ivens
948 Noel Ross-Russell
949 Richard Mayers
    FRICS
950 Dr R. Vaudrey
    Mercer
951 J.V.R. Cully
952 G.E.L. Yeandle
953 W.R.B. Foster
954 Dr. Colin R.
    Lattimore

955 H.E. Taylor
956 J.R.C. Quitman
957 Martin Ellis
958
959 P.A. Meecham
960 V.J. Fullforth
961
962 R.D. Anderson
963 John Barton
964 John R. Owen-
    Ward
965 Howard Johnson
966 A.E. Cook
967
968 A.J. Gillett
969 John R. Baxter
970 M.I. Danischewsky
971
972 Alan Jessup
973 Cdr M.F.R. Ainslie
    DSO, DSE, RN
974 Peter E. Braxton
975 J.R. Garrett
976 Michael Henderson-
    Begg
977 Cyril Hodge
978 R.A. Rowbotham
979 D. Siberry
980 Ian Louis Rodgers
981 G.A.G. Pulman
982 Dudley Saward
983 G.A.G. Pulman
984 Allan J. Marr
985 Sir Neil Wheeler
986 G.H. Richardson
987 K. Beaumont TD
988
989 P.H. Cresswell
990 David R. Mauleverer
991 J.A. Bearman
992 S.K.C. Attenborough
993 Alan E.C. Bennett
994 H.L. Triggs
995 R.M. Fisher
996 Anthony S. Jolliffe
997 C.R. Driver
1000
1001 Paul and Sharon
     Housden
1002 Robert McLean
1003 R.B. McFarlane
1004 J.F. Lachlan
1005 F. Ashe Lincoln
1006
1007 E.B. Kitchen
1008 Ivan Tomlin
1009 J.H.C. Mackmin
1010 Terence C. White
1011 R.N. Singer
1012 J.K. Jones
1013 Stewart K. Riddick
1014 Sydney Rust
1015 C.J. Rose
1016 D.G.M. Roberts
1017 Peter William Racey

1018 Stuart J. Lines
1019 E.M. Conway
1020 J.G. Ouvry
1021 James W. White
1024
1025 V. Larvan
1026 Andrew Pearmain
1027 Dr V. Powell-Smith
1028 J.W. Miskin
1029 P.R. Mitchell
1030 C.E. Mitchell
1031 David Selbie
1032 P.V. Radford
1033 N.P. Radford
1034 J.D. Radford
1035 James L. Seccombe
1036 Brian Scruby CBE
1037 John H. Adams
1038 G.R.A. Andrews
     FIB, FCIS
1039 A.W.J. Appleton
1040 Norman W. Andrews
1041 K.W. Aspinall
1042 T.J. Sargent
1043 E.M. Holmes
1044 A.C. Gardner
1045 Christopher Gold
1046 John N. Horne
1047 Patrick Gilbert
1048 F.W. Graham
1049 A.S. Grimes
1050 Denzil Henry Jacobs
1051 Lindsay Jones
1052 R.F. Johnson
1053 A.F. Stevens
1054 P.B.D. Sutherland
     MA
1055 H.J. Sims-Hilditch
1056 S.M. Haines
1057 Sebastian Benoit
     Salama
1058 C. Harry Short
1059 Capt F.E. Holmes
1060
1061 C.R.P. Ward
1062 Dorian Williams
1063 Alan Taylor
1064 R. Merrick & Burrell
     & Partner
1065 Noel Mander
1066 Mr & Mrs T.G. Torry
1067 Mr & Mrs N.J. Torry
1068 Eric G. Sage
1069 John Schroder
1070 Mollie Kate Stone
1071 Arthur Smith
1072 J.D. Harris
1073 V.S. Ghersie
1074 Euro Training
1075 M.A. Grayburn
1076 Geo M. Gould
1077 Victor Fleming
1078 P.G. Ellement
1079 Thomas B. Dwyer
1080 Capt R.J. Cormican

1081 David L. Cobbold
1082 P.A. Corby
1083 A.C. Clarke
1084
1085 R.A. Hartland
1086 C.A. Hadley
1087 Richard W. Hayward
1088 P.H. Purchon
1089 Michael Cobham
1090 Michael Cowen
1091 Julian Cowen
1092 Nichola Cowen
1093 Capt T.R. Pidgen
1094 R.G. Puttick
1095 J.E. Phillips
1096 Col H.H. Broadbent
     OBE, TD, DL
1097 Harvey M. Bird
1098 Deryck Botterill FCA
1099 K.P. Bennett
1100 Dr K.J. Brown
1101 R.S. Bowman
1102 N.O. Aston
1103 John William Bishop
1104 L.L. Kenchington
1105 Wm David Todd
1106 C.P.M. Gomm
1107 Chas F. Stone
1108 W. Charles Williams
1109 Howard J.C. White
1110 W.P. Warner
1111 John Williams
1112 B.A. Watson
1113 Peter R. Hodgson
     MA, FCA
1114 R.I. Hopkins
1115 Lynn Walters
1116 J.J.G. Waller
1117
1118 R.L. Martin
1119 William G. Carter
1120 J.R. MacWhirter
1121 Roy Vaughan
     Williamson
1122 G.H. Robinson
1123 N. Smyth
1124 Elwyn Edwards
1125 Reynold Wiles
1126 R.H.W. Lindsay
1127 Peter Anthony
     Sturgess
1128 John Owen Hibling
1129 Michael Allen
1130 Bernard Paddick
1131 C.L.S. Cornwall-Legh
1132 G.D. Draycott
1133 R. Sancroft-Baker
1134 Michael C. Oram
1135 R.C. Case-Green
1136 K.S.A. Davis ARIBA,
     FFB
1137 Rita Reed
1138 Christopher Prit-
     chard-Barrett

1139	F.J. Millard	1198	Richard Vergette
1140	J.T. Macleod	1199	Richard Tydeman
1141	William P. Padbury	1200	G. Ostler
1142	Angus M.E. Carmichael	1201	J.L. Osborne
1143	A.F. Bennett	1202	H.K. Thompson
1144	Maj Derek Allhusen	1203	P.H. Cordle
1145	Rennie Simpson	1204	Dr. W.B. Maile
1146	Dr F.M.S. Muller	1205	G. Courtauld
1147	N.E. Simons	1206	D.V.S. Burroughs
1148	D.L. Glatzel	1207	D.R.P. Johnson
1149	R.L. Petchey	1208	Halden E. White
1150		1209	Paul Harris OBE
1151	Roy A. Cadman BSc, DCU	1210	R.J. Percival
1152	R.J.B. Keene	1211	E.J.A. Colley
1153	H.P. Joscelyne	1212	Raymond A. Shard
1154	R.H. Randle	1213	Henry F. Howard
1155	D.M. Turnbull	1214	Michael Harvey
1156	Christopher Brown	1215	R. Ellis
1157	George Timms	1216	J.L. Mercer
1158	Roland Freeman	1217	Geoffrey H. Bell
1159	Brian A. Carte	1218	P.E. Newnham
1160	Maj P.W.M Lancaster	1219	Bernard G. Hippsley
1161	Peter M. Olley	1220	A.C. Street
1162	F.E. Birch	1221	D.G.E. Hilton
1163	George Raymond Speed	1222	Malcolm Bennett
1164	Gelena Christina Speed	1223	William A. Gregory
1165	Dr J. Stein	1224	D. Tudor Williams
1166	Michael Biscoe	1225	C. Graham Willett
1167	Gordon S. Planner MBE	1226	J.W. Homer FCA
1168	J.R. Oakley	1227	I.F. McLay TD
1169	J.H.P. Roberts	1228	Eric Tobitt
1170	Peter J. Lord-Smith	1229	Arthur R. Bray
1171	Terence Hopegood	1230	A.J. Everard
1172	P.A. Everett	1231	G.R. Jones
1173	Peter D. Marsh	1232	Oliver Elsom
1174	David J. Marsh	1233	C.D.L. Smith
1175	Peter J Le Bosquet	1234	Stanley Field
1176	Christopher Mitchell	1235	S.A. Brown
1177	Derek Sutton	1236	A.J. Field
1178	Col R.V. Blott OBE, TD, FGA	1237	P.W. Wyatt
1179	Dr W.W. Abbott	1238	M.A.H. Willett
1180	Keith F.C. Baker	1239	Alan Shave
1181	Alan J. Ray	1240	R.F.B. Marshall
1182	K.I. Wilson	1241	W.I. Baverstock Brooks CC
1183	Peter J. Le Bosquet	1242	P.E. Brown
1184	S.A. Greer	1243	W.H. Smith
1185	T.H. Wareham	1244	E.G.S. Groves
1186	Sir Bernard Scott	1245	B.R. Paton
1187	Graeme A. Living	1246	R.C. Hetherington
1188	D.C. Morgan	1247	A.H. Allt
1189	A.M. Fraser	1248	J.L. Wallworth
1190	S.J. Rowbotham	1249	G.M.J. Williams
1191	K.B. Drew	1250	J.J.G. Rowley
1192	D.M.F. Scott	1251	A.C. Fowler
1193	A.E. Ford	1252	C. Wildin
1194	E.R. Parker	1253	Michael F. Barford
1195	J.E. Neary	1254	Robert A. Sice
1196	John & Sylvia Reid	1255	Ralph G. Covell
1197	F.E. Lee	1256	P.F.L. Dandy
		1257	F.G. Browning
		1258	L.R. Knott
		1259	C.A. Hicks
		1260	Ian O. Baden
		1261	A.V. Coulson
		1262	D.L. Lindsay

1263	David Starkey	1323	Brian D.S. Burgess
1264	Robert J. Double	1324	Spencer T. Cooper
1265	Ian Coombs	1325	David A. Blaikie
1266	Norman V. Slatter	1326	Philip Sherling
1267	Lt Col J.A.E. Heard	1327	R.A. Garrett
1268	C.J. Allflatt	1328	D.G. Williams
1269	C.C. Beverly	1329	G.B. Lancashire
1270	J.V. Dabbs	1330	L.J. Cardew Wood BSc, FCG
1271	Michael L. Poster	1331	T.W. Moore
1272	G.W. Pingstone	1332	R.A. Easthill
1273	L.R. Ponder	1333	H.J.C. Pepperell
1274	Alan Gordon Fagg	1334	Gerald Simmons
1275	R.A. Bailey	1335	P.E.K. King-Scott
1276	Peter Scott	1336	Robert Graham Faithfull Henderson
1277	A.G. Gould	1337	Charles Robert Henderson
1278	M.L. Leigh	1338	Maj Gen Sir Leslie Tyler
1279	G.N.L. Leigh	1330	Maurice E. Pickering
1280	C.W. Osborn	1340	M.S. Ross Collins
1281	Henry M. Cohen	1341	Rodney Dennys CVO, OBE, FSA
1282	J.H. Rhodes	1342	A. Coline Cole, Garter King of Arms
1283	M.S. Ross Collins	1343	James T. Howat
1284	R.J. Crocker	1344	Stanley Lee
1286		1345	Mrs E.R. Wheatley-Hubbard
1287	D.J. Barham	1346	D.C. Topham
1288	R.J.C. Hiller	1347	L.M.Hohmann
1289	Robert Chapman	1348	Wilfred Fell
1290	Michael G. Bartlett	1349	A.J. Ellis
1291	R.J. Corben	1350	J.L. Harvey
1292	John M. Powell	1351	R.W. Manners
1293	N.H. Russell	1352	J.K. Golightley MA
1294	Ian MacDonald	1353	D.L. Farrant
1295	F.E. Neighbour	1354	William S.Y. West
1296	Joseph A. Denman	1355	J.F. Link RSS
1297	Gerald Thomas Uzzell	1356	J.A. Bardsley
1298	Mrs M. Benson	1357	Lionel V. Phillips
1299	Kenneth H. Lewis OBE	1358	Paul Broadbent
1300		1359	Sir David & Lady Pryke
1301	Lorrimer Silver	1360	Mr & Mrs K. Pettit
1302	N.D. Freethy	1361	Mr & Mrs E. Lightstone
1303	P.D. Esslemon	1362	J.D.G. Gabriel
1304	Vice Admiral Sir Frank Mason	1363	Lt Col H.A. Johnson TD
1305	K.F. Lipscombe	1364	S.B. Southcombe
1306	C.N. Kenyon	1365	Richard Butterworth
1307	P.C. Poland	1366	John H. Harper
1308	C.R.C. Hawkes	1367	Peter H. Santley-Dilley
1309	Ralph Cecil Chapman	1368	Don Mason
1310	R.E. Castell CBE	1369	J.T. Woolhouse
1311	Robert Claude Orme	1370	Keith O. Sims
1312	City of London Freemens School, Ashtead	1371	Edward Arthur Connell
1313	Maj R.A.J. Fowler MC, BAR	1372	J. Benjamin
1314	L.W. Andrews	1373	Bernard P. Bareham
1315	Donald Mack OBE	1374	C.N.G. Arding
1316	B.J. Griffith	1375	Chas E. Gostling
1317			
1318	Stanley Costin		
1319	Brig R.K. Hudson		
1320	D.N. Warner		
1321	Thomas Lloyd Barker		
1322	D.W. Pittard		

1376 R.H.G. Ring	1440 J.L. Macey	1501 D.A. Ward	1560 Denis Stevens
1377 Charles W. Farrance	1441 D.W.H. Galbraith	1502 R.H. Chambers	1561 Simon Duckworth
1378 S.N. Baldwin-Purry	1442 H. Terence Kaye	1503 Jack Hubbard	1562 John Day
1379 Roger W. Cork	1443 W.G. Cooper	1504 David Asdell	1563 Sheila Lightbody
1380 John M. Lock	1444 Gordon J. Lihou	1505 A.S. Raimes	1564 Edward A. Newby
1381 M.G. Stewart	1445 A.D. Smith	1506 Lt Col R.A. Payne	1565 S.P. Hallam
1382 R.J.M. Pickance	1446 R.A. Vincent	KStJ. JP	1566 John Bullock
1383 John Gratwick OBE	1447 Gavin Benbow	1507	1567 Sir Geoffrey
1384 Dr George Walker	1448 Mrs Joan Pinker	1509 John H. Penton	Errington
1385 Michael P. May	1449 Brian V. Burdett	1510 Richard D.E. Mant	1568 P.J.F. Croset
1386 Dr J.D. Ramshall	1450 Dr Hugh Malet	1511 David R. Crabtree	1569 Charles Vowles
1387 John M. Donner	1451 J.H. Gaze	1512 J.G. Baxter	1570 Dr Eric M. Hunt
1388 F.G. Hankins	1452 L.C. Lavers	1513 C.K. Makin-Taylor	1571 J.N. Harrington
1389 D.M. Henderson	1453 Alan R. Brown	1514 Dr A. Mackenzie	1572 John E. Jones
1390 John Heller	1454 Master of The	1515 Mary Macleish	1573 R.L. Wilson
1391 R.F. Gulliford	Bowyers Company	1516 Derek Baker	1574 Capt F.J. Turk
1392 G.G. Bannerman	1455 D.J. Rogers	1517 J.W.J. Freeston	1575 P.L. Young
1393 A.L. Darbey	1456 J. Eric Hunt	1518 His Excellency N.	1576 Edwin Evans
1394 B.A. Cohen	1457 K.S. Curlewis	Parker GCIG,	1577 Derek Edwards
1395 H.S. Dodson	1458 R.O. Harvey	GCCY	1578 Ronald T. Barnfield
1396 George C. Stead	1459 B.W. Pinker	1519 C.D. Cradock	1579 Peter Maslen
1397 Sir Hugh Linstead	1460 Col H.A.C.	1520 Lt Cdr P. Murray-	1580 Mathew Mitchell
1398 C.W. Lake	Mackenzie	Jones	1581 J.A. Durkin
1399 K.J. Ward	1461 Dr R.W. Covill	1521 Roland P. Lay	1582 A.C.H. Crisford
1400 A.V. Hall	1462 R. Lewis	1522 S.F. Brown	1583 Anthony Masters
1401 Mrs Gwendoline	1463 J.H. Hutchinson	1523 Frederick A. Biggs	1584 David Wiseman
Torry	1464 B.H. Gilkison	1524 S.P. Hallam	1585 R.J. Skuse
1402 C. Collett	1465 Eric Barber	1525	1586 Ian B. Bowerman
1403 W.G. Ellis	1466 Alfred Weekes	1526 John Bullock	1587 T.D.D. Hoffman
1404 John Howard	Holmes	1527 Alan I.R. Dow	1588 John A. Line
1405 Geoffrey Perfect	1467 A.W.C. Edwards	1528 Ellis Wood & Co	1589 Judith Beale
1406 Ian E. Baird	1468 L.H. Lockley	1529 J.H. Carlill	1590 Dr Marshall Wilson
1407 Anthony Foord	1469 H.E. Baker	1530 The Rev A. Tanner	1591 Arthur Herbert
1408	1470 I.M. Thompson	1531 R.P. Druett	1592 H. Kremer
1409 L.G. Pierson	1471 J.A. Roll Pickering	1532 British Jewellery &	1593 Anthony Paxford
1410 N. Longe	1472 J.R. Backshall	Giftware	1594 J.B.G. Carpenter
1411 John Sylvester	1473 J.R. Oliver	Federation	1595 E.J.D. Hewitt
1412 J.J. Rouse	1474 D.B. Watkinson	1533 F.A.J.B. Everard	1596 N.C. Nullis
1413 J.W. Watson	1475 Paul Lacey	1534 Rear Admiral A.J.	1597 E.C. Prest DFC
1414 Renault Breakbane	1476 Dr T. Douglas	Cooke	1598 Alan N. Griffin
1415 John M. Donner	Whittet	1535 C.K. Howe	1599 P. Gordon Spencer
1416 Cdr D.B. Cairns	1477 John Jeffery	1536 E.S. Pearson	1600 The Glaziers
RD, RNR	1478 E.S. Harborne	1537 Peter W. Jenkinson	Company
1417 J.V.H. Robins	1479 A.J. Heyworth	1538 R. Mansell Ltd	1601 M.C. Farrar-Bell
1418 T.H. Salter	1480 G.J. Wallis	1539 P. Cruikshank	1602 C.F.R. Barclay
1419 R.H.I. Dossetter	1481 Hillier B.A. Wise	1540 Charles A. King	1603 R.J. Rowles
1420 Ralph P. Anderson	1482 C.W. Lloyd	1541 G.J. Wallis	1604 Edmond Shipway
1421 E.G. Cornish	1483 Bryan Essenhigh	1542 M.J. Whittaker	1605 A.F.J. Rixon
1422 M.W. Miles	1484 Sir Geoffrey	1543 E.G. Barnes	1606 G.D. Adams
1423 R.G.L. Welham	Errington Bt	1544 R.A.H. Arnold	1607 George M. Gee
1424 C.H.W. Storer	1485 Girdlers Company	1545 Philip & Marjorie	1608
1425 L.L. Brace	1486 Graham Crompton	Blamey	1609 G.D. Trentham
1426 S.W. Bickford-Smith	1487 Dennis Turner	1546 Harold K. Stark	1610 T.R. Robinson
1427 Clive A. Harrington	1488 F. Stevens	1547 J.L. Smale	1611 Alan M. Marshall
1428 A.J. Clarke	1489 B. Stevens	1548 D.S. Jenkins	1612 Ronald T. Barnfield
1429 R.G. Peters	1490 W.D. Corkish	1549 P.D. Esslemont	1613 Bryn Williams
1430 John J.L. Corkill	1491 K. Corkish	1550 Dr Rodney Leach	1614 Dr Valerie Pearl
1431 A.G.W. Scott	1492 N. Corkish	1551 D.R.C. Bell	1615 Miss Betty Masters
1432 Richard Lawrence	1493 Max Beaumont	1552 William Marle	1616 Judy & Dennis
1433 A. John Hall	1494 A.J. Tattersfield	1553 John H. Drew	Bloodworth
1434 David I. Moor	1495 M. St. C. Baird	1554 J.L.C. Pratt	1617 Mark Hope
1435 James A. Moore	1496 A.G. Wooler	1555 John Large	1618 Diana & Alexander
1436 Vanessa J. Hunt	1497 Ian P. Bethwaite	1556 Paul Adorian	Good
1437 Alan Cope	1498 W.J.W. Courtney	1557 George Clarke	1619 Janet & Lawrence
1438 M.A.P. Simons	1499 J.T. Norman	1558 Martin C. Tubbs	Miller
1439 Francis Griffin OBE	1500 Derek S. Gillingham	1559 I.C.N. Seaton	1620 Josephine Bentley

1621 A.C. Mann	1657 Simon Richard Birch	1688 Stewart R. Green-berg	1720 W.J. Meakin
1622 A.E. Torry	1658 Caroline Birch		1721
1623 W.T.F. Austin	1659 James William Birch	1689 L.A. Bailey	1722 Jane Redman
1624 A. Torrance Law	1660 Emma Charlton Birch	1690 Alfred Student-Cuming	1723
1625 R.R. St. J. Barkshire	1661 Katie Doble		1724 Michael Montgomery
1626 R. Viner	1662 Jamie Doble	1691 J.S.L. Horsfall	1725 Major J.S.W. Powell
1627 R. Dick-Larkham	1663 F.W. Underhill FSMC	1692 Wilfred G.B. Colls	1726 H.F.V. Arbery FSMC
1628 Eric N. Lloyd		1693 R.J.W. Waterman	
1629 David P. Stewart	1664 L.R. Underwood	1694 Brian H. Ellis	1727 H.W. Spooner
1630 Hugh Insley-Fox	1665 Ernest B. Judge	1694 Mr & Mrs K.C. Holland	1728 T.G.J. Lawrence
1631 G.W. Mills	1666 Una K. Smith		1729 Edward J. Webb
1632 J.R. Penny	1667 The Revd J.A. Morrison	1696 Philip J. Cole	1730 David Woods
1633 J.G. Mann		1697 A. Glen Barr	1731
1634 J.B. Walsby	1668 Richard J. Allen	1698 Martin S. Goldman	1732 L.H. Hebditch
1635 T.F. Gostling	1669 Pamela Osborne	1699 E.V. Pearce	1733 Charles Samuel Bussin
1636 Alan Lucas	1670 Ernest B. Judge	1700 D.J. Scannell	
1637 S.I. Shapland	1671 Vernon Wigmore	1701 Laurence B. Lauder	1734 George G. Geyman
1638 P.S. London	1672 Timothy Tucker	1702 Eric Arthur Rudd	1735 M.J. Banes
1639 T.F. Phillips	1673 Amanda Mary Hill	1703 N.W. Gunn	1736 A.R.E. Mason
1640 Stephen G.B. Baker	1674 C.H. Lawrence FSMC	1704 T.A. Wadsworth	1737 K.C. Stratford
1641 Mrs Audrey P. Biggs		1705 George Purdom FSMC	1738 T.F. Torbett
1642 John Ewen Troup Horne	1675 A.L. Vickers		1739 Nicholas Elliott
	1676 Charles Bollen Blore FSMC	1706 Michael N. Henly	1740 Ian R.V. Morrow
1643 John R.N. Travis		1707 Eric Bateman	1741 R.L. Martin
1644 J.H. Rhodes	1677 Elizabeth Pearson	1708 J.K. Adams	1742 Derek Allen
1645 Gordon W. Smith	1678 Fredk J. Price	1709 Clive B. Roffe	1743 Len Wilmott
1646 B.D. Gilroy	1679 Martin F. Adlam	1710 Paul Zetter	1744 David Sands
1647 T.J.L. Cookman	1680 T.H. Motson	1711 Mrs B. Cheeseman	1745 Valerie Baskwill
1648 D.P. Collins	1681 B.L. Berry	1712 W.S. Topliss	1746 R. Crossley Bilborough
1649 R.C. Martin	1682 Frank W. Yeoman	1713 J. Paul Dodd	
1650 The National Association of Toastmasters	1683 Mrs H.P.B. Cox	1714 G. Stafford-Bloor	1747 Sophie Walpole
	1684 Richard John Hensley	1715 C.R. Norwood	
		1716 D.H. Drennan	
1651 John R.N. Travis	1685 C.E. Desborough	1717 Stanley Lowe	
1652 J.A. Mack	1686 Anthony Solomon	1718 Leslie Ross	
1653 Guildhall Library	1687 Andrew Parkhouse SMC (Disp) FADO FFDO	1719 Stephen Harvey Davis	*(Remaining names unlisted)*
1656			

ENDPAPERS: FRONT — Engraving of the 1572 map of London by Braun and Hogenberg showing the City and Westminster. (ML) BACK — St Paul's Cathedral and the modern City. (HP)